First World War
and Army of Occupation
War Diary
France, Belgium and Germany

21 DIVISION
Divisional Troops
Machine Gun Corps
21 Battalion
1 March 1918 - 31 March 1919

WO95/2145/2

The Naval & Military Press Ltd
www.nmarchive.com
Published in association with The National Archives

Published by

The Naval & Military Press Ltd

Unit 10 Ridgewood Industrial Park,

Uckfield, East Sussex,

TN22 5QE England

Tel: +44 (0) 1825 749494

www.naval-military-press.com

www.nmarchive.com

This diary has been reprinted in facsimile from the original. Any imperfections are inevitably reproduced and the quality may fall short of modern type and cartographic standards.

© Crown Copyright
Images reproduced by permission of The National Archives, London, England, 2015.

Contents

Document type	Place/Title	Date From	Date To
Heading	2145/2 21 Battalion Machine Gun Corp.		
Heading	21 Bn Machine Gun Corps 1918 Mar-1919 Mar		
Heading	21st Div. War Diary 21st Battalion. Machine Gun Corps. March 1918		
Miscellaneous	21st Division	07/04/1918	07/04/1918
War Diary		01/03/1918	14/03/1918
War Diary	Battalion H.Q At Longavesnes Battalion In Line In Epeny-Vaucelette Farm Chapel Hill Sector	14/03/1918	15/03/1918
War Diary	Epeny Sector	16/03/1918	21/03/1918
War Diary	Longavesnes & Haut Allaines	22/03/1918	24/03/1918
War Diary	Bray	25/03/1918	25/03/1918
War Diary	Chipilly	26/03/1918	26/03/1918
War Diary	Bresle	27/03/1918	27/03/1918
War Diary	Franvillers	28/03/1918	30/03/1918
War Diary	Cardonette	31/03/1918	31/03/1918
Heading	Report On M.G. Operations From Midnight 20/21st Midnight 28/29th March.		
Miscellaneous	21st Division.	08/04/1918	08/04/1918
Map			
Heading	21st Divisional Troops. 21st Battalion Machine Gun Corps April 1918.		
War Diary	Amiens	01/04/1918	01/04/1918
War Diary	Locre	02/04/1918	30/04/1918
Miscellaneous	29th Bde.		
Miscellaneous	Appendix A. 21st Batt G. Corps		
Miscellaneous			
Miscellaneous		30/04/1918	30/04/1918
Miscellaneous	21st Bn M.G.C. Social Order No. 4	15/04/1918	15/04/1918
Miscellaneous	21st Bn. M.G.C. Special Order No. 8	14/04/1918	14/04/1918
Miscellaneous	21st Bn. M.G.C. Order No 2	03/04/1918	03/04/1918
Miscellaneous	21st Bn. M.G.C. Order No 3	07/04/1918	07/04/1918
Miscellaneous	21st Bn. M.G.C. Order No 4	07/04/1918	07/04/1918
Miscellaneous	21st Bn. M.G.C. Order No. 5	09/04/1918	09/04/1918
Miscellaneous	21st Bn. M.G.C. Order No. 6	11/04/1918	11/04/1918
Miscellaneous	21st Bn. M.G.C. Order No. 7	14/04/1918	14/04/1918
Miscellaneous	21st Battn M G C Order No. 8	14/04/1918	14/04/1918
Miscellaneous	21st Bn. M.G.C. Order No. 9	15/04/1918	15/04/1918
Miscellaneous	21st Bn. M.G.C. Order No. 10	20/04/1918	20/04/1918
Miscellaneous	21st Bn. M.G.C. Order No. 11	21/04/1918	21/04/1918
Miscellaneous	21st Bn. M.G.C. Order No. 12	24/04/1918	24/04/1918
Miscellaneous	21st Bn. M.G.C. Order No. 13	25/04/1918	25/04/1918
Miscellaneous	21st Bn. M.G.C. Order No. 14	27/04/1918	27/04/1918
Miscellaneous	21st Bn. M.G.C. Order No. 15	30/04/1918	30/04/1918
War Diary	Middlesex Camp. G.17.d.4.4 Sheet 28 Belg France 1-40.000	01/05/1918	02/05/1918
War Diary	Bois de Beauvoorde	03/05/1918	03/05/1918
War Diary	Arques	04/05/1918	04/05/1918
War Diary	Train	05/05/1918	05/05/1918
War Diary	Cuisles	06/05/1918	11/05/1918
War Diary	Prouilly	12/05/1918	15/05/1918

Type	Description	Start	End
War Diary	Vaux Varennes	13/05/1918	27/05/1918
War Diary	Sapicourt	28/05/1918	28/05/1918
War Diary	Sarcy	29/05/1918	29/05/1918
War Diary	La Neuville	30/05/1918	30/05/1918
War Diary	Givry	31/05/1918	31/05/1918
Miscellaneous			
Miscellaneous	21st Battn. M.G.C. Order No. 19	03/05/1918	03/05/1918
Miscellaneous	21st Battn. M.G.C. Order No. 18	20/05/1918	20/05/1918
Miscellaneous	21st Battn. M.G.C. Order No. 17	02/05/1918	02/05/1918
Miscellaneous	21st Battn. M.G.C. Order No. 16	01/05/1918	01/05/1918
Miscellaneous	21st Division Special Order Thursday 2nd May 1916.	02/05/1918	02/05/1918
Operation(al) Order(s)	21st Bn. M.G.C. Operation Order No. 22	19/05/1918	19/05/1918
Operation(al) Order(s)	21st. Bn. M.G.C. Operation Order No. 21	12/05/1918	12/05/1918
Operation(al) Order(s)	21st. Bn. M.G.C. Operation Order No. 20	11/05/1918	11/05/1918
Miscellaneous	To all recipients of 21st. Bn. M.G.C. Order No. 19		
Miscellaneous	Headquarters, 21st. Division.	11/06/1918	11/06/1918
Miscellaneous	Report on Operations Berry Au Bac-Loivre (both exclusive) Commencing 27th May 1918 Appendix A		
Miscellaneous	21st Battn. Machine Gun Corps.	10/06/1918	10/06/1918
Miscellaneous	Narrative.	27/05/1918	27/05/1918
War Diary	Givry-Les-Loisy (Chalons-1,100.000)	01/06/1918	02/06/1918
War Diary	Courjeonnet	03/06/1918	08/06/1918
War Diary	Vindey (Arcis 1:80.000)	09/06/1918	11/06/1918
War Diary	Vindey	12/06/1918	15/06/1918
War Diary	Boencourt	16/06/1918	17/06/1918
War Diary	Forceville (Dieppe 1:100.000)	18/06/1918	21/06/1918
War Diary	Sept Meules	22/06/1918	30/06/1918
Operation(al) Order(s)	21st Bn. M.G.C. Operation Order No. 24	09/06/1918	09/06/1918
Miscellaneous	Administrative Instructions No. 1 for move of 21st Battn. Machine Gun Corps. from French Area.	12/06/1918	12/06/1918
Miscellaneous	21st Bn. M.G.C. Operation Order No. 25	13/06/1918	13/06/1918
Operation(al) Order(s)	21st Bn. M.G.C. Operation Order No. 26	17/06/1918	17/06/1918
Operation(al) Order(s)	21st Battn. Machine Gun Corps Operation Order No. 27	21/06/1918	21/06/1918
Operation(al) Order(s)	21st Battn. Machine Gun Corps Operation Order No. 28	20/06/1918	20/06/1918
Map			
Heading	21 Bn M G Corps Vol 5		
Miscellaneous	On His Majesty's Service.		
Heading	D.A.G. G.H.Q. 3rd Echelon M745		
War Diary	Sept Meules (Dieppe Map 1/100.000)	01/07/1918	01/07/1918
War Diary	Gamaches	02/07/1918	02/07/1918
War Diary	Le Quesnoy	03/07/1918	25/07/1918
War Diary	Acheux	26/07/1918	31/07/1918
War Diary	21st Battn. Machine Gun Corps.	04/07/1918	04/07/1918
Miscellaneous	Amendments to 21st Bn. M.G.C. Defence Scheme	21/07/1918	21/07/1918
Miscellaneous	21st Battn. Machine Gun Corps.	08/07/1918	08/07/1918
Miscellaneous	Appendix 1		
Miscellaneous	To All Recipients of 21st Bn. M.G.C. Defence Scheme.	21/07/1918	21/07/1918
Miscellaneous	Appendix 2.		
Miscellaneous	Appendix 3.		
Miscellaneous	Appendix 4.		
Miscellaneous	Appendix 5		
Miscellaneous	The Following Arrangements Will Apply To Appendices 1-5		
Miscellaneous	Appendix 6 The enemy has attacked on the front Albert-Arras.		
Miscellaneous	Appendix 7 First Line Transport		

Miscellaneous			
Miscellaneous	St Mann M C		
Miscellaneous	21st Bn. M.G.C. Appendix 9		
Miscellaneous	21st Battn. Machine Gun Corps Operation Order No. 29	10/07/1918	10/07/1918
Miscellaneous	21st Battn. Machine Gun Corps. Administrative Instructions In Connection with Operation Order No. 29		
Miscellaneous	Officer Commanding, 21st Battn. M.G.C.	13/07/1918	13/07/1918
Operation(al) Order(s)	21st Battn. Machine Gun Corps Operation Order No. 31	21/07/1918	21/07/1918
Operation(al) Order(s)	Administrative Instructions With Reference To 21st. Battn. M.G.C. Operation Order No. 31	22/07/1918	22/07/1918
Operation(al) Order(s)	21st Battn. Machine Gun Corps, Operation Order No. 32	27/07/1918	27/07/1918
Miscellaneous	All Os. C. Coys. Forward. All Os. C. Coys. Rear Quartermaster. (for Infn.)	28/07/1918	28/07/1918
Operation(al) Order(s)	21st. Battn. M.G.C. Operation Order No. 33	28/07/1918	28/07/1918
Miscellaneous	21st Bn MGC Vol 6		
War Diary	Acheux	01/08/1918	23/08/1918
War Diary	Mailly-Maillet	24/08/1918	24/08/1918
War Diary	Grandcourt	25/08/1918	29/08/1918
War Diary	Lesars	30/08/1918	31/08/1918
Operation(al) Order(s)	21st Battn. Machine Gun Corps Operation Order No. 34	03/08/1918	03/08/1918
Miscellaneous	To:-All Os. Coys (Forward)	04/08/1918	04/08/1918
Miscellaneous	Addendum No. 1 To 21st Battn. M.G.C. Operation Order No. 34 Dated 3rd August 1918	04/08/1918	04/08/1918
Operation(al) Order(s)	21st Battn. Machine Gun Corps Operation Order No. 35	08/08/1918	08/08/1918
Miscellaneous	All Os. C. Companies.	12/08/1918	12/08/1918
Operation(al) Order(s)	21st Battn. Machine Gun Corps Operation Order No. 36	11/08/1918	11/08/1918
Miscellaneous	Administrative Instructions. Appendix "A"		
Miscellaneous	Purple System (20 Guns		
Miscellaneous			
Miscellaneous	21st Battn. Machine Gun Corps. Defence Scheme "Mailly Sector"	11/08/1918	11/08/1918
Miscellaneous	All Recipients Of 21st. Bn. M.G.C. Defence Scheme.	13/08/1918	13/08/1918
Operation(al) Order(s)	21st Battn. Machine Gun Corps Operation Order No. 37	13/08/1918	13/08/1918
Operation(al) Order(s)	21st. Bn. M.G.C. Operation Order No. 38	13/08/1918	13/08/1918
Miscellaneous	21st. Battn. Machine Gun Corps. Operation Order No. 39	14/08/1918	14/08/1918
Miscellaneous	All Recipients Of 21 Bn. M.G.C. Order No. 38		
Operation(al) Order(s)	21st Battn. Machine Gun Corps Operation Order No. 40	16/08/1918	16/08/1918
Operation(al) Order(s)	21st. Bn. M.G.C. Operation Order No. 41	20/08/1918	20/08/1918
Operation(al) Order(s)	21st Battn. Machine Gun Corps Operation Order No. 42.	21/08/1918	21/08/1918
Miscellaneous			
Miscellaneous	To 21 M.G. Battn.		
Miscellaneous	Telegram-Urgent Operations Priority To Bdes.		
Miscellaneous	Telegram-Urgent Operations-Priority.		
Miscellaneous	Telegram.		
Miscellaneous	Telegram-Urgent Operations Priority To Addresses.		
Miscellaneous	GX. 494		
Operation(al) Order(s)	Telegram-Urgent Operations Priority		
Miscellaneous	To O.C. "C" Coy.		
Miscellaneous	21st Division Order No. 210	23/08/1918	23/08/1918
Miscellaneous	Major Hardinge. MC.	24/08/1918	24/08/1918
Miscellaneous	Messages And Signals.		
Miscellaneous	Appendix III To 21st Division Order No. 210		
Miscellaneous	Lieut. Athol. O.C. "B" Coy. (Forward)	24/08/1918	24/08/1918

Miscellaneous	Urgent Operations Priority.		
Miscellaneous	Urgent Operations Priority To Bdes D.M.G.C. C.R.A. & Flank Divs.		
Miscellaneous	Urgent Operations Priority.		
Miscellaneous	Urgent Operations Priority To 110th Bde.		
Miscellaneous	O.C. "C" Coy. O. C. "A" Coy.-62nd Inf. Bde.		
Miscellaneous	Urgent Operations Priority. To Brigades.		
Miscellaneous	Messages And Signals.	27/08/1918	27/08/1918
Miscellaneous	21st Division Special Order Wednesday 28th August 1918.	28/08/1918	28/08/1918
Miscellaneous	Urgent Operations Priority To Bdes And D.M.G.C.		
Miscellaneous	O.C. "C" Coy.	28/08/1918	28/08/1918
Miscellaneous	Urgent Operations Priority To 3 Bdes.		
Miscellaneous	Position Code Calls.		
Miscellaneous	Urgent Operations Priority		
Miscellaneous	Messages And Signals.		
Miscellaneous	Medical Arrangements. Appendix "B"		
Heading	21 Bn M G Corps Vol 7 September 1918		
Miscellaneous	The Officer i/c A.G's Office The Base		
War Diary	Lesars	01/09/1918	02/09/1918
War Diary	Lesars M.15.a.Central	03/09/1918	04/09/1918
War Diary	Morval	05/09/1918	05/09/1918
War Diary	Morval T10.b.0.9	06/09/1918	07/09/1918
War Diary	Sunken Road U.10d.7.6	06/09/1918	08/09/1918
War Diary	Mesnil	09/09/1918	26/09/1918
War Diary	Fins	27/09/1918	30/09/1918
Miscellaneous	A Coy. O.Order 22	01/09/1918	01/09/1918
Miscellaneous	Urgent Operations Priority		
Miscellaneous	21st M.G. Battn.		
Miscellaneous	Urgent Operations Priority		
Miscellaneous	Priority		
Operation(al) Order(s)	21st. Bn. M.G.C. Operation Order No. 45	05/09/1918	05/09/1918
Miscellaneous	21st. Bn. M.G.C. Operation Order No. 45	05/09/1918	05/09/1918
Miscellaneous	Messages And Signals.	05/09/1918	05/09/1918
Miscellaneous	Messages And Signals.	06/09/1918	06/09/1918
Miscellaneous	To:-O.C. "D" Coy. (Forward)		
Miscellaneous	Urgent Operations Priority To 64th Bde.		
Miscellaneous	To:-O.C. "D" Coy.		
Miscellaneous	Urgent Operations Priority To 64th Bde. 62nd Bde.		
Miscellaneous	Urgent Operations Priority To 62nd And 64th Bdes.		
Miscellaneous	Urgent Operations Priority To Bdes.		
Miscellaneous	Urgent Operations Priority To 64 And 110 Bdes.		
Operation(al) Order(s)	21st. Bn. M.G.C. Operation Order No. 46	10/09/1918	10/09/1918
Miscellaneous	Urgent Operations Priority To 64 & 110 Bdes.		
Miscellaneous	Messages And Signals.		
Miscellaneous	Position Code Calls.		
Miscellaneous	62nd Inf. Bde.	10/09/1918	10/09/1918
Miscellaneous	O.C. "A" Coy. (Fwd)	11/09/1918	11/09/1918
Miscellaneous	To:-All Os. C. Coys. (Forward).	12/09/1918	12/09/1918
Operation(al) Order(s)	21st Battn. Machine Gun Corps Operation Order No. 47	13/09/1918	13/09/1918
Miscellaneous	Urgent Operations Priority To 110th And 19th Inf. Bdes.		
Miscellaneous	21st Division Special Order. Sunday 15th September 1918.		
Miscellaneous	21st Division Order No. 233	16/09/1918	16/09/1918
Miscellaneous	21st Battn. Machine Gun Corps Operation Order No. 48	16/09/1918	16/09/1918

Miscellaneous	To:-O.C. "A" Coy. Fwd.	16/09/1918	16/09/1918
Miscellaneous	Messages & Signals.		
Operation(al) Order(s)	In Continuation Of 21st. Battn. M.G.C. Operation Order No. 48	17/09/1918	17/09/1918
Miscellaneous	Barrage Time Table For Attack On Brown Line.		
Miscellaneous	O.C. "C" Coy. Forward With Tracing.	17/09/1918	17/09/1918
Map			
Miscellaneous	Addenda To 21st. Bn. M.G.C. O.O. No. 48	17/09/1918	17/09/1918
Miscellaneous	To:-O.C. "A" Coy. 33rd Bn. M.G.C.	17/09/1918	17/09/1918
Miscellaneous	62nd Inf. Bde.	17/09/1918	17/09/1918
Miscellaneous	21st. Division Special Order. Friday 20th September 1918.	20/09/1918	20/09/1918
Miscellaneous	All Recipients Of Divl. Order No. 233	17/09/1918	17/09/1918
Miscellaneous	Urgent Operations Priority To Brigades.		
Miscellaneous	21st. Bn. M.G.C. Operation Order No. 49	18/09/1918	18/09/1918
Miscellaneous	Messages & Signals.		
Miscellaneous	21st Division Order No. 235	19/09/1918	19/09/1918
Operation(al) Order(s)	21st. Bn. M.G.C. Operation Order No. 50	19/09/1918	19/09/1918
Miscellaneous	O.C. "C" Coy. Forward.	19/09/1918	19/09/1918
Miscellaneous	Copy Of Telegram Received From General Shute d/18.9.18	19/09/1918	19/09/1918
Miscellaneous	21st Division Order No. 236	23/09/1918	23/09/1918
Miscellaneous	Proceedings Of Conference Held At Divisional Headquarters, 23rd Sept, 1918	23/09/1918	23/09/1918
Operation(al) Order(s)	21st. Bn. M.G.C. Operation Order No. 51	24/09/1918	24/09/1918
Miscellaneous	Plan For Attack Along Quentin Ridge And On Gonnelieu.	24/09/1918	24/09/1918
Miscellaneous	21st Division Order No. 237	26/09/1918	26/09/1918
Miscellaneous	All Recipients of Divl. Order No. 237	26/09/1918	26/09/1918
Operation(al) Order(s)	21st. Bn. M.G.C. Operation Order No. 52	26/09/1918	26/09/1918
Miscellaneous	In Continuation of 21st. Bn. M.G.C. Operation Order No. 52		
Miscellaneous	21st. Battn. Machine Gun Corps.		
Miscellaneous	Amendment to 21st. Bn. M.G.C. Barrage Time Table No. 2		
Miscellaneous	21st. Bn. Machine Gun Corps.		
Miscellaneous	21st Battalion M.G. Corps.		
Miscellaneous	Appendix "A" to 21st. Bn. M.G.C. O.O. No. 52		
Miscellaneous	Appendix "B" to 21st. Bn. M.G.C. O.O. No. 52		
Miscellaneous	All Recipients Of Div. Order No. 237	27/09/1918	27/09/1918
Miscellaneous	Urgent Operations Priority To Bdes H. I. F.		
Miscellaneous	Messages And Signals.		
Miscellaneous	D. R. L. S. 5th Div.		
Miscellaneous	Urgent Operations Priority to 3 Bdes.		
Miscellaneous	Forecast Of Future Policy.	29/09/1918	29/09/1918
Miscellaneous	Messages And Signals.		
War Diary	Fins	01/10/1918	05/10/1918
War Diary	Gouzeaucourt		
War Diary	Gouzecourt	05/10/1918	06/10/1918
War Diary	Gratte Panche Farm	07/10/1918	10/10/1918
War Diary	Walincourt	11/10/1918	22/10/1918
War Diary	Inchy	22/10/1918	22/10/1918
War Diary	Neuvilly	22/10/1918	23/10/1918
War Diary	Neuvilly	24/10/1918	24/10/1918
War Diary	Vendegies au Bois		
War Diary	Vendegies	24/10/1918	26/10/1918

War Diary	Neuvilly	26/10/1918	29/10/1918
War Diary	Vendegies	29/10/1918	31/10/1918
Heading	War Diary 21st Bn. Machine Gun Corps. October 1918		
Miscellaneous	Messages And Signals.		
Miscellaneous	21st Division Order No. 242	02/10/1918	02/10/1918
Miscellaneous	Urgent Operations Priority to 3 Bdes.		
Operation(al) Order(s)	21st Battn. Machine Gun Corps Operation Order No. 53	03/10/1918	03/10/1918
Miscellaneous	Urgent Operations Priority to 3 Bdes		
Operation(al) Order(s)	21st Battn. Machine Gun Corps Operation order No. 54	05/10/1918	05/10/1918
Miscellaneous	Urgent Operations Priority		
Miscellaneous	Messages & Signals.		
Miscellaneous	Messages And Signals.		
Miscellaneous	21st Division Order No. 246	07/10/1918	07/10/1918
Miscellaneous	Urgent Operations Priority.		
Miscellaneous	Messages And Signals.		
Miscellaneous	21st Division Special Order. Saturday 12th October 1918.	12/10/1918	12/10/1918
Miscellaneous	21st. Battn. M.G. Corps Administrative Instructions No. 4 for forthcoming Operations.	20/10/1918	20/10/1918
Miscellaneous	Reference 21st. Bn. M.G. Corps Administrative Instructions No. 4 for Forthcoming Operations.	21/10/1918	21/10/1918
Operation(al) Order(s)	21st Battn. Machine Gun Corps Operation Order No. 55	18/10/1918	18/10/1918
Miscellaneous	21st Division Order No. 247	21/10/1918	21/10/1918
Miscellaneous	All Recipients of Div. Order No. 247	21/10/1918	21/10/1918
Miscellaneous	To All recipients of Div. Order No. 247	21/10/1918	21/10/1918
Miscellaneous	21st Battn. Machine Gun Corps Administrative Instructions No. 5	21/10/1918	21/10/1918
Operation(al) Order(s)	21st Battn. Machine Gun Corps Operation Order No. 56	21/10/1918	21/10/1918
Miscellaneous	Priority		
Miscellaneous	Urgent. Operations priority to Brigades.		
Miscellaneous	Urgent Operations Priority 3 Bdes. D.M.G.C.		
Miscellaneous	Messages & Signals.		
Miscellaneous	Urgent Operations Priority 3 Bdes.		
Miscellaneous	Urgent Operations Priority To Bdes.		
Miscellaneous	Messages & Signals.		
Miscellaneous	GX. 228		
Miscellaneous	21st Division Order No. 253	26/10/1918	26/10/1918
Miscellaneous	Table To Accompany 21st Division Order No. 253		
Operation(al) Order(s)	21st Battalion Machine Gun Corps. Operation Order No. 57	26/10/1918	26/10/1918
Miscellaneous	21st Division Order No. 254	28/10/1918	28/10/1918
Operation(al) Order(s)	Operation Order No. 58 21st Battalion Machine Gun Corps.	28/10/1918	28/10/1918
Miscellaneous	21st Battalion Machine Gun Corps.	28/10/1918	28/10/1918
Miscellaneous	62 Inf. Bde.	30/10/1918	30/10/1918
Miscellaneous	21st Division Order No. 255	31/10/1918	31/10/1918
Heading	War Diary Of 21st Battn. Machine Gun Corps. From 1st November 1918 To 30th November 1918 Vol 9		
War Diary	Vendegies	01/11/1918	02/11/1918
War Diary	Neuvilly	03/11/1918	04/11/1918
War Diary	Poix	04/11/1918	05/11/1918
War Diary	Locquienol	05/11/1918	07/11/1918
War Diary	Berlaimont	07/11/1918	11/11/1918
War Diary	Bachant		
War Diary	Bachant	12/11/1918	12/11/1918
War Diary	Aymeries	13/11/1918	15/11/1918

War Diary	Berlaimont	16/11/1918	30/11/1918
Miscellaneous	21st Division Order No. 256	01/11/1918	01/11/1918
Miscellaneous	Table to accompany 21st Division Order No. 256		
Operation(al) Order(s)	21st Battalion Machine Gun Corps Operation Order No. 59	02/11/1918	02/11/1918
Miscellaneous	21st. Battalion Machine Gun Corps. Administrative Instructions No. 6		
Miscellaneous	21st Division Order No. 257	02/11/1918	02/11/1918
Miscellaneous	21st Battn. Machine Gun Corps Operation Order No. 60	03/11/1918	03/11/1918
Miscellaneous	21 Bn. M.G.C. Assembly Instruction No. 1	03/11/1918	03/11/1918
Miscellaneous	21st Battalion Machine Gun Corps.	03/11/1918	03/11/1918
Miscellaneous	Ref. 21 Bn. M.G.C. Operation Order No. 60	03/11/1918	03/11/1918
Miscellaneous	All Recipients of 21st Bn. M.G. Corps Order No. 60	03/11/1918	03/11/1918
Miscellaneous	21st Battalion Machine Gun Corps.	03/11/1918	03/11/1918
Miscellaneous	Urgent Operations Priority 3 Bdes.		
Miscellaneous	Telegram.		
Miscellaneous	SDR Bdes 33rd. Div.		
Miscellaneous	Urgent Operations Priority To Bdes. HIF.		
Miscellaneous	Messages And Signals.		
Miscellaneous	21st Division Special Order. Monday 11th November 1918.	11/11/1918	11/11/1918
Miscellaneous	C Form Messages And Signals.	11/11/1918	11/11/1918
Miscellaneous	Copy of telegram received from Lieut-General C.D. Shute Commander of Vth Corps,		
Miscellaneous	Priority to 62 Bde.		
Miscellaneous	To all recipients 21st Div. Order No. 263	11/11/1918	11/11/1918
Miscellaneous	Messages And Signals.		
Miscellaneous	Messages And Signals		
Miscellaneous	War Diary of 21st Batt. Machine Gun Corps. From December 1st.To December 31st 1918 Vol 10		
War Diary	Berlimont	01/12/1918	12/12/1918
War Diary	Vendiges	13/12/1918	13/12/1918
War Diary	Inchy	14/11/1918	17/11/1918
War Diary	Breilly	18/11/1918	30/11/1918
Operation(al) Order(s)	21st. Bn. M.G.C. Operation Order No. 61	09/12/1918	09/12/1918
Miscellaneous	Administrative Instructions in Connection With 21st. Battalion Machine Gun Corps Order No. 61	10/12/1918	10/12/1918
Miscellaneous	21st Battalion Machine Gun Corps. Special instructions re "Staging of Battn. Transport"	10/12/1918	10/12/1918
Operation(al) Order(s)	21st Battn. Machine Gun Corps Operation Order No. 62	15/12/1918	15/12/1918
Miscellaneous	Table to Accompany 21st. Bn. M.G.C. Order No. 62 for embussing 17-12-18		
War Diary	Breilly	01/01/1919	31/01/1919
Heading	War Diary Of 21st Batt. Machine Gun Corps. From 1st February 1919 To 28th February,1919 Vol 12		
War Diary	Breilly Sur Somme	01/02/1919	28/02/1919
Miscellaneous	H.Q. 21st Division.	03/04/1919	03/04/1919
War Diary	Breilly Sur Somme	01/03/1919	31/03/1919

2145/2

21 Battalion Machine Gun Corp.

21ST DIVISION

21 BN Machine Gun Corps

~~23rd Machine Gun Coy~~
~~Sept 1916 – Mar 1918~~
1918 MAR — 1919 MAR

~~Machine Gun Coy~~
~~1917 — 1918~~

21st Div.

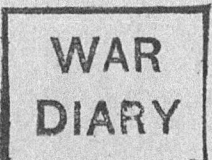

21st BATTALION, MACHINE GUN CORPS.

M A R C H

1 9 1 8

Attached:-

Report on M.G. Operations
from midnight 20/21st -
midnight 28/29th March.

21st Division

CORPS.
X 82

Herewith War Diary of this unit for the month of March 1918.

A.C. Bothwick, Major.
Cmdg. 21st Bn Machine Gun Corps.

7 April 1918.

Army Form C. 2118.

Place	Date	Hour	Summary of Events and Information	Remarks and references to Appendices
	1918 March 5 to March 6		"A", "B" and "D" Companies in the line. Situation normal. Disposition of Companies:- "A" Company on LEFT Sector. "B" Company in CENTRE Sector. "D" Company on RIGHT Sector. "C" Company at Batt'n HQrs in reserve.	
	March 7		"C" Company relieved "B" Company in the CENTRE Sector. Disposition of A and D Companies remain unaltered. B Company relieved to Battalion HqQrs at LONGAVESNES. Situation on the Divisional Front quite normal.	
	March 8		Nothing of note occurred today. The work of digging and improving old mine workings and improving old mine continued. "B" Company highly employed in work on Battalion HqQrs. qualities.	
	" 9		The situation continues to be normal. Enemy artillery active during remainder of day.	
	" 10		Enemy Artillery active this evening, our trench line between THRUSH VALLEY and FINNEY VALLEY being shelled with heavy shrapnel. A dump to W. of the BEET FACTORY was blown up by an artillery at 10.15 p.m.	
	" 11		The situation still normal. Desultory shelling on both sides.	
	" 12		Very heavy shelling well to our left. Lines down and very but the situation on our front remains normal. Several hostile aeroplanes were engaged by	

A6945 Wt.W17422/M1160 350,000 12/16 D.D. &L. Forms/C/2118/14.

INTELLIGENCE SUMMARY

(Erase heading not required.)

Place	Date	Hour	Summary of Events and Information	Remarks and references to Appendices
	1918			
	March 10		nil fire. Between 12.30 a.m. and 2.30 a.m. the enemy put over about 60 gas shells but the Battalion sustained no casualties. At 9.30 am a few more gas shells fell in EPEHY. Visibility was good today, and several hostile aeroplanes were engaged by our Machine Gun fire. Work on Battalion Headquarters and the Reserve Company's Camping still proceeding, and excellent progress is being made. Huts have been erected and the surrounding ground dug preparatory to being placed under cultivation.	
	" 11th		Artillery on both sides was markedly active today but little activity was shown in the air. Visibility was bad. Orders for relief being sent from a large number of emissionary patrols up by us of no avail as no one representative showed himself from the enemy. Our Arc lights & M.Gs would be a hindrance at 11p.m. the movements of the enemy B.E.F trench about the Jones West of Knoll & Brigade in a frontage of about 50 yards fourteen men of the Battalion fired an excellent of the casualty of 2 2000 rounds were expended	

Army Form C. 2118.

WAR DIARY
or
INTELLIGENCE SUMMARY.
(Erase heading not required.)

Instructions regarding War Diaries and Intelligence Summaries are contained in F. S. Regs., Part II. and the Staff Manual respectively. Title pages will be prepared in manuscript.

Place	Date	Hour	Summary of Events and Information	Remarks and references to Appendices
Battalion Hd	1918 March 14th (cont)		At 11 P.M. 10ff the guns opened on Nivelle at L angle 20.11.1 p.m. The remainder of guns fired fire on areas about suspected lines of approach & were to dissuade the enemy as to the front to be raided & to retard the ready reserves from any intervention & prevent	
Longuesnes				
Bullecourt			the Battery & trenches extensively the enemy replied	
Epéhy			9 a.m. German officer and rank were explored. The enemy artillery was very quiet. Many Sos. signals were sent up. Probably 3 given by us being made. The enemy SOS signals appeared unsuccessful.	
Villeselve Farm	March 15th		At 6 & 5 a.m. the S.O.S. went up on our front side at G.19 of him but was responded immediately. No reinforcements reported. Apparently the enemy in alarm at news of enemy raid would be quiet of our seem the S.O.S. situation of artillery & M.G. machine at 7.6 seem to be mostly fired by our own General activity resumed during the day. 15 bombs aeroplanes located near our new rebel huts	

WAR DIARY
or
INTELLIGENCE SUMMARY.

(Erase heading not required.)

Army Form C. 2118.

Place	Date	Hour	Summary of Events and Information	Remarks and references to Appendices
EPEHY	March 16"		Nothing of special interest occurred. Enemy aeroplanes very active.	
			Enemy shelled VILLERS GUISLAIN tonight.	
	17.3.18		Situation normal. About 8am enemy aircraft very active & fire was [exchanged]. One hostile aeroplane was brought down. [illegible]. Between 4.30pm & 9pm 3 large enemy aeroplanes flew over the camp near N of PEIZIERE. A large enemy camp was seen South of GUISCARD about 15km S.E. of PEIZIERE. Enemy balloons very high. "B" Company relieved "D" Company. Relief completed by 4 a.m. Guns heard night.	
	18.3.18		Enemy aeroplane activity was again noted as was shelling around our [lines]. Guns and rifle fire heard every 3 hours [illegible]. 9.30 p.m. hostility of enemy aircraft [illegible]. [illegible].	
	19.3.18		Report of enemy trench mortar fire at 5 a.m. [illegible] artillery [illegible] activity over our [lines] early in the morning. Enemy aeroplanes frequently [illegible] during the morning. [illegible] hostile M.G. defence fire became active.	

A6945 Wt. W1422/M1160 350,000 12/16 D. D. & L. Forms/C./2118/14.

Army Form C. 2118.

WAR DIARY
or
INTELLIGENCE SUMMARY.
(Erase heading not required.)

Instructions regarding War Diaries and Intelligence Summaries are contained in F. S. Regs., Part II. and the Staff Manual respectively. Title pages will be prepared in manuscript.

Place	Date	Hour	Summary of Events and Information	Remarks and references to Appendices
	20.3.18	6	A very thick ground mist. Enemy attack. Enemy expected heavy enemy shelling but take place. Enemy infantry advancing if the mercy of	
	21.3.18		On this date enemy offensive started. As it is impossible to give a detailed statement of its movements if the daily enemy movements up to 9 pm their work is attached to war Diary	
	21.3.18		Enemy offensive started. Longuedo moved to Bus. 2nd Batt. did not go far as Longueau station being shelled.	Ref 12
			No news of men up to 6 am. 2nd Btn had dispersed when the enemy advanced on only. Lieut Bell leaving to a further enemy attack.	Appx "
LONGUEAU	22.3.18		B Division on refuge of the Can. & Byron aims about noon. Albert close between Rev our Byron aim of the enemy to Rubenpre fugitives ever appear way in the G.T. Embyre moving down from Quesnoy	"
QUESNOYAUXMONTS				"

Army Form C. 2118.

WAR DIARY
or
INTELLIGENCE SUMMARY.
(Erase heading not required.)

Instructions regarding War Diaries and Intelligence Summaries are contained in F. S. Regs., Part II. and the Staff Manual respectively. Title pages will be prepared in manuscript.

Place	Date	Hour	Summary of Events and Information	Remarks and references to Appendices
	22.3.18		Great mist - one mile E of Azy Over to Hast - Battalion H.Q. moved to HOUDRICOURT. Transport at HAUT BOSQUET	
	23.3.18		Early morning Battle inspected under Major 4.0. to Direct all summer as Transport moved from HAUT BOSQUETS to CREVECOEUR through HUS. In the end I coy was ordered up to moved up with the advance selected heavy cavalry + unit of infantry holding the new rear defence saved. Advanced cavalry + infantry defeated. Both never	
	24.3.18		units days 24th to the Marne area. Heavy fighting Lieut Cleary h.M. Scott D.S.O M.C aylorted own red a enemy machine gun. Laplace took over command of the Battalion however relieved from the line + if the Battalion had supplied and suffered immense Sentences to Capt Walker to moved to rest	
	25.3.18		Battalion marched to BOAY under the command escorted also known to bivouac. A conference emerged of I guns under Capt Batcroft on are future course of the advance ordered to reinforce is 32 division who have	

A6945 Wt W14742/M1160 12/16 D. D. & L. Form/C./2118/14.

WAR DIARY
or
INTELLIGENCE SUMMARY.
(Erase heading not required.)

Army Form C. 2118.

Instructions regarding War Diaries and Intelligence Summaries are contained in F. S. Regs., Part II. and the Staff Manual respectively. Title pages will be prepared in manuscript.

Place	Date	Hour	Summary of Events and Information	Remarks and references to Appendices
	25.8.15		remainder of no ?? ?? left ??	
			Regt. to ?? ?? march train to ??	Map
BERGUETTE				
CAMBLAIN	26.	8.15	In the morning about 9am of pair of ?? ?? ?? ??	Armies
			also marched from the B.H.Q. attached to B.H.C. 1 battalion of	it
			when [illegible] the [illegible] Battalion moved to	
			BRECKENROUGE. B.H.Q. of [illegible] of [illegible] were at	
			[illegible] guns & 6 vickers guns the reinforcement up	
			[illegible] the enemy [illegible] it's airplanes of the 3rd	
BRESSE	27.	3.15	[illegible] up men cyclist from Co [illegible]	
			a [illegible] [illegible] infantry [illegible] at [illegible]	
			they [illegible] in their [illegible] no casualty & [illegible] regard to [illegible] H.Q.	
			ST LAURENT [illegible] [illegible] late to BAILLEUL'S 4.P. [illegible]	
			regt. Encountered enemy [illegible] of infantry who	
FOUQUIERES	28.	3.15	[illegible] cleaned up [illegible] at ?? [illegible] & [illegible]	
			a Bay regiment claim 2ct [illegible] [illegible] Engrs	
			shortly of [illegible] [illegible] [illegible] received	
	29.	3.15	a [illegible] of [illegible] [illegible] [illegible] marched from Bert [illegible]	

WAR DIARY
or
INTELLIGENCE SUMMARY.
(Erase heading not required.)

Army Form C. 2118.

Instructions regarding War Diaries and Intelligence Summaries are contained in F. S. Regs., Part II. and the Staff Manual respectively. Title pages will be prepared in manuscript.

Place	Date	Hour	Summary of Events and Information	Remarks and references to Appendices
FROMELLES	9/3/18 (cont)		order Capt Thomson 4 ordered 2 gun of 4 section forward. Helby fired which acted as a possible measure	
	10.3.18		Capt Chapman with remainder of B section joined B Battalion. Proposed to move 2 guns when weather would be cooler nearer our lines.	
COMMILLETTE	11.3.18		Position shared to refused 2 to cover rd running through our stuff of Coz. Helby was to a trickled 2 + trickled 3 came forward as 4 I second reported Guns were also sent up.	

R.C. Bathurst Major.
Commanding 21st Bn. Machine Gun Corps

Report on M.G. Operations from Midnight 20/21st - midnight 28/29th March.

28th Division.

Report on the Operations from midnight
20th/21st — midnight 28th/29th March.

Map Ref.
VILLERS GUISLAIN 57c SE
EPEHY 62c NE

DISPOSITIONS   The Sector held by the 21st Lancers
was supported by three M.G. Companies
in the line, and one Company in Reserve.
The defence was organised in depth to
an extent of 2,000 yds. guns being
grouped in Pairs in the Forward Area
and Batteries in the Rear Area, each
Pair and Battery being under the
control of an Officer. On operations
commencing, each odd or pairs of guns
came under the control of the Battalion
Commander in whose Sector they were
situated. The Batteries were controlled
from Group H.Q. by telephone.

Preparations   Owing to the fact that the intention
of the enemy to attack was known every
precaution had been taken to ensure
that the M.G. defence was sound and that
all ranks thoroughly understood what
would be expected of them.
S.A.A. Dumps, Reserves of Personnel and
Oil were formed and as far as could
be foreseen, everything was in readiness
to make a determined resistance in the
event of an attack.

The Attack   Throughout the night 20th/21st, the
March 21st   enemy artillery which had been
previously abnormally active at the present
increased until 4:45 A.M. when a
terrific bombardment was opened on
our trench system and back areas

- 2 -

Shells of all calibres including a large proportion of gas shells were fired, the latter necessitating the gun teams wearing Gas Masks up to 3½ hours. Unfortunately a thick mist rendered all observation impossible, with the result that from the majority of gun positions no S.O.S. was observed, neither was it possible to ascertain the position of either our own or the enemy's troops. All M.Gs were therefore very severely handicapped, and it is impossible to over-estimate the disadvantages under which the defence was thus placed.

At 10 A.M. it was reported that VAUCELLETTE FARM had fallen, and that the enemy was advancing along CHAPEL HILL towards CAVALRY SUPPORT TRENCH. The fire of three Batteries (9 guns) was therefore directed on to VAUCELLETTE FARM and the open ground to the West. At the same time a report was received that the 16th Division had been heavily attacked, and was falling back. This latter information was as once sent to all guns on our right, with orders to watch the exposed flank and engage all visible targets. At 11 A.M. the mist have lifted sufficiently to enable guns to get direct shooting and heavy casualties were inflicted on the enemy on CHAPEL HILL VAUCELLETTE - PEIZIERE RIDGE, and the vicinity of LEMPIRE.

Throughout the day all M.Gs kept up effective fire although in cases almost surrounded by the enemy, and continued inflicting tremendous losses until eventually silenced by sheer weight of numbers. The guns at CHAPEL CROSSING and on CHAPEL HILL held their ground all day, and especially the Battery just East of GENIN WELL COPSE

deserve recognition. One gun firing from
W.23.a engaged a target of about 80 at
the Haystacks. About 40 of them were
killed and the remainder surrendered.
During the evening counter attacks by
the 2nd Lincolns and 7th Leicesters supported
by M.G. fire successfully drove the enemy
back and cleared PEIZIERE. However the
night of 21st/22nd was quiet on the
Divisional front.

The morning of 22nd was again misty
and it was not until 10.30 A.M. that M.G.
were able to observe their fire. The enemy's
main intention then appeared to be to
envelope EPEHY from the North and South.
M.G's at TOTTENHAM POST and No.3 Battery
caused appreciable casualties as the enemy
attempted to advance on PEIZIERE from
Sunken Road in W.30.b and Railway in
X.25.a. The guns at No.1 Battery and
4 guns at F.7.a inflicted ...... losses
as he advanced on the Southern flank.
At about 1.0 P.M. orders were received to
withdraw from our advanced posts and
occupy the Brown Line. This was carried
out under heavy rifle & M.G. fire from
PEIZIERE and EPEHY with slight casualties.
On taking up position on this line a
determined stand was made by 8 guns of
the Battalion in front of HEUDECOURT until
both flanks were turned and all
ammunition expended. A prolonged
resistance of this line was impossible owing
to the enemy's occupation of GUYENCOURT.

From this onwards M.G's became too
scattered to enable any connected report
to be rendered. Guns usually working in
pairs fought their way back in gallant
style, stands being made at the Aerodrome

/LONGAVESNES

- 4 -

LONGAVESNES, GREEN LINE, AIZECOURT-LE-HAUT, HAUT ALLAINES, CLERY. On arrival at [?] on the 25th March, a Company of 8 guns was attached to General Headlam's Force. These guns were posted to command the approaches to BRAY from the East, and obtained many excellent targets. Other Sections were detached from the Battalion as guns allowed, and in all cases where they got into action heavy casualties were inflicted. All ranks throughout the operations displayed the utmost gallantry and self-sacrifice, at all times covering the withdrawal of our infantry, and remaining in action until ordered to withdraw or annihilated. All reports show that the losses inflicted on the enemy were undoubtedly very severe, and in no case did he capture a defended area without paying a heavy price in men. The morale of the men was at all times excellent, in spite of the most trying conditions.

R C B [?] Major
Comdg 21st Batn M G C

8/4/18.

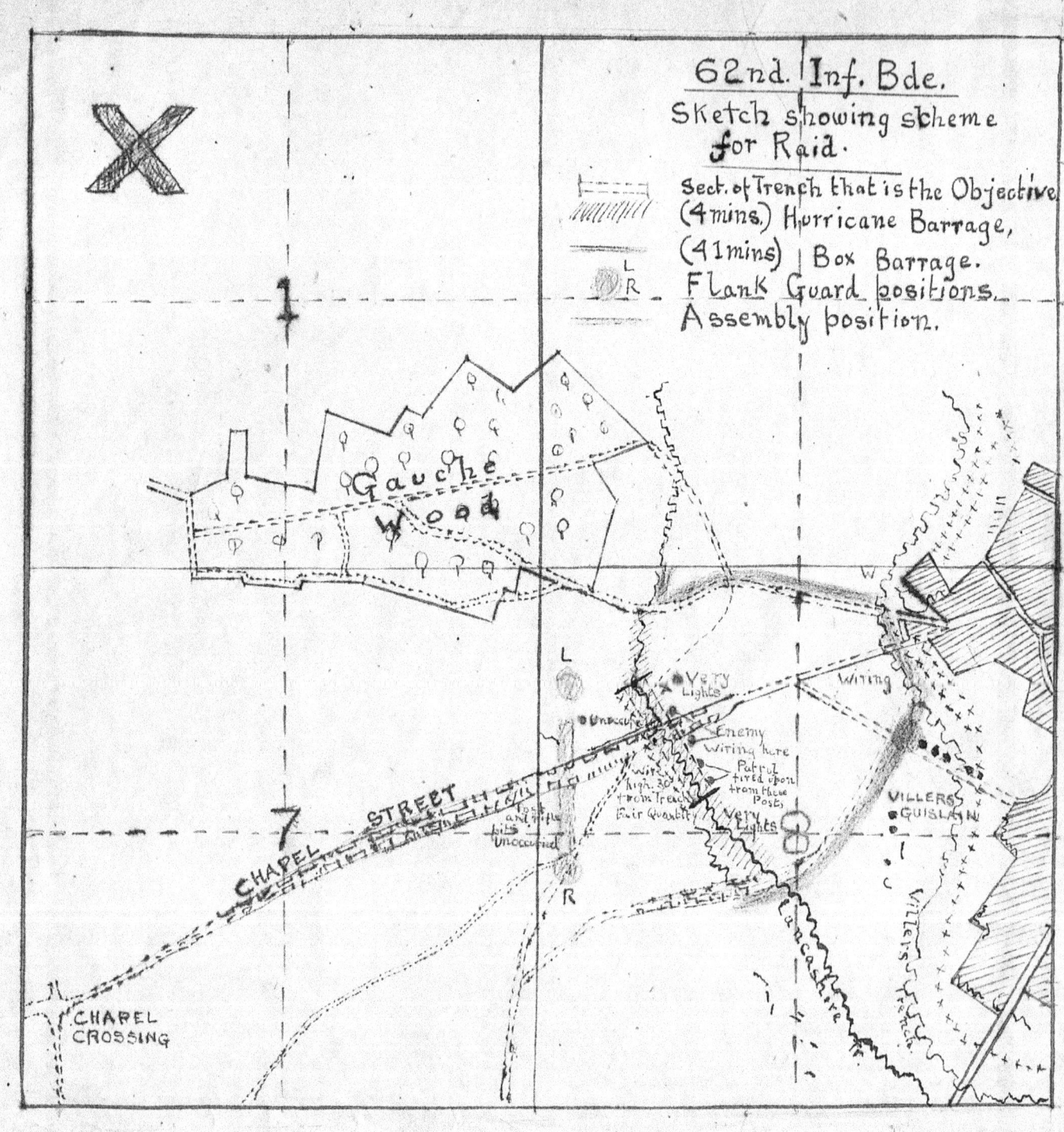

21st Divisional Troops.

21st BATTALION MACHINE GUN CORPS

APRIL 1918.

Army Form C. 2118.

WAR DIARY
or
INTELLIGENCE SUMMARY.
(Erase heading not required.)

21st Bn R. Battalion

Instructions regarding War Diaries and Intelligence Summaries are contained in F.S. Regs., Part II. and the Staff Manual respectively. Title pages Ap 1st - 30th 1918 will be prepared in manuscript.

Place	Date	Hour	Summary of Events and Information	Remarks and references to Appendices
AMIENS	Ap 1st 1918		Battalion moved from CARDINETTE to Belgium. Two Companies AT Bn train at LaVaire d'Road. AMIENS at 10 a.m. with transport. Two Companies at C.T.O at 10.50 pm and Bn Headquarters at 7.50 pm.	
LOCRE	Ap 2		Battalion arrived at LOCRE & encamped in BIRR CAMP. Poor accommodation. Bn HQ opened at 12 noon M.29.b 50.70. (Sheet 28 France & Belgium 1/40,000) afternoon spent in cleaning up, reorganizing etc.	
	Ap 3		C.O. with C.O. of 1st Aus Bn 9 Batt to arrange relief accompanied by O.C. "B" Coy. Maj Ryland with new C.O. C.O. attended conference at DIV. 10 Officers + 250 O.R. arrived from Base as reinforcements. 2/Lt Stace reported from leave.	
	Ap 4		10-3.00 - 1 Officer + 70 O.R. per Coy were inspected by G.O.C 2nd Army. B.O.C Division inspected Batt at 9.15 a.m. 9.30 a.m. C.Os conference of Coy comm? Y.O T.O.M. B. + C. Coy relieved 1st Batt Aus Bn R.C. in the line. Platoon pkts Remainder of Battalion including transport moved to GLASGOW CAMP 1-15 a.m. 5-4-18. KEMMEL & Bn HQ opens at N.20.a 90.30 at 4 pm (Belgium Sheet 28 1/40,000) Accommodation limited. No Lewis guns in line 18.	
	Ap 5		Work carried by by Companies. Co. went round line + selected positions for 6 new guns which were sent up during the evening. 10 Officers + 5 O.R. reinforcements.	
	Ap 6		50 O.R. arrived as Reinforcements. Two Platoons at BOLLER CAMP under command of 2/Lt Lakin	
	Ap 7		Lt Col B.D.Ray reports to take over command of the 21st Bn R.B attn. Capt V.S Samuels D.S.O. 4th Batt D.E Queens reported for duty. Two Coys at Reignor Camp carried on reorganization.	
	Ap 8		Companies carried on training under Coy arrangements.	

D.D. & L.td, London, E.C.
(N700) W.W.1771/M2031 750,000 5/17 Sch.52 Forms C2-16/14

Army Form C. 2118.

WAR DIARY
or
INTELLIGENCE SUMMARY.
(Erase heading not required.)

Instructions regarding War Diaries and Intelligence Summaries are contained in F.S. Regs, Part II. and the Staff Manual respectively. Title pages will be prepared in manuscript.

Place	Date	Hour	Summary of Events and Information	Remarks and references to Appendices
	9-4-18		A Coy (16 Guns) + 2 Guns B Coy took over Left Sector of Line from 49th Bn R. Batt in HOOGE Sector. Reliefs complete at 10 am - without casualties. Coy HQ. JACKDAW TUNNELS.	
	10-4-18		D Coy (16 Guns) took over Right Sector of the Line, B Head Quarters, B.T.C. Coy; together with details of A.D. Coy move to BRISTOL CAMP - H35A 50.50 (Sheet 28. Bel France 1/40,000) Transport to Ouderdom Camp H32 A 50.30. Transport brought up to BRISTOL CAMP for "STAND TO". 2/Lt Ruckles 147B uckles sent to Divisional rest Station for Inoculation.	
	11-4-18		Battalion "Stood to" at 5 am. throughout day ready to move at 6 mins notice. C.O. visited Left Sector. 2 Officers per Coy made reconnaissance of Corps Line.	
	12-4-18		Work carried on by Companies Commanding. Officers reconnoitred Rt Coys lines indicated are gun positions to be manned by gun withdrawn from forward positions. These positions at I 30. 1. H 30 3 by D Coy gun team by 8-15 pm. C.O. interviewed by G. in charge J. Coy D.Hd army Helt Battalion Commander. Capt cation in Army line produced report. Casualties OR 3 wounded Divisional Rest. 2 Officers reconnoitred Army Line.	
	13-4-18		Coy Coy stood to at 5 am. Companies carried out training on the 25 yd Tank gun butt places at 2-6 p.m. C.O. inspected Battalion. whole of the Battalion take out Holiday.	
	14-4-18		Church Parade also here. B.T.C. Coy fired on 25 yd Range. Two gun B Coy were relieved by 2 A theorned Coy at BRISTOL CAMP. Coy Commander reconnoitred new outpost line. C.O. at DIVISION received instruction as withdrawal	

Army Form C. 2118.

WAR DIARY
or
INTELLIGENCE SUMMARY.
(Erase heading not required.)

Instructions regarding War Diaries and Intelligence Summaries are contained in F. S. Regs., Part II. and the Staff Manual respectively. Title pages will be prepared in manuscript.

Place	Date	Hour	Summary of Events and Information	Remarks and references to Appendices
	15.4.18		In early hours Retreat guns -7½ A + 2 D Coyours withdrawn & returned BRISTOL CAMP. C.O. + 2½ reconnoitred the most front line for gun positions. B + C Coys placed B + 15 gun respectively into position – Coys by 11.45pm. Remainder return camp.	
	16.4.18		Platt HQ. Transport moved to MIDDLESEX GHP. C17A 10.10. A Coy 12 guns – B Coy 9 guns. C.O. reconnoitred DICKEBUSCH line to the "A" line. Borrowed guns [A + D Coys] returned to camp leaving 4 guns placed by in Corps line. C.O. + 2½ reached Division re. R.B. disposition.	
	17.4.18		C.O. visited Divisional Commander D.A. + staff Division. Machine Gun Corps billets well hit. HV shells from 10.30am to 3.30pm (2 killed – 7 wounded) Shell mandible into meal sections. A quantity of trapped for equipment destroyed Coys + Coy Bivouacs just beyond shelled area. 2 Lt Snow reported from leave. 1 Officer 9 & O.R. casualties [?] arrived at 3pm – Casualties OR 20 killed, wounded, missing	
	18.4.18		C.O. visited Division – received instructions & defence of BEDFORD HOUSE & VOORMEZEELE and instructed Capt. Thomas reconnoitred DICKEBUSCH LINE with special reference to defence of left flank of Division.	
	19.4.18		C.O. visited VOORMEZEELE – BEDFORD HOUSE. Both ½pt bomb shell & ½pt shell or A.T. look on long as possible. Two On G allotted to each place. Saw MGC's R des Commande who distribution of M.G. vickers in Battalion. Commander B/G/alter + Two Coy Commanding 2.Lt G.R.Roth. Gun run medically N.2 KRUISTRAAT HOEK – VOORMEZEELE. Rd was blown up. Lambert killed. A Coy (8 guns) reduced Play (4 guns) + Play (4 guns) in Corps hire R.O. left complete 9.15pm. Cas – B.L. OR 1Dn OR 1 2 wounded.	

D. D. & L., London, E.C.
Wt. W1271/M2971 750,000 5/17 Sch. 52 Forms C2.–6/14
(A 001)

WAR DIARY
or
INTELLIGENCE SUMMARY.
(Erase heading not required.)

Army Form C. 2118.

Place	Date	Hour	Summary of Events and Information	Remarks and references to Appendices
	20.4.18		Heavy shelling of "C" Coy HQ. at CHATEAU SEGARD. C.O. & 30th Bn G Batt visited C.O. of 20 gun Bty Comd by Capt Boyle - placed under control of 21st Division and occupying position on right flank of Divisional front. Orders to Zone. C.O. visited G.O.C. Division & received order to place 10 guns at disposal of B.G.C. 110 Bde. & Bann H.Cy. 1B, 10 details Capt Boyle started Batt. H.Q. Cosmidden. V.C.R. 1 Rabbit missing.	O.O.R. O/C Coby 9.0.10 Mr M Col
	21.4.18		10 Guns in detail yesterday shook to at 5am moved off at 9pm to vicinity of 110th Bde. H.Q. H27 central, under command of Capt Howard. C.O. visited Division formed D.A.A. & V.M.B. dispositions taken to G.O.C. Division & B.G.C. left four guns in Corps line relieved by C.M. Division. 2 reinforces own Corp line & two relieved Camp. Relieved plate 4, 8-45 pm Casualties OR 1 wounded. L/CR Ball & L/CR Shaw reported for duty. Major Anderton (Capt Bn.) having been returned to Camp took on command of D Coy.	O.O.R. O/C Coby 9.0.11 O.O.H
	22.4.18		by Capt Boswell, relieved Capt Howard who returned to Camp.	O.O.H
	23.4.18		C.O. visited B & C Coy in line, including several guns position in rear forward lines. line held by 21st I Bde & covered with special officers in M.G. positions informed OC Manchester 1st M.G. Coy. Returned to 21st I Bde reported suggested changes.	O.O.R.
	24.4.18		Quiet day. Received orders for Division redistribution of front Operation order drawn up affecting B, C & D Coys for the main & relief. These orders were subsequently cancelled owing to enemy attack pending.	O.O.R. O/C Coby 9.0.12 O.O.H
	25.4.18		Early in morning Enemy attacked in region of KEMMEL & advanced as far as SIEGE FARM & YORK HOUSE at 1-15 pm 18 guns (16D, 1B, 1C.) proceeded to WALKER CAMP H15 a from placed under order of B.G. C/Nor Rd. Capt Howard in command. 4 Guns of Aty (Maj Anderton) sent to defend S bank DICKEBUSCH LAKE & MILLE BAST CORNER. 2 Guns sent to locality between RIDGE WOOD & BRISTOL CAMP. Casualties OR 1 wounded.	O.O.R.

WAR DIARY or INTELLIGENCE SUMMARY

Army Form C. 2118.

Place	Date	Hour	Summary of Events and Information	Remarks and references to Appendices
	25.4.16		15 Guns of D Coy were sent to strengthen the night flank shortly. C.O. of Bns. moved up day. Casualties O.R. 2 killed, 13 wounded (1 rem. duty). Capt 2nd THOMSON - C.M. HOWARD appointed A/MAJ. Lt C.W.R. BALL M.C. to be A/CAPT.	no 15 OOH
	26.4.16		Enemy captured BLUFF & SPOIL BANK. Gun position were heavily shelled. Lieut Regt L'Adelechot did very good work firing on an average 2000 rounds per gun. One Boche with Mr B attached was killed 50 how on front line. Men were seen on getting tangled in GERMAN FARM - JOCK'S shoot. Corps Line Det 2 Pdrs withdrawn from trees line. WOORMEZEELE - VOORMEZEELE SOUTHERN SWITCH to SJ RIDGE WOOD as front line. 12 Guns of 89 Bde placed under 21st DIV order. C.O. visited Bs. G.C. 110th — 62nd & 89th Bdes & O.C. A&D Coy. 6 Guns from Corps Line returned to WALKER CAMP. Casualties - O.R. 12 wounded (1 rem. duty).	OOH
	27.4.16		Four guns A Coy SJ RIDGE WOOD relieved by 4.9 K. Div. 4 ret to WALKER CAMP. C.O. to DIV - 21/c to 89th Bde. 11 Guns of A&D Coy were relieved by 89th Bde on night of 27/28. Lt Campbell - MISSING.	Summary of Operations 27th - 29th Ap. in Appendix marked A OOH
	28.4.16		On night of 28/29 A Gun B Coy was relieved by guns of 89th Bde. Relief complete 11-30 pm. 2 Guns were sent from D Coy to take up position at Huff Rd. W of BEDFORD HOUSE. Lt SHAW WOUNDED.	OOH
	29.4.16		2 Guns from WALKER CAMP were ordered by B.G.C. 89th Bde to take up position strengthening front line. Orders were done under orders issued by Maj Ardehem. Four guns were placed in Bedebut Line under 2nd Lt LESLIE forming a salient formed of the 2 LG Bars of LOCK & HANKHOF FARM. A/MAJ HOWARD WOUNDED. LT MASLIN	no 14 OOH

Army Form C. 2118.

WAR DIARY
or
INTELLIGENCE SUMMARY.
(Erase heading not required.)

Place	Date	Hour	Summary of Events and Information	Remarks and references to Appendices
	30.4.18		15 Guns (6D - 4A) relieved 10 Jormal guns I/C Coy. Maj Walker 19th M.G. Batt. visited HQ. to obtain information about the line before taking over.	O.C. Codes Posts 19th

LIEUT-COLONEL,
COMMANDING 21st BN. MACHINE GUN CORPS.

29th April

2nd Cav of 3rd Division relieved the
remaining guns of B Cy in the Rt Bde Sector
& left complete by 1-30 a.m. 29th.

At 3. a.m. Enemy bombardment commenced
along whole Divisional Front. It was a
terrific intensity & was followed at 5 a.m.
by Infantry attacks but nowhere with
any success despite repeated efforts.
At the end of the day the line remained
intact. Prisoners captured state that a
marked proportion of their casualties was
caused by M.G. fire which seemed to
come from all directions.

Left Sector
Two guns T 25 c did splendid work
all day firing over 6000 rounds direct at
the advancing enemy inflicting heavy
casualties. Much assistance was
rendered by the Infantry who filled belts
for the team.

Guns in BEDFORD HOUSE fired on
VOORMEZEELE (indirect) during the attack
firing 5000 rounds. Two other guns in
T 25 c 00.80 also did similar work &
Forward Observation Officers of the Artillery
report that many casualties were
inflicted in this manner.

APPENDIX A.

2/2 Batt'n G. Corps.   REF {SHEET 28 1/40000

Ap 25th
Gun east) RIDGE WOOD. (A1.) out of action though still fires. Replaced by gun from R4.
Enemy shelling exceedingly heavy. R9 (near canal I.19.d.50.50) slightly damaged by shrapnel but remained in action.

Ap 26th
B/Coy Headquarters BRISTOL CAMP blown in at 9 a.m. HQ moved to H.29.c.00. No 1 gun SNIPERS BARN lost No 2 withdrew to H.36.d.80.50.
Small parties of the enemy penetrated to EIZENWALLE. Owing to thick mist prevailing it was impossible to see in the early morning for more than 50x. Communications were badly disorganised and casualties among runners.
Some guns of B Coy did excellent work. R4 H.36.d.80.50 allowed a Boche with a M.G. to approach within 50x when he was dealt with effectively. Guns in N.6.a each fired 1000 rounds into good targets.

Lewis in N5a in co-operation with Australians did useful work in clearing parties of the enemy from NISSEN HUTS in N11b.

Very heavy barrage was put down on RIDGE WOOD at 4 pm. A feeble attack on the SCOTTISH RIFLES (N4d) was easily repulsed. Men exceedingly keen on getting targets.

Capt. Clay

Left Bde Sector.

Lt Campbell with two guns arrived at SPOIL BANK at 9 am to take up positions there but found parties of the enemy there, consequently withdrew to LANKHOF FARM.

All guns in the sector intact despite heavy shelling.

Guns in H23d report that Infantry evacuated line for a period but returned late in the day.

Section Officers have remained in close touch with Infantry Commanders throughout.

27th April.

Reports received up to 9 am state that one gun in H30d was damaged by shell fire but remained in action.

Left Bde Sector

About 4 pm a heavy barrage was put down from I.25.a.1550 to VOORMEZEELE until 8.30 pm. Campbell. Two guns at LANKHOF FARM were captured in a raid between 8+9 pm.

Two guns at BEDFORD HOUSE engaged targets during the day firing 1000 rds.

The gun at LOCK 8 held out until being compelled to move his position owing to our own artillery having smashed his gun & making his position generally untenable. His position was apparently untenable after LANKHOF FARM had been lost.

A party of the enemy approached the gun & called upon him to surrender but the cpl in charge dispersed them with M.G. fire. He withdrew for reasons already given with his gun completely out of action but he brought with him together with his complete team & gun equipment. He reported to his Coy Commander at Belgian Chateau on the afternoon of the 25th.

Rt Bde Sector

VOORMEZEELE was lost during the day

the enemy being in possession of the village or Tower but fighting for the KEEP continued until a late hour. The Officer in charge 2Lt Hunt to withdraw at 10pm with 6 OR and one gun, all that remained of 3 teams that had been placed in VOORMEZEELE. They had been subjected to very heavy bombardment throughout the period & withdrew only with much difficulty after conflict with Bombing parties of the enemy.

Gun A.3. north of RIDGE WOOD was engaged by artillery + completely knocked out - four casualties being caused to troops manning the position.

Much direct firing was done by the guns in RIDGE WOOD & good results were obtained.

April 28th.

Guns of the 89th Bde relieved 11 guns in the Right Sector on the night of 27th-28th. On the evening of the 28th a very heavy bombardment was started by the enemy but no infantry attack developed. The Guns in BEDFORD HOUSE fired direct at troops in LANKHOF FARM between 8 & 9 pm. 5000 rounds being fired.

The total rounds fired were 17.000. The guns in the Right Sector also did most useful work in repelling the attack & also late engaged several enemy working parties.

30th April

During the day numerous parties of the enemy were dislodged from huts etc by the Artillery & our M.G.s engaged the enemy during his attempts to seek fresh cover. Total rounds fired were over 15.000 & infantry commanders complimented the team on their excellent work & gave them credit for taking a great share in holding up the attack on the previous day. The day ended quietly.

LIEUT-COLONEL,
COMMANDING 21st BN. MACHINE GUN CORPS.

Second Army telegram dated 29th April, timed 8.20 p.m. Begins.

"Following from Commander-in-Chief. Begins. Please inform General CAMPBELL and the Officers and Men of the 21st Division that the share taken by them in the recent fighting North of the LYS following so closely upon their gallant action on the battle front South of ARRAS reflects credit alike on their Division and upon the British Army. I thank them for the great courage and devotion they have already displayed and am confident that any further test which the future may bring will be met by them with the same unflinching resolution. Ends"

A.H.Macdougall. Major.
General Staff
21st Division.

30th April 1918.

Copy No. 1

21st Bn. M.G.C. Special Order No. 7.

15th April 1918.

1. In continuation of 21st Bn. M.G.C. Special Order No. 3 dated 14th April 1918, further withdrawals of Machine Guns will be carried out on 15th inst as follows:-

    A Coy.   7 8 8A R 6 R 17

    D Coy.   R 1 R 2 R 3 R 4 R 5 R 6 R 7 R 8 R 9 R 10

    The withdrawal of these guns must be completed by noon.

2. Carrying parties will report to Company H.Q. as follows:-

    A Coy.   1 Officer 20 other ranks   8.0 p.m.

    D Coy.   1 Officer 20 other ranks   8.0 p.m.

3. Limbers for transporting gun equipment will be at Company H.Q. as follows:-

    A Coy.   4 Limbers   11.0 p.m.

    D Coy.   6 Limbers   11.0 p.m.

4. On the above guns being withdrawn the following guns will be in position in the Corps Line.

    A Coy.   R 18 R 19 R 22 R 23

    D Coy.   2 guns at strong point L 30 1. and L 30 3. respectively.

    Officers Commanding A and D Companies will each leave two Officers in charge of these guns.

5. Capt. Stoward will remain in command of 8 guns and will assume command of these guns at A. Coy.

S E C R E T.   Copy No......

        21st Bn. M.G.C. Special Order No. 6.

                                                        16th April 1918.

1.   The following machine guns will be withdrawn from the
        MOTHER on the morning of 18th April.

        "A" Coy.   A.11, A.12, A.14, A.16, A.17, A.18, A.19,
                    A.19, A.20, A.21.

        "B" Coy.   The 2 guns at strong point at J.1.b.4.

2.   The withdrawal of these guns will commence not later
        than 3 a.m. The utmost care will be exercised in
        removing these positions before enemy observation is
        possible.

3.   On withdrawal, these gun teams will return by the most
        direct route to Battalion H.Q., J.1.b.3. cent.

4.   O.C. "A" Coy. ~~and~~ will remain in charge of his
        remaining guns.

        O.C. "B" Coy. and 2 other officers will remain in
        charge of the remaining guns of own Coy.

        ──

5.   It is important that as much S.A.A. to have as possible
        is removed. Limbers for this purpose will be available
        as follows:

        2 Limbers at KEMMEL TERRACE at 4 a.m.

        2   "   " JUNC 60 at 2 a.m.

        M.G. Coys. will arrange for loading up rifles on back
        limbers, and for the S.A.A. to be alongside a trench or
        road where limbers can approach.

        No S.A.A. will be withdrawn from gun positions
        not being vacated.

6.   .... Coys. will report to respective Coy. H.Q.
        as follows:

        "A" Coy. H.Q.   1 Officer, 40 O.R. at 4 a.m.
        "B" "   "   1 Officer, 20 O.R. at 7 a.m.

7.   Limbers for transporting Coy. equipment will be at
        respective Coy. H.Q. as follows:

        "A" Coy. H.Q.   2 Limbers   3 a.m.
        "B" "   "   1 Limber   4 a.m.

        All Coy equipment, including camp beds, S.A.
        magazines and signboards will be withdrawn.

8.   Companies in the line will acknowledge the receipt of
        these instructions by telephoning the code word "Clog
        to Banks".

                                                V. F. Samuelson
                                                        Capt. & Adjt.
                                                21st Bn. Machine Gun Corps.

DISTRIBUTION.
Copy No 1. O.C. "A" Coy.
     " 2. O.C. "B" Coy.

31st Bn M.G.C. Order No 2.

5th April 1918

1. The 31st M.G. Bn. will relieve the 1st Australian M.G. Bn. in the WYTSCHAETE Sector on the 5inst.

2. Eight Guns of B Coy will relieve the following eight guns of the Southern Group.
   S.13 S.14 S.15 S.16 S.19 R.8 R.19 R.22

3. Ten Guns of C Coy will relieve the following ten guns of the Northern Group.
   S.20 S.22 S.23 S.24 S.26
   R.23 R.24 R.25 R.27 R.28

4. As many gun positions as possible will be relieved by day. This includes the majority of reserve Posted Guns.

5. Gun teams for those Positions stated in para 4 will meet Company Guides at LANPOST CORNER (0.10.b.45) at 2. noon.

6. Gun teams for all other Positions will meet Guides at OOSTTAVERNE FARM at 6.0 p.m.

7. All other details of relief will be arranged between Company Commanders concerned.

8. All Maps Tracings Aeroplane Photographs Dispositions, S.O.S. & Battle plans & Trench Stores will be taken over with receipts exchanged.

9. Completion of relief will be reported to Battn H.Q. by…

10. Battn H.Q. will open at S.20.d.3.10. & 6 p.m.
    PLEDGE

11. ACKNOW—

(Contd).

6. On withdrawal being completed, Major Ashton will report as soon as possible at Battn. H.Q., BRISTOL CAMP.

Gun teams will return by the most direct route to Battn. H.Q.

7. The platoon referred to in para 3. will carry out as much S.A.A. as can possibly be carried. No S.A.A. must be withdrawn from Gun Position until being vacated.

8. All gun equipment, including Zero Pots, A.A. Mountings, and sightboards will be withdrawn.

9. Companies in the line will acknowledge the receipt of these instructions by code word ROBEY.

Copy no 7.   SECRET.

21st Bn. M.G.C. Order no 3

7th April 1918

1/ The 21st M.G. Bn will be relieved on the night of April 8/9th by the 19th M.G. Bn.

2/ The following Gun Positions of the <u>Right Sector</u> will be withdrawn :-

   S12   S17   R20   R21

The following Gun Positions of the <u>Left Sector</u> will be withdrawn :-

   S.21   R.26

3/ The withdrawal of the Gun Positions as stated in para. 2 will not commence before 7.30 p.m.

All S.A.A. and Stores at these Positions will be handed over to relieving Companies and receipts obtained.

4/ No position under enemy observation is to be relieved until after dark.

5/ All Battle, S.O.S lines & Dispositions, 12 Belt Boxes per Gun, maps, Tracings, aeroplane Photographs and Trench Stoves will be handed over and receipts obtained.

6/ Company Commanders will notify Battalion H.Q. of limber requirements by noon 8th April.

7/ All other details of relief including guides will be arranged between Company Commanders direct.

8/ On relief or withdrawal Gun teams will return to Battalion H.Q. GLASGOW CAMP.

(2)

9/ Completion of relief will be reported to Battalion H.Q.

10/ <u>Acknowledge.</u>

L S Bathurst, Major
Comdg 21st Bn Machine Gun Corps

Issued at 6pm.

Distribution
Copy No 1 - OC A Coy
       2 - OC B Coy
       3 - OC C Coy
       4 - OC D Coy
       5 - T.O.
       6 - O.M.
       7 - War Diary
       8 -
       9 - File
      10 - 21 Div
      11 - 19 Inf Bn.

Copy No. 10 SECRET.

[illegible] Order No. 4

8th April 1918.

1. A. Company together with 2 Gun Teams of B Company of the 33rd M.G. Bn. will relieve 18 guns of the 49th M.G. Bn. in the left Bde. Sector of the MENIN ROAD Sector on the 9th inst.

2. Guides for these guns will be at BIRR Crossroads at 6.0 pm.

3. The personnel of the relieving Gun teams will proceed to BIRR Crossroads by lorry leaving CYCLIST CAMP at 5.0 pm.

4. The Company transport will proceed under the 2nd in Command of A Coy by march route to arrive at BIRR Crossroads at 6.0 pm.

5. Belt boxes for all Gun Positions ~~[illegible]~~ will be taken over and receipts given [illegible]

6. Gun Lockers, S.O.S. Lines, Dispositions, maps, drawings and trench stores will be taken over and receipts exchanged.

7. All other details of relief will be arranged between Coy Commanders direct.

8. Acknowledge.

[illegible]

Copy No. 10.   SECRET.

21st Bn. M.G.C. Order No. 5.

Ref. Map Sheet 28.   9th April 1918.

1. "D" Coy. 21st.M.G.Bn. will relieve a Company of the 49th.M.G.Bn. in the Right Brigade Sector of the MENIN ROAD Sector on the 10th inst.

2. Guides for these guns will be at ZILLEBEKE CHURCH at 2.30 p.m.

3. The personnel of the relieving Gun Teams will proceed to ZILLEBEKE CHURCH by Light Railway, leaving LA POLKA M.21.c.8.9. at 1.30 p.m.

4. The Company Transport will proceed under the 2nd in Command of "D" Coy. by march route, to arrive at ZILLEBEKE CHURCH by 2.30 p.m.   Route: KEMMEL .. VIERSTRAATE .. KRUISSTRAATHOEK .. SHRAPNEL CORNER.

5. Six belt boxes per gun will be carried in by relieving teams, and six belt boxes per gun will be taken over and receipts given.

6. No gun position which is under enemy observation will be relieved until after dark.

7. DRESS: Fighting Order. Overcoats, en bandoleer.

8. All Battle, S.O.S. Lines, Dispositions, Maps, Tracings and Trench Stores will be taken over and receipts exchanged.

9. All other details of relief will be arranged between Company Commanders direct.

10. Completion of relief will be reported by wire to Battalion H.Q.

11. Battalion H.Q. will open at BRISTOL CAMP, H.35.d.8.6. at 5.0 p.m.

12. A C K N O W L E D G E.

                                              Captain & Adjutant,
                                           21st Bn. Machine Gun Corps.

Issued at 6 p.m.

Distribution:

    Copy No. 1 ... "A" Coy.
           2 ... "B" Coy.
           3 ... "C" Coy.
           4 ... "D" Coy.
           5 ... T.O.
           6 ... Q.M.
           7 ... 21 Div.
           8 ... 49th M.G.Bn.
           9 ... War Diary.
          10 ...   "   "
          11 ... File.

25th Bn M.G.C. Order No 6

11th March 18

1. The following Machine Guns will be relieved to-night by Lewis Guns of the 110th Inf. Bn.

No. of Positions	Map Reference
1	31 . a 1 9
2	23 . a 4 5
3	15 . a 6 8
4	26 . a 4 5
5	20 . a 6 0
6	21 . a 1 6

2. On relief, these guns will take up following position in the CORPS LINE

   No 1 & 2   to Strong point I 30
   3 & 4   I 30 . 3
   5 & 6   I 9 .

3. Approximate positions and direction of fire are shown on attached Map.

4. These guns will be used for direct fire only.

5. O.C. D Coy will forward to Battn H.Q. as soon as possible exact locations of these guns and their fields of fire.

6. All other details of relief will be arranged between O.C. D Coy and Battalion Commanders direct.

7. Completion of relief will be reported to Battn H.Q. by code word CHARLIE stating hour at which relief is completed.

8. ACKNOWLEDGE

SECRET.   Copy No...12.

                21st Battn. M.G.C. Order No. 7.

                                              14th April 1918.

1.   The following M.G. reliefs will take place on
        the 15th and 16th inst.

2.   On April 15th, "B" Coy., less 1 sub-section, will
        relieve 16 guns of "A" Coy. in the Left sector.
        O.C. "A" Coy. will arrange for 4 gun teams (to include
        the attached sub-section of "B" Coy.) to remain in
        position until orders of O.C. "B" Coy.

3.   On April 16th "C" Coy. will relieve the 16 guns
        of "D" Coy. in the Right sector.

4.   All battle and S.O.S. lines, dispositions,
        programmes of harrassing fire, maps, tracings and
        trench stores will be taken over and receipts obtained.
        These receipts will be forwarded to Battalion H.Q. by
        9 a.m. on the day following relief.

5.   No gun under enemy observation will be relieved
        until after dark.

6.   All other details of relief will be arranged
        between Company Commanders direct.

7.   On relief "A" Coy., less 1 sub-section, and "D"
        Coy. will return to Battalion H.Q., BRISTOL CAMP.

8.   Completion of relief will be reported by code
        word STRAFFING, stating time.

9.   ACKNOWLEDGE.

                                    VF Samuelson
                                    ....
                                    Major.,
                                21st Battn. Machine Gun Corps.

DISTRIBUTION.

Copy No. 1 ... O.C. "A" Coy.
         2 ... O.C. "B" Coy.
         3 ... O.C. "C" Coy.
         4 ... O.C. "D" Coy.
         5 ... Quartermaster.
         6 ... Transport Officer.
         7 ... 182nd Inf.Bde.
         8 ... 183rd Inf.Bde.
         9 ... 61st Division.
        10 ... Signals, 61st Div.
        11 ... War Diary.
        12 ... "   "
        13 ... File.

21st. Batt'n M.G.C. ORDER No. 8.

1. The Sub Section of B Company attached A Company are to be withdrawn to Battalion H.Q. to-night, 14th inst.

2. If the above guns are at R.14 and R.15, they will be replaced by 2 guns from strong point J.142 and put in position at R.14 and R.15 vacated by B Company.

   If the 2 guns are not at R.14 and R.15, it is left to Company Commander's discretion whether to replace the vacated position or not.

3. Withdrawal complete will be sent to Battalion H.Q. by code word "SAM".

4. A report will be sent as soon as possible stating the alterations made.

14.4.18

SECRET.   Copy No......

21st Bn.M.G.C. Order No. 9.   18th April 1918.

1.   The undermentioned guns in the CORPS LINE under Capt.
HOWARD will be relieved on the 19th inst. by 8 guns from
"A" Coy., and Major ASHERTON will take over command on
completion of relief;

        I.30.1 (2 guns)
        I.30.3 (2 guns)
        R.22,
        R.23, and
        2 guns on NINTH ROAD.

2.   The relieving gun teams of "A" Coy. will proceed to
BRISTOL CAMP, arriving about 12 noon, and have hot mid day
meal there, proceeding to new positions at 2 p.m.

3.   Capt. HOWARD will detail one guide per gun position
to be at DILLEBEKE CHURCH at 2.30 p.m. to guide relieving
guns to positions. Each guide must have written instructions
naming gun position, etc.

4.   All S.A.A., belt boxes, tripods, maps etc. will be
handed over on relief, and copies sent Battalion H.Q. of
all stores, etc. handed over.

5.   "A" Coy. will take Transport as far as SHRAPNEL CORNER,
and the Transport will return to BRISTOL CAMP and await guns
coming out of the line, and convey them to MIDDLESEX CAMP,
G.17.d.4.4.

                                    and 22nd (3 days)
6.   Rations for the 20th and 21st/ will be taken in the
line by the relieving sections.

7.   O.C. "A" Coy. will detail one Officer per two guns,
and each gun team will consist of one gun commander and
six other ranks.

8.   Relief complete will be reported to Battalion H.Q.
by code word "HARVEY" by telephone and runner.

9.   A C K N O W L E D G E.

                                    V.Samuelson
                                    Capt. & Adjt.,
                                21st Battn. Machine Gun Corps.

DISTRIBUTION.

Copy No. 1 .. "A" Coy.
        2 .. "B" Coy. (for information)
        3 .. "C" Coy.   "   "
        4 .. "D" Coy.   "   "
        5 .. Capt. HOWARD.
        6 .. Q.M. & T.O.
        7 .. 21st Division.
     8 to 10 .. War Diary & File.

SECRET.   COPY .11.

21st. Bn. M.G.C. ORDER No. 10.

20th. April, 1918.

1. A composite company under Capt. HOWARD, and Lieut. ROSWELL 2nd. in command, consisting of 10 guns, will be formed at once and will "stand to" at 5. 0 a.m. tomorrow 21st. inst. ready to move at 10 minutes notice. This company will come under the orders of G.O.C. 110th. Inf. Bde. WALKER CAMP, H.27.b., from 5. 0 a.m. 21st. inst.

2. Guns will be provided as follows:

   "A" Coy.   8 guns and 2 Officers. (subalterns)

   "B" Coy.   1 gun and 1 Officer. (subaltern)

   "C" Coy.   1 gun and 1 Officer. (subaltern)

3. The Headquarters of "A" Coy. and all "A" Coy. transport will be at the disposal of Capt. HOWARD.

4. O.C. "B" Coy. will provide 1 Fighting Limber for the 2 guns of "B" and "C" Coys. "A" Coy. will carry the S.A.A. for these 2 guns on their S.A.A. limbers.

5. This company will move to the vicinity of WALKER CAMP, H.27.b. and be billeted there on orders to be issued later.

6. Rations will be carried by each man for the 21st. inst.

7. ACKNOWLEDGE.

                         (Sgd.)V.F.SAMUELSON.

                                                 Capt. & Adjt.
Issued to: 21st. Battn. Machine Gun Corps.

    Copy No. 1 ... O.C. 'A' Coy. (nucleus)
            2 ... O.C. 'B' Coy.   "
            3 ... O.C. 'C' Coy.   "
            4 ... O.C. 'A' Coy.
            5 ... O.C. 'B' Coy.
            6 ... O.C. 'C' Coy.
            7 ... Capt. Howard.
            8 ... 21 Div. 'G'.
       9 and 10 ... War Diary
      11 and 12 ... File.

S E C R E T.   Copy No. 5

21st Bn.M.G.C. Order No. 11.

21st April 1918.

1. In accordance with Division Order No. 176, the 6th Division will take over the sector held by 2 Coys. astride the MENIN ROAD, April 20th/21st.

   On the night of the 21st/22nd the 6th Battn. M.G.C. will relieve 4 guns in the following positions:

   R.22, R.23, 2 guns on MENIN ROAD.

2. All details of relief will be arranged between Coy. Commanders concerned.

3. On relief, 2 guns at R.22, R.23 will return to Battalion H.Q., MIDDLESEX CAMP, G.17.d.4.4.

   The 2 guns at MENIN ROAD will be placed in position near JACKDAW TUNNELS, as suggested in your Intelligence Report of today's date.

4. A report, showing actual Gun Positions, Map References, Fields of Fire and all other information, will be forwarded to Battalion H.Q. as soon as possible.

5. The completion of redistribution of guns will be wired to Battalion H.Q. by code word "HENRY".

6. All ranks will carry out unexpended portion of rations.

7. One limber to be detailed by O.C. "D" Coy. will be at SHRAPNEL CORNER at 9 p.m. tonight, and await arrival of teams to carry back guns etc. and act as guide to Battalion H.Q.

8. One Officer will come out of the line with the guns.

9. On arrival in camp, the Gun Teams will be accommodated and rationed by O.C. "D" Coy.

10. The new Northern Boundary will run as follows:

    J.19.b.4.4. .. I.24.a.8.5. .. I.22.d.7.6 (ZILLEBEKE exclusive) .. I.28.a.2.9. .. I.21.c.6.0. .. I.19.d.5.6. (bridge inclusive) .. M.16.d.1.1.

11. A C K N O W L E D G E.   V F Samuelson

                                            Capt. & Adjt.,
                                      21st Battn. Machine Gun Corps.

DISTRIBUTION.

Copy No. 1 .. Major ASSHETON.
       2 .. O.C. "D" Coy.(Nucleus)
       3 .. 6th Division.
       4 .. 21st Division.
       5 .. War Diary.
       6 .. War Diary.
       7 .. File.

Secret.

21st Bn M.G.C. Order No 12.

24th April 1918

Ref. Map Sheets:
28 N.W. 1/20,000
28 S.W.

1. The following M.G. reliefs and redistribution will take place on the 25th and 26th April 1918.

2. On 25th inst. six guns of "D" Coy will relieve the following six guns of "C" Coy in the Left Sector:
   6, 7, 8, 10, R.5, R.10.

   One guide for each of the above guns, less R.5, will be at BRIDGE at I.19.a.5.6 at 3.0 pm.

   One guide for R.5 will be at SEGARD CORNER, H.30.c.3.8 at 2.30 pm.

   On relief the gun teams of "C" Coy will return to Batt'n HQ. MIDDLESEX CAMP.

   O.C. "C" Coy will withdraw the following guns at 0.0 pm 25th inst. to Batt'n HQ:
   A.6, A.7, A.8, R.6, R.7, R.8, 9.

   O.C. "C" Coy will report to Batt'n HQ. on completion of these moves.

   O.C. "D" Coy will also place 7 guns in position in the KNOLL RIDGE Sector. The exact positions will be notified later.

3. On night of 25th/26th, the following 6 guns of "B" Coy will vacate their present positions
   A.1, A.2, A.3, A.4, A.5, R.2;
   and will at once relieve 6 guns of 21st Coy. in the following positions:
   2, 4, 17, 18, 19, 20.

   Two guns of "D" Coy from Divisional Reserve will be attached to "B" Coy and will relieve two guns of 21st M.G. Coy. at gun positions 1 and 3.

4. No gun positions which are under enemy observation will be relieved until after dusk.

5. All other details of relief will be arranged between Coy Commanders direct.

(1)

6.   O.C. D Coy, 30th M.G. Battn. will retain the following positions:
6, 8, 9, 10, 11, 12, 13, 14, 15, 16,
and will also place two guns in position at about I 28 c Central, covering THE RAVINE in I 34 a. and b.

Two guns will also be placed about I.35 a 8.8 to cover Railway Cutting running S.E. from HILL 60.

The remaining six guns will be withdrawn into Bde Reserve under orders of B.G.C, 21st Bde.

7.   On completion of relief, Coy. H.Q. will be established as follows:

Right Coy.   VOORMEZEELE   I 31 c 2 5.
Centre "   SPOIL BANK   I 33 d 2 7
Left   "   WOODCOTE HOUSE   I 20 c 4 2

8.   Completion of relief these moves will be wired by Coy Commanders to Battn HQ by code word "ZENA", stating time.

9.   ACKNOWLEDGE

(Sgd) N Hamilton, Capt. Adjt.
21st Battn M.G. Corps.

Copy No _____   SECRET

21st Bn. M.G.C. Order No 13.

25th April 1918.

1/ The following guns of "D" Coy are to be placed in position as follows on receipt of these instructions:—

2 guns in SPOIL BANK and 1 Officer to shoot in direction SOUTH and SOUTH EAST. These guns will be known as E1 and E2, and will come under orders of Capt. Blackman.

2/ The following Guns are to be doubled and will be found by "D" Coy.

		(Map Ref)
(a)	R.1.	N.5.d.8.6.
(b)	R.4.	H.36.c.9.6.
(c)	R.10. (Woodcote House)	
(d)	A.1.	N.5.a.45.80.
(e)	A.2.	N.5.c.45.90.
(f)	A.3.	N.5.c.35.80.

3/ 2 Guns of "D" Coy will take up positions at M.G. Ranges East of DICKEBUSCH LAKE, firing SOUTH and SOUTH-EAST.

4/ 4 Guns of either "A" or "D" Coy will be at disposal of B.G.C. 62nd Bde. and will receive instructions from Brig. Genl. Gater. O.C. Section will report at once to Genl. Gater WALKER CAMP.

5/ 12 Belt Boxes and as much S.A.A. as possible with a minimum of 2000 rounds will be at each gun position.

6/ Acknowledge by bearer and wire by code word LAKE.

(Sgd) V.F. SAMUELSON.
Capt. & Adjt.
21st Bn. M.G.C.

21st Battn. M.G.C. Order No. 14.

29th April 1918.

Four Guns under Lt. Leslie will move at once and take up position on the DICKIEBUSCH line as follows:-

(1) H 29 a 55. 65 ⎫ Pair
(2) H 29 a 80. 60 ⎭
(3) H 23 d 75. 60 ⎫ Pair
(4) H 23 d 75. 80 ⎭

These positions are approximate & are sited to suit the following conditions.

No. 1 Gun — To shoot on canal & in a Southerly direction & also guard road in H 29 Central.

No. 2 Gun — To shoot in a S.E. & N.E. direction.

No. 3 Gun & No. 4 Gun
To shoot N.E. & S.E. especially to flank road in H.24 a & b.

The exact position selected must fulfil the above condition.

Ten Belt Boxes per Gun to be taken & one Auxiliary Mounting per Subsection

These Guns will come under the orders of Capt. Blackman who will furnish Headquarters with the Map locations when guns are definitely sited.

Lt. Leslie will report to 'L' Coy Headquarters on arrival.

ACKNOWLEDGE by code word "ISOBEL".

SECRET.   Copy No....

21st Bn. M.G.C. ORDER No. 15.
                                                                30th April 1918.

Ref. Map Sheets:
28 N.W., 1/20,000.
28 S.W.,   "

1.   The following M.G. reliefs in the Left Sector will take
     place tonight, 30th inst.

2.   Six guns of "D" Coy. will relieve six guns at:

         2 Guns at BEDFORD HOUSE.
         2 "   " WOODCOTE HOUSE.
         1 Gun at BANBURY.
         1 "   " WRENCH FARM.

3.   Four guns of "A" Coy. will relieve four guns at R.5., R.6.,
     R.7., R.8.

4.   Guides for above guns will be at BELGIAN CHATEAU at 9.30 p.m.

5.   Two Officers from "D" Coy. and one Officer from "A" Coy.
     will relieve three Officers in charge of these gun teams.

6.   Capt. BLACKMAN will remain in Command of this Sector.

7.   Tripods and belt boxes will be handed over.

8.   On relief, the relieved teams will return to Battalion H.Q.
     MIDDLESEX CAMP.

9.   The two limbers which convey guns to the line, will remain
     at BELGIAN CHATEAU, and transport guns of relieved teams to
     Battalion H.Q.

10. Completion of relief will be sent to Battalion H.Q. by code
     word "NIXON".

11. A C K N O W L E D G E.

                                        V F Samuelson

                                                Capt. & Adjt.,
                                        21st Battn. Machine Gun Corps.

DISTRIBUTION.

Copy No. 1 .. "A" Coy. (Rear)
         2 .. O.C. "A" Coy. Forward (for information)
         3 .. "D" Coy. Rear.
         4 .. "D" Coy. Forward (for information)
         5 .. "B" Coy. Rear.
         6 .. O.C. "B" Coy. Forward.
         7 .. H.Q., 110th Inf. Bde.
         8 .. File.
         9 .. War Diary.
        10 .. War Diary.

Army Form C. 2118.

WAR DIARY
or
INTELLIGENCE SUMMARY.
(Erase heading not required.)

Place	Date	Hour	Summary of Events and Information	Remarks and references to Appendices
MIDDLESEX CAMP G.17.d.4.4. Sheet 28 Belg. France 1:40,000	1-5-18		Remainder of C Coy and 4 guns of D Coy were relieved. Guns of D Coy now the only guns not in camp. Still acting as mobile reserve at WALKER CAMP. Coy Commander & 2nd i/c Scott relieving Ratt visited HQ prior to regarding the line. Message No. 29 from Brass & manned position of night bar. Casualty - LCpl wounded.	On GCR Grder No. 16 [illegible] GC Grder No. 18
	2-5-18		Orders to move received from Brigade. H.Q. B Coy moved to transport lines G/30/c (Sheet 28 Belg.) Transport & Billets Major BORTHWICK and Billeting Officer handing over made of 2nd inst.	
BOIS de BEAUVOORDE	3-5-18		Batt moved from MIDDLESEX CAMP to BOIS de BEAUVOORDE (K.31 L.V.G Sheet 27 S4 France) arrived 10:30 am. Conferences of Coy Commanders orders is now to LEDERZEELE FRED (a few miles) until moved in action. 2nd i/c BURTON proceeded to see billets VI - Branch Army.	to GC Order No. 14
ARQUES	4-5-18		Four Coy transport moved to WIZERNES. Batt & transport to ARQUES. Personnel to repatriate town by Bus. Major BORTHWICK in command of HARNESS.	
TRAIN	5-5-18		Whole Batt entrained at places & times mentioned in Sch. 20 & III W.D.M. & then Marches for duty as per Batt.	
MIDDLES	6-5-18		Headquarters detrained at BOULOGNE (SOISSONS - 15:100:500) Companies at NOYON H.Q. & pushed at CUISSES & CUFFIES at 9 pm Billets excellent.	
	7-5-18		Conference reorganising & clearing up.	
	8-5-18		Batt marched to Training area formed on forming by Coy.	
	9-5-18		Batt carried on Training under Coy arrangement.	
	10-5-18		Training under Coy arrangement.	

Army Form C. 2118.

WAR DIARY
or
INTELLIGENCE=SUMMARY.
(Erase heading not required.)

Place	Date	Hour	Summary of Events and Information	Remarks and references to Appendices
CUISLES	11.5.18		C.O, O.C. A Coy, Signalling Officer & Intelligence Officer went to French Officer i/c of the Infantry for Coy in the line (near VERGEUR). Gunners of A Coy taken to positions for Coy Commanders who were relieving in the field by day. Arranged to take over gun position.	Map of dispositions 1-100,000
PROUILLY	12.5.18		Batt. moved by train from VIDRAINE to SAVIGNY, thence by march route to PREP 59. BE PROUILLY. Transport by road. 3 Coy Commanders (A, C, D) & B Echelon Officers preceded march the line.	O.C. Orders No. 20
VAUX VARENNES	13.5.18		A Coy with 16 guns relieved French O.R. in centre sector. Relief complete by 11.30am (14th) Remnants of Batt. together with H.Q. moved to West Camp VAUX VARENNES HQ arrived at 7 pm	Orders No. 21
"	14.5.18		C & D Coy relieved French on Right + Left Sectors respectively. Reinforcement of 1 or 2 (15th) NCOs & 3 men (2 p/Coy) were taken under instruction by Coy Officers. Coys went to 12 morning. Remnant of Batt. — former transport took up training under R.S.M.	
"	15.5.18		C.O. reported to 110 Bde HQ 1 Soc. Burnand with meeting under Brdr. Chain Preston on guns and sectors. B. Coy trained. (Authority - 21 Div. A/1112/14-5-18)	
"	16.5.18		C.O. visits right sectors — gun positions. B. Coy training. Lt RICHARDSON took up duty as Adjutant	O.B.H
"	17.5.18		C.O. visited Left Sector Gun positions & observes Enemy Barrage by Commanding Artillery. B. Coy training. B. Coy wild scale artillery barrage	O.B.H
"	18.5.18		Quiet day. Coy training continued.	O.B.H
"	19.5.18		C.O. attended Divisional Conference. Lt held meeting of Co Commanders to also 2nd called on 8 Bde, 9 Bde, L.E.I. with a view to co-operate on different occ. Lt. PORTHWICK Burr APPAR 12	
	20.6.18		B. Coy went through War Scheme at Divisional H.Q. C.O. held a conference with Coy Commanders in the line. C. Overfield 6th Berks Regt. Joined. Berks Co. Coy. J.S. gifted 2 VARENNES to Batt. 2 Lt Pol. West Hanna. Wilson reported for duty.	

WAR DIARY
or
INTELLIGENCE SUMMARY

Army Form C. 2118.

Place	Date	Hour	Summary of Events and Information	Remarks and references to Appendices
VAUX VARENNES	21.5.18		Maj. relieved C.O.in Right Sector. C.O. interviewed Lt. Coy Commdrs. Reps. to Gun (sight Sendbach) re. on R.C. Scheme placing them in CAUROY. Word received that attack was probable on the front MARAEUIL to PRAIZE village. Major Hardinge, Capt. W.H. Sword, Capt. J. Gearman, Lt. J.W. Parker told me reported for duty with C.O. and Capt. F. General Duplanali also posted to our group defending CAUROY. Latter works liaison Coy Commander in the Chateau-Porcial gun position. 2Lt. Searle to Pure Leave.	Re. on R.C. Scheme No. 2
"	22.5.18		Quiet day.	
"	23.5.18			
"	24.5.18		Capt V.F. SAMUELSON M.C. joined 1st Lincolns. Co-makes Lt. Peden & Coy DHQ move to CHAPELLE, M.W. CORMIER. Co. marks 110 L-Bde. 62 Wilde 1 Bn.	
"	25.5.18		Co. marks Sussex. Capt W.E.A. BLACKMAN to Pune.	
"	26.5.18		C.O. Scout Command to C. Coy makes Royal Andre Section Information of attack preparation made.	Schedule APPENDIX "A"
"	27.5.18		Enemy attacked on DIVISION at 1 a.m. H.Q. moved to SAPICOURT. Casualties K W M Missing 1 - 4 - 3 - OR 12 - 47 89 64	
SAPICOURT	28.5.18		H.Q. moved to SARCY at 11 a.m. Casualties OR 3 Killed 6 wounded 4 missing.	
SARCY	29.5.18		Transport move to CHAUMUZY. DHQ moved to LANEUVILLE. d 3 pm. Transport to FLEURY 1.30. Casualties 1 Killed 5 Wounded 1 missing (O Rank)	
LA NEUVILLE	30.5.18		H.Q. Transport to MONTEUIL. Coln. leaves at 11.30 am. to proceed to TROUENNES (CHALONS 1.100.000) Arrive at 3 pm Bivouacs. Reorganised & Completed 12 gun Coy.	
GIVRY	31.5.18		Batt. moved to GIVRY (CHALONS 1.100.000). Arrived 3 pm. Billets. Emergency Coy under Major Hardinge was formed under New Division.	

J. H. ? , LIEUT-COLONEL,
COMMANDING 21st BN. MACHINE GUN CORPS.

4. (Cont'd)

Personnel will report at the entraining Station ½ hour and Draught 3 hours before their trains are to start.

All trains must be loaded up ready to start, half an hour before they are due to start.

The Senior Officer on each train will be O.C. Train, where one is detailed travelling on the same train.

Loading Parties for each train have been detailed for the Infantry.

5. (A) The journey will take about 24 hours. Detraining Station will be notified at MARQUIZE-SUR-DOURS.

(B) There will be "halts" at Noyelles (near Abbeville) & Pontoise (near Paris) for 1 hour.

(C) A hot meal & hot water for tea will be provided at these places.

(D) Trains consist of:-

1 Officers Coach.
22 Covered Trucks.
4 Flats.

plus Brake Van(s) to the rear for Guards (or Others)

Each covered truck will take 40 men, 6 M.D. or 8 L.D. Horses or Mules.

(2)

10. **LEAVING THE TRAIN.**

No man is to get out of the train without permission from the O.C. Train. At each halting place picquets must be provided to prevent the men from wandering too far from the train, and to see that they are all back in the train before it starts.

These picquets will also watch each side of the train to assure that there is no looting of stores.

11. **PRECAUTIONS AGAINST ACCIDENT.**

No one will enter or leave the train while it is in motion. Men must not climb on to the roofs of the trucks or sit with their legs outside. They must not climb from one truck to another. All doors of covered trucks and carriages on the right hand side of the train, when on the main line, must be kept closed.

12. **AMMUNITION.**

All ammunition echelons will be entrained full.

13. **FIRES.**

No braziers or fires will be allowed in the trucks. If there is any straw or hay in the trucks, no candles or lights except those provided by the Railway Authorities will be allowed.

14. **SALVAGE.**

Great care must be taken that no clothing or other salvage is left in present billets or camps.

15. **CAMP.**

All bivouacs and horse lines must be left scrupulously clean. A certificate that this has been done will be sent to Battn. H.Q. by 10 a.m. for Transport Lines; 2.15 p.m. for Bivouacs.

16. **DAMAGE.**

Special care must be taken that no damage is done to the property of the inhabitants of the new area.

17. **MARCHING OUT STATE.**

Company Commanders will submit to the Orderly Room by 9 a.m. sharp a Marching Out state, showing:

(a) No. of Officers & Other Ranks who will proceed by bus;
(b) No. of Officers & Other Ranks, No. of animals (by classes), and vehicles (by types) proceeding by road.

18. **ACKNOWLEDGE.**

Capt. & Adjt.,
21st Battn. Machine Gun Corps.

Copy No ...12...   S E C R E T.

21st. Battn. M.G.C. ORDER No. 19.

Ref. Maps: Sheet 27.   3rd. May, 1918.
          Hazebrouck 5a.

1.   Reference 21st. Bn. M.G.C. Order No. 18, para. 1, the
Battalion will not move to the LEDERZEELE area tomorrow, but
personnel will embuss at N.25.d.6.2. at 3. 0 p.m. for WIZERNES
and ARQUES.   All Transport will proceed by road as under.

2.   The Battalion, less Transport, will be formed up in front
of present Bivouacs at 2.45 p.m. 4th. inst., ready to embuss at
above point.

     Dress: Full marching Order, and each man will carry one blanket.

          Headquarters Coy. will debuss at ARQUES.   "A", "B", "C"
and "D" Coys. will debuss at WIZERNES.

          The Battalion will billet for the night at above places,
prior to entraining at those towns on the morning of the 5th. May,
as per para. 4.

          The Battalion Transport will parade ready to move at
10. 0 a.m. 4th. inst., to proceed by road as under:
              H.Qrs. Transport to ARQUES.
              All remaining transport to WIZERNES.
2/Lt. CARTWRIGHT, with 2/Lt. JONES, will be in charge of the Coy.
Transports.   Lieut. WEARING will proceed with H.Qrs. Transport.
          Each Coy. and Battn. H.Q. will detail 1 N.C.O. and 2 men
to accompany the Transport to give any help that is required on
route.   These men will rejoin Coys. on arrival.

3.   Os.C. "A" and "B" Coys. will each detail 1 Sergeant; Os.C.
"C" and "D" Coys. each 1 Officer, to report to the Adjutant at
9.30 a.m. to proceed to WIZERNES and report Area Commandant on the
4th. inst. for accomodation for the 4 Coys. and Transport.   The
above party will report at road junction South of S in WIZERNES
at 6.30 p.m. and await arrival of busses.
          Lieut. HARVEY will proceed with above party as far as
ARQUES and arrange for accomodation for Battalion H.Q., reporting
at the Church West of E in ARQUES at 6 p.m. and await busses
     (Reference above: HAZEBROUCK, Sheet 5a.)

4.   TRAINS.
          Battalion Headquarters and Transport will entrain at ARQUES
at 6.49 a.m. 5th. inst.

          "A" and "C" Coys. and Transport will proceed by train
leaving WIZERNES at 3.12 a.m. 5th. inst.

          "B" and "D" Coys. and Transport will proceed by train
leaving WIZERNES at 7.12 a.m. 5th. inst.

                                (1)

                                                                   /Personnel ...

2.

12. ACKNOWLEDGE.

V. Hamilton
Capt. & Adjt.,
21st Battn. Machine Gun Corps.

Issued by Runner at 5.30 p.m.

DISTRIBUTION.

Copy No. 1 .. O.C. "A" Coy.
         2 .. O.C. "B" Coy.
         3 .. O.C. "C" Coy.
         4 .. O.C. "D" Coy.
         5 .. Major Sedgewick.
         6 .. 21st Div. M.G.
         7 .. Q.M. & T.O.
         8 .. R.S.M.
     9 & 10.. War Diary.
    11 & 12.. File.

SECRET.   COPY NO......

                    51st Battn. M.G.C. ORDER No. 12.

                                                         2nd May 1918.
Ref. Map sheets:
27 & 52.

1.   The 51st Battn. Machine Gun Corps will move by route march
     3rd May to the WATOU Area, and bivouac in the B. de BERTHOEN
     Area on the night 3rd/4th May, continuing march to INGHELBELD
     Area on the 4th May.

2.   The Battalion, less Transport lines and "B" Coy. will leave
     present area in following order:-

          Battn.H.Q. .. "A" Coy .. "C" Coy .. "D" Coy.

     Head of column will pass starting point G.17.d.4.6 at 6 a.m.

     Companies will move by half companies, and section limbers
     behind respective half companies. Interval of 50 yards will
     be kept between company personnel and Transport.

3.   "B" Coy. will move by route march on the 2nd May, and
     bivouac the night 2nd/3rd May in Transport lines.

4.   Route: G.17.d.4.4 .. BUSSEBOOM .. Right handed to cross
     roads G.13.b.1.6 .. Left to cross roads B.25.a Central ..
     Then to Sheet 27 join at B.16.c.00.10 .. Y Roads B.17.D.2.1 ..
     Thence main road to ARNEKE .. R.24.d.95.45, and await orders.

5.   Transport and "B" Coy. at G.13.d.1.5 will rejoin Battalion on
     the line of march at G.13.d.9.1.
     The Transport Officer will arrange that all Transport at
     above camp is formed up, so as to join respective companies
     on line of march without checking column.
     Company 2nd in command will supervise the march discipline of
     his Transport. 2/Lieut. CARRINGTON will move with Battn. H.Q.
     and 2/Lieut. JONES in rear of battalion with Major POMFRET.
     Q.M.Stores & H.Q. Transport will move in rear of M.G.
     Company.
     "B" Company will join column at above point in rear of "D"
     Company.

6.   The strictest march discipline will be observed on the line
     of march.

7.   All huts, trenches etc. must be left scrupulously clean, and
     a certificate sent Battn. H.Q. by 8.30 a.m. to this effect,
     except Transport lines and "B" Coy. who will render it on the
     line of march.

8.   Breakfasts must be served before moving off, and mid day meal
     at 12 noon in new area.

9.   Dress: Full marching order. All officers must be mounted
     who have horses.

10. Halts will be at ten minutes to the hour, first halt at
     6.50 a.m. Company commanders at STARTING TAPE will synchronise
     watches with the Adjutant at 5.50 a.m.

11. Company commanders will render a marching out state to
     Battn. H.Q. by 5.30 a.m.

SECRET.   Copy No. 10.

H.Q. 185th. M.I.B. ORDER No. 17.

                                                            2nd May 1918.

Ref. Map Sheet:
BELGIUM, 1/20,000.

_____

1.   The machine guns of the 20th Machine Gun Battalion in the
     Right Sector will be relieved by the 19th Machine Gun Battalion
     on the night of 2nd/3rd May.

2.   All details of relief will be arranged between Divisional
     Machine Gun Commanders concerned.

3.   Completion of relief will be reported to Headquarters,
     21st Battalion, Machine Gun Corps, at G.17.d.4.4 by telephone
     and runner by code word "GAIN".

4.   The Command of all machine guns in the Divisional Sector
     passes from D.M.G.O., 21st Division, to D.M.G.O., 19th Division,
     at 12 midnight 2nd May.

5.   ACKNOWLEDGE.

                                        V.F. Samuelson
                                        Capt. & Adjt.,
                                    21st Battn. Machine Gun Corps.
                                    _____

DISTRIBUTION.

Copy No. 1 .. 19th Bn. M.G.C.
       " 2 .. 20th Bn. M.G.C.
       " 3 .. 21st Division.
       " 4 .. 19th Division.
       " 5 .. 49th Bn. M.G.C.
       " 6 .. 20th Inf. Bde.
       " 7 .. 25th Inf. Bde.
       " 8 .. File.
   " 9 & 10.. War Diary.

2.

9. Command of the Machine Guns in the Divisional sector will pass from D.M.G.C., 21st. to D.M.G.C., 19th., on completion of relief night 2nd/3rd May.

10. A C K N O W L E D G E.

                                                    Capt. & Adjt.,
                                        21st Battn. Machine Gun Corps.

DISTRIBUTION.

Copy No.1 .. O.C. "A" Coy. Forward.
     2 .. O.C. "A" Coy. Rear.
     3 .. O.C. "B" Coy.
     4 .. O.C. "C" Coy. Forward.
     5 .. O.C. "C" Coy. Rear.
     6 .. O.C. "D" Coy.
     7 .. H.Q., 62nd Inf. Bde.
     8 .. H.Q., 56th Inf. Bde.
     9 .. H.Q., 21st Division.
    10 .. 6th Bn.M.G.C.
    11 .. 19th Bn.M.G.C.
    12 .. 30th Bn.M.G.C.
    13 .. O.M. & T.O.
14 & 15 .. File.
16 & 17 .. War Diary.

SECRET.   Copy No......

21st Battn. M.G.C. ORDER No. 16.

                                                                1st May 1918.
Ref. Map Sheets:
28 N.W., 1/20,000.
28 S.W.,   "

1. The 19th Division has been ordered to relieve the 21st Division in the Line.
    The 21st Division will withdraw to a back area to rest and re-organise.

2. The 19th M.G.Battn. will relieve machine guns of this Battn. in the Left Brigade Sector on the night 1st/2nd May, and the Machine Guns of 30th Battn. in the Right Brigade Sector on the night 2nd/3rd May.
    The Battn., less Transport and Special Guns detailed in para.3, will concentrate in MIDDLESEX CAMP, and await orders. Transport will remain at present camp.

3. The eight guns of "A" Coy. under Major ASSHETON will remain at WALKER CAMP until orders to withdraw are issued from Battn.H.Q.

4. 19th Battn.M.G.C. will relieve the undermentioned 18 guns tonight 1st/2nd May as follows:

    1 Gun .. FRENCH FARM.   R.5., R.6., R.7., R.8.,
    2 Guns .. BEDFORD HOUSE,   A.6., A.7., A.8.,
    2 Guns .. WOODCOTE HOUSE,   2 Guns M.23.d.
    1 Gun .. I.19.d.50.40.(N.9)   2 Guns M.29.a.
    1 Gun .. I.19.d.80.40.

    The undermentioned guns will be withdrawn:

        1 Gun, No.9, formerly at HAZELBURY.
        1 Gun .. I.19.d.40.30.

    The 19th Battn. will place one additional gun in FRENCH FARM and one at A.6.

    Guides for above guns will be at Cross Roads N.16.d. *Belgian Chateau* at 9.30 p.m. tonight, to be detailed by Capt. BLACKMAN.

    Capt. BLACKMAN will detail an officer to be at N.16.d. *Belgian Chateau* at 9.30 p.m. to supervise the guides.

    On relief these guns will return to Battalion H.Q., MIDDLESEX CAMP.

5. All other arrangements of relief will be arranged between Coy. Commanders concerned.

6. All maps, photos, tracings, dispositions and Trench stores, and 14 belt boxes per gun will be handed over and receipts obtained.

7. Completion of relief will be reported on arrival at Battn.H.Q. by code word "WILKIE".

8. Four limbers of "B" Coy. will be at BELGIAN CHATEAU at 11 p.m. to convey gun equipment of relieved teams to Battn. H.Q.

    O.C. "A" Coy. (Rear) will detail one officer to accompany above limbers to BELGIAN CHATEAU, and supervise the loading of limbers etc., and return with last limber to Battn. H.Q.

War Diary

21st DIVISION SPECIAL ORDER.

Thursday, 2nd May 1918.

During the past six weeks the Division has earned for itself a world wide reputation. It has twice been specially mentioned in Despatches, and was also included in the mention accorded to the 9th Division for fighting round WYTSCHAETE. It is of especial gratification to me, to feel that the esprit de corps of the whole Division is so great that, whether fighting with the Division or alongside troops of another, the same splendid spirit and devotion to duty animates all ranks.

The work performed by the Division has earned a special congratulatory telegram from the Commander-in-Chief. In reply to that message I have informed Field Marshal Sir Douglas HAIG that whatever may be required of the Division in the future he can confidently count on all ranks displaying the same spirit as they have shown in the past. I further said that the Division is out to beat the Hun and that no sacrifice will be considered too great to accomplish that object.

In thus pledging the Division I know I am only expressing the full determination of every Officer, N.C.O., & Man to see this fight through. Whatever trials the future may have in store for you I know that, having such splendid men under my command, I can look forward to that future with the most absolute confidence, and I know full well, from what you have already done, that my confidence cannot be misplaced.

David M Campbell

Major-General
Commanding 21st Division.

V. J Samuelson Capt
ADJUTANT,
21st BN. MACHINE GUN CORPS.

Copy No. 14

SECRET.

21st Bn. M.G.C. OPERATION ORDER No. 22.

19th May 1918.

Ref. Maps:
BRIMONT, 1/20,000.
BERRY AU BAC, 1/20,000.

----

1. "B" Coy. will relieve "C" Coy. in the Right Sector of the Divisional front on the night 21st/22nd May.

2. On relief "C" Coy. will return to Battalion Headquarters Camp at VAUX VARENNES.

3. All details regarding the relief will be arranged between Company Commanders concerned.

4. All aeroplane photographs and documents relating to the Sector, and trench stores, will be handed over, and receipts obtained. These receipts will be forwarded to Battalion Headquarters by 11 a.m. on the day after relief.

5. Completion of relief will be reported by the code word "ARTHUR".

6. A C K N O W L E D G E.

W.C. Hobson

Lieut. & Adjt.,
21st Battalion, Machine Gun Corps.

Copy No. 1 .. "A" Coy.
2 .. "B" Coy.
3 .. "C" Coy.
4 .. "D" Coy.
5 .. H.Qrs.Coy.
6 .. Transport Officer.
7 .. Quartermaster.
8 .. 21st Div. 'G'.
9 .. 21st Div. Signals.
10 .. 62nd Inf. Bde.
11 .. 64th Inf. Bde.
12 .. 110th Inf. Bde.
13/14 .. War Diary.
15/16 .. File.

Copy No: 12   S E C R E T.

21st. Bn. M.G.C. OPERATION ORDER No. 21.

Ref. Maps:
BRIMONT, 1/20.000.
BERRY AU BAC, 1/20.000.   12th. May, 1918.
----

1.   "A" Coy. will relieve the CENTRE Sub-Sector of the 74th.
     French Division on the night 13/14th. May.
       The following Gun Positions <u>in pairs</u> will be taken over:-

       9 - 10 - 11 - 12 - 13 - 14 - 15 - 16.

       Company H.Q. will be situated at P.C. FRANCE, 223.80 291.63.

2.   On the night 14/15th. May, "C" Coy. will relieve the RIGHT
     Sub-Sector and take over the following positions <u>in pairs</u>:-

       1 - 2 - 3 - 4 - 5 - 6 - 7 - 8.

       Company H.Q. will be situated at P.C. GEORGES, 225.10 290.00.

3.   "D" Coy. will relieve the LEFT Sub-Sector on the same night
     and take over the following positions in pairs:-

       17 - 18 - 19 - 20 - 21 - 22 - 23 - 24.

       Company H.Q. will be situated at P.C. CAMILLE, 222.35 294.12.

4.   All arrangements re reliefs will be arranged between respective
     Coy. Commanders concerned.

5.   12 belt boxes per gun and 2 S.A.A. boxes per gun will be carried
     into the line. A further 4 belt boxes per gun and 2 S.A.A. will be
     carried in on the night following the relief.
       Teams will consist of 1 N.C.O. and 5 men per gun
       1 box containing 12 hand grenades will be at each gun position.

6.   All ranks must be warned that there must be no movement in the
     vicinity of these gun positions, whether misty or not, and no firing
     of any description must be done from these emplacements except in
     case of attack.

       Harassing Machine Gun fire is not to be employed unless a
     definitely agressive policy is initiated by the enemy. In the event
     of the enemy seriously annoying our troops by fire of any description,
     the strongest possible retaliatory fire is at once to be opened on
     the offending locality.

       By day, no matter how foggy the weather may be, movement above
     ground East of the road running from HERMONVILLE via CAURCY to CORMICY
     and thence North-Westwards is strictly forbidden.

(1)

/Every ....

Every precaution is to be taken to prevent unnecessary movement in the trenches, by day, and means are to be adopted to prevent smoke etc. from attracting the enemy's attention.

Digging, which involves throwing earth outside the trench, will not take place during daylight.

All new work is at once apparent to the enemy, owing to the chalky nature of the soil; care must be taken to hide the traces of any excavation work done during the night.

7. Os.C. Coys. will select suitable positions for their rear guns for dealing with enemy aircraft. These must be a reasonable distance from the permanent gun positions.

8. Receipts must be given for all trench stores and ammunition etc. taken over from the French. Receipts should be signed by the French Officer from whom stores are taken over as well as by the Officer receiving the stores. Copies of receipts will be forwarded to this Office.

9. Os.C. Coys. will report daily to the Os.C. Battalions whose Sector they are in, and will acquaint the B.G.C. Brigade Sub-Sector and Battalion Commanders of all gun positions within 24 hours of relief.

10. Completion of relief will be sent to Battalion H.Q. by runner and wire by code word "ROBEY."

11. Command of the CHALONS LE VERGEUR Sector passes to G.O.C. 21st. Division at 9. 0 a.m. May 15th., at which hour Divisional H.Q. will open at CHALONS LE VERGEUR.

12. Tracings showing resected gun positions will be sent to Battalion H.Q. within 48 hours of relief.

13. A C K N O W L E D G E.

V.G. Samuelson
Captain & Adjutant.
21st. Battn. Machine Gun Corps.

Issued at 9.30 p.m. to:

Copy No. 1 ... O.C. "A" Coy.	Copy No. 8 ...	H.Q's. 62nd. Inf.Bde.
2 ... O.C. "B" Coy.	9 ...	" 64th. "
3 ... O.C. "C" Coy.	10 ...	" 110th. "
4 ... O.C. "D" Coy.	11 ...	War Diary.
5 ... Quartermaster.	12 ...	" "
6 ... Transport Officer.	13 ...	File.
7 ... H.Q'S. 21st. Divn.	14 ...	"

Copy No. 9

SECRET.

21st. Bn. M.G.C. OPERATION ORDER No. 20.

11th. May, 1918.

1. The 21st. Division will relieve the 74th. French Division in the left (CHALONS LE VERGEUR) Sector of the XXXVIIIth. French Corps, - LOIVRE (exclusive) to BERRY AU BAC (exclusive) between the 13th. and 16th. May.

2. The 21st. M.G.Battn. will move to Area No. 55 near PROUILLY on the 12th. May. Personnel will proceed by train. Hour of movement from CUISLES to be notified later. The Battalion Transport will move as a whole, leaving present area at 9.45 a.m. The Transport Officer will issue instructions re Starting Point and Order of March, notifying Battn.H.Q.

Each Company Commander will detail one Officer to accompany Transport. Lieut. CARTWRIGHT will be in charge of Column and H.Q's Transport.

Route to be taken:

ROMIGNY (not to enter before 11 a.m.) - LHERY - FAVEROLLES - SAVIGNY - BRANSCOURT, where Lt. FAIRLIE will be at CHURCH at 3.45 p.m. and direct to Camps.

Troops will march to attention through JONCHERY.

Each Coy. including Bn.H.Q's. will detail 1 N.C.O. (Corporal) and 12 men to accompany Transport and give any assistance required.

3. The Battalion will commence the relief of French Machine Guns in the line commencing with those in the Centre Sector on the night 13/14th. May and completing on the night 14/15th. May. Further orders will be issued.

4. Units will take over all maps, aeroplane photographs, Defence Schemes etc. from units they relieve.

5. Arrangements must be made to serve midday meal and teas without Cookers.

6. Battalion H.Q. will be situated at CAMP du MOULIN CUISSAT.

7. The strictest march discipline is to be maintained throughout the march.

8. All billets, huts etc. must be left scrupulously clean, and the Battalion Orderly Officer will inspect all billets 2 hours before the Battalion moves.

(2)

9. All billets, Coy. Messes etc. will be paid for under Bn.H.Q's arrangements.

10. A C K N O W L E D G E.

                                                      (sgd) V. F. SAMUELSON.
                                                                Capt. & Adjutant.
                                                  21st. Battn. Machine Gun Corps.

Issued by runner at 9.30 p.m. to:

    Copy No. 1 ... O.C. "A" Coy.
             2 ... O.C. "B" Coy.
             3 ... O.C. "C" Coy.
             4 ... O.C. "D" Coy.
             5 ... Transport Officer.
             6 ... Quartermaster.
             7 ... 21 Div. H.Q.
             8 ... H.Q's. Coy.
             9 ... War Diary.
           10 ... "   "
           11 ... File.
           12 ... "

SECRET.

To all recipients of 21st. Bn. M.G.C. Order No.19.

In continuation of 21st. Bn. M.G.C. Order No. 19:-

1. The Division is being transferred by rail from the XXII Corps, Second Army, to the IX Corps, 6th. French Army, between May 4th. and May 6th.

2. RATIONS.

   (a) The ration position on entrainment will be as follows:- ('Z' represents day of entrainment)

On the man	unexpended portion of the day's ration. Rations for Z plus 1 day. Iron Ration.
On the man or on First Line Transport	Rations for Z plus 2 day.
On Supply Wagons	Rations for 'Z' plus 3 day.

   (b) In order to make this possible the following procedure will be adopted on Z minus 1 day., i.e.,
   (1) Train wagons will replenish Units in the morning.
   (2) Train wagons will refill in afternoon and join Units (moving with them loaded up on Z day).
   (3) One days rations will be drawn from refilling points by First Line Transport at 4 p.m.

   (c) Rations for M.G.Battn. will be issued to the Battalion at WIZERNES on Z minus 1.

   (d) Railhead will open in the new area on May 5th.

3. AMBULANCES.

   Motor Ambulances will probably proceed by road.

4. CENSORSHIP.

   Special attention of all ranks will be drawn to the Censorship Regulations.

5. DISTANCES.

   The usual distances will be observed on the march to entraining stations, namely, 50 yards between Sections and 50 yards between Transport Sections.

6. ADVANCE PARTY.

   O.C. 'A' Coy. will detail 1 Officer and each Coy. Commander 1 Sergeant to report Battn. Headquarters at 7. 0 a.m. 4th. inst. This party will proceed to WIZERNES Station on bicycles and report to the D.A.Q.M.G. 21st. Div. and proceed with first train at 11.14 a.m. and act as Advance Party for the Battalion. On arrival at MAROUIL SUR OURCQ they will detrain and report to Major HOOPER, D.A.A.G. 21st. Div. asking for instructions as to where the Battalion will be accomodated. O.C. "A" Coy. will detail 1 bicycle and Bn. Signal Officer 4 bicycles.

Capt. & Adjutant.

(4)

Issued at 6.30 p.m. by Runner to:

Copy No. 1 ... O.C. 'A' Coy.
        2 ... O.C. 'B' Coy.
        3 ... O.C. 'C' Coy.
        4 ... O.C. 'D' Coy.
        5 ... Quartermaster.
        6 ... Transport Officer.
        7 ... 51st Div. H.Q.
        8 ... Major BORTHWICK.
        9 ... R.S.M.
       10 ... War Diary.
       11 ...   "
       12 ... File.
       13 ...   "

Headquarters,
    21st. Division.

SX 552

       Will you please cause attached Report on Operations (Appendix 'A') to be added to War Diary of this Unit for the month of May, forwarded under this Office M.34 of 9-6-18.

11th., June 1918.

D A Kay
Lieut.Colonel.
Commanding 21st. Bn. Machine Gun Corps.

APPENDIX A

CONFIDENTIAL.

Report on Operations BERRY AU BAC - LOIVRE
(both exclusive) commencing 27th May 1918.

Ref. Maps:
  BERRY AU BAC, S.E., 1/10,000.
  BRIMONT S.O.,   " 1/10,000.
  JONCHERY   " 1/20,000.
  SOISSONS   " 1/100,000.

The Sector held by 21st Division was taken over from the French on the 13th and 14th May 1918, and covered a frontage of approximately 5 miles, from BERRY AU BAC exclusive - Point ½ mile N.W. of LOIVRE inclusive. The original dispositions of Machine Guns were taken over in the first instance, but changes were later on necessitated in order to secure more depth and improved fields of fire. By May 24th all these changes were complete and the Machine Gun defence considerably strengthened. All guns were sited in pairs with all round defence, and echeloned to a depth of 5,000 yards from the Front Line. 8,000 Rounds S.A.A. for each forward gun, and 10,000 for rear guns were maintained at gun positions in boxes, 16 belts were reserved for direct fire up to 1,000 yards, the remainder of the belts for long range harassing fire. In addition, dumps of 20,000 rounds were formed at each Company H.Q. A box of French bombs was also taken over with each gun position.

The Divisional Sector was supported by 3 Machine Gun Companies in the Line and one in Reserve. In addition, the Sector was strengthened by 18 ST. ETIENNE guns of the French Territorials, placed primarily for the defences of CORMICY and CAUROY. Communications were established between Battalion H.Q. - Division by buried cable, thence to Company H.Q. by telephone. Runners, Mounted and Cyclist Orderlies also maintained communication between all Headquarters.

During this period, the Sector was exceptionally quiet, and no hostile attack was anticipated. This permitted a very careful daily reconnaissance, which was very essential on account of the extent of the Sector and the exceptionally large number of communication trenches. At 9.30 p.m. on 26th May, warning was received from Divisional Headquarters that an attack was imminent, and the order "Man Battle Stations" immediately issued. Company Commanders at once reported to their respective Brigade Headquarters, a Liaison Officer being left at the Company H.Q. The Commanding Officer with Adjutant and Orderlies proceeded to Divisional H.Q. At 1.0 a.m. on May 27th a very heavy bombardment by guns of all calibres was opened on our Trench System and Back Areas. This included a very large percentage of gas shells, which necessitated the wearing of Box Respirators for a considerable time, and in places up to five hours. Very few casualties, however, were caused by this gas shelling. This bombardment continued with great intensity until 4.30 a.m. when the infantry attack developed. Early reports showed that the weight of the attack was directed against the CHEMIN DES DAMES, which was captured in a surprisingly short time. The loss of this necessitated a

(1) /withdrawal....

(2)

withdrawal on our left, thus seriously exposing our Left Flank and ultimately forcing a withdrawal on our part. The Machine Guns became seriously involved from the outset of operations and resisted with the greatest determination, always covering the withdrawal of our Infantry and in cases fighting until overwhelmed by sheer weight of numbers. Many cases occurred of Machine Guns being put out of action by enemy bombers who made the utmost use of the "warren" of communication trenches which existed in the Sector. Where, however, "local protection", found by the gun teams themselves in the shape of one or two men being pushed out to a flank with rifles or revolvers, occurred, sufficient delay was caused to enable the remainder of the gun teams to keep their gun in action and make successive withdrawals later. All reports both from Infantry and Machine Gun Commanders show that very heavy casualties were inflicted on the enemy, and exceptionally good work was done in covering Infantry withdrawals and giving them every assistance. These operations undoubtedly proved that the value of Machine Guns is appreciated by the Infantry, and the presence of even one gun in their locality has a very decided moral effect. As a result of the good record of the Battalion both at EPEHY and YPRES, the moral of all ranks was of a very high standard throughout.

The detail of Machine Gun Operations is attached.

--------oOo--------

LIEUT-COLONEL,
COMMANDING 21st BN. MACHINE GUN CORPS.

21st Battn. Machine Gun Corps.

LESSONS LEARNT.

1. The great difficulty of maintaining the ammunition supply for guns which were in the original Trench Sector and making a gradual withdrawal with continual change of gun positions. During these operations, S.A.A. was sent in limbers from Battalion H.Q. to Brigade H.Q. From there it was man-handled to gun positions: surplus men from Battalion H.Q. should be utilised for this. Later on, when in open country, the S.A.A. supply was facilitated, and was by means of limbers direct to vicinity of gun positions.

2. The enemy made use at every opportunity of the numerous communication trenches in the Sector, thereby avoiding the good field of fire of the Machine Guns. It would, therefore, be a great benefit from the Machine Gun point of view that either no, or a very few, communication trenches exist. If any communication trenches in the vicinity of gun positions do exist, provision should be made for a straight piece of trench about 100 yards in length to be defended by Lewis Gun fire.

3. It is suggested that it is preferable to keep one Section of Machine Guns at Brigade H.Q. in each Brigade Sector, as a Mobile Reserve, and to be used at discretion of Brigades: than to place full complement of guns in the trenches - The Section on no account to be taken from the Divisional Reserve, which must be kept intact.

Main Advantages.

(a) Brigade Commander has Section at his disposal to move to any threatened point.

(b) Internal reliefs can be effected inside Company in a Brigade Sector, thus providing means of training under supervision of Company Commander.

(c) Prevents necessity of Sections being sent from Divisional Reserve Company, thus avoiding casualties in the movement up to Brigade.

(d) Better opportunities for reconnaissance of areas in the vicinity of Brigade.

Disadvantage.

Less guns in the line. This, however, still further enhances the principle of guns being distributed in depth.

4. Spare Parts Cases **must** be attached to the traversing handles of the gun, as this would have been the means of saving them in many cases.

5. The importance of fighting limbers being employed tactically with the Section was successfully carried out and proved entirely satisfactory.

LIEUT-COLONEL
COMMANDING 21st BN. MACHINE GUN CORPS

---oOo---

10.6.18.

NARRATIVE.

27.5.18.

Right Brigade Sector.

Guns in this Sector dealt mainly with parties of the enemy who attempted to cross ROUTE 44. In this they were successful until at 9 p.m. they were compelled to withdraw owing to the remainder of the line having been forced back.

Three especially good targets were engaged:-

(1) Transport bringing up supplies just E. of the Canal beyond BOIS DE COUDE. In several instances wagons were turned back, and one at least was put out of commission.

(2) In the afternoon, the enemy was seen to be using the roads leading into CAUROY from the N.E. for the purpose of bringing up S.A.A. and bombs, and our Machine Guns inflicted heavy casualties among these parties.

(3) An enemy Machine Gun was located at MOULIN DEREAUX at 4 p.m. and was knocked out by enfilade fire at a range of 700 yards. This was confirmed by observers with field glasses.

At least 7 guns out of the 16 in this Company were destroyed or rendered useless by shell fire or bombs.

The guns in this Sector took up position in the prepared line North of HERMONVILLE at 9 p.m.

Centre Sector.

Two guns at OUVRAGE RIGA did excellent work and fought to the end, continually engaging parties crossing between the canal and ROUTE 44. No one returned from these guns. They are known to have been in action at 4 p.m.

A gun due W. of P.C. LOUISE knocked out a limber on ROUTE 44 at 7 p.m.

Five guns at least in this Sector were destroyed by shell fire or bombs. Two were in BOYAU de la SOMME and two in BOYAU ANTOINE.

Left Sector.

Four guns East and North of MOULIN de CORMICY fought to a finish and no one returned. Reports of their good work were given by an Officer in charge of two guns N.W. of MOULIN de CORMICY.

Four guns took up position on the Railway Embankment S.W. of CHAPELLE, and engaged parties of the enemy crossing the flat ground to the N.E. of CHAPELLE.

Towards 5 p.m. these guns formed a protective flank covering the withdrawal of the infantry on the left.

Four guns W. of MOSCOU assisted in covering the infantry withdrawal, engaging parties of the enemy who tried to follow closely.

/The....

Left Sector (Continued).

The guns in this Sector fought their way back step by step (under harassing fire) from 62nd Brigade through CHALONS LE VERGEUR to VAUX VARENNES, and about midnight 27th/28th a position was taken up on the high ground N.W. of PEVY, and the teams stood to all night.

Guns in Support.

Four guns were sent to B.G.C. 110th Brigade at 11 a.m. An unlucky shot put two teams with their Officer out of action at once. The remaining guns at 1 p.m. occupied positions between CAUROY and CORMICY, and excellent targets were engaged, parties of the enemy crossing the open being effectively dealt with.

These guns were ultimately withdrawn at midnight to Cross Roads N.E. of VAUX VARENNES.

The Second Section arrived at 110th Brigade at 12 noon, and were also sent to reinforce the CAUROY - CORMICY Line. Two guns, firing down the valley, FOND DE CORMICY, did excellent work from 3 - 6 p.m. and caused considerable casualties to the enemy. The other pair had few targets.

The Section reporting to the 62nd Brigade were put in action on the Left Flank. The Officer in charge was killed almost immediately, and the guns worked in conjunction with the Section at CHAPELLE.

At midnight the general line occupied was - RIDGE LUTHERNAY FARM - N. of PEVY.

28.5.18.

During the whole day the Machine Guns were fighting rear-guard actions, and numerous targets were engaged. Two guns in position on the high ground about 1,000 yards N.W. of TRIGNY supporting our own and French troops had good targets most of the day.

Another pair of guns N.E. of LUTHERNAY FARM fired on waves of infantry advancing in a N.E. direction on LUTHERNAY FARM.

The Section sent to the Tile Works on the JONCHERY - RHEIMS Road, took up a position at the E. corner of the wood N.W. of the Tile Works. These guns were instrumental in preventing the enemy from entering the wood from the N. and dealt effectively with parties who attempted it.

Conforming with the general withdrawal, guns on the left were brought back to the JONCHERY - RHEIMS Road.

29.5.18.

Machine Guns again continued to fight rear-guard actions during this day, and several good targets were engaged, among these being Field Artillery at 1,000 yards range, which was taken on by guns at a point 1,000 m. S.W. of SAPICOURT, firing in a N.W. direction. These guns also effectively stopped Infantry and Motor Transport from crossing the open, and remained in action for several hours until being finally relieved by the French at 5 p.m.

At the close of active operations as far as the Division was concerned, the Battalion had 12 Machine Guns and 3 Mk.IV Tripods intact, the remainder of the 64 which took part being for the most part destroyed by shell fire and bombs.

WAR DIARY or INTELLIGENCE SUMMARY

Army Form C. 2118.

Month: June
Unit: 91st Bn M.G. Corps

Place	Date	Hour	Summary of Events and Information	Remarks and references to Appendices
GIVRY-EN-ARGONNE	1/6/18		Composite Coy. moved at 6 a.m. to SOULIÈRES for Entrainment. Destination unknown. B.G.C. 21st Independent Bde - Gen Oates D.S.O. Central dump of all stores established & removed to Corps.	A.3
LES-LOISY (CHÂLONS 1:100,000)	2/6/18		Reorganization of Coys as far as possible. Draft of 40 arrived which included some stragglers.	A.3
COURTEONNET	3/6/18		The Bn moved to COURTÉONNET via ÉTOGES, for actual forms part of 110th Bde Group. Officers' billets very poor — men's — moderate.	A.3
	4/6/18		8 guns received from Ordnance. 2 Sections under Capt Ball M.C. proceeded to form Composite Coy.	A.3
	5/6/18		The Commanding Officer visited the Independent Bde training by Coys.	A.3

WAR DIARY or INTELLIGENCE SUMMARY

Army Form C. 2118.

Place	Date	Hour	Summary of Events and Information	Remarks and references to Appendices
COURTEONNET	6/6/18		The Commanding officer returned from his visit to the Independent Bde in the line. Capt V.F. Samuelson M.C. reported to the Bn. Training by Coys continues.	A.B.
	7/6/18		Capt V.F. Samuelson M.C. took over the duties of Adjt to the Bn from Capt R.G. Hobson M.C. who was struck off the strength of the Bn accordingly. Training by Coys continues.	A.B. A.B.
	8/6/18		School for young N.C.O.s started — Training as before.	A.B.
VINDEY (ARCIS 1:80,000)	9/6/18		The Bn marched to VINDEY via SOIZY-aux-BOIS & SEZANNE. Left 10 a.m, arrived 5-30 p.m. Bn HQ opened at the Mairie on arrival. Billets poor for officers otherwise good.	21st Bn Mac of Cdr No 24 A.B.
	10/6/18		Coy training & School of N.C.O.s continues	A.B.
	11/6/18		Training as before — Warning received of move to a British Zone.	A.B.

Army Form C. 2118.

WAR DIARY
or
INTELLIGENCE SUMMARY

(Erase heading not required.)

Place	Date	Hour	Summary of Events and Information	Remarks and references to Appendices
VINDEY	12/6/18	—	Administrative orders received — Training continued.	Order "Instr" No 1.
	13/6/18		Transport of the Bn (less 'A' Coy) moved to staging area. HQ + 'C' Coy to CONNANTRAY, 'B' + 'D' Coys to CORROY. Coy training as usual.	do
	14/6/18		Companies moved to their respective entraining stations by bus, + the whole Bn entrained at the places + times mentioned in Op" order No 25.	Op" order No 25 do
	15/6/18		Bn moving by rail to ABBEVILLE area.	do
BOENCOURT	16/6/18		Bn detrained at LONGPRÉ + PONT RÉMY (ABBEVILLE 1:100,000), + marches to billets as follows:- HQ + 'C' Coy at BOENCOURT, 'A' Coy at LES CROISETTES, 'B' Coy at BIENFAY, 'D' Coy at YONVAL.	do
	17/6/18		Coy training + school of N.C.O's continued	do

WAR DIARY
or
INTELLIGENCE SUMMARY

Army Form C. 2118.

Place	Date	Hour	Summary of Events and Information	Remarks and references to Appendices
FORCEVILLE. (DIEPPE : 1:100,000)	18/6/18		Bn. moved to FORCEVILLE by route march. Billets for officers very poor, otherwise good.	Op. ordr. No. 26.
	19/6/18		Training by Coys continued. Independent Brigade returned from the line, detraining at OISEMONT. (DIEPPE 1:100,000).	
	20/6/18		Training continued. Capt Evans proceeded to base & struck off the strength accordingly.	
	21/6/18		Training. Lts Thomas & Steele + 2t. Foster reported for duty from the base.	
SEPT MEULES.	22/6/18		Bn marches to CUVERVILLE area, halting for 6 hours at GAMACHES. H.Q. + 'A' Coy billeted at SEPT MEULES. "B", "C", & "D" Coys at CUVERVILLE. Billets excellent.	M.G.C. Op ordr. No 27.
	23/6/18		Miniature ranges sited. Capt the Rev. F.S. March to England on leave. 164 O.R. reported for duty	

Army Form C. 2118.

WAR DIARY
or
INTELLIGENCE SUMMARY
(Erase heading not required.)

Place	Date	Hour	Summary of Events and Information	Remarks and references to Appendices
SEPT MEULES	24/6/18		Training continued. Lt Barker Mill M.C. proceeded to Grantham + struck off the strength accordingly. Lt P.G.S. Holmes reported for duty	A.F
	25/6/18		Miniature ranges completed, firing commenced.	A.F
	26/6/18		Training - Lt A. Huxley to England on leave.	A.F
	27/6/18		Training by Companies.	A.F
	28/6/18		Commanding officer attended a Divisional Conference - Training continued	A.F
	29/6/18		Warning received of a move to a new area. The Commanding Officer visited the 8th Bn M.G.C.	A.F
	30/6/18		A portion of the Transport moved by road to the OISEMONT area en route for the PUCHEVILLERS area. Training continued.	M.G.C. A.F Order N° 20

S E C R E T. Copy No. 12

21st Bn. M.G.C. OPERATION ORDER No. 24.

Ref. Maps CHALONS) 9th June 9 18.
        MEAUX) 1/80,000.
        PROVINS)
        ARCIS.)

----

1.   The Division, less Divisional Artillery and 21st Independent Brigade, will move to the LES ESSART area today.

2.   The Battalion will parade in following order, and head of column pass Starting Point at Road Junction, "B" & "D" Coy. Officers' billet, at 10.30 a.m.

      H.Q.Coy. - "D" Coy. - "B" Coy. - "C" Coy. - "A" Coy. -

    Transport in same order, except that each Coy. will have Coy. Cooker and one limber with Coy. Mess Stores on in rear of each Coy.

    Interval of 100 yards will be kept between Coys. personnel and Transport personnel.

    One Officer per Coy. will accompany each Coy. Transport.

    Dress: Battle Order.

3.   Billets will be left scrupulously clean, and a certificate rendered to Headquarters to this effect.

    The Battalion Orderly Officer will report at Battalion H.Q. at 10 a.m. to receive special instructions.

4.   Mid-day meal will be served en route.

    Strictest march discipline will be maintained on the march.

5.   A C K N O W L E D G E.

                                                    Capt. & Adjt.,
                              21st Battn. Machine Gun Corps.

Issued by Runner at 9.15 a.m.

Copy No.1 & 2 .. File.
       3 .. O.C. "A" Coy.
       4 .. O.C. "B" Coy.
       5 .. O.C. "C" Coy.
       6 .. O.C. "D" Coy.
       7 .. H.Q.Coy.
       8 .. Q.M.
       9 .. T.O.
      10 .. 21st Division H.Q.
      11 .. 110th Inf. Bde.
  12 & 13. War Diary.
      14 .. R.S.M.

SECRET.   Copy No. 12

Administrative Instructions No. 1 for move of 21st BATTN. MACHINE GUN CORPS from French Area.

1. **STATIONS.**

    Entraining Stations and times of departure of trains will be notified later.

2. **OFFICER TO REPORT TO ENTRAINING OFFICERS.**

    Lieut. BARKER MILL, M.C., will report to the Entraining Officer 3½ hours before the departure of train or trains with an accurate return of the numbers of Officers, Other Ranks, Animals (by classes) and Vehicles (by types) which are to proceed by each train. The entraining Officer will issue orders as regards entraining to this Officer.

3. **LOADING & UNLOADING TRAINS.**

    Transport accompanied by a Loading Party of at least 60 men per train in addition to the drivers will be at the Station 5½ hours before the time of departure of each train.

    A party of 60 men on each train will be told off to unload the train on arrival. The O.C. Train will be responsible that this party is told off and is ready to start work immediately the train arrives.

    Further orders will be issued regarding this.

4. **WATER.**

    All men will entrain with their water bottles full. Watercarts will be entrained full.

5. **TRANSPORT.**

    (a) Baggage and supply wagons will entrain with Units.

    (b) Breast ropes for horses must be provided by Units. Ropes for lashing vehicles will be provided by the Railway Authorities. Canvas buckets will be carried in each horse truck.

    (c) Horses will be entrained saddled up.

    (d) Transport men and grooms will travel in the trucks with their animals.

5. TRANSPORT (Continued).

(c) If possible, cinders or gravel will be spread on the floors of trucks occupied by animals.

6. AMMUNITION.

All ammunition echelons will be entrained full.

7. LEAVING THE TRAIN.

No man is to get out of the train without permission from the O.C. Train. At each halting place picquets must be provided to prevent the men from wandering too far from the train, and to see that they are all back in the train before it starts.

These picquets will also watch each side of the train to ensure that there is no looting of stores.

8. PRECAUTIONS AGAINST ACCIDENT.

No one will enter or leave the train while it is in motion. Men must not climb on to the roofs of the trucks or sit with their legs outside. They must not climb from one truck to another. All doors of covered trucks and carriages on the right hand side of the train, when on the main line, must be kept closed.

9. FIRES.

No braziers or fires will be allowed in the trucks. If there is any straw or hay in the trucks, no candles or lights except those provided by the Railway Authorities will be allowed.

10. DISCIPLINE.

The O.C. Train is responsible that strict discipline is maintained on the train and at all stopping places. He will see that all instructions issued by the Railway Authorities are carried out.

11. SALVAGE.

Great care must be taken that no clothing or other salvage is left in present billets or camps.

(3)

12. BILLETS & CAMPS.

   (a) All camps, billets and horse lines must be left scrupulou[sly] clean. If possible, a certificate that this has been done will be obtained from the Major de Cantonnement, or Maire.
   (b) Trench Shelters will be handed over to D.A.D.O.S. before moving.
   (c) No tents or trench shelters except those allowed by Mobilization Store Tables will be removed from this area.
   (d) The Orderly Officer will remain behind at the Mairie to receive any claims from the Inhabitants. This Officer will rejoin the Battalion in time to entrain with Battalion - on last train if more than one train.

13. A C K N O W L E D G E.

                                                   V. F. Samson
                                                   Capt. & Adj[t]
12.6.18.   21st Battalion, Machine Gun Corps.

DISTRIBUTION.

Copy Nos. 1 & 2 .. File.   Copy No. 7 .. H.Q. Coy.
          3 .. O.C. "A" Coy.   8 .. Quartermaster.
          4 .. O.C. "B" Coy.   9 .. Transport Offic[er]
          5 .. O.C. "C" Coy.   10 .. 21st Div. H.Q.
          6 .. O.C. "D" Coy.   11 & 12 .. War Diary.

SECRET.   Copy No. 12

21st Bn. M.G.C. OPERATION ORDER No. 25.

Ref Maps: 13th June 1918.
  PROVINS)
  ARCIS   ) 1/80,000.

---

1.   The Division less 21st Independent Brigade and Divisional Artillery will move by rail to the ABBEVILLE Area on June 14th. The 21st Independent Brigade and Divisional Artillery will move by rail to the same area on dates to be notified later.

2.   Entraining Stations will be:-

        62nd Bde. Group   )
        "A" Coy., 21st M.G.Bn) .. SEZANNE.

        64th Bde. Group   .. FERE CHAMPENOISE.

        110th Bde. Group   .. SOMMESOUS.

        14th North'd Fus.   .. SEZANNE.

3.   For the purposes of this move,

        64th Bde. Group will consist of:-

        64th Inf. Bde.
        No. 4 Coy. Train.
        "B" & "D" Coys., 21st M.G.Bn.
        64th & 65th Field Ambulances.
        Mobile Veterinary Section.

        110th Bde. Group will consist of:-

        110th Inf. Bde.
        No. 3 Coy. Train.
        98th Field Coy. R.E.
        H.Q. & "C" Coy., 21st M.G.Bn.

                                                      P.T.O.

(2)

4. (a) Infantry and dismounted personnel of 64th and 110th Bde. Groups will be bussed to entraining stations under orders to be issued later.
62nd Bde. Group will receive further orders.

(b) Transport of these Groups will march to staging areas today, June 13th, as under: One Officer per Company will accompany each Company's transport.

    (i) 110th Bde. Group to CONNANTRAY.
        To be clear of SEZANNE by 2 p.m.
        Route - FERE CHAMPENOISE.

    (ii) 64th Bde. Group to CORROY.
        Not to enter SEZANNE before 2.15 p.m.
        Route - CONNANTRE.

Special Orders will be issued later.

5. The strictest march discipline will be observed. Intervals as laid down in IXth Corps Traffic Orders will be observed on the line of march.

6. Dress: Full marching order.

7. G.Os.C. Brigade Groups will report completion of moves to Divisional Headquarters.

8. A C K N O W L E D G E.

V.F. Samuelson
Capt. & Adjt.,
21st Battalion, Machine Gun Corps.

To All Recipients of Administrative Instructions No. 1.

SECRET.   Copy No......

21st Bn. M.G.C. OPERATION ORDER No.26.

Ref. Maps:
ABBEVILLE,
DIEPPE.   17th June 1918.

1. The Battalion, less personnel with Independent Brigade, will move independently by route march to FORCEVILLE on the 18th inst.

2. Companies will pass Starting Point at Road Junction W. of X in ZALLEUX on Main ABBEVILLE - BLANGY Road as under:-

   "A" Coy. 10 a.m.   -   Bn.H.Q. 10.5 a.m.   -   "C" Coy. 10.10 a.m.
   "B" Coy. 10.15 a.m. -   "D" Coy. 10.20 a.m.

   Interval of 50 yards between Company and Transport.

3. Route: BOENCOURT - HUPPY - DOUDELAINVILLE - MARQUENNEVILLE VAUX - NEUVILLE-au-Bois - FORCEVILLE. (Distance about 7 miles).

4. Mid-day meal will be cooked en route and served on arrival.

5. Lieut. G.O.Fairlie, M.C., 4 C.Q.M.Ss., R.Q.M.S., will report Bn. H.Q. at 8 a.m. to proceed as Advance Prty to Billet. All will be mounted on bicycles now in Company possession.

6. Personnel etc. now with the Independent Brigade will rejoin the Battalion on the 19th or 20th inst. in new area.

7. All billets will be left scrupulously clean.

   An Officer will be left behind at the Mairie, in each village, for 3 hours after departure of troops to receive claims; he will obtain a certificate that there are no claims for damage and that billets have been left clean. This certificate will be sent Battalion H.Q. on arrival in new area.

8. Arrival in new area will be reported to Battn. H.Q. by Coys.

9. Halts will be at 10 minutes to clock hours, first halt 10.50 a.m. Watches will be synchronised by first D.R.L.S.

10. A C K N O W L E D G E.

                                                    V.F. Samuelson
                                                    Capt. & Adjt.
                                                    21st Battn. Machine Gun Corps.

Issued by Runner.

Copy No. 1 .. O.C. "A" Coy.
          2 .. O.C. "B" Coy.
          3 .. O.C. "C" Coy.
          4 .. O.C. "D" Coy.
          5 .. Q.M.
          6 .. T.O.
          7 .. H.Q.Coy.
          8 .. 64th Inf. Bde.
          9 .. Commanding Officer.
         10 .. File.
    11 & 12 .. War Diary.

SECRET.   Copy No. 13

21st Battn. Machine Gun Corps
OPERATION ORDER No. 27.

21st June 1918.

Ref. Map.
DIEPPE, 1/100,000.

1. The Division will move on 21st and 22nd inst. to GAMACHES Area (South).

2. The Battalion will parade ready to move at 6 a.m., 22nd inst. by route march to CUVERVILLE and SEPT MEULE in following order:-

   Bn. H.Q. .. "B" Coy. .. "C" Coy. .. "D" Coy. .. "A" Coy.

   Head of Battalion to be at Road Junction due North of the 1st E in FORCEVILLE.

   "A" Coy. can remain in Coy. area off main road, and join column.

3. Route:-
   FORCEVILLE - OISEMONT - TRANSLAY - GAMACHES - GUERVILLE - MELLEVILLE - VILLY LE BAS - SEPT MEULES - CUVERVILLE.

4. The strictest march discipline will be maintained on the march, and regulation hourly halts will be observed.
   100 yards interval will be kept between respective Coys. and Coy. Transports.

5. Advance Party.
   Lieut. G. O. FAIRLIE, M.C., Lieut. A.A.F.SEARL, 4 Coy. Qr.Mr.Sgts, and 1 N.C.O. Battn. H.Q.Coy. will report Battn. H.Q. at 5.30 a.m. on bicycles, to proceed to new area and take over billets.
   Lieut. G.O.FAIRLIE, M.C., is appointed Billeting Officer.

6. All billets will be left scrupulously clean, and a certificate sent Battn. H.Q. by 5.30 a.m. to this effect.
   Lieut. D. L. SCOTLAND will report to the Mairie, FORCEVILLE, after the Battalion has moved, and get usual certificate, and rejoin Battalion.

7. Dress: Battle Order. Water Bottles filled.

8. Breakfasts will be served at 5 a.m. Mid-day meal cooked on route and served at 12.30 p.m. Teas on arrival in billets about 7.30 p.m.
   The Battalion will rest short of GAMACHES, between 10 a.m. and 4 p.m.

9. Motor Lorries have been asked for, and further instructions will be issued.

10. A C K N O W L E D G E.

V. F. Samuelson
Capt. & Adjt.,
21st Battn. Machine Gun Corps.

Issued by Runner at 11.30 a.m.

SECRET.   Copy No. 13

                    21st Battn. Machine Gun Corps
                    OPERATION ORDER No. 27.

                                                21st June 1918.
Ref. Map.
    DIEPPE, 1/100,000.
    ----

1.   The Division will move on 21st and 22nd inst. to
GAMACHES Area (South).

2.   The Battalion will parade ready to move at 6 a.m.,
22nd inst. by route march to CUVERVILLE and SEPT MEULE in
following order:-

    Bn. H.Q. .. "B" Coy. .. "C" Coy. .. "D" Coy... "A" Coy.

Head of Battalion to be at Road Junction due North of the 1st
E in FORCEVILLE.

          "A" Coy. can remain in Coy. area off main road, and
join column.

3. Route:-
          FORCEVILLE - OISEMONT - TRANSLAY - GAMACHES - GUERVILLE
          - MELLEVILLE - VILLY LE BAS - SEPT MEULES - CUVERVILLE.

4.   The strictest march discipline will be maintained on
the march, and regulation hourly halts will be observed.
          100 yards interval will be kept between respective
Coys. and Coy. Transports.

5. Advance Party.

          Lieut. G. O. FAIRLIE, M.C., Lieut. A.A.F.SEARL,
4 Coy. Qr.Mr.Sgts, and 1 N.C.O. Battn. H.Q.Coy. will report
Battn. H.Q. at 5.30 a.m. on bicycles, to proceed to new area
and take over billets.
          Lieut. G.O.FAIRLIE, M.C., is appointed Billeting Officer.

6.   All billets will be left scrupulously clean, and a
certificate sent Battn. H.Q. by 5.30 a.m. to this effect.
          Lieut. D. L. SCOTLAND will report to the Mairie,
FORCEVILLE, after the Battalion has moved, and get usual
certificate, and rejoin Battalion.

7.   Dress: Battle Order. Water Bottles filled.

8.   Breakfasts will be served at 5 a.m. Mid-day meal
cooked on route and served at 12.30 p.m. Teas on arrival in
billets about 7.30 p.m.
          The Battalion will rest short of GAMACHES. between
10 a.m. and 4 p.m.

9.   Motor Lorries have been asked for, and further instructions
will be issued.

10.   A C K N O W L E D G E.

                                        V. F. Samuelson
                                                Capt. & Adjt.,
                                    21st Battn. Machine Gun Corps.

Issued by Runner at 11.30 a.m.

SECRET.   Copy No. 9.

                     21st Battn. Machine Gun Corps
                         OPERATION ORDER No. 20.

                                                        30th June 1918.

Ref. Map DIEPPE, } 1/100,000.
         LENS,   }

1.   The Division will move from the GAMACHES Area to PUCHEVILLERS
        Area by road and train, commencing 30th June 1918.

             The marching portion of Transport will move by road today,
        30th June, to OISEMONT Area, and continue march following day.

2.   All personnel of the Battalion, plus 3 limbers each of
        Battalion Headquarters and "A" Coy, 2 limbers each of "B", "C" &
        "D" Coys. will move by rail, probably 1st July. Further orders
        will be issued.

3.   All transport except that mentioned in para. 2, will move
        today, and pass Starting Point at 9.45 a.m., namely, Cross Roads
        due North of S in SEPT MEULES in following order:-

        Battn. HQ. - "A" Coy. - "B" Coy. - "C" Coy. - "D" Coy.

        Usual intervals will be maintained.

             The Column will join the 62nd Inf. Bde. Group, passing 2nd
        Starting Point at 12.5 p.m., where eight roads meet on the main
        GRANDCOURT - RIEUX - BLANGY Road in HAUTE FORET D'EU.

        Order of march:

             2nd Lincoln Regt. - 21st Bn.M.G.C. - 1st Lincoln Regt. -
             12/13th Northumberland Fus. - 62nd Inf. Bde. HQ. - 63rd
             Field Ambulance - 97th Field Coy. R.E.

             A distance of 300 yards will be maintained between Transport
        of Units.

             The Brigade Group are under orders of the Brigade Transport
        Officer.

             Rations and forage for the 1st July will be carried if
        issued in time.

4.   All Lines must be left clean.

5.   A C K N O W L E D G E.

                                                V.J. Cameron
                                                       Capt. & Adjt.,
                                           21st Battn. Machine Gun Corps.

Issued by Runner at 7.45 a.m.

Copy No. 1 .. O.C. "A" Coy.
         2 .. "   "B" Coy.
         3 .. "   "C" Coy.
         4 .. "   "D" Coy.
         5 .. M.O.
         6 .. Q.M.
         7 .. H.Q.Coy.
         8 .. File.
     9 & 10 .. War Diary.

21 Bn M E Corps
Vol 5

On His Majesty's Service.

SECRET.

D.A.G.
G.H.Q.
3rd Echelon.

M745

Army Form C. 2118.

WAR DIARY
or
INTELLIGENCE SUMMARY
(Erase heading not required.)

2nd Bn Rifle Corps

July 1916

Place	Date	Hour	Summary of Events and Information	Remarks and references to Appendices
SEPT-EN-EQUIHEN (DIEPPE MAP)	1/7/16		Posture [?] brought away Ord inst relating to this – OO No 38. Battn moved to GAMACHES at 3 P.m. for entraining	OO No 38 Appx 1 Appx 2
GAMACHE	2/7/16		Battn entrained at 1:30 am & left at 5 am, arrived PUCHEVILLERS (Somme) 12 noon, marched to I.E. QUESNOY and bivouac at MAY CAMP. 9/16 Reserve 93rd Anglo-Reserve. R.C. Cath. Luth. tea party at C. CATHOLIC Lieuts H.V. SCOTT, T. HUNTER & J. BULLARD reported for duty, posted to B, A, B, & C Coys respectively	Appx 3 Appx 4
I.E. QUESNOY	3/7/16		C.O. visited C.R.E. Coys	
	4/7/16		C.O. + 6 Coys reconnoitred BROWN LINE (Coy of 2nd WR Surrey) 2nd Battn Rifle Defence Scheme issued	Appx 5 Appx 6 A
	5/7/16		Training	Appx 7
	6/7/16		Training & 6 Coys reconnoitred [?] (front & rear)	Appx 8

WAR DIARY
or
INTELLIGENCE SUMMARY
(Erase heading not required.)

Army Form C. 2118.

Place	Date	Hour	Summary of Events and Information	Remarks and references to Appendices
LE QUESNOY	7/4/18		Church Parade. 2/Lieuts. J.B. WALKER, T.O. WATES & A.J. WEBBER (m.g.) reported for duty & were posted to "D", "C" & "D" bys respectively.	JRM
	8/4/18		Training. Lecture by Brigade Officer to all Officers & N.C.O's.	JRM
	9/4/18		Training	
	10/4/18		18pounder "B" Bty proceeded to line to Special barrage. 2/Lt R.M. FAIRHURST & 60 O.R's also "B" Bty, also 60 O.R's taken on strength.	O.O. No. 21 B JRM
			reported for duty. 9 horses to "B" Bty.	
	11/4/18		C.O. + O.C. by reconnaissance line B - co-operated with 38th Div in raid	JRM
			to HAMEL. Railway successful. Casualties 2 O.R's killed 4 O.R's	
			wounded all "A" bty. Casualties.	
	12/4/18		"C" Bty party returned to KAY CAMP from line.	
			Lieut. C.B. WATSON (M.G.) died of wounds received some morning.	JRM

WAR DIARY
INTELLIGENCE SUMMARY

Army Form C. 2118.

Place	Date	Hour	Summary of Events and Information	Remarks and references to Appendices
LE QUESNOY	13/4/18	1PM	Training. B's attached to 38th M.G. unit for co-operation in raid on HAMEL.	See M.G.U. Narrative
		7PM	2nd Lieut. C.B. WATSON pro. buried at Military Cemetery. N21c S.W. Shts. 51D & 57D (1 of 10,000)	J.P.M
	14/4/18		Church Parade. C.O.'s Inspn. The No. 8. 38M.G.B's reconnoitred under R.M. L.S.H. of A. by burial at Military Cemetery N21c S.W. (Shts. 57D & 51D 1 of 10,000)	J.P.M
	15/4/18		Training. 3rd M.G. Course commenced under R.M.R. 2.6 by station. Officers reconnoitred line.	J.P.M
	16/4/18		G.O. Inspected "C" Sqn.	J.P.M
	17/4/18		Training. D.O.6. 21st Sup. addressed all Ranks on re-joined Br. announcing T. Montagu. C.O. Inspected A, B & D Sqns.	J.P.M
	18/4/18		Training.	J.P.M

WAR DIARY
or
INTELLIGENCE SUMMARY.

(Erase heading not required.)

Army Form C. 2118.

Place	Date	Hour	Summary of Events and Information	Remarks and references to Appendices
I.E. QUESNOY	19/4/18		Training firing on Long Range. Inspection by 5. Army Commander Gen Julian Byng in afternoon. B.C. & firing order during afternoon. Lieut T.S. CLAPHAM & Lieut H. HAIGH E.O. CLEMENSON dynasty duty & all post on A. by 6 & 8 O.P's in duty 6 hrs.	J.S.M.
	20/4/18		Training. All boys firing on Long Range. 29 O.R's rejoined from Tropical wastage. (or strength)	J.S.M.
	22/4/18		Saluting Parade. G.O. visited 63rd M.G. Bn. Hdrs at 11 & B & Hdrs at 11 & met D.I.M.G.O. Colonel Blake & H.Q. at 63 M.G.Bn Hdrs. 3 Army.	J.S.M.
	23/4/18		All Officers reconnoitred line in front (Chuignes) 1000' Aep taps state instead of spray.	J.S.M.
	23/4/18		In training. Heavy rain. G.O. Conference with all Officers at 9 am at B. Hdrs.	O.O. N°31 J.S.M.
	24/4/18		Training "G.O.B." Coy moved into the line.	J.S.M.

WAR DIARY
or
INTELLIGENCE SUMMARY

Army Form C. 2118.

Place	Date	Hour	Summary of Events and Information	Remarks and references to Appendices
LE QUESNOY	23/4/18		A.D. Coys into line. Bn. HQrs moved from LE QUESNOY to ACHEUX. C.O. reconnoitred PURPLE LINE & Right B Sector.	O.O. No 31. C. J.D.N.
ACHEUX	24/4/18		C.O. reconnoitred Centre B Sector. Bn. attended explosion of Mine at 4 pm	J.D.N.
	25/4/18		C.O. reconnoitred Reg¹ B Sector	J.D.N.
	28/4/18		Church Parade. C.O. reconnoitred Right B Sector. Bn. HQrs C.O. attended conference at Bn. HQrs at 4 pm of Coy 2nd Rifle Bde relieved 10/R.B. & to be attached for one month's probation to 3rd Light Infantry	J.D.N.
	29/4/18		C.O. reconnoitred line with D.I.M.G.O. Colonel Leyshon, 3rd Army. S.O. 3 3rd Army visited Purple Line during afternoon	J.D.N.

Army Form C. 2118.

WAR DIARY
or
INTELLIGENCE SUMMARY.
(Erase heading not required.)

Place	Date	Hour	Summary of Events and Information	Remarks and references to Appendices
ACHEUX	30/4/18		Heavy gas shelling on MAILLY-MAILLET during night 29/30. Sn. O.O. No 32333. Anticipated attack at 9 a.m. 18 - 6,000 rds fired on selected targets. D/E. Slight retaliation. Enemy did not 2.O.R. attempt to open an attack.	
	1/5/18		Heavy gas shelling (Mustard gas) around MAILLY-MAILLET during night. 18 gas casualties during both nights	

J. McCoy
LIEUT-COLONEL
COMMANDING 21st BN. MACHINE GUN CORPS.

SECRET. Copy No. 17

21st Battn. Machine Gun Corps.

PROVISIONAL DEFENCE ARRANGEMENTS.

Ref.Map Sheet:
57d, 1/40,000.

4th July 1918.

1. The Vth Corps Front, extending from W.16.d.5.0 to Q.4.a.9.5, is held with three Divisions in the line and two in Reserve.

   The 21st Division is at present in G.H.Q. Reserve, and is also left Supporting Division to Vth Corps.

2. Whilst in G.H.Q.Reserve:-

   (a) Companies will be at one hour's notice to move from 6 a.m. to 9 a.m. daily, and at three hours' notice for the remainder of the day.

   (b) Training and route marches will proceed as usual. In the event of the Tactical situation not permitting of training and marches, notice will be sent from this Office.

   (c) The Battalion will be at 9 hours' notice to leave the Third Army Area.

3. In addition to above, the Battalion being left Supporting Division, Companies will be at one hour's notice to move from midnight to 5 a.m. daily.

Action of 110th Inf.Bde. plus "A" & "C" Coys. 21st Bn.M.G.C. in case of attack.

1. On the alarm being given, the Brigade plus "A" & "C" Coys 21st Bn.M.G.C. will "Stand to" in its present area.

2. In the event of orders being received to move, the following action will be taken:-

   (a) The Bde. plus "A" & "C" Coys.M.G.C., and 1 Coy. Field Coy.R.E. will move and occupy the Brown System from FORCEVILLE to BEAUSSART (both inclusive), i.e. from P.28.a.5.0 to P.5.central. Bde. H.Q. at ACHEUX.
   A Liaison post will be established about P.5 central with IVth Corps by 110th Inf.Bde.

   (b) Detailed instructions as to dispositions to be taken up etc. will be issued later.

Action of 64th Inf.Bde. plus "B" Coy. 21st Bn.M.G.C.

1. On the alarm being given, the Brigade plus "B" Coy. 21st Bn. M.G.C. will "Stand to" in the open country just EAST of PUCHEVILLERS and SOUTH of the RAINCHEVAL Road, N.22.d.
   "B" Coy. will move independently to this area, and report on arrival to H.Q. 64th Inf. Bde.
   The most probable move that will be ordered is to a position of readiness in O.17.c.
   The Brigade will be called upon to attack and recapture ENGLEBELMER.

(2)

4. **Action of 62nd Inf. Bde. plus "D" Coy. 21st Bn. M.G.C.**

   In event of attack, the Brigade plus "D" Coy. would probably move to a position of readiness in O.17.a. (N.W. of LEAIVILLERS). Further orders will be issued.

5. Battalion H.Q. will move to Advanced Divisional H.Q. in O.17.b.

6. Gun Teams will consist of 1 N.C.O. and 5 Men.

   1 Officer or full N.C.O. will be in charge of each pair of guns.

7. All Battalion Details, including Company 2nds. in Command and Transport Officers will "Stand to" in present area, and be ready to move at ¼ hour's notice.

8. A C K N O W L E D G E.

V.F. Samuelson

Capt. & Adjt.,
21st Battn. Machine Gun Corps.

DISTRIBUTION:-

Copy No. 1 .. Commanding Officer.
        2 .. Bn. 2nd in Command.
        3 .. O.C. "A" Coy.
        4 .. "   "B" "
        5 .. "   "C" "
        6 .. "   "D" "
        7 .. 62nd Inf. Bde.
        8 .. 64th   "   "
        9 .. 110th "   "
       10 .. 21st Division.
       11 .. H.Q.Coy.
       12 .. Quartermaster.
       13 .. Intelligence Officer.
       14 .. Medical Officer.
       15 .. File.
    16 & 17 .. War Diary.

SECRET.

AMENDMENTS to 21st Bn. M.G.C. Defence Scheme dated 8th July 1918.

Para. 3.(b) should now read:

No. 1 Brigade plus "A" Coy. M.G.Bn. (Occupy BROWN ~~LINE~~ SYSTEM. H.Q. at ACHEUX).

"C" Coy. 21st M.G.Bn. .. Joins No. 1 Brigade, (Moves from QUESNOYE) and takes over positions in Left Sector from "A" Coy. (as in Appendix I).

Appendix 6, para. 7 - Action of Machine Guns.

(c) .. For "A" Coy. substitute "C" Coy.

(d) .. For "C" Coy. substitute "A" Coy.

21st Bn. M.G.C.
21-7-18.

D.F. Kay Lt.Col.,
Comdg. 21st Bn. M.G. Corps.

S E C R E T.   Copy No... 14

21st Battn. Machine Gun Corps.

DEFENCE SCHEME.

                                                                8th July 1918.

Ref. Map Sheets:
57d, 1/40,000 &
57d.S.E., 1/20,000.
----

1. In continuation of 21st Bn.M.G.C. 'Defence Arrangements', the following appendices are attached, shewing the detailed action of units in the case of certain eventualities. Company Commanders, Section and Transport Officers, will at once reconnoitre all Tracks, Assembly Positions, Machine Gun Emplacements and Trench Systems, according as they affect the Company concerned.

2. For the purposes of this Defence Scheme, Infantry Brigades are referred to as follows:-

110th Infantry Brigade	..	No. 1 Brigade.
64th -do-	..	" 2 "
62nd -do-	..	" 3 "

3. In the case of alarm, the message "Move to Assembly Positions" will be sent out from this office. On receipt of this message, Companies will act as follows:-

   (a) Advanced Divisional H.Q.)   Move to O.17.b.8.9.
       H.Q., 21st Bn.M.G.C.   )

   (b) No. 1 Brigade.   Occupy BROWN SYSTEM.
       "A" & "C" Coys. M.G.Bn.   Occupy positions in BROWN SYSTEM.

   (c) No. 2 Brigade.   Move to O.17.c.
       "B" Coy. M.G.Bn.   Move with No. 2 Brigade.

   (d) No. 3 Brigade.   Move to O.17.a.
       "D" Coy. M.G.Bn.   Move with No. 3 Brigade.

4. ROADS & TRACKS.

   (a) Troops and Horse Transport will, as far as possible, move by Cross Country Tracks. The following are allotted to the Division:-

   M.21 .. PUCHEVILLERS - LEALVILLERS.
   M.16 .. BEAUQUESNE - ARQUEVES - ACHEUX.

   (b) Roads are allotted as follows, but will only be used by Horse Transport if Tracks are impracticable owing to bad weather:-
       ROSEL CROSS ROADS - BEAUQUESNE - RAINCHEVAL - LEALVILLERS.

                                              J. H. Kay.
                                              Lieut. Colonel,
                                   Commanding 21st Bn. Machine Gun Corps.

DISTRIBUTION.
To All Recipients of "Provisional Defence Arrangements".

APPENDIX 1.

1. In the event of the Division being ordered to occupy either all or part of the PURPLE or BROWN Systems within the Divisional Boundaries, the probable dispositions and Headquarters will be as follows:-

(a) **PURPLE SYSTEM.**

Advanced Divl. H.Q. & H.Q. 21st Bn.M.G.C. .. Q.17.b.6.9.

Right Sector.

No. 2 Brigade,   } .. H.Q., - FORCEVILLE.
"B" Coy. 21st Bn.M.G.C.} .. 2 Sections in position in depth
                            2 Sections in Reserve with
                            Support Battalion.

Left Sector.

No. 3 Brigade,   } .. H.Q., - BEAUSSART.
"D" Coy.21st Bn.M.G.C.} .. 2 Sections in position in depth
                           2 Sections in Reserve.

Reserve.

No. 1 Brigade,   } .. H.Q., - ACHEUX.
"A" & "C" Coys. 21st Bn.   } .. 3 Sections of each Company in
  M.G.C.   position in BROWN SYSTEM.
                                1 Section of each Company in
                                Reserve in ACHEUX WOOD.

The Dividing Line between the Right and Left Sectors is the Grid Line Q.15 Central - Q.14 Central.

(b) **BROWN SYSTEM.**

Advanced Divl. H.Q. and H.Q., 21st Bn.M.G.C. .. ARQUEVES.

Right Sector.

No. 2 Brigade   } .. H.Q. - ACHEUX.
"A" Coy. 21st Bn.M.G.C.} .. 3 Sections in position in depth
                           1 Section in Reserve with
                           Support Battalion.

Left Sector.

No. 1 Brigade,   } .. H.Q. - ACHEUX.
"C" Coy. 21st Bn.M.G.C } .. 3 Sections in position in
                           BROWN SYSTEM (Left Sector).
                           1 Section in Reserve,
                           ACHEUX WOOD.

ACHEUX WOOD LINE.

"B" Coy. will take up positions in this Line.

Reserve.

No. 3 Brigade,   ) Bde. H.Q.) Concentrated in
"D" Coy. 21st Bn.M.G.C) LEALVILLERS) G.17.a and c.

The Dividing Line between Right and Left Sectors is the Grid Line P.14 Central - P.16 Central.

SECRET.

M. 242

To All Recipients of
21st Bn. M.G.C. Defence Scheme.

Reference 21st Bn. M.G.C. Defence Scheme dated 8.7.18:

1. In the event of the Division being ordered to hold the RED LINE, the following dispositions will be taken up:

Right Sector.   O.30.a.5.0 - O.18.a.2.0.

    No. 2 Brigade (64th Inf. Bde.) .. H.Q. ARQUEVES.
    "B" Coy. 21st Bn. M.G.C.

Left Sector.   O.18.a.2.0 - O.5.b.1.0.

    No. 3 Brigade (62nd Inf. Bde.). H.Q. ARQUEVES.
    "D" Coy. 21st Bn. M.G.C.

Divisional Reserve.

    No. 1 Brigade (110th Inf. Bde). with "A" & "C" Coys. 21st Bn. M.G.C. would remain in the BROWN LINE.

2. Company Commanders will reconnoitre the RED LINE and determine the exact positions to be taken up by their Companies.

                                L.C. Bathwick Major for.

                                Lieut. Colonel,
              Commanding 21st Bn. Machine Gun Corps.

21.7.18.

APPENDIX 2.

1. The enemy has captured the high ground on the Line Hill 142 - AUCHONVILLERS, and has advanced on the PURPLE SYSTEM and captured ENGLEBELMER - MAILLY-MAILLET.

The Divisional Commander intends to recapture ENGLEBELMER and MAILLY-MAILLET, and re-occupy the PURPLE LINE to the East.

2. The attack will be carried out by Nos. 2 and 3 Brigades simultaneously as follows:-

(a) **No.2 Brigade.**

Objective: ENGLEBELMER and PURPLE LINE to the East.

Assembly Position.

 Preliminary - 0.17.c.
 Secondary - Bde. H.Q. P.27.b.3.2.
      Advanced Bde.H.Q.(Report Centre) P.22.a.5.7.
      Battalions: Hollow East & South of
        FORCEVILLE, P.20.b, P.15.c.
        and 21.a.

Boundaries.

 Right - Q.25.b.Central - P.17.c.0.0.
 Left - Q.20.a.Central - P.17.b.Central.

O.C. "B" Coy. will detail one section to each flank of the attack to cover the advance of the infantry. Particular attention is to be paid to looking out for, and dealing with advanced hostile L.G's.

These two sections will go forward and assist in consolidation of PURPLE LINE as soon as it is known that this is captured.

Eight guns will be in reserve, remaining in the first instance in P.22.b. and moving forward later to the positions vacated by the forward sections.

(b) **No.3 Brigade.**

Objective: MAILLY-MAILLET & PURPLE LINE to the East.

Assembly Position:

 Preliminary - 0.17.a.
 Secondary - Bde. H.Q., COPSE P.8.b.
      Battalions - P.4.c. and e.

Boundaries.

 Right - P.5.d.Central - Q.14 Central.
 Left - P.6.a.9.4 - Q.8.b.0.4.

"D" Coy. M.G.Bn. will be at disposal of No.3 Brigade.

"A" & "C" Coys. M.G.Bn. will provide Long Range Covering Fire from suitable positions in the BROWN SYSTEM.

/Divisional......

(2)

Divisional Artillery Programme is as follows:

ENGLEBELMER.

Zero - Zero plus 80.	S.W. and N.W. edges of village.
Zero plus 80 to Zero plus 85.	Main Street running N.E. and S.W. through centre of village.
Zero plus 85 to Zero plus 95.	PURPLE SYSTEM.
Zero plus 95 onwards.	Protective Barrage.

MAILLY - MAILLET.

Zero to Zero plus 80.	W. and N.W. edges of village.
Zero plus 80 to Zero plus 85.	Main Street running N.E. and S.W. through village.
Zero plus 85 to Zero plus 90.	Street running N.E. and S.W. through Q.7. Central.
Zero plus 90 to Zero plus 95.	Trenches in Q.7.b. and d.
Zero plus 95 onwards.	PURPLE SYSTEM until Protective Barrage is ordered by B.G.C., No. 3 Brigade.

O.C. "D" Coy. will detail one section to each flank of the attack to cover the advance of the Infantry. Particular attention is to be paid to looking out for, and dealing with, advanced hostile M.G's.

These two sections will go forward and assist in consolidation of PURPLE LINE as soon as it is known to be captured.

Eight guns will be held in Reserve and used for further consolidation in depth, or on orders of B.G.C., No. 3 Brigade.

APPENDIX 3.

1. The enemy has captured the Ridge along HILL 142 - AUCHONVILLERS. The PURPLE SYSTEM to the West is still intact.
   The Divisional Commander intends to recapture HILL 142 - AUCHONVILLERS, and the intervening ground.

2. The attack will be carried out by Nos. 2 and 3 Brigades simultaneously as follows:-

   (a) **No.2 Brigade.**

   Objective. Hill 142 between Q.27 Central and Q.15.d.00.

   Assembly Position.

   Preliminary .. O.17.c.
   Secondary .. Bde. H.Q. P.24.d.3.3.
   Battalions. P.24.c. P.24.a.

   Boundaries.

   Right. - Q.27 Central - Q.27 Central.
   Left - Q.14.d.0.0. - Q.15.d.0.0.

   The Right Battalion will advance round South end and Left Battalion round ~~West~~ NORTH end of ENGLEBELMER.

   O.C. "B" Coy.M.G.Bn. will detail one section to each flank of the attack to cover the advance of the infantry.
   Particular attention will be paid to looking out for and dealing with advanced hostile M.G's.
   These two sections will go forward to the ridge during consolidation.
   Eight guns will be in Brigade Reserve in P.19.a.

   (b) **No.3 Brigade.**

   Objective: Line Q.9.d.0.0. - AUCHONVILLERS (inclusive - Q.3 Central.

   Assembly Positions.

   Preliminary .. O.17.a.
   Secondary. .. Brigade H.Q.) BEAUSSART.
   "D" Coy.M.G.Bn.)
   Battalions: VALLEY P.18.a., P.12.b.

   Boundaries.

   Right. .. Q.8.d.0.0. - Q.9.d.0.0.
   Left :: Q.2 Central - Q.3 Central.

   O.C. "D" Company M.G.Bn. will detail one section to each flank of the attack to cover the advance of the infantry.
   Particular attention will be paid to looking out for and dealing with advanced hostile M.G's.

   "A" & "C" Coys. will carry out Long Range Covering Fire from positions in the BROWN SYSTEM.

/The........

The Divisional Artillery Programme is as follows:-

Zero to Zero plus 60. Ridge between Q.9.d.0.0. - Q.3 Central (including AUCHONVILLERS).

Zero plus 60 to Zero plus 70. Western outskirts of AUCHONVILLERS.

Zero plus 70. Barrage sweeps Eastwards by Lifts of 100 yards every 3 minutes, till it forms a Protective Barrage on line Q.23.c.0.0. - Q.4.c.0.0.

APPENDIX 4.

1. The enemy has captured AUCHONVILLERS and MAILLY-MAILLET, including the PURPLE SYSTEM from about Q.14 Central - Q.2 Central. The Divisional Commander intends to recapture MAILLY-MAILLET, the PURPLE SYSTEM and AUCHONVILLERS.
Our troops still hold HILL 142 & ENGLEBELMER.

2. The attack will be carried out by Nos. 2 and 3 Brigades as follows:-

(a) No. 3 Brigade.

Objective: MAILLY-MAILLET and PURPLE LINE between Q.8.d. and Q.2 Central.

Assembly Position:

Preliminary .. O.17.a.
Secondary .. Bde.H.Q.) COPSE P.8.b.
"D" Coy.M.G.Bn.)
Battalions - P.4.a. and c.

Boundaries:

Right. .. P.5.d Central - Q.8.d.0.0.
Left .. P.6.a.9.9. - Q.2.d.0.5.

O.C. "D" Coy. M.G.Bn. will detail one section to each flank of the attack to cover the advance of the Infantry.
Particular attention will be paid to looking out for, and dealing with, advanced hostile M.G's.

(b) No. 2 Brigade.

During the operations by No. 3 Brigade, No. 2 Brigade will be assembled in ACHEUX WOOD.
On its completion the Brigade will move to assembly positions in the valley in P.12.d and P.18.b. by Cross Country Track North of FORCEVILLE.
Brigade H.Q. will be in BEAUSSART.

At Zero Hour the Brigade will move forward from this assembly position, cross the Southern portion of MAILLY MAILLET, reform for assault outside the wire of the PURPLE SYSTEM (gaps in which will be reconnoitred) and attack AUCHONVILLERS.

Boundaries:

Right. .. Q.8.d.0.0. - Q.10.d.0.0.
Left .. Q.2 Central - Q.3 Central.

The Advanced Brigade Report Centre will be established at Q.7.d.6.4.

O.C. "B" Coy. M.G.Bn. will detail one section to each flank of the attack to cover the advance of the Infantry.
Particular attention will be paid to looking out for, and dealing with, advanced hostile M.G's.
These two sections will go forward beyond AUCHONVILLERS during consolidation of objective.
Eight guns will remain in Brigade Reserve in P.12.d.

APPENDIX 5.

1. The enemy has driven in our centre, and occupied HILL 142 and ENGLEBELMER.
   The Divisional Commander intends to recapture HILL 142 and ENGLEBELMER.

2. The attack will be carried out in the first place by No. 2 Brigade, and subsequently by No. 3 Brigade.

   (a) No. 2 Brigade will retake ENGLEBELMER and the PURPLE SYSTEM as detailed in Appendix 2.
   No. 3 Brigade will then pass through No. 2 Brigade and retake HILL 142.
   "B" Coy. M.G.Bn. will co-operate with this Brigade, as laid down in Appendix 2, or as detailed by B.G.C., No. 2 Brigade.

   (b) No. 3 Brigade

   Objective: HILL 142 between Q.27 Central, and Q.15.d.0.0.

   Assualting Position.

   Preliminary .. O.17.a.
   Secondary .. Bde. H.Q.) P.27.b.3.2.
   "D" Coy.M.G.Bn.)
   Battalions: Valley West of MAILLY-MAILLET down to P.18.b.

   Boundaries.

   Right. .. Q.20.c.2.6. - Q.27 Central.
   Left. .. Q.14.d.2.7 - Q.15.d.0.0.

   O.C. "D" Coy. will detail one section to each flank of the attack to cover the advance of the Infantry.
   Particular attention will be paid to looking out for, and dealing with, hostile M.G's.
   The remaining two sections will be held in Reserve for consolidation in depth, or at the disposal of B.G.C. No. 3 Brigade.

THE FOLLOWING ARRANGEMENTS WILL APPLY TO APPENDICES 1 -56.

SYNCHRONISATION OF WATCHES.

Synchronisation of watches will be carried out by an Officer of the General Staff at CROSS ROADS P.13.b.3.7 in ACHEUX at Zero minus 4 hours in all cases.

ZERO HOUR.

ZERO will be the time appointed for Infantry Brigades to move from their Secondary Positions of Assembly.

In the case of Appendix No. 4, the zero hour for the attack by No. 2 Brigade will be the time appointed for leaving the Third Position of Assembly.

TANKS.

The Third Light Tank Battalion will co-operate with the Supporting Division of the Vth Corps in the event of counter-attack.

Tanks, when returning to our lines, will fly a Red, White and Blue Flag.

The following Signals from Tanks to Infantry are now in use:-

Green & White Flag.   ..   "Come on".

Yellow & Red Flag.   ..   "I am broken down, go on."

War Diary

APPENDIX C.

1. The enemy has attacked on the front ALBERT - ARRAS.

    The V Corps has been shaken, but the enemy has not been able to pierce the front, and has not reached the PURPLE SYSTEM except on the right, where the Right Supporting Division restored the situation.

    One Brigade of the Left Supporting Division has occupied the BROWN LINE from FORCEVILLE to BEAUSSART. The remaining two Brigades, Pioneer Battalion and Field Coys. have moved forward to assembly positions about LEALVILLERS.

    Definite news is received from the IV Corps that their front has been driven back and that the enemy has occupied SAILLY AU BOIS and BAYENCOURT. At the same time reports are received that enemy troops are in COLINCAMPS and COURCELLES, and are apparently moving on BUS LES ARTOIS, which is held by the French.

    No. 1 Brigade of the Left Supporting Division, which was in the BROWN LINE has now formed to its left and is holding the line BEAUSSART - BERTRANCOURT. Its right is in touch with the Left Division holding the line at MAILLY MAILLET.

2. The Divisional Commander intends to advance North and South of FORCEVILLE, form up West of MAILLY MAILLET - ENGLEBELMER WOODS and thence attack Northwards, retake COLINCAMPS and COURCELLES, making use of all three Infantry Brigades in doing so, and attack the enemy's /flank between HEBUTERNE and SAILLY AU BOIS.
    left

3. GENERAL SCHEMES OF ATTACK.

    (a) The 21st Division will attack with No. 2 Brigade on the right, No. 3 Brigade in the Centre and No. 1 Brigade on the left.

    The first objective will be a line from the Spur in K.33.a to J.23.c, including the Villages of COLINCAMPS and COURCELLES AU BOIS.

    The Second objective will be the line running round the Spur in K.27., K.21 and the Quarries in K.21.b.(which forms a defensive flank to the East) - K.15.d. and c. - SAILLY AU BOIS inclusive.

/The....

The attack will be carried out in two bounds.

Nos. 3 and 1 Brigades will each leave a Battalion to hold COLINCAMPS and COURCELLES AU BOIS respectively.

No. 2 Brigade will form a defensive flank to the Eastwards from the SUGAR FACTORY to their final objective.

4. ARTILLERY ACTION.

From the moment of the receipt of orders, the G.O.C., R.A. Vth Corps is arranging to keep APPLE TREE HILL, COLINCAMPS, COURCELLES AU BOIS, and the areas in the neighbourhood of those places, known to be occupied by the enemy, under a continuous bombardment of all available heavy guns and howitzers & Divisional Artillery until Zero hour.

Divisional Artillery.

The C.R.A. will divide such artillery as is at his disposal less 3 Batteries, into 3 groups, each group supporting the advance of 1 Brigade. Each Infantry Brigade will have 1 Battery affiliated to it to deal with special targets, under the orders of the Brigadier General concerned.

A Barrage will be formed along the line APPLE TREE HILL - OLD CHALK PIT - Cemetery South of COLINCAMPS - Southern edge of COURCELLES AU BOIS. This barrage will lift at Zero plus 100 minutes and artillery groups will come under the orders of their respective Infantry Brigadiers. In the absence of special instructions, the barrag will creep back at the rate of 100 yds. in 3 minutes to the line LA SIGNY FARM - K.25.a Central - J.23 Central, when it will form a protective barrage at Zero plus 140 minutes.

At Zero plus 155 minutes, the barrage will concentrate on the line of this protective barrage in the three Zones allotted to each Infantry Brigade, accelerating its rate of fire. At Zero plus 160 minutes it will lift and Artillery Groups will once more revert to the orders of Infantry Brigadiers. In the absence of special instructions the barrage will creep back within these Zones at the rate of 100 yards in 3 minutes to the line K.15.d.8.8 - K.8 Central - J.12 Central - when it will again form a protective barrage for 15 minutes and then cease.

/5........

(3)

5. ACTION OF ATTACKING BRIGADES.

(a) No. 2 Brigade:-

Objective.

(i) APPLE TREE HILL, SUGAR FACTORY, Spur in K.32.b and K.33.a.
(ii) Spur in K.21.a and b. connecting with No. 3 Brigade in K.15.c and forming a defensive flank back to the Sugar Factory.

Positions of Assembly.

(i) Preliminary Assembly Position - O.17.c.
(ii) Secondary Assembly Positions - Valley in P.24.a - P.18.c. Brigade H.Q.   P.22.b.8.6.

Method of Attack.

The Brigade will attack from a forming up line between the cross roads Q.7.b.2.6 to Q.6.d.7.3.

Right Boundary: Q.7.b.2.6 - K.33 Central - K.21.b.8.8.
Left Boundary: P.6.d.7.3 - K.32.a.8.8. - K.14.d.9.4.

(b) No. 3 Brigade:-

Objective.

(i) COLINCAMPS.
(ii) High ground in K.14.b and a., connecting with Brigades on either flank.

Positions of Assembly.

(i) Preliminary Assembly Position - O.17.a.
(ii) Secondary Assembly Position - VALLEY South of BEAUSSART P.10 and 11.   Brigade H.Q. - ACHEUX.

Method of Attack.

The Brigade will attack from a forming up line between P.6.d.8.8 and P.6.a.0.8.

Right Boundary: P.6.d.8.8 - K.26.c.0.0. - K.14.b.4.3.
Left Boundary: P.6.a.0.8 - J.30.b.8.0 - K.13.b.3.8.

/(c).......

(4)

(c) <u>No. 1 Brigade</u>:-

<u>Objectives</u>.

(i) COURCELLES AU BOIS.
(ii) SAILLY AU BOIS, connecting with troops attacking on the left.

<u>Positions of Assembly</u>.

The line BEAUSSART - BERTRANCOURT.   Brigade H.Q. - ACHEUX.

<u>Method of Attack</u>.

The Brigade will attack between Boundaries:-

P.5.a.5.0.   J.30.a.8.0.   K.13.a.6.6.
J.34.c.0.8.   J.29.a.4.0.   J.12.c.7.0.

6. <u>ZERO HOUR</u>.

Zero hour will be the time appointed for Infantry Brigades to move from their secondary positions of assembly.

Zero plus 100 minutes will be the time at which the Artillery barrages begin creeping from the line given in para. 4(b), i.e., the line APPLE TREE HILL - OLD CHALK PIT - Cemetery South of COLINCAMPS - Southern edge of COURCELLES AU BOIS.

Infantry movements must be so regulated that they will be ready to carry out the assault at that moment.

7. ACTION OF MACHINE GUNS.

(a) "D" Coy. 21st M.G.Battn. will at once take up Battery Positions of 8 guns in the PURPLE LINE as follows:-

　　No. 1 Battery .. Q.2.c.6.4. (Left Gun).
　　 " 2   "   .. Q.2.a.3.9. ("   ")

and will protect the right flank of No. 2 Brigade, especially watching the approaches from BEAUMONT HAMEL and SERRE.

(b) "B" Coy. 21st M.G.Bn. will assemble with No.2 Brigade in Valley in P.24.a - P.18.c, and will proceed by cross country route East of MAILLY MAILLET to Orchard at Q.1.d.8.6. On the barrage of Heavy & Divisional Artillery lifting off APPLE TREE HILL at Zero plus 100 minutes, "B" Coy. will proceed to Banks in Q.2.b. in order to obtain direct fire on approaches from SERRE. On the successive Infantry Battalions' Objectives being captured, O.C. "B" Coy. will detach a Section to each for the purpose of consolidation.

(c) "A" Coy. is placed at the disposal of B.G.C. No. 3 Brigade for covering fire and consolidation purposes, and will assemble with No. 3 Brigade in Valley South of BEAUSSART in P.10 and 11.

(d) "C" Coy. is placed at the disposal of B.G.C. No. 1 Brigade, and will conform with the movements of No. 1 Brigade when taking up the BEAUSSART - BERTRANCOURT Line.

APPENDIX 7.

1. **FIRST LINE TRANSPORT.**

    (a) First Line Transport will concentrate as under as soon as any of the moves ordered in 21st Divisional Defence Scheme are made.

    62nd & 64th Inf. Bdes. will remain in present positions.

    21st M.G.Battn. move to Eastern outskirts of PUCHEVILLERS and join 64th Inf. Bde. Group.

2. **SUPPLY OF S.A.A.**

    (a) S.A.A. is dumped as follows:-

    <u>Brown Line.</u>   10 Boxes S.A.A. in each M.G. position.

    <u>Red Line.</u>   10 Boxes S.A.A. in each M.G.position.

    (b) 21st M.G. Battalion will be responsible for the S.A.A. in M.G. positions, and 110th Inf. Bde. will be responsible for the remainder of the S.A.A.

    (c) The following ammunition dumps have been formed in the forward area, and may be drawn on in case of necessity:-

    Q.16.c.2.4.   Q.3.d.3.4.
    Q.9.c.5.4.   Q.2.d.1.0.
    Q.15.b.5.9.   Q.7.d.7.4.

    (d) 250 Boxes ordinary S.A.A. and 250 boxes M.G. S.A.A. are stored at each of the following places:-

    O.5.d.9.4.   O.2.d.   N.5.c.

3. **RATIONS.**

    (a) If possible, men will go into action carrying rations for the following day.

    (b) Refilling points remain as at present.

4. **WATER POINTS.**

    There are water points at the following places:-

    MAILLY-MAILLET, BEAUSSART, ACHEUX, LOUVENCOURT, ENGLEBELMER, FORCEVILLE, RAINCHEVAL, PUCHEVILLERS, and BEAUQUESNE.

(3)

(b) "A" Coy. will take up positions in the Left Sector, BROWN SYSTEM, and will come under the orders of B.G.C. RAINCHEVAL Brigade.

(c) Battalion H.Q. and "B" and "C" Coys. will proceed to either of the Advanced Divisional H.Q. for the Right or Left Sector, BROWN SYSTEM, as ordered.

21st Bn.M.G.C.   A P P E N D I X   9.

1.   Until further orders, the Division, as Supporting Division Vth Corps, will be prepared to occupy either or both Sectors of the BROWN SYSTEM.

2. (a)   In the event of the Division being ordered to occupy the Right Sector of the BROWN LINE, the order "MOVE RIGHT" will be sent from Divisional Headquarters.

   On receipt of this order, the following moves will take place:-

   (i)   The "TOUTENCOURT" Brigade with 2 Companies Machine Gun Battalion and 1 Field Company R.E. will occupy the BROWN SYSTEM and the SENLIS Village Defences holding localities as under:-

   'A' Battalion - BROWN SYSTEM (SENLIS Sector) from Southern Corps Boundary, V.14.d.1.0 to Grid Line V.3 Central - V.2 Central.

   'B' Battalion - BROWN SYSTEM, from Grid Line V.3 Central - V.2 Central to FORCEVILLE (exclusive).

   'C' Battalion (less 1 Coy.) in SENLIS Village Defences, 1 Company in trenches East of the Village, 2 Companies in Support in trenches West of the Village. 1 Company 'C' Battalion in Switch from Southern Corps Boundary, V.15.d.2.0 to V.15.a.0.5. Suggested Battalion Headquarters about V.16.a.8.4.

   (ii)   The "RAINCHEVAL" Brigade to assembly positions in U.11.c. & d.

   (iii)   The "PUCHEVILLERS" Brigade to assembly positions in U.10.c. & d.

   (iv)   Advanced Divisional Headquarters to U.11.d.1.5.

/Action......

(2)

Action of Machine Guns.

(a) 'C' & 'D' Coys. will be placed at the disposal of B.G.C. TOUTENCOURT Brigade (62), for the defence of the Right Sector & SENLIS Village. 'C' Coy. will take up position covering the Left Battalion and 'D' Coy. the SENLIS Sector.

(b) 'A' Coy. will be placed at the disposal of B.G.C. RAINCHEVAL Brigade (110), and will assemble with this Brigade in U.11.c. & d.

(c) 'B' Coy. will be placed at the disposal of B.G.C. PUCHEVILLERS Brigade (64), and will assemble with this Brigade in U.10.c. & d.

(b) In the event of the Division being ordered to occupy the Left Sector of the BROWN LINE, the order "MOVE LEFT" will be sent from Divisional Headquarters.

On receipt of this order, moves will take place in accordance with para.5, 21st Division Defence Scheme.

(c) In the event of the Division being ordered to occupy both Sectors of the BROWN LINE, the order "MOVE BOTH" will be sent from Divisional Headquarters.

On receipt of this order the following moves will take place:-

(i) The TOUTENCOURT Brigade with 1 Coy. Machine Gun Battalion and 1 Field Company R.E. will occupy the Right Sector, BROWN SYSTEM as in (a) (i).

(ii) The RAINCHEVAL Brigade with 1 Coy. Machine Gun Battalion and 1 Field Company R.E. will occupy the Left Sector, BROWN SYSTEM.

(iii) Advanced Divisional Headquarters and the remainder of the Division will be prepared to move to Advanced Headquarters and Assembly Positions of either the Right or Left Sectors, BROWN SYSTEM, as may be ordered at the time.

Action of Machine Guns.

(a) "D" Coy. will take up positions in the Right Sector, BROWN SYSTEM, and will come under the orders of B.G.C. TOUTENCOURT Brigade.

/ (b).......

War Diary.

SECRET.   Copy No. 9

21st Battn. Machine Gun Corps
OPERATION ORDER No. 29.

                                                           10th July 1918.
Ref. Map Sheet:
57d.S.E., 1/20,000.

1. The 2nd Bn. Royal Welsh Fusiliers (115th Inf. Bde) will carry out a raid on the night of July 11th/12th.

2. The objective will be the village of HAMEL.

3. The limits of the Raid will be approximately:

   <u>To The East.</u> Railway Line running through Q.23.b and d.

   <u>To the North.</u> A line drawn through Q.24.a.0.3 - Q.23.b.0.8.

   The Raiding Battalion is forming up outside HAMEL OUTPOSTS, and advancing in a N.E. direction.

4. Zero Hour will be notified later.

5. Machine Guns of 21st, 38th and 63rd (R.N.) Battalions, Machine Gun Corps, will co-operate.

6. The Machine Guns of 21st Battalion will be divided into 2 Groups of 4 Eight-Gun Batteries, with dispositions and tasks as follows:-

   <u>RIGHT GROUP</u>, under Command of Major C.M. HOWARD, M.C.

   <u>Group Headquarters .. Q.22.c.1.8.</u>

Battery Position.	Battery Commanders.	Time.	Target.	Rate of Fire.
"B" Battery Q.28.b.2.6.	Lieut. C.C. ATHOL.	Zero plus 3 to Zero plus 70.	"B" Q.30.b.30.15 to Q.30.b.30.80	100 R.P.M. for 1st 10 Minutes. 75 R.P.M. remainder.
"K" Battery Q.23.b.3.9.	2/Lt. V.G. HUNTER, M.C.	-do-	"K" Q.18.c.30.65 to Q.17.b.80.10	-do-
"D" Battery Q.22.d.4.4.	Lieut. W.E. CHAMBERLAIN	-do-	"D" Q.24.d.50.40 to Q.24.b.50.00	-do-
"C" Battery Q.22.c.1.5.	Lieut. A.A.F. SEARL.	-do-	"C" Q.30.b.00.80 to Q.24.d.03.45	-do-

(1)   /Left........

(2)

LEFT GROUP under Command of Major R.T.ASSHETON.

Group Headquarters .. Q.22.c.1.8.

Battery Position.	Battery Commanders.	Time.	Target.	Rate of Fire.
"A" Battery. Q.22.b.1.1.	Lieut.R.H. THOMAS.	Zero plus 3 to Zero plus 70.	"A" Q.30.c.75.00 to Q.30.b.05.15.	100 R.P.M. for 1st 10 minutes. 75 R.P.M. for remainder
"F" Battery. Q.22.b.0.4.	Lieut.C.B. WATSON,M.C.	-do-	"F" Q.24.b.65.25 to Q.24.b.65.90.	-do-
"J" Battery Q.22.c.1.8.	Lieut.E.C. STEELE.	-do-	"J" Q.18.c.85.40 to Q.18.a.60.00.	-do-
"E" Battery Q.22.a.1.7.	2/Lt. S.A. ENGLISH.	-do-	"E" Q.24.c.85.55 to Q.24.a.90.20.	-do-

7. REPORT CENTRE.

   Report Centre will be Centre Group H.Q. at Q.21.d.2.4.

8. SYNCHRONISATION OF WATCHES.

   A Liaison Officer will take synchronised time to Group Commanders.

9. All Machine Gun fire will commence at Zero plus 3 minutes, and the time will be taken from the commencement of the Field Artillery Barrage. Artillery fire ceases at Zero plus 60, Machine Gun fire at Zero plus 70.

10. Group Commanders are responsible for the checking of all calculations.

11. The near danger area of Batteries must be picketed if firing over trenches, tracks etc.

12. Each gun will have 24 filled belts.

13. All Machine Guns cease fire at Zero plus 70, when both Groups will withdraw and return to Battalion Headquarters at QUESNOYE under Administrative Instructions already issued.

14. All guns will be taken in on the night 10th/11th July. Lorry and detailed arrangements have been issued to all Battery and Group Commanders.

(3)

15. Eight Guides from 38th Battalion, M.G.C., will be at corner of wood P.23.d.85.85 at 9. 0 p.m., 10th inst. This point will be the rendezvous for the Battalion, who will be guided to the Prisoners Cage Q.21.c.9.4 by Batteries, from which point Battery Commanders will be responsible for conducting their Batteries to their positions.

16. MEDICAL.

R.A.P. Q.28.c.6.2, for Stretcher Cases., Walking wounded will proceed by CUTHBERT AVENUE, thence up the MARTINSART - ENGLEBELMER Road, where they will be directed.

17. A C K N O W L E D G E.

D. Kay.
Lieut. Colonel,
Commanding 21st Battn. Machine Gun Corps.

DISTRIBUTION.

Copy No. 1 .. O.C. "A" Coy.
2 .. O.C. "B" Coy.
3 .. O.C. "C" Coy.
4 .. O.C. "D" Coy.
5 .. 21st Division.
6 .. 38th M.G.Bn.
7 .. Corps M.G.O.
8 .. File.
9 & 10 .. War Diary.

SECRET.   Copy No....
                    21st Battn. Machine Gun Corps.
                      ADMINISTRATIVE INSTRUCTIONS
                  in connection with Operation Order No.29.

1.   All personnel proceeding line will report Adjutant
        at N.29.d.2.2 at 5.30 p.m. to embuss.

2.   Transport will move independently under each Group
        Commander's Orders, and proceed to P.23.d.85.85, not
        arriving there before 9 p.m. 10th inst.
            The same transport will report at above point Zero
        plus 4 hours on the night 11th/12th July to bring back
        guns. If personnel unable to get out that night, then
        the Group Commanders will send special orders to
        Transport Officers at above place.

3.   Rations for the 11th inst. will be carried. Tea etc.
        will be sent up by the Transport on the night 11th/12th
        in case of necessity emergency.

4.   Company Transport Officers will accompany Transport
        on each occasion. One Officer per Group will proceed
        with Transport on 10th inst., to be detailed by each
        Group Commander.

5.   Lorries to convey personnel back from line will be
        at FORCEVILLE 6 a.m. 12th inst., unless special order
        received that Companies unable to get out of line, when
        they will report same place (P.27.b.5.3) 11 p.m. 12th inst.

                          (Sgd) V.F.SAMUELSON, Capt. & Adjt.,
                                 21st Bn. Machine Gun Corps.

Issued to:
O.C. "B" Coy.
O.C. "C" Coy.
O.C. "D" Coy.
O.C. "A" Coy.
File.
War Diary (2)

COPY.   M.G.B. 291.

Officer Commanding,
    21st Battn. M.G.C.

    Would you please express my thanks to all who assisted in the operations of the 11th inst.

    Officer Commanding 2nd R.W.F. reports that the Artillery and the Machine Gun Barrage left nothing to be desired.

                            (Sgd) A.G. LYTTELTON, Lieut. Colonel,
                        Commanding 38th Battn. M. G. C.
                        ─────────────────────────

13th July 1918.   Certified True Copy
                    V. Samuelson Capt &
                                        ADJUTANT,
                    21st BN. MACHINE GUN CORPS.

SECRET.   C   Copy No. 17   War Diary

21st Battn. Machine Gun Corps
OPERATION ORDER No. 31.

Ref. Map Sheets:
57d.
----

1. The Division, less Artillery, will relieve the 63rd (R.N.) Division, less Artillery, in the MAILLY Sector, Vth Corps Front between 24th and 26th July.

2. The 21st Bn.M.G.C. will relieve the 63rd Bn.M.G.C. as under:-

   (a) <u>24th July 1918.</u>

   "C" Coy. 21st Bn. will relieve "A" Coy. 63rd Bn. in the PURPLE LINE and take over the following gun positions in pairs:-

   Q 1.1 - Q 2.2 - Q 7.2 - Q 8.1 - Q 13.1 - Q 20.1 -
   Q 25.1 - Q 14.1.

   This relief to be complete by 7 p.m. 24th inst.

   (b) <u>Night 24th/25th July 1918.</u>

   "B" Coy. 21st Bn. will relieve "B" Coy. 63rd Bn. in the Centre Sub-Sector, taking over the following gun positions in pairs:-

   Q 10.1 - Q 16.1 - Q 16.2 - Q 15.1 - Q 15.2 - Q 15.3
   Q 15.4 - Q 15.5.

   "A" Coy. 21st Bn. will be relieved by "A" Coy. 63rd Bn. in the BROWN LINE. Relief to be complete by 9 a.m. 25th inst.
   On completion of this relief, "A" Coy. 21st Bn. will proceed to a position of readiness in the vicinity of ACHEUX WOOD. Location to be notified to 21st Bn. H.Qrs.

   (c) <u>25th/26th July 1918.</u>

   "A" Coy. 21st Bn. will relieve "D" Coy. 63rd Bn. in Right Sub-Sector, and take over the following gun positions all in pairs:-

   Q 14.2 - Q 21.1 - Q 21.2 - Q 21.3 - Q 27.1 - Q 27.2.
   Q 27.3 - Q 22.1.

   "D" Coy. 21st Bn. will relieve "C" Coy. 63rd Bn. in the Left Sub-Sector, and take over the following gun positions in pairs:-

   Q 3.3 - Q 3.4 - Q 3.2 - Q 3.1 - Q 9.3 - Q 9.2 - Q 9.1 -
   Q 2.1.

   H.Q. Coy. will move from KAY CAMP at 2 p.m. 25th inst. to new Battalion H.Q.

3. All details of relief will be arranged between Company Commanders concerned, and a copy of Company Operation Orders sent this office as soon as possible.

/4.........

4. Details of work in hand, Photos, Defence Schemes, Trench Stores etc. will be taken over, and a list of same sent Battn. H.Q. within 24 hours of relief.
All Defence Schemes for the present area will be handed over to Companies of 63rd Bn.M.G.C.
Companies relieving each other will take over Camp standing.

5. Completion of reliefs will be reported to H.Q. 63rd Bn. M.G.C. and repeated to H.Q. 21st Bn.M.G.C. by code word "VIOLA".

6. Command of M.G. Positions passes to O.C. 21st Bn.M.G.C. on completion of relief.

7. Battalion H.Q. closes at KAY CAMP, N.35.b.5.7 at 4 p.m. 25th inst., and open at 4 p.m. same date at ACHEUX, P.13.a.6.6.

8. Administrative Instructions will be issued later.

9. A C K N O W L E D G E.

Capt. & Adjt.,
21st Battn. Machine Gun Corps.

21st July 1918.

DISTRIBUTION.

Copy No. 1 .. O.C. "A" Coy.
        2 .. O.C. "B" Coy.
        3 .. O.C. "C" Coy.
        4 .. O.C. "D" Coy.
        5 .. H.Q. Coy.
        6 .. 63rd Bn.M.G.C.
        7 .. 62nd Inf. Bde.
        8 .. 64th   do.
        9 .. 110th   do.
       10 .. 21st Division 'G'.
       11 .. 21st Division Signals.
       12 .. Quartermaster.
       13 .. Intelligence Officer.
       14 .. Commanding Officer.
       15 .. Major Borthwick.
       16 .. File.
    17-18 .. War Diary.

SECRET.

ADMINISTRATIVE INSTRUCTIONS
with Reference to
21st. Battn. M. G. C. Operation Order No.31.

1. ACCOMMODATION & TRANSPORT LINES.

   Companies will arrange to take over all accommodation and Transport Lines from the Units which they relieve.

2. TENTS & TRENCH SHELTERS.

   (a). 63rd., Battn. M. G. C. will leave all tents and bivouacs standing. Relieving Companies will give receipts for Tents and Trench shelters, and will report numbers taken over to Battn. H.Q's. Advanced parties will be sent to take over the day before Companies arrive.

   (b) All Tents and Trench shelters in this Area will be handed over standing to 63rd., Battn. M. G. C. Receipts will be taken and forwarded to Battn. H.Q's

3. TRENCH STORES.

   All Trench and Area Stores will be taken over and receipts given. A list of articles taken over will be forwarded to Battn. H.Q's.

4. S.A.A. & GRENADES.

   The Divisional S.A.A. and Grenade Store is at O.6.d.5.5. Lieut. Verity, 21st, D.A.C. will take this Store over at mid-day, July 25th., 1918.

5. BATHS.

   Baths are situated at FORCEVILLE, CLAIRFAYE, ACHEUX, and LOUVENCOURT, (6. 5.a.7.7.)
   Applications for use of these Baths will be made to Battn. H.Q's 5 6 hours before they are required.

6. GAS CHANGING ROOM.

   A Room in which men who have had their clothing infected by Gas can change, has been established at ACHEUX.

7. WATER.

   Water Points are situated as follows:- BEAUSSART, FORCEVILLE, LOUVENCOURT, (O.5.a.5.0.) ACHEUX, O.12.a.4.8. O.6.c.5.3.

8. SALVAGE DUMP.

   A Salvage Dump will be formed at Q.M.Stores, ACHEUX.

9. MOBILE VETERINARY SECTION.

   The 33rd., Mobile Veterinary Section will remain at RAINCHEVAL.

(2)

10. CANTEENS.

    The Battalion Canteen will be established at ACHEUX. There is a Y.M.C.A. Hut at ACHEUX.

11. All lines must be left scrupulously clean, and a certificate sent to Battn. H.Q's,4 hours before the Compnay vacates the Camp,to this effect.

V. L. Samuelson
Capt. & Adjt.
21st., Battn. Machine Gun Corps.

22/7/1918.

DISTRIBUTION

To all recipients of Operation Order No.31.

SECRET.   Copy No. 20

                        21st Battn. Machine Gun Corps,
                        OPERATION ORDER No. 32.
                        ─────────────────────

Map Reference: 27th July 1918.
France - Sheet 57d.S.E., 1/20,000.
─────────────────────────────────

1.   At a date and hour to be notified later, Raids to penetrate the enemy's defences will be carried out along the Corps Front.

2.   Attached Tracing "A" shows areas to be raided by this Division, also areas to be barraged by Machine Guns.

3.   Machine Guns of 21st Battn. and 63rd (R.N.) Bn. M.G.Corps will co-operate on this Divisional Front.

4.   The following subsidiary operations will be carried out as a preliminary to the above operation:-

   (a) From now onwards the enemy will be subjected to a bombardment of heavy artillery and such Field Artillery as may be available to search and block all approaches to the enemy's garrison West of the Line RIVER ANCRE - STATION ROAD - WAGON ROAD, with the object of lowering his moral by starvation tactics.
       Field Artillery (18 Pdrs.) will cut wire.

   (b) 21st Bn. M.G.Corps, supplemented by Machine Guns of 63rd (R.N.) Bn. will co-operate in (a) above by day and night with harassing fire on known enemy lines of approaches. Special care will be taken that this Machine Gun fire is maintained uninterruptedly during the normal quiescent period immediately prior to and after dawn, so as to prevent the enemy utilising these hours for relief or replenishment of stores. To minimise the chance of the enemy withdrawing from the areas to be raided, undue attention will NOT be paid during this period of preliminary bombardment to the enemy trenches within the zone specified in (a) above.
       Patrolling, however, will be very active.

   (c) At 9. 0 a.m. on July 30th a sham attack will be made along the entire Corps Front. This will comprise a Smoke Screen by Artillery and Trench Mortars, and as soon as it is considered that the enemy has had time to man his defences, an Artillery and Trench Mortar bombardment to simulate an Infantry attack will be put down.
       All available Machine Guns will barrage approaches and selected targets.

5.   As any retaliation the enemy may make will probably be with the object of rendering areas impracticable as assembly positions, concentrations of Mustard Gas must be expected, and every precaution taken to prevent casualties.

6.   Company Commanders will at once make all necessary calculations and arrangements for the allotted targets (shown on Map "A") to be engaged. Copies should be forwarded to Battalion Headquarters on completion of this.

7.   Further instructions will be issued later.

                                                    /8..........

(2)

8. ACKNOWLEDGE.

J.T.Kay.
Lieut. Colonel,
Commanding 21st Battalion, Machine Gun Corps.

DISTRIBUTION.

Copy No. 1 .. "A" Coy. (Rear)
2 .. "A" Coy. (Forward).
3 .. "B" Coy. (Rear).
4 .. "B" Coy. (Forward).
5 .. "C" Coy. (2)
6)
7 .. "D" Coy. (Rear).
8 .. "D" Coy. (Forward).
9 .. Commanding Officer.
10 .. 2nd in Command.
11 .. H.Q. Coy.
12 .. Quartermaster.
13 .. 63rd (R.N.) Bn.M.G.C.
14 .. 21st Division.
15 .. 62nd Inf. Bde.
16 .. 64th Inf. Bde.
17 .. 110th Inf. Bde.
18 .. Intelligence Officer.
19 .. File.
20) .. War Diary.
21)

SECRET.

All Os.C. Coys. Forward.
 "   "   "   "   Rear.
Quartermaster. (for infn.)

SX. 980.

Reference 21st. Bn. M.G.C. Operation Order No.3 2 dated 27-7-18:-

1. The 10,000 rounds per gun now in gun positions must be left complete as reserve, and the following will be sent up to Coys. under Coy. arrangements. This can be drawn from Q.M. Stores daily on indenting direct.

2. On nights 28/29th., 29/30th., 30/31st., 31/1st. Aug., 1/2nd. Aug., 2/3rd. Aug. - to be used for harassing fire:

   "A" Coy.- 6 guns each 5,000 rounds   = 30,000 rounds.
   "B" Coy.- 14 guns each 5,000   "   = 70,000   "
   "D" Coy.- 14 guns each 5,000   "   = 70,000   "

   If Coy. Commanders find they have enough S.A.A. for use on 3rd. Aug. then above need not be taken up on night 2/3rd.

3. The following rounds to be taken up and used in para. 4 (c) on night 29/30th. inst:

   "A" Coy.- 6 guns each 3,000 rounds   = 18,000 rounds.
   "B" Coy.- 14 guns each 3,000   "   = 42,000   "
   "D" Coy.- 14 guns each 3,000   "   = 42,000   "
                                          102,000 rounds.

4. The following to be taken up at Coy. Commanders' discretion, all to be complete by night 2/3rd. Aug. for use in para. 1:

   "A" Coy.- 6 guns each 6,000 rounds   = 36,000 rounds.
   "B" Coy.- 14 guns each 6,000   "   = 84,000   "
   "D" Coy.- 14 guns each 6,000   "   = 84,000   "
                                          204,000 rounds.

5. Coy. Commanders will render a return commencing 29th. inst. to Battn. H.Q's by 10 a.m. giving the amount of S.A.A. in bulk at each gun position at 5 a.m. daily until further orders.
   This need not include 14 belt boxes and 10,000 rounds per gun now at gun positions.

28th. July, 1918.

Capt. & Adjt.
21st. Bn. Machine Gun Corps.

Copy No .....   S E C R E T.

E *War Diary.*

21st. Battn. M.G.C. OPERATION ORDER No. 33.

28th. July, 1918.

1.   With reference to 21st. Bn. M.G.C. Operation Order No.32 of 27th. July 1918,- para. 1 is hereby CANCELLED.

2.   The subsidiary operations detailed in para. 4 and subsequent paragraphs of above order culminating in the sham attack at 9 a.m. on the 30th. July will however continue to be carried out. On conclusion of the sham attack, operations on the Divisional Front will revert to normal trench warfare.

3.   A C K N O W L E D G E.

V.F. Samuelson
Capt. & Adjutant.
21st. Battn. Machine Gun Corps.

Issued by Runner at 3.30 p.m.

To all recipients of O.O. No. 32.

(6339) Wt. W150/M3016 1,500,000 10/17 McA & W Ltd (E 1898) Forms W3091.   Army Form W.3091.

Cover for Documents.

Nature of Enclosures.

21st Bn MGC

Notes, or Letters written.

WAR DIARY 21st Bn. M.G. Corps. August 1918

INTELLIGENCE SUMMARY

(Erase heading not required.)

Army Form C. 2118.

Place	Date	Hour	Summary of Events and Information	Remarks and references to Appendices
ACHEUX	1st		C.O. and C.R.E. visited the newer overall positions being made in the MARIETT SECTOR. C.O. attended Conference at Div HQ's RAINCHEVAL at 4 P.M. on front line quiet.	V.F.C. Cpt.
-do-	2nd		Casualties P/N R.H. Hospital — 2 O.R. wounded — Enemy Aircraft over Village — 1 O.R. Gunshot flesh	V.F.C. Cpt.
-do-	3rd	5 P.M.	C.O. attended Conference Div H.Q.'s RAINCHEVAL 4 P.M. Operation Order No 34 issued. Quiet day.	O.O. 34 attd. V.F.C. Cpt.
-do-	4th	4 P.M.	Church Parade - Y.M.C.A. Hut ACHEUX 10.30 A.M. — C.O. visited Offr Bde Public Umpires — attended Conference at Div HQ's at 4 PM. Casualties ag 16 & 92 39 wounded. (Memo M 312) — Deserves 10 R. wounded — Enemy 2 O.R.'s gunshot from Base	attended Conference V.H.S Cpt.
-do-	5th	2 P.M.	C.O. recieved off Bde 2 O.R. 7 AM. Attd Conference Div HQ's RAINCHEVAL 2 PM — Memo M/34/57/A V.F. S. Cpt.	Memo M/34/57/A V.F.S Cpt.
-do-	6th		C.O. H.Q. 34 Casualties (Memo A/L/5/M) Deserve — 15 O.R. — 15 O.R. went — 38 O.R. Bn. J. Cpt.	V.H. Cpt.
-do-	7th		Quiet day — B.O. and Major Rockwell visited front line — Right and Center Sector.	
-do-	8th		C.O. visited 6 Bde Point.	17.F.C.Cpt.
-do-	9th	10 A.M.	Quiet day — Attempts 2 O.R. wounded left. G.O.C. Div visited Bn H.Q.'s 9 P.M.	
-do-	10th		Opn. Or. No 35 issued. — Deserves 1 O.R. Injury by fall. C.O. visited Bn H.Q.'s and Div H.Q.'s and B.G.C.679 Bde — Regts found R.C. Cullagh.	O.O.35 attd. V.H.C. Cpt. V.F.C. Cpt.
-do-	11th		Quiet day	V.F.C. Cpt.
-do-	12th	9 A.M.	Church Parade at Y.M.C.A. ACHEUX at 10.30 A.M. Front line quiet. C.O. visited Bd to HQ's right and left — Bde ticker wop'd out. — Promoed 2 Lieut - T.R. Parnell and Lieut FRASER joined. — 1 O.R. Wounded — 1 O.R. to 39 aux. Enemy 3rd Div USSR A.B.C. arms Batt - Lieut offtg.	V.F.C.Cpt. D.O.40 35 attd V.F.C.Cpt.
-do-	13th	10 P.M.	Quiet day Bn. Defence Scheme of MAILLY Sector issued. — Efforts atvlath 27 wounded and 2 Joined.	9937+38 attn'd
-do-	14th	12 noon	C.O. visited Right and Left Bde Sectors at 7 AM. 6 junction Order No 39 issued. — 6 1/2 PM from A/1/25/10 A/5/5/10 Deserved - Deserve 10.R. wounded sick	Memo A/1/25/10 40.9 39 attd V.H. Cpt.
-do-	15th		Quiet day —. Deserve 10.R. to Base to hosp. C.O. visited all front line —	V.F.C.Cpt.
-do-	16th	8 A.M.	Opn. Order No 40 issued — 2 Lieut T.R. Parnell C/D Wounded.	O.O.40 attd V.F.C.Cpt.

WAR DIARY 21st Bde R.G. Corp August 1918

INTELLIGENCE SUMMARY

(Erase heading not required.)

Army Form C. 2118.

Place	Date	Hour	Summary of Events and Information	Remarks and references to Appendices
ACHEUX	17th		C.O. visited front line – Lieut. C. BROWNE and 2nd Lieut. M.R.S. YOUNG joined, afft. strength Lieut. J.B. WALTER proceeded to sheltering huts fe[?]. Quiet day.	V.F.S.Cpt
– do –	18th		Church Parade – Y.M.C.A. AHEUX 10 A.M. Capt. W.C. VIBERT proceeded on leave to U.K. Guest on the Rad. – 6. O.R's. joined from Base Depot – One O.R. Evacuated sick – 2 O.R's wounded. C.O. and Major Booth visited front lines. Major C.M. HOWARD M.C. admitted hospital	V.F.R Cpt
– do –	19th		C.O. attended Conference at Div. Hdqrs 3 p.m. – 2nd Lieut. S.E.C. SLAYMAKER and C.E. HARDWICK joined Bde and posted to 'C' and 'D' Coys respectively.	Copy of O.O No 41 attd. V.F.R Cpt V.F.R Cpt
– do –	20th	8 A.M.	Oper. Order No 41 Issued. – Capt. A.F. HARVEY admitted hospital – Recon party for Rail head –	V.F.R Cpt
– do –	21st	6 A.M.	Operation Order No 43 Issued – Operation commenced.	
		5 A.M.	Position of guns – A'By 16 Guns under 116" Inf Bde – 'B' By in Toumpe Trench under 64th Inf Bde – 'D' By under 64th Inf Bde – 16 Guns 'B'Cy first Barrage from 0.5.a.80–85 (about 57 – N.W) – 8 guns of Cs attd of D Cys attd under 62nd Inf Bde	V.900 Cpt V.F.R Cpt
		9 A.M.	Closed B.G. of 62 Bde on leaving BEAUCOURT. Captured for D coy guns to take up following position – section on left flank of fresh Posn.	V.F.C Cpt V.F.R Cpt
			8 Centl Meter 6-1 pdr Q.7.a.37. to guard BEAUCOURT – one Stn. gun in 62 Bde Posn.	
		9.5 A.M.	Placed Capt Harper's B Coy 6 and 12 guns at once to be at disposal of B.G. 62 Inf Bde remaining 6 guns B Cy to remain with Major Harding 'C' Coy	V.F.R Cpt V.F.R Cpt V.F.C Cpt
		9.20 A.M.	The 1/2 Coys of B Coy under Major Hugo Harding to be in Rdn [?] 64th Inf Bde.	Copy of message with Cpt?
		12.50 P.M	O. Order No 42 issued	Copy of O.O.attd
		1 P.M.	21st Div Order No 208 received	V.F.R Cpt
		1.30 P.M.	Major Booth 'A' Cy wired – 6" Casualties mostly wounded by opposite crossing R. Ancre – boys withdrawing and fighting patrols being pushed forward on his G. [?] not in action yet.	Copy attached V.F.R Cpt
		2 P.M.	Wire G.X.455 received	

Sheet 2.

Army Form C. 2118.

WAR DIARY 21st Bn. M.G. Corps. AUGUST

INTELLIGENCE SUMMARY

(Erase heading not required.)

Place	Date	Hour	Summary of Events and Information	Remarks and references to Appendices
22nd ACHEUX	21st	2.10PM	Wire S & 26 received	Appx Wire attached V.T.R. Capt.
	do.	6PM.	21st Div Order No 207 received	Copy attached V.T.R. Capt.
		8.45PM	Div Order No 208 Received	Copy attached V.T.R. Capt.
		8 PM	Location of guns — 'A'Coy with 110th Bde Hd Qr ZUSTER Trench Q.19.a — Hd Qr ZUSTER Reserve Q.19.a — Section ZUSTER	V.A.R. Capt.
		-do-	guns at Q.17.d — "A"Coy Reserve at Coy HQ's Q.19.c —	N.R. Capt.
		-do-	'B'Coy, 1 section at Q.14.b — 2 Sections at Q.12.b — Hd Qr Coy HQ's Reserve Q.5.d all attached 64th Inf. Bde	M.A. Capt.
		-do-	'C'Coy, 1 Sect attached Bgd at R.3.C. — 1 gun in Div Reserve — Ridge trench — Auchonvillers — Hamel Road — Coy HQ's Q.16.b.90.40 V.A. Capt	V.A. Capt.
		-do-	'D'Coy attached 62nd Inf Bde — Hd Qr at R.2.E. — 1 sec at R.3.E. — 1 sec at Q.6.d at gun line — 1 sec R.6.e.d guns line — Coy HQ's Q.6.C.4.5.	V.A. R. Capt. V.A. Capt.
			Casualties — Lieut R.FREUTER (A Coy) — Lieut S.HALL (A Coy) wounded — Lieut M. FOSTER (D Coy) also wounded —	V.Y. Capt.
			1 O.R. Killed — 5 O.R. Wounded — 10 O.R. Wounded gas.	N.R. Capt.
	22nd	7AM.	Situation unchanged —	N.R. Capt.
		10.10AM	G.S.487 Wire (D.W) received, Known points ANCRE bombarded — Enemy gas ware all troops not to drink	N.R. Capt. Copy attached
		11AM.	Wire M.G. 150 Sent out.	V.R. Capt.
		11.30AM	O.C. 'B' Coy Wire, Coy situated as follows — 2 guns in Trity Alley Q.12.b.35. — 2 guns ZUSTER Q.12.a centred — 4 guns in GRANDCOURT — 4 guns at Bn HQ's in BEAUCOURT	V.R. Capt.
			Enemy — 4 guns in R.2.C.30.50 attached g. Royal firing on GRANDCOURT — 4 guns at Bn HQ's in BEAUCOURT.	N.R. Capt.

Sheet 4

WAR DIARY August 1st 21st Bn. Rn. G Corps.

or

INTELLIGENCE SUMMARY.

Army Form C. 2118.

(Erase heading not required.)

Place	Date	Hour	Summary of Events and Information	Remarks and references to Appendices
ACHEUX	2.2nd	1.30 P.m.	"C" Coy wired - Coy HQrs closed at Q16.c.64 and opened at Q.9.q.7.2.	V.H. Cpl
	Cont	4 P.m.	Capt W BALL M.C (D Coy) wound - 1 Sec of C Coy attached 1st London Rgt att in yellow line - R.2.d.70.55 - 1 Sec D Coy in reserve on left flank at R.2.a.5 to 2.0.	V.H. Cpl / V.H. Cpl
		4.10 P.m	Major Coulter A Coy wired over the hald Blue line - One platoon under Lieut LESLIE ordered across to A.N.C.R. to with flank	V.H. Cpl / V.H. Cpl
			defence - Lt LESLIE wounded crossing River.	V.H. Cpl
		4.12 P.m	Capt BALL M.C. wired I went AT HOR with one platoon B Coy attacked w/3rd Montl Stronchies) from N of approx	V.H. Cpl
			R.7.a.40.08 - R.7.a.30.05. - R.7.a.40.12. - R.7.a.40.14 in junction to protect flank of Blue line	V.H. Cpl
		5 P.m	C.O and 2nd Lieut MANN M.C. visited front line	V.H. Cpl
		5 P.m	21-Dil Orden No 209 received	Copy attached
		5.15 P.m	Major Coulter wired "A" Coy - situation - no 1 & 2 Coy Q.18.c.29. - no 2 & 3 Coy unchanged - no 3 platoon Q16.7.3C.10.	V.H. Cpl
			No 4 Plt Q.18.C. central and no 4 section mounts guns by night in the 12 platoons in Q.18.C. to general	V.H. Cpl / V.H. Cpl
			Bridge head Q.18.d.37.	V.H. Cpl
		7.30 P.m	Wire from Div. GX494 received w Bomby Trps.	Copy attached / Copy attached
		8.45 P.m	Wire Div 496 received - "A" Coy relieved by A Coy 17th Bn M.G.Cps - A Coy concentrate at ANCHONVILLERS.	W.H. Cpl / V.H. Cpl
			Casualties 2 Lieut A D LESLIE wounded "A" Coy - 10 R Rank Wound (Gas) -	

Sheet 5

WAR DIARY August 1918 21st Bn. R.B. Corps
or
INTELLIGENCE SUMMARY
(Erase heading not required.)

Army Form C. 2118.

Place	Date	Hour	Summary of Events and Information	Remarks and references to Appendices
ACHEUX	23rd	9.30 a.m.	Wire O.i/c (B'Coy) received. "Enter ATHOE sports having recounted portion & coys opposite to BEAUCOURT	V.H. Coy.
—	—	—	from trenches of R.9 a.d aa & fin will be moved to nightime to Bty R9 & 06.62. Coys Plys in R9 and	V.H. Coy.
—	—	—	Longueval Railway as far as R.8.c. on far at R.7.6.26.73. Coys opposite along Railway — in addition to above	V.H. Coy
—	—	—	Left flank our A & B fire into R.15a, then covering left flank of our line in R.14 a&b.	V.H. Coy
—	1.35		Orders received for Advance. Bn. HQrs to open at CHATEAU — MAILLY MAILLET 8.7.c. 90.95 (Batty) & 8E) at 7 p.m.	V.H. Coy. O/c D Coy. e.W.C. Coy.
—	3 p.m.		Div Order No. 210 received.	V.H. Coy.
—	5 p.m.		Affiliation to Brigade to stand as M.G. at present.	V.H. Coy.
MAILLY-MAILLET	7 p.m.		Advanced Br. HQ closed at ACHEUX and opened at Chateau — MAILLY - MAILLET	
—	7.10 p.m.		Operation Order No 43 issued.	Copy attached App:
—	8.50 p.m.		Sitrep Wire & X. 5.29 received by informed of contents.	V.H. Coy
—			Casualties 3 O.R.'s wounded (gas)	V.H. Coy
—	24th	1.30 a.m.	Wire G.R. 476 from D10 — "We are in COURCELLES continuously with Essanne — Hargicourt all Corps.	V.H. Coy.
—	—	4 a.m.	Wire received from A Coy — Red Line captured together with about 30 prisoners.	V.H. Coy.
—	—	4.5 a.m.	Wire received from A Coy — G.3. H.Qrs at Q.12.d.1.8. will no '10 Bde hope to be in Beauc in Divn Valley 8.12 a.	V.H. Coy.
—	—		Objective — hostile wire Y Section (B.15.d.0.0.) — in touch with 5 Leicesters (on our left) — no touch with 1st Wilts	V.H. Coy.
—	—		(on our right) — HQrs will move later to BATTERY VALLEY later —	V.H. Coy.

WAR DIARY August 21st Bn In G Corps.

Army Form C. 2118.

Sheet 6

Place	Date	Hour	Summary of Events and Information	Remarks and references to Appendices
MAILLY-MAILLET	24th	7 A.M.	Aby Wir DX 2 - Hot botn with 7 Leinster orders to assist in formation of defensive flank from River along GRANDCOURT-MILLY	J.P. Cpl.
-	-	-	-THIEPVAL WOOD to Bn AT Boundary.	J.P. Cpl.
-	-	8 A.M.	Div Order No 211 received	Copy attached V.P.Cpl.
-	-	8.5 A.M.	Remainder of Bn HQ' and G all Coy Rear HQ' arrived at Wood MAILLY-MAILLET R.11.a.9.5.	J.P. Cpl.
-	-	11 A.M.	Wire from Bde - 2nd Bott Inf Advance Bn G Echelon attached - Orders by HQ Q.12 & 10.59. 2nd Lieut V.G. HUNTER M.C.	V.P.Cpl.
-	-	-	received -	J.P.Cpl.
-	-	11.15 A.M.	Memo No 390 issued	Copy attached V.P.Cpl.
-	-	12 P.M.	Bn. Runners post established at Crossroads R.7.K.9.1.	V.P.Cpl.
-	-	1.45 P.M.	O.C. 13th moving HQ' to GRENDICOURT	Copy attached V.P.Cpl.
-	-	4 P.M.	Memo No 391 sent out	Copy attached V.P. Cpl.
-	-	4.45 P.M.	Div Order No 212 received	V.P. Cpl.
-	-	10.40 P.M.	Div Order No 213 received	V.P. Cpl.
-	-	-	Casualties 1 O.R. Killed - 7 O.R's Wounded - 2nd Lieut V.G. HUNTER M.C., M.M. Wounded BG.	V.P. Cpl.
-	25th	3.45 A.M.	'A' Coy wired 110th Bde orders that night to push forward to line M. 20. Central - M. 10. Central - fine of 'A'G. followed.	V.P. Cpl.
GRANDCOURT	-	8.30 A.M.	Bn HQ's and all Coy Rear HQ' moved to GRANDCOURT R.11.a.99. Transp Sunken Road R.3.C.	V.P. Cpl.
-	-	9 A.M.	'C' Coy HQ' at R.9.a.9.2.	J.P. Cpl.

Sheet 7

WAR DIARY August 1918. H.Q. C.P.L.
21 Br. M.G. Corps

INTELLIGENCE SUMMARY

Army Form C. 2118.

(Erase heading not required.)

Place	Date	Hour	Summary of Events and Information	Remarks and references to Appendices
GREVILLERS	25	2 P.M.	Bty moved - 16 guns with Iron Lt/Inf into Div Reserve into BOOM VALLEY.	1 P.L. Cpt.
"	"	4 P.M.	Runners Post Closed at R.7.2.19. opened at R.5.d.o.8.	V.P. Cpt.
"	"	9.15P	Aft'n Wire - by HQ at 110th Bd. HQ, M.B.A. 6.6. - Coy got guns and limbers to bid. off Reserve - relief but no Casuals.	V P H Cpt.
"	"	—	Casualties 1 O.R. Killed — 5 O.R. Wounded — Guides from Bn. 12 ORs	1 P H Cpt.
"	26	7.30 A.M.	A Coy moved Coy HQ at M.R.a.66.	V PL Cpt.
"	"	7.35 AM	D Coy moved - Every morning with M.6's along Road M.24.a. - M.18 a. at approx — Coy HQ in Quarry M.17.a.5t. - one section with 1st/10 North'd Fusiliers M.11.t. 80.10. - 3 Section in Reserve at Coy HQ.	V P H Cpt.
"	"	8 A.M.	Bty report Line but inf't ran as follows. LA BARQUE along Ruse Cut. approx to EAUCOURT D'ABBAYE — thence artillery way action about FEPARI and ALBERT — BAPAUME Road	1 P.H. Cpt.
"	"	12 noon	A Coy wire - Strike 3.45 PM 25th inst - 110th 94 Bde was a horseway in accordance with L.W. Johns on EAUCOURT on leaving considered held over Ridge in M.18 and M.24 Guides that repulsed - 3 guns of A Coy engaged.	1 P.L. Cpt.
"	"	8.30 PM	Liv Order No 215 Received	1 P.L. Cpt.
"	"	3 P.M.	Wire to 5.70 R's received re relief of C & D Coys	"
"	"	11 PM	Liv Order No 216 Received	"
"	"	11.50 PM	Wire at 652 received	"
"	"	—	Casualties — Lt LW KEATING KILLED R.I.P. — 2 OR Killed — 10 OR Wounded — 2 OR Ca. & LA Filt. List 9th AD.N.S.D [?] — 10 OR Wounded — 20 OR En. to LH Filt.	1 P H Cpt.

Sheet 8

WAR DIARY August 1918 2.1 Bn. Sr. G Gds.
or
INTELLIGENCE SUMMARY.

Army Form C. 2118.

(Erase heading not required.)

Instructions regarding War Diaries and Intelligence Summaries are contained in F. S. Regs., Part II. and the Staff Manual respectively. Title pages will be prepared in manuscript.

Place	Date	Hour	Summary of Events and Information	Remarks and references to Appendices
GRANDCOURT	27	10AM	B'dy Report — Situation quiet and nothing i.e. along Blue Line M12 C and M17 d and Eng Ins G Staffing	O'H G/R
—	—	—	very scattered shelling. Casualties — Enemy attack rep'd action on found south and on ALBERT-BAPAUME Road	O/P G/R
—	—	10.10AM	D Cy Report — One G'tn into posn M.17.d. 4.5" Learning Valley running down E of EARL at ZARBAYS	O.H.G/R
—	—	—	One G'tn in M.12.c. and M18.a. — One below in M18.c. 5.4. — 1 Pack at M.15.a.g.1 and by HQrs in Reserve	V.T.G/R Gds.
—	—	4.47AM	Liv Order to 217 Received	V.T.G/R
—	—	4.30AM	Memo AN/339/G received	O.V.G/R
—	—	7.17AM	O.V. Order to 217 Received	O.V.G/R
—	—	—	Casualties. 4 O.R. wounded sick — Lieut A.A.V. SEARLE proceeded Leave U.K. — Capt A.S. HARVEY signed from Base Sick	V.V.G/R
28	—	—	Quiet Day — G.O.C. 2I.D. Visited Batn	O/P G/R
—	—	9AM	B'dy Report — We have advance posts & Lichen near LIVERPOOL FARM — Fred 150 Yds on Enemy going	V/H G/R
—	—	—	EAST about H2C. — Caused several Casualties — 64" Bde are in Div Reserve — by HQrs at MIRAUMONT	O/H G/R
—	—	4PM	Liv Order to 217 Received	Capt Stanley
—	—	7.30PM	Liv Order to 2B Received	Capt Crighton
—	—	—	Casualties Nil — 1 OR Evacuated sick	O/P G/R
29	—	7AM	O.C. D Coy Rang up and reports Relief complete	V/T G/R
—	—	—	Coys attached A Cog 110" Bde — B Cog 64" Bde — C Cog 62" Inf Bde — D Cog Div Reserve	V.T.G/R

WAR DIARY

Sheet 9

August 21st Bn. Dr. G C/ps

Army Form C. 2118.

INTELLIGENCE SUMMARY.

(Erase heading not required.)

Place	Date	Hour	Summary of Events and Information	Remarks and references to Appendices
GRANDCOURT	29	9.30 AM	West 6 & 65th Received	Appendices V.H.C/pr
—	—	12.10 PM	West 6 & 66th Received	Appendices V.H.C/pr
—	—	12.30 PM	"A" Coy with 110" Bde observers on Road N9c — N3a —	V.H.C/pr
—	—	9 PM	Coy HQrs at 17 "A" Coy N12 & 7.8. "B" Coy Butte de WARLENCOURT N17 a 20.60 - "C" Coy to B.Gp in Quarry	V.H.C/pr
—	—	—	at M.15.a.9.7	V.H.C/pr Appendices
—	—	11 PM	Lieut Baker & 219 Received	V.H.C/pr
—	—	11.30 PM	"A" Coy was — the 3 section in front with 7th Lincolns form at M6 a b.d.t forward. No 2 section protecting left flank of 7th Lincolns —	V.H.C/pr
—	—	—	The 3 section with 1 Vickers gun at line N16.a.05 — N16.c.05 for close support — hostile bckn in Bde Reserve at N13.c.7.5.	1.A.C/pr
—	—	—	Casualties Nil — L/Cpl Leavesitt Sick	M.A.C/pr
—	30	—	Quiet day	1.A.C/pr
LESARS	—	8 AM	Adv. Bn HQrs moved at GRANDCOURT and opened at M15a 5.8 at 8 AM.	M.A.C/pr 4/-
—	—	9 AM	Rear Bn H.Coy HQ's left Sandre Road R2 e at 8.45 arriving M2d at 11 AM.	V.H.C/pr
—	—	9 AM	Runner Post opened at BUTTE de WARLENCOURT N17 a 20.60.	V.H.C/pr
—	—	3 PM	A Coy N12 - to 3 fee in Trench N21. b.0.7 - N15.d.k. & to 3fee in Trench N18 to.0.8 - N15 to control —	V.H.C/pr
—	—	—	2 Secs in Bde Reserve near G.Coy Bde. HQ's in TRUGENHOF FARM N13.d.6.9.	V.H.C/pr
—	—	—	Casualties Nil — 2 ORs reported sick — 2/Lieut W.E.F. ELHORN 1st Bn. Rif. Bde rejoined his unit	V.H.C/pr

Sheet 10

WAR DIARY August 21st Bn. M.G. Corps
INTELLIGENCE SUMMARY

Army Form C. 2118.

Place	Date	Hour	Summary of Events and Information	Remarks and references to Appendices
THE CARS	31	8 AM	Quiet day — Coys attached 'A' Coy 110th Bde. Tuilennoy Farm N.13.d.69. — 'B' Coy 4th th Bde — Battn. H.Q. WARLENCOURT N.17.a.20.b.0. — C' Coy Quarry M.15.a.9.9. attached 62nd Bde — S.Coy in Bde Reserve at Quarry M.15.a.9.9.	V.A.P.Cpt V.A.P.Cpt
		3:30 PM	Transfers Lieut R. Phillips — Lieut Hoc Barrowclough Kelt — 10 O.R killed — 5 O.R. wounded	V.A.P.Cpt V.A.P.Cpt V.A.P.Cpt
		10 PM	Div Order 220 received —	V.A.P.Cpt
			Casualties as above — Lieut S. Pitt and Lieut R.G. Somerford reported for duty and posted Coys B & D respectively	V.A.P.Cpt V.A.P.Cpt
			Change C.M. to W.H.R reported from Sick Base. Strength of Battn: 42 Officers 851 other Ranks.	

R.C. Barlow Major for.

LIEUT-COLONEL,
COMMANDING 21st BN. MACHINE GUN CORPS.

SECRET.   Copy No.....

                    21st Battn. Machine Gun Corps
                    OPERATION ORDER No. 34.
                    ─────────────────────────
                                                        3rd August 1918.

1.   In connection with a local attack to be carried out at a
future date, by the Division on our Right, the following
preparatory operations will be undertaken.
        The date of this attack will be communicated separately to
all concerned.

2. ARTILLERY.

        From now onwards the fire of Heavy and Field Artillery will be
maintained by day and night at a gradually increasing intensity,
to be developed to the fullest limit two or three days prior to
the date fixed for the attack. The aim will be to demoralise the
enemy by destructive shoots on his trenches, and by starvation
shoots against his communications.

        The Heavy Artillery will pay special attention to keeping all
bridges over the ANCRE destroyed, and to continuous and slow
harassing fire on the enemy's communications and crossings over
the River. Destructive shoots on enemy trenches and sunken roads
will also be put down in crashes at frequent and odd intervals.

        To allow the enemy no rest, 6" Stokes Mortars, from well
separated positions, will commence forthwith a steady slow
bombardment of enemy's trenches and sunken roads.

        Destructive shoots will be directed mainly on trenches and
localities in the area to be attacked, or from which the enemy can
interfere with the attack, and shoots by Heavy Artillery on areas
other than these will be limited to keeping the enemy in doubt as
to where to expect attack.

        Wire cutting by day and harassing fire by night on communications
and working parties, will be carried out by Field Artillery as far
as possible along the entire Corps front.

        The following sham attacks will be made along the entire Corps
front:-

                4th August   ...   Zero hour 4.30 a.m.
                6th August   ...   Zero hour 8 p.m.
                8th August   ...   Zero hour 10 a.m.

        These will consist of:-

(i)   A smoke screen opposite both Northern and Southern
        Divisional Sectors.

(ii)   As soon as smoke screen has been formed, Artillery and
        Trench Mortars will bombard the enemy's trenches to simulate
        an Infantry attack.

MACHINE GUNS & STOKES MORTARS.

        The disposal of Stokes Mortars in depth will be dispensed with
and all Mortars of Divisions in the line will be employed especially
to harass the enemy by night to allow him no rest by bombardments
from varying positions in our Front Line trenches or No Man's Land.
Brigade Commanders will make all necessary arrangements, and steps
will be taken to send up sufficient ammunition to enable the 3"
Stokes Mortars to be employed to their full capacity.

                                                        /Harassing...

-2-

3. (Continued).

Harassing fire by Machine Guns will be co-ordinated with Field Artillery by programmes.
Company Commanders will make their own arrangements with respective ~~Battery~~ Commanders and B.Gs.C.
Artillery Brigade

4. PRECAUTIONS.

Enemy gas bombardments must be specially guarded against. Positions normally occupied by Machine Gunners, which experience has shown to be likely targets for a gas attack may be vacated and alternative positions allotted, Battalion Headquarters being informed of any alterations. Positions must not be changed unless absolutely essential. B.Gs.C. will be consulted as to this paragraph.
Any re-adjustments entailed will be communicated to Battalion Headquarters.

5. A C K N O W L E D G E.

V.F. Samuelson
Capt. & Adjt.,
21st Battn. Machine Gun Corps.

DISTRIBUTION.

Copy No. 1 to O.C. "A" Coy. (Forward)
    "   2 " "   "A" " (Rear)
    "   3 " "   "B" " (Forward)
    "   4 " "   "B" " (Rear)
    "   5 " "   "C" "
    "   6 " "   "C" "
    "   7 " "   "D" " (Forward)
    "   8 " "   "D" " (Rear)
    "   9 "   H.Q.Coy.
    " 10 " Commanding Officer.
    " 11 " Major Borthwick.
    " 12 " Quartermaster.
    " 13 " Intelligence Officer
    " 14 " 21st Division 'G'.
    " 15 " 62nd Inf. Bde.
    " 16 " 64th Inf. Bde.
    " 17 " 110th Inf. Bde.
    " 18 " War Diary.
    " 19 " "   "   "
    " 20 " File.

To:- All Os.Coys (Forward)
    All   Coys (Rear)
      H.Q's Coy.
        Quartermaster.
                                                  AX/57/M

Order No.34 is cancelled.

                                                (Sgd.) V. F. Samuelson
                                                       Capt. & Adjt.
4/8/1918.   21st. Battn. Machine Gun Corps.

SECRET.

M. 312.

ADDENDUM No. 1 to 21st Battn. M.G.C. OPERATION ORDER
No. 34 dated 3rd August 1918.

1. **Reference paragraph 2.**

    The dates and hours for the sham attacks will be as under:-

        4th August .. Zero hour 6 p.m.

        6th August .. Zero hour 4.50 a.m.

    and not as therein stated.

2.   Please acknowledge.

V. J. Pemmerton
Capt. & Adj
21st Battn. Machine Gun Corps.

4.8.18.

Copies to all recipients of Order No. 34.

SECRET.   Copy No. 15

                    21st Battn. Machine Gun Corps
                    OPERATION ORDER No. 35.
                    ─────────────────
                                                    8th August 1918.
Ref. Sheet
57d, 1/40,000.
─────────────

1.   The Divisional Front will be reorganised as under on the night 9th/10th inst:-

   (a)   110th Infantry Brigade will extend its left up to Q.17.a.5.3. relieving troops of 64th Infantry Brigade.

   (b)   64th Infantry Brigade will extend its left up to Q.4.d.0.4 (NEW BEAUMONT ROAD inclusive), relieving troops of 62nd Infantry Brigade.

   (c)   62nd Infantry Brigade will withdraw one Battalion into Brigade Reserve to a position to be notified later.

2.   On completion of reorganisation, boundaries between Brigades will be as follows:-

Between 110th and 64th Infantry Brigades.

   Q.17.a.5.3 - Q.16.b.5.4 - Q.16.c.0.6 - Q.15.c.9.6 (South half of locality 30 to 110th Infantry Brigade) - Q.15.c.0.9 - Q.14.c.4.5 (locality 6 to 110th Infantry Brigade) - thence to original boundary.

Between 64th and 62nd Infantry Brigades.

   Q.4.d.0.4 - NEW BEAUMONT ROAD (inclusive to 64th Infantry Brigade) to Station Q.8.b.5.0 - Q.8.a.8.1 (Road inclusive to 64th Infantry Brigade) - Q.7.d.7.5 - Q.7.d.0.5 - thence original boundary.

3.   There will be no alteration as regards re-allotment of Machine Guns to new Group Commanders, but all remain under the present Groups.

4.   A C K N O W L E D G E.

                                            V.F. Samuelson
                                            Capt. & Adjt.,
                                            21st Battn. Machine Gun Corps.
                                            ─────────────

DISTRIBUTION.

   Copy No. 1 .. O.C. "A" Coy. (Forward).
             2 .. O.C. "B" Coy. (Forward).
             3 .. O.C. "D" Coy. (Forward).
             4 .. O.C. "C" Coy.
             5 .. 110th Inf. Bde.
             6 .. 62nd Inf. Bde.
             7 .. 64th Inf. Bde.
             8 .. 21st Division "G".
             9 .. Commanding Officer.
            10 .. Intelligence Officer.
            11 .. O.C. "A" Coy. (Rear).
            12 .. O.C. "B" Coy. (Rear).
            13 .. O.C. "D" Coy. (Rear).
       14 & 15 .. War Diary.
            16 .. File.

War Diary

All Os.C. Companies.
62nd, 64th & 110th Inf. Bdes.
21st Division 'G'.
C.R.A., 21st Division.
A.D.M.S., 21st Division.
Signals, 21st Division.
Commanding Officer.
2nd-in-Command.
38th Bn.M.G.C.
42nd Bn.M.G.C.
War Diary (2)
File.

M. 350.

Herewith 21st Bn.M.G.C. DEFENCE SCHEME of the MAILLY SECTOR.

Please acknowledge.

V. F. Samuelson
Capt. & Adjt.,
for O.C. 21st Battn. Machine Gun Corps.

12th August 1918.

SECRET.	Copy No. 21

War Diary.

21st Battn. Machine Gun Corps
OPERATION ORDER No. 36.

11th August 1918.

Ref. Map Sheet
- 57d. -

1. The following guns will be withdrawn tonight, 11th/12th August 1918, from the positions:

   "A" Coy.   Q.27.3.   -   Q.21.2.

   "B" Coy.   Q.10.1. - Q.16.1, 1 gun - Q.16.2, 1 gun,

   and will be in Divisional Reserve in or around BEAUSSART. Company Commanders will use their own discretion as regards hour of withdrawal.

2. Capt. VIBERT, MC, will be in Command of these guns, and will report to Battalion Headquarters when all Gun Teams are at BEAUSSART by code word "WILKIE"

3. One Guide for each above pair of guns, and one for each single gun, will be at P.11.b.80.20 (on road) at 11 p.m. tonight. These will be supplied by O.C. "C" Company.

4. All Range Cards, Order Boards, Gun Equipment and Belt Boxes will be carried out. Reserve S.A.A. and Bombs will be handed over to the nearest Infantry Commander, and receipts obtained.

5. Os.C. "A" & "B" Companies will each detail one Officer to be in charge of above 4 guns respectively.

6. Capt. VIBERT, MC, will notify Battalion Headquarters as soon as possible where his Headquarters will be, and recipients of this order will be notified at once from this office.

7. Company 2nds-in-Command will make all arrangements re rations etc.

8. Os.C. Companies will notify respective Infantry Commanders and B.Gs.C. the hour that above guns will be withdrawn.

9. A C K N O W L E D G E.

V. F. Samuelson
Capt. & Adjt.,
21st Battn. Machine Gun Corps.

DISTRIBUTION.

Copy No. 1 .. O.C. "A" Coy. (Forward).   Copy 16 .. 9th K.O.Y.L.I.   )
         2 .. "   "   "   (Rear).   17 .. 15th Durham L.I.) for
         3 .. "   "B" "   (Forward).   18 .. Quartermaster.   ) Inf'n.
         4 .. "   "   "   (Rear).   19 .. Intelligence Offr)
         5 .. "   "C" Coy.   20 & 21 .. War Diary.
         6 .. 64th Infantry Brigade.   22 .. File.
         7 .. 110th   "   "
         8 .. 21st Division 'G'.
         9 .. 62nd Inf. Bde.   )
        10 .. O.C. "D" Coy. (Forward)
        11 .. Commanding Officer.   )
        12 .. 6th Bn. Leic. Regt.   )
        13 .. 7th "   "   "   )
        14 .. 1st Bn. Wilts. Regt,   )   for
        15 .. 1st E. Yorks. Regt.   )   information.

APPENDIX "A".

ADMINISTRATIVE INSTRUCTIONS.

AMMUNITION.

    Divisional Grenade Dump .. O.12.d.9.9.

    250 Boxes of M.G. S.A.A. .. At O.2.d and N.5.c.

SUPPLIES.

    Railhead .. .. ROSEL.

    Refilling Points .. O.8.a.9.1.
                                  O.4.a.2.4.
                                  O.3.b.8.2.
                                  O.11.d.9.1.

WATER.

    Water Points:-

        MAILLY-MAILLET .. Q.7.c.6.0.

        BEAUSSART .. .. P.5.c.5.5.

        ACHEUX .. .. .. P.14.c.4.1.

        LOUVENCOURT .. .. O.5.c.2.9.

                            O.6.c.5.3.

        ENGLEBELMER .. .. P.24.c.3.6.

        FORCEVILLE .. .. P.27.b.5.5.

        RAINCHEVAL .. .. N.12.d.2.9.

ANTI-GAS DEFENCE.

    (a) Baths at which men, whose clothes have been infected by gas, can change and wash, are established at ACHEUX WOOD P.14.c.6.7 and FORCEVILLE P.27.b.4.8.

    (b) Each man will carry an iron ration of ½ oz of Bicarbonate of Soda. 2 lbs per 50 men will be maintained at Battalion Headquarters.

STRAGGLERS POST.

    Stragglers Posts will be established at:

        P.8.b.5.1.
        P.9.c.4.5.
        P.14.d.5.3.
        P.21.d.7.7.

--oOo--

15. (Cont'd.) PURPLE SYSTEM (20 Guns

Number.	Location.	Type of emplacement.
Q.1.1.	Q.1.a.2.0.	Champagne emplacement to be contructed. Guns at present at P.12.a.4.8.
Q.2.2.	Q.2.c.9.3.	Camouflaged Slit.
Q.2.3.	Q.2.c.4.8.	do do
Q.7.2.	Q.7.b.7.8.	100 ton Pill Box under construction.
Q.8.1.	Q.8.a.7.3.	Camouflaged Slit.
Q.13.1.	Q.13.d.9.1.	100 ton Pill Box under construction.
Q.14.1.	Q.14.c.9.1.	Champagne emplacement. Deep dugout.
Q.20.1.	Q.20.a.8.4.	Camouflaged Slit.
Q.25.1.	Q.25.a.7.4.	100 ton Pill Box under construction.
Q.26.1.	Q.26.a.1.8.	Camouflaged Slit.

COMMUNICATIONS.

16. Gun Positions — Section H.Q. ... Runner.

    Section H.Q. — M.G.Company H.Q.)
    "   "   — Inf. Battn. H.Q.)   ... Runner.

    M.G.Company H.Q. — M.G.Battn. H.Q. ... Runner & Telephone.
    (Buried Cable).

    M.G.Battn.H.Q. — Brigade H.Q.)   Telephone.
                     Divisional HQ) ... (Buried Cable).

    Report Centres are established at Q.8.d.2.2. and Q.15.c.3.4. From there messages are transmitted by telephone (Buried Cable).

    In the event of active operations, Mounted and Cyclist Orderlies would be at the disposal of Company Commanders for communication to Battalion Headquarters.

S.A.A. SUPPLY.

17. A Reserve of 10,000 S.A.A. is maintained at each Gun Position.

    A Reserve of 50,000 S.A.A. is maintained at each Company H.Q.

    A General Reserve of 288,000 S.A.A. is maintained at Machine Gun Transport Lines.

/18 ....

HEADQUARTERS.

18. Right Machine Gun Company ... P.24.d.3.5.
    Centre   "   "   "   ... P.11.b.5.3.
    Left   "   "   "   ... P.5.d.3.1.
    Battalion Headquarters.   ... ACHEUX.
    Transport Lines.   ... O.6.a.

ACTION IN CASE OF S.O.S.

19. If the "S.O.S." is seen on the Divisional Front, all guns will open fire on their S.O.S. lines as follows:-

    For THREE minutes ... Rapid.
    "   FIVE   "   ... 150 rounds per minute.

    Then cease fire unless the signal is repeated, or it is clear that a serious attack is in progress.
    In foggy weather, or when visibility is bad, and the enemy puts down a barrage on our Front or Support Trenches in any Sector, Machine Guns will open on their S.O.S. lines. Duration and rate of fire as above.

ANTI-TANK DEFENCE.

20. In the event of enemy tanks being employed, it is the role of Machine Guns to fire at the Infantry following the tanks, while the tanks themselves are being engaged by specially detailed Artillery.

D.F.Kay,
Lieut.Colonel.
Commanding 21st. Battn. Machine Gun Corps.

6. The "Battle Zone" will be the area between the PURPLE Line (inclusive) and the BROWN Line (exclusive).
   The "Main Line of Resistance" will be the PURPLE Front Line.

GENERAL PRINCIPLES OF DEFENCE.

7. The policy of the Division is to maintain the ground now held under all circumstances, and to break and definitely hold up any enemy attack preparatory to the counter-attack being launched either by troops of this Division or by troops of Supporting Divisions.

8. Troops occupying defensive positions must realise that there is no question of our withdrawing from the lines we are now holding, and that every post and locality must be held to the last man and last cartridge.

METHOD OF HOLDING SECTOR.

9. The Front will be held by 3 Infantry Brigades in the Line, supported by 3 Machine Gun Companies, plus 2 Sections.

   1 Company, less 2 Sections will be held in Divisional Reserve.

PROBABLE DIRECTIONS OF ATTACK.

10. Although a frontal attack across the ANCRE against the front of this Sector is the least likely of the possible directions of attack, dispositions must be made with this primary object in view. The most probable directions of attack, however, are:-

                                       Defensive Flank:

   (a) Break through on left of Left Brigade and capture of COLINCAMPS RIDGE. — To be arranged by G.O.C. Left Flank Brigade.

   (b) Break through on left of Centre Brigade. — AUCHONVILLERS SWITCH.

   (c) Break through South of AVELUY WOOD and attack from direction of MARTINSART against HILL 142 and ENGLEBELMER. — To be arranged by G.O.C. Right Flank Brigade.

ACTION TO BE TAKEN ON THE ORDER "MAN BATTLE STATIONS".

11. (a) At one hour before Dawn, the Infantry will start to evacuate certain portions of our front line, observation parties being left at certain selected points.
      At one hour before Dusk, the Infantry will start reoccupying those trenches which were cleared in the morning.

    (b) From three quarters of an hour before Dawn until 1½ hours before Dusk, should an "S.O.S." be sent up the Field Artillery barrage will come down in rear of those portions of the front trench which have been evacuated, lanes being left for two minutes for the withdrawal of observation parties. The Machine Gun barrage will also be drawn closer. Details will be issued in an Appendix.

      Except between the above hours, the barrage will come down in its normal place., i.e. in front of the front line throughout.

      The hours of Official Dawn and Dusk will be published from time to time.

SECRET.   Copy No......

21st Battn. Machine Gun Corps
DEFENCE SCHEME "MAILLY SECTOR".

Ref. Map Sheet: 11th August 1918.
57d. S.E., 1/20,000.

DESCRIPTION OF DIVISIONAL SECTOR.

1. The principal feature of the Divisional Sector is the AUCHONVILLERS RIDGE which runs midway between the GREEN and PURPLE Systems in the Northern half of the Sector, and forms a Southern branch of the higher ground in the Divisional Sector on our left.

   In the Southern half of the Sector, the Ridge branches out into three Spurs:-

   (a) The Ridge which runs S.E. to Q.17.a and thence Southwards along the GREEN Line to LESNIL.

   (b) The Ridge which runs South to HILL 142.

   (c) The Ridge which runs S.W. to ENGLEBELMER and thence Southwards along the PURPLE Line.

2. Minor Spurs are thrown off (a), the most important of which are:-

   (i) The Spur running East from AUCHONVILLERS towards BEAUMONT HAMEL (HAWTHORNE RIDGE).

   (ii) The Spur running East through Q.17.a and b.

   (iii) The Spur running East through Q.17.c and Q.23.a.

3. These minor Spurs form reentrants across which the Divisional Forward Defences run at right angles, viz.,

   (i) The Valley from Q.3 Central to BEAUMONT HAMEL.

   (ii) The "Y" Ravine (Q.10.d. and Q.11.c.)

   (iii) The Valley Q.17.c and d.

4. The highest ground in the Sector is at AUCHONVILLERS, and the retention of the higher ground to the North of the Sector from LE SUCRERIE (K.33) - APPLE TREES HILL - to MAILLY MAILLET is vital to its successful defence.

ORGANIZATION OF DEFENCES.

5. The "Forward Zone" will be the area between the Front Line and Battle Zone (exclusive) and will include:-

   (a) The "Front Zone" or area East of the Line BARN SUPPORT - RIDGE SUPPORT - READING TRENCH - BEAUMONT RESERVE (all inclusive).

   (b) The "Intermediate Zone" or area between the Forward Zone and the Battle Zone (both exclusive).

   The Line of Resistance of the "Forward Zone" will be the trench immediately East of HILL 142 - BOVET TRENCH to point Q.9.b.2.3. - OCEAN TRENCH.

/6............

15. --- MACHINE GUN DISPOSITIONS ---

FRONT ZONE. (12 Guns).

Number.	Location.	Type of Emplacement.
Q.3.1.	Q.3.d.2.2.	Champagne.
Q.3.2.	Q.3.d.2.8.	"
Q.3.4.	Q.3.a.3.0.	Camouflaged Slit.
Q.9.3.	Q.9.b.7.6.	Champagne.
Q.16.2.	Q.16.c.4.6.	"
Q.22.1.	Q.22.d.3.0.	"

INTERMEDIATE ZONE (24 Guns).

Number.	Location.	Type of Emplacement.
Q.2.1.	Q.2.b.1.9.	Champagne Emplacement under Construction.
Q.3.3.	Q.3.c.3.3.	Moir Pill Boxes (Dug-out under Construction).
Q.9.1.	Q.9.d.1.9.	2 " " Deep Dug-out.
Q.15.1.	Q.15.c.9.3.	Camouflaged Slit.
Q.15.2.	Q.15.a.8.3.	2 Concrete Pill Boxes.
Q.15.3.	Q.15.a.9.9.	Camouflaged Slit. Deep Dug-out.
Q.15.4.	Q.15.a.0.0.	" "
Q.15.5.	Q.15.a.3.4.	" "
Q.14.2.	Q.14.d.8.0.	Moir Pill Box.
Q.21.1.	Q.21.a.8.8.	Camouflaged Slit.
Q.21.3.	Q.21.d.3.5.	"
Q.27.2.	Q.27.b.0.5.	"

12. The S.O.S. Signal in use is a Rifle Grenade bursting into three stars, GREEN over RED over GREEN.

PRINCIPLES OF MACHINE GUN DEFENCE.

13. The Basis of the Machine Gun defence of the MAILLY Sector is distribution in depth, the guns being so echeloned as to assist in breaking up any enemy attack on the Forward or Intermediate Zones, and subsequently repelling any successive advance against the PURPLE System.

Guns are therefore sited as follows:-

Front Zone	12 Guns.
Intermediate Zone	24 Guns.
Purple System	20 Guns.
Divisional Reserve.	8 Guns.

Guns in the Forward Zone are therefore sited to cover Tactical Features rather than Localities for the purpose of delaying the enemy in the event of a determined attack, and demoralising him prior to his assault on the Purple Line. These guns could also be used in supporting local counter-attacks in the event of the enemy obtaining a footing in the Forward Zone.

The Purple System is defended by guns sited primarily for Cross and Enfilade Fire, from and in rear of the Purple Front Line.

All guns are sited in pairs with a field of 600 yards Direct Grazing Fire, and in most cases an additional long range fire up to 1400 yards.

Certain guns in the Forward Zone are detailed for sniping and harassing purposes.

2 Sections are held in Divisional Reserve at BEAUSSART under orders of G.O.C., 21st Division.

LIAISON.

14. All Machine Gun Officers will keep in the closest touch with Infantry Commanders. In the event of attack, Machine Gun Section Officers will at once report to their respective Infantry Battalion Commanders, and Machine Gun Company Commanders to B.G.C. their Sector.

A Liaison Officer will be maintained at each Machine Gun Company Headquarters.

/15 ....

SECRET.

AX/230/0.

To:-
All recipients of 21st. Bn.M.G.C. Defence Scheme.

The following amendments will be made:

<u>Page 2, para. 11.</u>   (a) & (b) will be deleted.

<u>Page 3, para. 13, last line but one.</u>   Delete BEAUSSART and substitute "cross-roads 100 yards North of P.3.b.8.9."

V.F. Samuelson
Capt. & Adjt.

13th. Aug. 1918.   for O.C. 21st. Bn. Machine Gun Corps.

SECRET.   Copy No...... 10

                    21st Battn. Machine Gun Corps
                    OPERATION ORDER No. 37.
                    ─────────────────

                                                13th August 1918.
Ref. Map Sheet
57d.S.E, 1/20,000.
───────────────────

1.   The following alterations in Machine Gun Dispositions
        will be carried out on night 14th/15th August 1918.

2.   The 2 guns at present numbered Q.22.1 (co-ordinate
        Q.22.c.3.0) will be moved to Q.21.b.5.5 (old Q.21.2 position).

3.   The 2 guns at present numbered Q.21.1 (co-ordinate
        Q.21.a.8.8) will be moved to Q.16.c.7.3 (old Q.16.1 position)
        and Q.16.c.3.6. (old Q.16.2 position), making a pair of guns
        at each of these positions.

4.   All Range Cards, Order Boards, Gun Equipment and Belt
        Boxes will be removed to new positions.

5.   Company Commanders will notify their respective Brigade
        and Battalion Commanders concerned of these moves.

6.   Completion of above moves will be reported to Battalion
        Headquarters by code word "BILL" stating time.

7.   A C K N O W L E D G E.

                                    D F Kay
                                                Lieut. Colonel,
                        Commanding 21st Battn. Machine Gun Corps.

DISTRIBUTION.

Copy No. 1 .. O.C. "A" Coy.(Forward).
         2 .. "   "   "   (Rear).
         3 .. " "B" Coy.(Forward).
         4 .. "   "   "   (Rear).
         5 .. 110th Inf. Bde.
         6 .. 64th Inf. Bde.
         7 .. 21st Division 'G'.
         8 .. 38th Bn.M.G.C.
     9 & 10 .. War Diary.
        11 .. File.
        12 .. Commanding Officer.
        13 .. 2nd-in-Command.

SECRET.   Copy No. 8

21st. Bn. M.G.C. OPERATION ORDER No. 38.

Ref. Map 57.d. 1/40,000.   13th. August 1918.

1.   Gas Projectors and Stokes Bombs will be fired into the enemy's trenches in Q.5.c. and d. and Q.11. by 'N' and No. 3 Special Companies R.E. on the night 14/15th. August.

2.   Zero hour will be notified later.

3.   The Wind limits for this operation are:-

   S.W. to W.N.W. through W.
   Velocity - 1 to 5 miles per hour.

4. (a)   All trenches in the area marked GREEN on the attached Map will be cleared by Zero minus 15 minutes.
   Should the tactical situation not permit of this area being cleared, the Garrisons will be reduced to a minimum.

   (b)   All troops occupying trenches in the area marked RED, including any left in the area marked GREEN, will wear Box Respirators from Zero minus 2 minutes, until ordered to take them off by an Officer which will not be before Zero plus 30 minutes.

   (c)   The area marked GREEN will not be reoccupied before Zero plus 30 minutes.
   All troops reoccupying this area will be preceded by the Company Gas N.C.Os., who will advise the Officers concerned whether the trench is safe.

NOTE.- Coy. Commanders will ask their respective Brigade Majors to show them the Map referred to in above para.

   The only Gun Positions affected will be Q.9.3 which will withdraw to OCEAN TRENCH, - Q.3.2. and Q.3.1 will wear Box Respirators as per para. (b).

5.   The C.R.A. will arrange to harass all approaches to the gassed area from Zero plus 60 minutes onwards.

6.   The Os.C. 'N' and No.3 Special Companies R.E. will arrange direct with B.G.C. 64th. Infantry Brigade for the synchronisation of watches.

7.   Should conditions not be favourable, the code word "RUPERT" will be wired to all concerned.

8.   A C K N O W L E D G E.

                                                   V. F. Samuelson
                                                   Capt. & Adjutant.
Issued by runner at 5.30 p.m.   21st. Battn. Machine Gun Corps.

Distribution.-

   Copy No. 1 ... O.C. "A" Coy. Fwd.   Copy No. 5 .. Intell. Officer.
            2 ... O.C. "B" Coy. Fwd.   6 .. File.
            3 ... O.C. "D" Coy. Fwd.   7-8 .. War Diary.
            4 ... Commanding Officer.

SECRET.   Copy No. 21

21st. Battn. Machine Gun Corps
OPERATION ORDER No. 39.

14th August 1918.

Ref.Map Sheet:
57d.S.E., 1/20,000.

1. The following reliefs and redistribution of guns will take place tonight, 14th/15th August.

2. The undermentioned guns of "A" Coy. under 2/Lt. Scott, at present in Divisional Reserve, will relieve the following guns of "C" Coy. -

    Q.25.1.   Q.20.1.

On completion of relief, these 4 guns will report to O.C., 7th Leicesters at Q.19.b.55.30.
2/Lt. Watts will be in command of this Section.

3. The guns at Q.15.5 will relieve guns at Q.8.2. [Gun Position at Q.15.5 will not be occupied]
The guns at Q.7.2 will be evacuated at once.
On completion of these moves, the 4 teams from Q.7.2 and Q.8.2 under 2/Lt. Rowell will proceed at once to report to O.C., 9th K.O.Y.L.I. at Q.7.d.6.4. and come under his orders.

4. The undermentioned guns of "B" Coy. under 2/Lt. Hunter, MC, MM, at present in Divisional Reserve, will relieve the following guns of "C" Coy.

    Q.2.3.   Q.2.2.

On completion of relief, these guns will return to Divisional Reserve at BERTRANCOURT.

The undermentioned gun position will be evacuated at once, and teams return to Divisional Reserve at BERTRANCOURT.

    Q. 13. 1.

5. The guns at Q.14.2 will relieve guns at Q.14.1. On relief the teams of Q.14.1 will return to BERTRANCOURT. The position Q.14.2 will not be occupied.

6. The 8 guns at present in Divisional Reserve will commence relieving on receipt of these orders.

7. All moves and redistribution will be completed by 12 midnight. Completion will be reported to Battalion Headquarters by code word "BAILEY" by Company Commanders concerned.

8. Operation Order No. 37 still holds good.

9. All Range Cards, Order Boards, Gun Equipment and Belt Boxes will be either removed to new positions, or withdrawn to BERTRANCOURT.

10. O.C. "C" Coy. will make all arrangements regarding transport, and will notify Company Commanders concerned.

11. All personnel of "C" Coy. now at ACHEUX will move to BERTRANCOURT tonight under Company Commanders orders.

12. Divisional Reserve will be accommodated at Road Junction 100 yards North of P.3.b.7.9.

13. ACKNOWLEDGE.

V.F. Samuelson
Capt. & Adjt.,
21st Battn. Machine Gun Corps.

S E C R E T.

Copy No......

21st. Battn. Machine Gun Corps

OPERATION ORDER No. 28.

Ref. Map Sheet.
57d.S.E., 1/20,000.   14th August 1918.

Distribution:-

Copy No. 1 ... O.C. "A" Coy. Fwd.
         2 ... O.C. "B" Coy. Fwd.
         3 ... O.C. "C" Coy. Fwd.
         4 ... O.C. "D" Coy. Fwd.
         5 ... 2nd.-in-C. "A" Coy.
         6 ... 2nd.-in-C. "B" Coy.
         7 ... 2nd.-in-C. "C" Coy.
         8 ... 2nd.-in-C. "D" Coy.
         9 ... Tpt. Offr. "C" Coy.
        10 ... Quartermaster.
        11 ... Commanding Officer.
        12 ... 2nd. in Command.
        13 ... 21st. Division "G".
        14 ... 64th. Inf. Bde.
        15 ... 62nd. Inf. Bde.
        16 ... 110th. Inf. Bde.
        17 ... 9th. Bn. K.O.Y.L.I.
        18 ... 7th. Leicester Regt.
        19 ... File.
     20-21 ... War Diary.

TO:- All recipients of 21 Bn. M.G.C. Order No.38.

AX/253/O.   14th.   AAA

Order No.38 is CANCELLED aaa Acknowledge.

FROM: 21 Bn. M.G.C.
6.15 p.m.

S E C R E T.   Copy No. 15

21st Battn. Machine Gun Corps
OPERATION ORDER No. 40.

Ref.Map Sheets:
57d.N.E., 1/20,000.
57d.S.E., 1/20,000.

16th August 1918.

1. The 62nd Infantry Brigade will relieve the Forward Battalion of the 64th Infantry Brigade tonight August 16th/17th. under arrangements to be made between Brigadiers concerned.
   After relief, the 62nd Infantry Brigade will be responsible for keeping touch with the enemy from the STATION Q.18.b.8.8 to the Northern Divisional Boundary, and for the defence of the Northern and Centre Brigade Sectors.

2. 2 Battalions 64th Infantry Brigade will withdraw to the area RAINCHEVAL - ARQUEVES today, August 16th.
   The remainder of the Brigade will withdraw to this area tomorrow August 17th.

3. The 110th Infantry Brigade will be responsible for keeping touch with the enemy from the Southern Divisional Boundary to the STATION at Q.18.b.8.8, and for the defence of the Southern Brigade Sector.

4. "C" Coy. 21st Bn.M.G.Corps (less 2 Sections) at present under the orders of B.G.C. 64th Infantry Brigade, will come under the orders of B.G.C. 110th Infantry Brigade forthwith.
   The Forward Section of "C" Coy. in the 64th Infantry Brigade Sector will come under the orders of B.G.C. 62nd Infantry Brigade.
   The fourth Section of "C" Coy. is already with the 110th Infantry Brigade. Major Hardinge, MC, will get in touch with B.Gs.C. 62nd and 110th Infantry Brigades for instructions.

5. The 2 Sections in Divisional Reserve are accommodated at J.33.d.60.30 (BERTRANCOURT).

6. On completion of relief of the 64th Infantry Brigade by the 62nd Infantry Brigade, "B" Coy. 21st Bn. M.G.Corps will come under the orders of B.G.C. 62nd Infantry Brigade.

7. A C K N O W L E D G E.

V.F. Samuelson
Capt. & Adjt.,
21st Battalion, Machine Gun Corps.

DISTRIBUTION.

Copy No. 1 .. O.C. "A" Coy. (Forward).
       2 .. O.C. "B" Coy. (Forward).
       3 .. O.C. "C" Coy.
       4 .. O.C. "D" Coy. (Forward).
       5 .. "B" Coy. (Rear).
       6 .. 62nd Infantry Brigade.
       7 .. 64th Infantry Brigade.
       8 .. 110th Infantry Brigade.
       9 .. 21st Division 'G'.
      10 .. Quartermaster.
      11 .. Commanding Officer.
      12 .. 2nd in Command.
      13 .. File.
   14 & 15 .. War Diary.

SECRET.   Copy No. 15.

21st. Bn. M.G.C. OPERATION ORDER No.41.

Ref. Map 57.d. 1/40,000.   20th. August 1918.
----

1.   On a day and hour to be notified later the 21st. Division in conjunction with the 42nd. Division on the Left will:

   (a) Capture the Village of BEAUCOURT.

   (b) Prolong the Right of the attack of the 42nd. Division to the River ANCRE by capturing:

      (i) The YELLOW LINE connecting with the 42nd. Division at R.2.a.8.3.
      (ii) THE BROWN LINE connecting with the 42nd. Division at R.3.a.2.2.

   (c) Endeavour to exploit the success to the South of the River ANCRE.

2.   Operations (a) and (b) will be carried out simultaneously by the 62nd. Inf. Bde. under a Creeping Barrage at a Zero hour to be known as 'Z' (1).

        From 'Z' (1) minus 40 minutes till 'Z' (1) and while the troops are advancing on this objective a Smoke Barrage will be put down on the Line LOGGING SUPPORT - LUFF AVENUE - GRANDCOURT RD. at R.9.d.7.3.

        In addition from 'Z' (1) minus 40 minutes till 'Z' (1) a Smoke Barrage will be placed on the area River ANCRE - YELLOW LINE - Northern Divl. Boundary - Grid Line between R.1. and R.2. and between R.7. and R.8.

        During the pause on the YELLOW LINE, the area, Junction of LITTLE TRENCH and LUFF AVENUE - GRANDCOURT RD. at R.9.d.7.3. - R.9.central - Junction of Road and LITTLE TRENCH at R.13.b.5.7. will be bombarded with H.E.

3. Action of Machine Guns.

   (a) One Section of "C" Coy. will be at the disposal of B.G.C. 62nd. Inf.Bde. for the consolidation of the YELLOW and BROWN LINES.
   (b) "D" Coy. will also be at the disposal of B.G.C. 62nd.Inf.Bde. 8 of these guns will be placed in suitable positions in trench between Q.5.a.90.30. and Q.5.c.95.50, and will carry out indirect overhead fire on to Grid Line R.2.a.0.0 - R.2.a.0.9 for a period to be laid down by B.G.C. 62nd.Inf.Bde. On completion of this task, these 8 guns will move to high ground about Q.6. and will engage all visible targets by direct fire.
       The remaining 8 guns will be held in Brigade Reserve under orders of B.G.C. 62nd.Inf.Bde.

                                                    /c ....

3. (contd).

(c) "A" Coy. will be attached to B.G.C. 110th.Inf.Bde. for assisting in the consolidation in depth of the ground exploited S. of the River ANCRE.

(d) "B" Coy., and "C" Coy. (less 1 Section) 21st. Bn. M.G.C. and 2 Companies 17th. Bn. M.G.C. will put down the following Barrages:-

From Z (1) minus 40 minutes till Z.(2) the area CANDY AVENUE - LOGGING SUPPORT - LUFF AVENUE - Road at R.8.d.0.0 - ST. PIERRE DIVION.
Detailed tasks and Battery Positions are shown on attached tracing..
At Z.(2) these guns cease fire and remain in position in Divisional Reserve.

4. At a second Zero hour to be known as Z.(2). (i.e. time at which 62nd. Inf.Bde. leaves YELLOW LINE), Battle Patrols of 110th.Inf.Bde. on the Right and of the 62nd. Inf.Bde. on the Left will cross the River ANCRE and will advance on the BLUE LINE. The Smoke Barrage on this line will change to shrapnel at Z.(2) plus 15 minutes and lift forward 200 yards at Z.(2) plus 30 minutes, so as to allow patrols to reach the BLUE LINE, and will then remain stationary for 15 minutes.

From Z.(2) plus 45 minutes to Z.(2) plus 3 hours, the Artillery will fire bursts on selected targets between the BLUE and RED LINE.

5. After reaching the BLUE LINE the 62nd.Inf.Bde. will send further patrols to the BLUE DOTTED LINE to connect up with other troops on the BROWN LINE.

6. (a) At Z.(2) plus 3 hours patrols will advance under a Creeping Barrage to the RED LINE

(b) After a pause of 2 hours on the RED LINE patrols will renew the advance under a Creeping Barrage to the GREEN LINE.

7. The 38th. Division will send patrols across the River ANCRE should the enemy show signs of weakening on his front and will be ready to support those patrols and eventually to connect with our Right across the River.

8. Should Battle Patrols meet with serious resistance either on the line of the ANCRE or in their subsequent advance it is NOT the Divisional Commander's intention to deliver a costly attack on the THIEPVAL RIDGE.

9. The aeroplane signal to denote the assembly of the enemy to counter attack is the dropping of a Red Smoke Bomb over the place where the enemy are seen.

10. Watches will be synchronised at Brigade H.Qrs. between 6.30 p.m. and 7.30 p.m. daily.

11. Special attention is drawn to the absolute necessity of maintaining the utmost secrecy regarding the operation.

/12 ....

SECRET.   Copy No. 18

21st Battn. Machine Gun Corps
OPERATION ORDER No. 42.

21st August 1918.

Ref. Map:
57d.S.E.

1. Under instructions received from 21st Division, "C" & "D" Companies, 17th Bn. Machine Gun Corps, will take up the following defensive dispositions.

2. "C" Coy. 17th Bn.M.G.C. will on receipt of these instructions occupy gun positions as follows:-

Gun Position Nos.	Co-ordinates.
Q.25.1.	Q.25.a.70.40.
Q.20.1.	Q.20.a.80.20.
Q.14.1.	Q.14.c.98.10.
Q.15.1.	Q.15.c.95.10.
Q.15.2.	Q.15.a.85.15.
Q.13.1.	Q.13.d.88.20.
Q.26.1.	Q.26.a. .60.

   O.C. "C" Coy. 17th Battn. will arrange direct with Os.C. "A", "B" & "C" Coys. 21st Battn. about Guides.
   There are suitable Coy. H.Q. at Q.24.d.30.40 and P.11.b.50.40.
   1 Sub-Section will be held in Brigade Reserve in vicinity of Coy. H.Q.
   This office will be informed which Coy. H.Q. will be occupied.

3. "D" Coy. 17th Battn. will occupy positions as follows:-

Gunn Position Nos.	Co-ordinates.
Q.15.3.	Q.9.c.99.15.
Q.9.1.	Q.9.d.00.80.
Q.8.2.	Q.8.a.65.30.
Q.2.2.	Q.2.c.95.26.
Q.2.3.	Q.2.c.40.80.
Q.3.3.	Q.3.c.15.25.
Q.2.1.	Q.2.b.50.20.

   1 Sub-Section will be held in Brigade Reserve at Gun Position Q.1.1. Map Reference P.11.b.8.3.
   O.C. "D" Coy. 17th Battn will arrange direct with Os.C. "B" & "D" Coys. 21st Battn. about Guides.
   Coy. H.Q. can be established at P.5.d.30.10.

4. The above dispositions will be taken up as soon as possible. No position under enemy observation will be occupied during daylight.

5. Completion of the above moves will be reported to Battn. H.Q. by code word "ARTHUR", stating time.

F. Samuelson
Capt. & Adjt.,
21st Bn. Machine Gun Corps.

-2-

DISTRIBUTION.

1 .. O.C. "D" Coy, 17th Bn.M.G.C.)
2 .. O.C. "C" Coy.   -do-   ) To acknowledge.
3 .. O.C. 17th Bn.M.G.C.   )
4 .. 'G' 21st Division.   )
5 .. 64th Inf. Bde.   )
6 .. 62nd Inf. Bde.   )
7 .. 110th Inf. Bde.   )
8 .. 42nd Bn.M.G.C.   )   For
9 .. 38th Bn.M.G.C.   )
10 .. Commanding Officer.   )
11 .. 2nd in Command.   )   information.
12 .. O.C. "A" Coy, 21st Bn.(F'd).)
13 .. "   "B" "   "   "   )
14 .. "   "C" "   "   "   )
15 .. "   "D" "   "   "   )
16 .. File.   )
17 .. War Diary.   )
18 .. "   "   )

12. No dugout in the enemy's system will be occupied until it has been examined by Tunnellors, and a notice board erected to the effect that it is safe.

13. A C K N O W L E D G E.

V.F. Samuelson
Capt. & Adjutant.
21st. Battalion Machine Gun Corps.

Distribution:-

Copy No. 1	...	O.C. 'A' Coy. (Fwd).
2	...	O.C. 'B' Coy. "
3	...	O.C. 'C' Coy. "
4	...	O.C. 'D' Coy. "
5	...	21st. Division 'G'.
6	...	17th. Bn. M.G.C.
7	...	38th. Bn. M.G.C.
8	...	42nd. Bn. M.G.C.
9	...	Commanding Officer.
10	...	Second in Command.
11	...	'D' Coy. 17th.Bn.M.G.C.
12	...	' ' Coy. 17th.Bn.M.G.C.
13	...	File.
14-15	...	War Diary.

COPY. - Telegram.

To 21 M.G.Battn.
----

21 Divn. order No. 206 aaa 62 Bde. will attack and capture remainder of BROWN line at once and without waiting for Artillery support unless enemy holding wired position when Artillery bombardment must precede attack aaa 64 Bde. less portion already S. of ANCRE will assemble about R.1 and R.2 aaa 62 Bde. has been ordered as soon as BROWN Line is captured to establish line R.4.c.6.7 R.4.d.0.5 and picquet bridges over ANCRE in R.3 and R.4 aaa If 62 Bde. should fail 64 Bde. will take on operations aaa When operating complete 64 Bde. will cross ANCRE and move up SIXTEEN Road through R.16.a. & c on to GREEN Line with left flank guard along BOON RAVINE aaa 64 Bde. will act with boldness aaa ACKNOWLEDGE aaa Addsd recipients 21 Div Order 205.

From 21 Div.

12.20 p.m.

Certified True Copy
J.F. Samuelson Capt
ADJUTANT.
21st BN. MACHINE GUN CORPS.

COPY.

Telegram — Urgent Operations Priority to Bdes.

/   21   / aaa

JEZU Order No. 208 aaa JEZU Order No. 207 is cancelled aaa BUMA will maintain present positions with front line from R.4.a.5.1 to R.3.a.9.9, where touch must be gained with 42nd Div aaa Two Coys. in BEAUCOURT after relief by 1 Coy. from R.4.c will be withdrawn into reserve aaa BURA will establish Bridgeheads over ANCRE tonight at selected points between R.4.d.3.4. and YELLOW Line at R.9.a.1.9 with 1 Battalion aaa connecting with BUMA at R.4.a.5.1 aaa BUMA will form Bridgeheads from R.9.a.1.9 to BEAUCOURT inclusive aaa RUVE will form Bridgeheads from BEAUCOURT exclusive to MILL Bridge Q.24.a.5.3 aaa BURA less one Battalion will be in support to BUMA tonight in area Q.6, Q.12, R.1, R.7 aaa One Battalion RUVE remains attached to BURA aaa RUVE will remain in present positions in area Q.15, 16, 17, 18 aaa Active patrolling tonight to gain and keep touch with enemy aaa BURA will be prepared to operate South of ANCRE as ordered in D.O. 206 early tomorrow BUMA and RUVE be prepared to send Battle Patrols supported by Coys. across ANCRE early tomorrow aaa C.R.E. will detail two Sections R.E. to assist each Brigade with crossings over ANCRE aaa Pioneers will make road for Artillery as already detailed aaa M.G.Dispositions remain unaltered aaa ACKNOWLEDGE. Addsd All recipients JEZU Order No. 207.

JEZU
8.30 p.m.

Certified True Copy
J. Hamilton Capt

(Sgd) H.C.FRANKLYN, Lieut. Col.,
General Staff.

ADJUTANT,
21st BN, MACHINE GUN CORPS.

COPY.

Telegram — Urgent Operations — Priority.

G.X.464 / 21 / aaa

BUMA	WUMA	A/Q	42nd Div.	15th Sqn. R.A.F.
BURA	JENU	5th Corps. 38th Div.		
RUVE	FOLO	5th Corps RA. 17th Div.		

JEZU Order No. 207 aaa 63rd Division are going to attack IRLES this evening aaa Situation may then develop aaa BUMA will continue to hold their present line keeping touch with 42nd Div. aaa BURA will keep touch with situation to their front and take advantage of any chance presented to push forward to line ordered in GX 452.
aaa BURA will be in position so that BUMA may be supported and so that no delay will occur if enemy retires aaa RUVE remain in present positions aaa LOFO revert to RUVE and may rejoin now or wait till dark aaa Care must be taken to avoid overcrowding of troops in Area aaa ACKNOWLEDGE aaa Addressed all recipients of Order No. 206.

JEZU

6 p.m.

(Sgd) H.C.FRANKLYN Lieut. Col.
General Staff.

Certified True Copy
V.A. Samuelson Capt.
ADJUTANT,
21st BN. MACHINE GUN CORPS

COPY.

Telegram.

To FOLO

SK 26 / 21 / aaa

Action of 12 guns FOGA under BURA will be as follows aaa
4 Guns will report to O.C. HOLI forthwith and will remain
under his orders aaa 4 Guns will be in position of readiness
about R.2 cent aaa Remaining 4 Guns will be in reserve in
vicinity of Bde. H.Q. aaa Addsd FOGA reptd HOWI HOLI GOJO
FOLO

BURA

9.45 p.m.

Certified True Copy
V F Samuels Capt

ADJUTANT.
21st BN. MACHINE GUN CORPS.

COPY.

Telegram - Urgent Operations Priority to Addressees.

GX. 496 / 22 / aaa

RUVE less LOFO will be relieved by BUBU tonight (22/23) under arrangements to be made by Brigadiers aaa On relief RUVE will become Div. Res. with H.Q. at P.11.b.2.5 aaa Battalions of RUVE will take over present dispositions of HOKU H.Q. Q.7.d.6.3. and HOQI H.Q. Q.14.a.3.7 aaa LOFO will remain attached to BURA aaa FOTA will be relieved by one Coy. FOTU under arrangements to be made by FOLO and FOTU aaa On relief FOTA will bivouac in AUCHONVILLERS aaa H.Q. FOTA will not move aaa All reliefs to be complete by 5 a.m. 23rd aaa Command of Sector passes to JEVI on completion of relief aaa Boundary between JEZU and JEVI will be reported R.21.d.00 - R.14.a.0.0 - Q.12.c.6.0, thence West along Grid line between Q.11 and Q.17 aaa Completion of relief will be reported to JEZU AAA ACKNOWLEDGE AAA Addsd BUMA BURA RUVE WUMA FOLO JENU RORU JEKU JEMU A/Q 17th Div. reptd. 5th Corps 5th Corps H.A. 38th, 42nd Divs. 15th Sqn R.A.F.

JEZU   Certified True Copy   (Sgd) A.I.MACDOUGALL Major
                                                              for Lieut. Col.,
8.30 p.m.   General Staff.

ADJUTANT,
21st BN. MACHINE GUN CO.

COPY.

BUMA   WUMA
BURA   FOLO
RUVE   MOVI

GX. 494 / 22 / aaa

New form of booby trap consisting of large bomb actuated by a trip wire concealed in a thick mass of concertina and barbed wire across a road had been discovered aaa This was found on HAMEL - MESNIL Road aaa Similar barricades of wire should be avoided until examined.

JEZU.

7.30 p.m.

Certified True Copy
V Hamilton Cpt

ADJUTANT,
21st BN. MACHINE GUN CORPS.

COPY.

Telegram. — Urgent operations priority.

BUMA	WUMA	A/Q	5th Corps R.A.	17th Div.
BURA	JENU	JEKU	42 Div.	15th Sqn R.A.F.
RUVE	FOLO	5th Corps	38th Div.	MOVI

JEZU Order No. 209 aaa BURA will relieve 2 Coys. of BUMA in R.14.a. and b. tonight aaa Two Coys. BURA in R.9.b. will come temporarily under orders of BUMA aaa They will be relieved by BUMA when two Coys. now in ACHEUX rejoin that Brigade aaa LOFO will remain with BURA but will not be used except in case of urgency aaa LOFO will probably return to RUVE tomorrow aaa BUMA will be responsible for defence of Sector East of Grid line between R.1 and R.2 and BURA West of this line and for defence of BLUE Line in R.14.a and b.aaa Every effort will be made to establish line COMMON LANE from junction with THIEPVAL ROAD along LOGGING SUPPORT - LUFF AVENUE and BLUE DOTTED Line to join with YELLOW Line on ANCRE aaa Attack on RED and GREEN Lines will probably be made by BURA and RUVE tomorrow evening aaa Brigades will improve and if possible increase present crossings over ANCRE with aid of R.E.Sections attached aaa Pioneers will work on track for Artillery and will wire YELLOW Line aaa M.G.Dispositions unaltered except 12 guns in Div. Reserve moved today to AUCHONVILLERS aaa ACKNOWLEDGE. Addsd recipients JEZU order No. 208.

JEZU.

4. 35 p.m.

(Sgd) G.TOOTH, Capt. for Lt.Col.,
General Staff.

Certified True Copy

ADJUTANT.
21st BN. MACHINE GUN CORPS.

COPY.

To O.C. "C" Coy.

M.G. 100 / 22nd / aaa

Ref. conversation re your 12 guns in Divisional Reserve aaa These will be moved as soon as possible to vicinity of Cemetery at AUCHONVILLERS Your Headquarters will be established in cellar occupied by you before ("D" Coy's Section H.Q.) aaa The Sections must be concentrated so as to be in a position to move at a moment's notice aaa They will be prepared to move either in support of 64th Inf. Bde. or to occupy defensive positions EAST of AUCHONVILLERS aaa Bn. Signalling Officer is arranging communication aaa Your Headquarters at Q.16.1 will not close until communications have been established at your new H.Q. aaa Notify at once any further pack saddlery you require aaa Telephone completion of move aaa

---

FOLO.

(Sgd) V.F. SAMUELSON, Capt.

Certified True Copy
V.F. Samuelson Capt.
ADJUTANT,
21st BN. MACHINE GUN CORPS.

SECRET.   Copy No..........

21st DIVISION ORDER NO.210.

Ref.57.D.S.E. 1/20,000   23rd August 1918.

1.   The Vth Corps are to carry out two attacks on the enemy's position:-

   (a) "A" Attack.

          On the night 23rd/24th August, the Vth Corps are to capture the THIEPVAL RIDGE.

          Zero hour will be 1 a.m.

   (b) "B" Attack.

          At 5 a.m. August 24th, the 21st Division will make a second attack with the objective BLUE line (See Map)

          The attacks will be pushed with the greatest boldness and risks will be taken which, at other times, would be unjustifiable.

2.   "A" attack will be carried out by the 64th Infantry Bde.

        "B" attack will be carried out by the 110th. Infantry Bde.

        The general direction of both attacks will be due East.

"A" ATTACK.

3.   The 64th Infantry Brigade will attack at 1 a.m.

   (a) 1st Objective.   BROWN line from R.20.a.9.3. to R.O.b.7.2.

   (b) 2nd Objective.   RED line from R.21.d.0.0. through R.15 Central, to Railway at R.9.b.3.3.

        The 50th Infantry Brigade (17th Division) will be attacking on the right of the 64th Infantry Brigade.

        The left of the 64th Infantry Brigade will be on the ANCRE.

4.   (a)   The 1st Objective (BROWN line) will be reached at Zero plus 40 minutes, where there will be a pause of 10 minutes.

     (b)   The 2nd Objective will be reached at Zero plus 90 minutes.

5.   Both BROWN and RED Lines will be consolidated and on reaching the RED line the 64th Infantry Brigade will push out troops to the general line shown RED and BLUE on Map and exploit success and to cover consolidation.
        These patrols will be withdrawn by 5 a.m. to enable a creeping barrage for 110th Infantry Brigade to be brought down 300 yards East of the RED line.

/6............

- 2 -

6. The 64th and 62nd Infantry Brigades will effect a junction on their respective RED and BROWN lines at R.9.a.9.6.

"B" ATTACK.

7. (a) The objective for "B" attack to be carried out by the 110th Infantry Brigade is the BLUE line shown on Map from R.27.b.2.8. - along SIXTEEN Road to R.4.c.5.7. with bridgehead at R.4.d.2.4.

(b) After the capture of the BLUE line the 110th Infantry Brigade will exploit the success towards LE SARS and PYS, with the special object of capturing the high ground (marked GREEN DOTTED on Map).

(c) 2 The 17th Division are to advance their left to maintain touch with the 110th Infantry Brigade.

8. The 110th Infantry Brigade will pay particular attention to the guarding of their left flank along the ANCRE. When the BLUE line has been captured the 62nd Infantry Brigade will push on to the Road in R.4.a. and a junction between the two Brigades will be effected at R.4.c.5.7.

9. The 15th Squadron R.A.F. are arranging for a Contact Aeroplane to call for flares as early as possible and at even hours (i.e. 6 a.m., 8 a.m. etc) RED flares will be lit by the foremost troops at these hours and whenever called for by a Contact Aeroplane, sounding its Klaxon Horn.

If the supply of flares fails, the leading troops will show their position by using the using the tin discs which have been issued.

The Signal to denote "enemy concentrating for counter attack" will be a red smoke bomb dropped by the aeroplane over the position of assembly.

10. Both 64th and 110th Infantry Brigades will carry GREEN Very lights. These will be used by the 64th Infantry Brigade in "A" attack and by the 110th Infantry Brigade in "B" attack to show the position of their foremost troops to ground observers.

11. Compasses must be used to maintain direction. The compass bearing of the line of advance will be given in orders issued by all Units.

12. The position will be consolidated in depth. Machine guns will be pushed forward bodly to assist in the defence of the captured area.

13. Watches will be synchronized by an Officer from Divisional Headquarters between 6 p.m. and 7.30 p.m. on August 23rd.

/14..........

14.   Progress Reports (including negative reports) will be rendered every 20 minutes.

15.   Advanced Divisional Headquarters will open at the BREWERY, MAILLY MAILLET at 7 p.m. August 23rd 1918.

16.   ACKNOWLEDGE.

(Sgd.) H.C.FRANKLIN.

Lieut-Colonel.
General Staff.
21st Division.

Issued through Signals at   to:-

	Copy No.
62nd Inf.Bde.	1
64th " "	2
110th. " "	3
C.R.A.	4
C.R.E.	5
Pioneers.	6
D.M.G.G.	7
Signals.	8
A.D.M.S.	9
Train.	10
A/Q	11
5th Corps.	12
Vth Corps R.A.	13
do. H.A.	14
17th Division	15
38th Div.	16
42nd Div	17
15 Sqn.R.A.F.	18
War Diary	19
File.	20

Certified True Copy
/Hanrahan Capt

ADJUTANT,
21st BN. MACHINE GUN CORPS.

Major Hardinge, MC
O?C. "A" Coy. (Forward)
O.C. "B" Coy.   do.   For information.   M.391.
O.C. "D" Coy.   do.

      You will move with the Divisional Reserve on receipt of this order to Battery Valley. The exact location is left to yiu. There is reported to be a bridge in 17th Divisional Area which you can use for Transport at R.18.b.9.4. There are 4 guns of "B" Coy and 4 of "C" Coy which are moving to Battery Valley under Lieut. Athol today. Please collect them as they now pass from 62nd Infantry Brigade to Divisional Reserve, which will now consist of 20 guns. Please report as soon as possible location of Headquarters and personnel.

      A Report Centre has been established North of River at R.7.b.8.1.

      Battalion Headquarters will probably move to GRANDCOURT tomorrow.

      The 8 guns under Lieut. Athol may possibly be about R.9.d.6.4. (62nd Infantry Brigade Headquarters)

                    (Sgd.) D.H.KAY.
                                    Lieut-Colonel.
24th. August 1918.   Commanding 21st Battn Machine Gun Corps.

Certified True Copy
                                          ADJUTANT,
                              21st BN. MACHINE GUN CORPS.

MESSAGES AND SIGNALS.

TO:- FOLO.

GX 529   23   AAA

JEZU order No.210 amended as follows AAA There is every indication that enemy is withdrawing rapidly AAA The advance to the green dotted line will be carried out as soon as possible AAA New Divisional boundaries east of blue line are grid line R.22,23,24 Central and grid line between R.5. and R.11. and return R.66 and R.12 AAA BURA will advance with left on ANCRE with objective green dotted line in R.11 B and D AAA BURA will inform JEZU HQ of ZERO hour AAA RUVE will advance in rear of BURA and connect right of BURA with 17th.Div. on green dotted line AAA 42 Div are advancing through MIRAUMONT tonight and will connect with BURA at Mill R.11 B. AAA M.G. barrages cancelled AAA Orders for RE and Pioneers stand AAA BUMA remains in present positions AAA RURO will lay line to bridge over ANCRE R.9b.0.6. as soon as feasible for communication with Forward Brigades.AAA

Acknowledge AAA
Addressed to all recipients JEZU Order No.210.

FROM:- JEZU.   8.50 p.m.

Certified True Copy
/Hamilton Capt.

ADJUTANT,
21st BN. MACHINE GUN CORPS.

APPENDIX III to 21st DIVISION ORDER NO.210.

MACHINE GUN ARRANGEMENTS.

1. Barrages.

   (a)   16 Guns at R.2.c.8.4. to place barrage East of BROWN line in R.15.a. and lift on to R.15.d. R.16.a. etc.

   (b)   16 Guns at R.7.b.8.0. to barrage R.15.c. and R.21.a.

   These barrages will be co-ordinated with the Artillery barrage, so that there shall be a minimum distance of 400 yards between the near edge of the Artillery Creeping Barrage and the Machine Gun Barrage.

2. Consolidation.

   (a)   12 Guns are detailed to accompany and assist in consolidation of the ground won by the 64th Infantry Brigade.

   (b)   16 Guns are detailed to accompany and assist in consolidating the ground won by the 110th Infantry Brigade.

   (c)   On the completion of the barrages detailed in para(1) 20 guns will revert to the 62nd Infantry Brigade for the defence of the ground North of the ANCRE.

   12 Guns will revert to the Divisional Reserve.

Lieut. Athol.
O.C. "B" Coy. (Forward)
O.C. "C" Coy (Forward)
O.C. "D" Coy (Forward)

M.390.

16 Guns of "D" Company will move on receipt of these orders to a position of readiness in R.14.a., where they will remain under the orders of the B.G.C. 62nd Infantry Brigade. 8 guns composed of 4 of "C" Company and 4 of "B" Company will remain North of the ANCRE to support the Infantry holding BROWN line. Please report position of assembly taken up, and locality of Company Headquarters.

The 8 guns North of the ANCRE will be under the command of Lieut. Athol, who will get in touch with the Infantry Commander.

(Sgd.) D.H. KAY
Lieut-Colonel
24th Aug. 18   Commanding 21st Battalion Machine Gun Corps.

Certified True Copy.
J. Hannucka Capt.
ADJUTANT,
21st BN. MACHINE GUN CORPS.

TELEGRAM.

Urgent
Operations
Priority.

Words
Sent
At........m
To........
By........

/ 24th / AAA

BUMA	MOVI	A/Q	38th Div.
BURA	FOLO	5th.Corps	42nd Div.
RUVE	RORU	5th Corps R.A.	15th Sqn.R.A.F.
WUMA	JEZU	" H.A.	
JENU	JEKU	17th Div.	

Order No.211 AAA BURA have reached high ground in R.11.b. & d.
AAA RUVE will push on by easiest route possible irrespective of
left of 17th Division and get touch with right of BURA AAA
RUVE will protect BURAS right and endeavour to connect it to
left of 17th Division.

JEZU.
7.40 a.m.

H.F.MACDOUGALL.
Major for
Lieut-Colonel.

ADJUTANT
21st BN. MACHINE

TELEGRAM.

Urgent operations priority to Bdes.D.M.G.C. C.R.A. & Flank Divs.

Words.
Sent
At.................m
To..................
By..................

/ 24 / AAA

BUMA	MOVI	A/Q	38th DIV
BURA	FOLO	5th Corps	42nd Div.
RUVE	RORU		R.A. 15th Sq.R.A.F.
WUMA	JEMU		H.A.
JENU	JEKU	17th Div.	

JEZU Order No.213. AAA Advance will be continued tomorrow AAA JEZU on BEAULENCOURT AAA BUMA main body will cross road R.12. R.18. at 6 a.m. and moving through RUVE make good line of road M.24.a.3.0. - N.7.a.0.0. AAA When this line made good RUVE will advance through BUMA to line of road N.21.d.4.0. - N.9.b.6.0. AAA BUMA will then advance to BAPUME - SAILLY SAILLISEL Road establishing touch with 4th Corps at REINCOURT AAA Brigadiers to keep close touch with each other so as yo avoid delays between bounds AAA JUJA moves with and affiliated to BUMA AAA JUTU same with RUVE AAA Troop Div.Cav. on arrival with work with leading Brigade AAA One M.G.Coy with each Brigade 1 Coy. in Div.Reserve AAA BURA in Div.Reserve remains in present position AAA Flank Divs. advancing due East every effort must be made to keep touch with them but advance not to be thereby delayed AAA Line for Brigade report centres R.16.Central N.16.Central AAA Advanced Div.Report Centre opens GRANDCOURT 8 a.m. AAA Div.H.Q. opens same place later AAA ACKNOWLEDGE AAA Added recipients JEZU Order No.212.

JEZU

10.40.p.m.   (Sgd.) A.I.MACDOUGALL,Major.
                                                         for
                                                              Lieut.Col.
                                                                     G.S.
                        Certified True Copy
                        V. Hamilton Capt
                                    &
                                ADJUTANT,
                        21st BN. MACHINE GUN CORPS.

TELEGRAM.

Urgent		Words.	
Operations		Sent	
Prioity.		At............m	
Bdes.		To.............	
		By.............	

/ 24 /

BUMA	MOVI	A/Q	38 Div.
BURA	FOLO	V Corps	42 Div.
RUVE	RORU	V Corps R.A.	15 Sqn. R.A.F.
WUMA	JEMU	V Corps H.A.	
JENU	JEKU	17 Div.	

JEZU Order No.212 AAA 17 Div. are moving on COURCELLETTE and MARTINPUICH and 42 Div on WARLENCOURT AAA JEZU will advance on LE SARS AAA RUVE will advance forthwith and make good the line M.20.b.0.3. - M.15.central - M.10.central AAA Patrols will be sent forward through LE SARS and to DESTREMONT FARM AAA Arrangements have been made to meet parties of flank Divisions at DESTREMONT FARM and LITTLE WOOD AAA BUMA will concentrate on road R.12 R.18. ready to move through RUVE and take up advance or to hold line of road in case of need AAA BURA will reorganize in BOOM RAVINE AAA One Arty Brigade will move through MIRAUMONT to cover advance AAA New Northern Boundary runs R.5.Central - M.8. 9. 10. 11 Central AAA ACKNOWLEDGE. Added recipients Order No.211.

JEZU
4.55.p.m.

H.C.FRANKLYN
for
Lieut.Colonel
General Staff.

Certified True Copy
Hamilton Capt
ADJUTANT,
21st BN. MACHINE GUN CORPS

TELEGRAM.

Urgent Operations Priority to 110th Bde.

| | 26 | | AAA |

BUMA	POLO	5th Corps R.A.	A/Q
BURA	RORU	17th Div.	Div. Cav Troop
RUVE	JEKU	63rd Div.	Div. Cyclist Coy
WUMA	5th Corps	15th Sqn.R.A.F.	
JENU			

JEZU Order No.215 AAA 17th Division have reached general line M.24.c.1.7. - M.29.Central - M.35.a.0.0. AAA 63rd Division hold half of LE BARQUE AAA Dispositions for tonight as follows AAA BURA will find outposts on General Line now held AAA BUMA will Hold YELLOW CUT as Main Line of Resistance AAA RUVE will concentrate each unit and let men rest but be prepared to hold line DESTREMONT FARM - Road junction M.16.b.3.3. - WARLENCOURT AAA Reserve M.Gs same positions as last night AAA JEZU will continue to advance tomorrow August 27th on BEAULENCOURT AAA BURA will push advance guards in half light tomorrow morning to occupy line of road N.19.b. - N.7.b. AAA RUVE will on receipt of orders from JEZU H.Q. which will not be before 7 a.m. advance through BURA with objective high ground on general line N.20 Central - N.14.b.5.0. - N.8.central AAA BURA will be prepared on receipt of orders to advance through RUVE to line of ridge N.22.a.0.4. to N.16.c.4.8. thence along trench to main cross roads N.9.d.7.3. and along road to Boundary at N.9.b.8.0. AAA One Coy.Cyclists one troop Cavalry and one Mobile Newton Mortar will work with leading Brigade reporting in first instance to BURA H.Q. at BUTTE DE WARLINCOURT AAA JUTU will work under orders of BURA AAA JUJA will work under orders of RUVE AAA Div.H.Q. remains GRANDCOURT AAA ACKNOWLEDGE AAA Added all recipients JEZU Order No.214.

JEZU

8.30.p.m.

Certified True Copy

H.C.FRANKLYN
Lt.Col.
General Staff.

ADJUTANT,
21st BN. MACHINE GUN CORPS.

O.C. "C"Coy. O.C."A"Coy. - 62nd Inf.Bde.
O.C. "D" Coy. O.C."B"Coy. - 21st Div "G"

V.S.570.   27   AAA
----

16 guns of "C" Coy will relieve "D" Coy guns on the night of 28/29th.
August AAA All arrangements re relief of Forward and Rear positions
will be made between Coy. Commanders concerned AAA Relief of "D" Coy
guns will be complete by 12 midnight 28/29th inst AAA Lt.English will
see that the guns of "D" Coy are placed in correct positions and when
complete will report Battn.H.Qs before proceeding to relieve
Lt.Hacon AAA Lt.Hacon will remain with O.C."C"Coy until relieved by
Lt. English AAA O.C."D"Coy will report and take up his Coy.H.Qs.
at advanced Battn.H.Qs. at BOOM RAVINE AAA O.C."C"Coy will act under
the orders of B.G.C. 62nd Inf.Bde. after relief.

ACKNOWLEDGE

21st.Bn.M.G.C.   V.F.SAMUELSON
                                              Capt. & Adjt.

Certified True Copy
/Samuelson Capt
              ADJUTANT.
21st BN. MACHINE GUN CORPS.

TELEGRAM.

Urgent	:	Words.	:
Operations	:		:
Priority.	:	At................m	:
to Brigades.	:	To................	:
	:	By................	:

C.X.622   /   27   /   AAA

BUMA	FOLO	5th Corps	A/Q
BURA	RORU	5th Corps R.A.	Div.Cav.Troop
RUVE	JEKU	17th Div.	Div.Cyclist Coy.
WUMA	JENU	63rd Div.	
		15Sqn.R.A.F.	

JEZU Order No. 215 cancelled AAA BURA will make good LUISENHOF FARM and line of Road for 400 yards on each side of it connecting back with flank Divisions AAA This operation to be carried out by patrols AAA Garrisons will then take over ground gained AAA When above line made good patrols will be pushed forward to high ground N.14.b. and d.AAA If touch cannot be gained with Enemy Cavalry Troop will be used AAA BUMA will relieve BURA tonight Aug 27/28 and in addition will continue to hold YELLOW CUT AAA On relief BURA to valley M.9.15.14 AAA ACKNOWLEDGE AAA Added recipients JEZU Order No.215.

JEZU

11.50 p.m.

H.C.FRANKLYN
Lt.Col.
General Staff.

Certified True Copy
[signature] Capt
ADJUTANT,
21st BN. MACHINE GUN CORPS.

MESSAGES AND SIGNALS.

Office Stamp

POLO

27.8.18

Handed in at 21st Div. Office 10.10.p.m.   Recd. 11.30.p.m.

To:- 21 M.G.Battn.

/ 27 / AAA

21 Div Order No.216 AAA Bde withdraws tonight as already arranged and will in case of need be prepared to hold high ground in M.15 and 20 AAA Patrols as already ordered will keep touch with enemy throughout the night AAA Patrols and posts east of YELLOW CUT will be withdrawn by 4.30a.m. at which hour artillery will bombard area between LUISENHOFF Farm road and 400 yards E. of Yellow Cut also road in N.14.a. and c. and square N.8. AAA At 5.30 a.m. barrage will come down 400 yards east of Yellow Cut and advance at rate of 100 yards in 4 minutes AAA 62 Bde. will send forward advanced guard patrols to occupy LUISENHOF Farm road AAA 17 Div will be sending patrols to GUEDECOURT and 42 Div to THILLOY AAA If enemy is not encountered patrols will be sent to high ground N.14 15 and Cavalry troop will be utilised AAA If enemy has definitely retirred 62 Bde. followed by other Bdes will follow him up AAA If Divs. on either flanks fail to make progress flank of patrol line will be bent back in conformity AAA Cyclist and NEWTON mortar under 62 Bde. AAA Cavalry troops will be sent if required remaining in camp till ordered AAA Artillery under C.R.A. ACKNOWLEDGE AAA Added all recipients Order No.215.

21 Div.

10.10.p.m.

Certified True Copy

signature Capt

&

ADJUTANT.

21st BN. MACHINE GUN CORPS.

War Diary

21st DIVISION SPECIAL ORDER.

Wednesday, 28th August 1918.

The magnificent work done by the Division during the recent fighting equals, if it does not surpass, any previous performance done by it in the past. The manner in which the 64th Infantry Brigade occupied and, although completely surrounded, held the high ground South of MIRAUMONT will certainly rank as one of the finest deeds performed by any Brigade in this War.

That such deeds were possible, after the serious casualties which the Division has suffered during the past few months, clearly shows the fine spirit and determination which all ranks possess.

The Commander-in-Chief has called for a special effort in order to reap the fruits of our already great successes. I am confident that he will not call on this Division in vain, notwithstanding the great hardships which all ranks have already endured.

David M Campbell

Major-General
Commanding 21st Division.

TELEGRAM

Urgent operations
Priority to
Bdes.and D.M.G.C.

A.F.Macdougall
　　　Major.

Words

Sent

At................m:
To................:
By................:

BUMA	RORU	5th Corps R.A.	Div.Cyclist Coy.
BUMA	JEKU	17th Div.	
RUVE	A/Q	42 Div.	
REVE WUMA	JEMU	15 Squ.R.A.F.	
JENU	5th Corps	Div.Cav.Troop	

/   28   /   AAA

JEZU Order No.217 AAA RUVE will relieve BUMA in the line tonight 28th/29th inst. AAA Details will be arranged between Brigadiers AAA On relief BUMA will take over present dispositions and defence arrangements of RUVE AAA No troops of RUVE will cross the ALBERT - BAPUME road before 8.30 p.m. AAA Cyclists come under orders of RUVE on completion of relief AAA Acknowledge AAA Adssd recipients of JEZU Order No.216.

JEZU

4.15.p.m.

　　　　　　　　　　　　　　　　　　A.F.MACDOUGALL
　　　　　　　　　　　　　　　　　　　　　Major.
　　　　　　　　　　　　　　　　　　for
　　　　　　　　　　　　　　　　　Lt.Col. G.S.

Certified True Copy
V Hammer Capt
　　ADJUTANT,
21st BN. MACHINE GUN CORPS.

SECRET.

To:- O.C. "C" Coy.
O.C. "D" Coy.
62nd Inf. Bde.

AX/379/Q

1. The Division will not attack tonight or tomorrow morning but a Barrage Fire will be put down by 16 guns of "D" Coy and 8 guns of "C" Coy.

2. "D" Coy guns will fire from positions arranged verbally this morning. Centre of barrage on Grid line N.8. and N.14. bounded by N.8.d.0.8. to N.14.b.0.4.

3. "C" Coy will barrage high ground N.14.c. and d. from same positions as "D" Coy.

4. 100,000 rounds of S.A.A. will be dumped at QUARRY M.15.b.0.8. with Rations tonight for "C" & "D" Coys.

5. The above guns will put down a Barrage from 5.30 a.m. to 6.0.a.m. 29th. inst. Rate of fire : 100 rds per min.

6. Each Section will traverse only to the Right about 4 degrees Tracing of barrage herewith attached for "C" & "D" Coys.

7. O.C. "D" Coy will be with the guns.

8. After barrage, 8 guns of "C" Coy will return to the 62nd Inf. Bde. and "D" Coy will occupy rear positions recently vacated by "C" Coy.

9. ACKNOWLEDGE.

(Sgd.) V.F. SAMUELSON
Capt. & Adjt.
for O.C. 21st. Bn. Machine Gun Corps.

28th August 1918.

Certified true copy
V Hamilton Capt
ADJUTANT,
21st BN. MACHINE GUN CORPS.

TELEGRAM.

Urgent Operations Priority to 3 bdes.		Words. Sent At..............m: To.............: By............:	

BUMA	ROKU	5th Corps	15th Sqn.R.A.F.
BURA	JEKU	5th Corps R.A.	Div.Cav.Troop.
RUVE	JEMU	17th Div.	Div.Cyclist Coy.
WUMA	FOLO	42nd Div.	
JENU	A/Q	38th Div.	

/ 28 / AAA

JEZU Order No.218. AAA The 38th Div. are attacking tomorrow August 29th at 5.30.a.m. with objective the high ground East of GINCHY T.14. AAA To assist attack by the 38th. Div.artillery and M.G. barrages are being put down across the remainder of Corps front AAA 42nd. Div are not attacking tomorrow AAA Div.Arty. will fire under orders of WUMA AAA M.G.Battn will put down barrages unders orders issued personally to C.O AAA RUVE will be ready to push forward advanced guards on any slackening of the enemy's resistance AAA RUVES main body will not advance without orders from JEZU AAA Cav.Troop will remain in Camp ready to move at ½ hours notice. Acknowledge. AAA Addressed recipients JEZU Order No.217.

JEZU

7.15 p.m.

H.C.FRANKLYN.
Lt.Colonel.
General Staff.

Certified True Copy

V.Hamilton Capt

ADJUTANT,
21st BN. MACHINE GUN CORPS.

MESSAGES AND SIGNALS.

Urgent operations
priority to 3 Bdes.
remainder priority.

BUMA	FOLO	WOMA
BURA	17thDiv.	5 Corps.
RUVE	42nd Div.	RORU

G654.   29   AAA

---

38 Div. report they met no opposition this morning AAA There are other indications that enemy are retiring AAA RUVE will push forward advance guards followed if feasible by remainder of Bde and make good following successive bounds AAA LUISENHOF FARM Road AAA Road N.12.a. N.9.a. along road to N.9.b.8.0. Cross Roads N.24.a.5.1: BEAULENCOURT and Road from N.11.d.5.0. to N.11.b.7.0. AAA BUMA will support RUVE moving to LUISENHOF FARM Rd when RUVE has made good road N.21.a, N.9.a. AAA N.2. Spur N.22.a.0.0. Cross Roads N.9.d. when RUVE has reached BEAULENCOURT AAA Moves of BURA and RESERVE MGs will be oredred direct from Div.HQ.AAA Successive Report Centres at BUTTE DE WARLENCOURT LUISENHOF FARM and Sunken Road N.15.d.4.7. AAA
ACKNOWLEDGE.

JEZU
9.20.a.m.
                                        Sgd. H.C.FRANKLYN.
                                              Lt.Col.

Urgent operations   BUMA   WOMA   5CORPS
priority to 3 bdes. BURA   FOLO   17Div.
                    RUVE   RORU   42 Div.

GX 661   29   AAA

Ref G654 of today AAA BURA will become supporting Brigade instead of BUMA AAA BURA will be prepared to move to YELLOW CUT on receipt of orders from Div.HQ AAA JUTU will now come under orders of BURA AAA ACKNOWLEDGE.

JEZU
12.10.p.m.
                                        (Sgd.) H.C.FRANYLYN
                                              Lt.Col.

Certified true copies
V Hamilton Capt
                                              ADJUTANT,
                                        21st BN. MACHINE GUN CORPS.

POSITION CODE CALLS.

In reference to attached War Diary.

UNIT	STATION CODE CALL	UNIT	STATION CODE CALL
21 Div.H.Q.	JEZU	21 DIVL.ARTY.H.Q.	WUMA
62nd Inf.Bde.H.Q.	BUMA	94 Bde.R.F.A.	JUTU
		"A" Battery	JUGA
12/13 N.F.	MOHI	"B" do.	JULA
1st.LINCS.	JORE	"C" do.	JUHA
2nd.LINCS	JOPE	"D" do.	JUVA
62LTM.Batty.	LILI		
		93rd Bde.R.F.A.	JUQU
64th Inf.Bde.H.Q.		"A" Battery	JUDU
		"B" do.	JUBU
1 E.YORKS.	HOWI	"C" do.	JUFU
9 K.O.Y.L.I.	HOLI		
15 D.L.I.	QOJO	95th.Bde.R.F.A.	JUJA
64thLTM.Batty.	LIVI	"A" Battery	JUZA
		"B" do.	JUNA
110thInf Bde.HQ	RUVE	"C" do.	JUKA
		"D" do.	JUSA
6 LIECTR.REGT.	JONE		
7 do do	JOKE	315 Bde.R.F.A.	GUNA
1 WILTS REGT	LOFO	"A" Battery	GUKA
110 LTM Batty.	LIQU	"B" do.	GUSA
		"C" do.	GUMA
21st M.G.BATTN.	FOLO	"D" do.	GUWA
"A" Coy	FOTO		
"B" Coy	FOGA		
"C" Coy	FOHO		
"D" Coy	FOVO		

TELEGRAM.

Urgent
operations
Priority

	Words
	Sent
	At..................
	By..................
	To..................

BUMA	RORU	5th Corps.	15 Sqn.R.A.F.
BURA	JEKU	5th Corps. R.A.	Div.Cyclist Coy.
RUVE	JEMU	17th Div.	Div.Cav.Troop
WUMA	FOLO	42nd Div.	
JENU	A/Q	38th Div.	

/ 31 / AAA

JEZU Order No.220 AAA Confirming verbal instructions AAA RUVE will capture BEAULENCOURT tonight AAA Infantry forming up line N.10. central. N.11.b.2.9. AAA 18 pdr. barrage will come down on line N.16.b.9.6. N.11.b.8.0. at 2 a.m. AAA Barrage will lift at 2.20.a.m. by which time Infantry will be closed up to it AAA Inf.objective N.23.b.4.8. to N.18.central. AAA Arty barrage will move at rate of 100 yards in six minutes until 300 yards beyond objective where it will halt for 12 minutes and then cease AAA Heavy Arty will barrage 500 yards ahead of 18 pdrs. and will also engage high ground O.13.c. O.19.a. and c. between Zero plus 30 and Zero plus 140 AAA 42 Div.Arty will be bombarding area N.12.a. and d. and N.E.portion of N.18.b. from Zero to Zero plus 140 AAA The O.C.Machine Gun Battn will arrange M.G.barrages with all available guns to co-ordinate with artillery barrage AAA RUVE will carry out a second attack in conjunction with 17th Div.AAA 17th Div are attacking LE TRANSLOY AAA Zero hour for 17 Div is 5.40.a.m. AAA RUVE will capture Sugar Factory N.24.central AAA Forming up line for Infantry N.23.a.5.0. to N.23.a.7.6. AAA From 5.40 a.m. to 6.20.a.m. artillery will put smoke barrage on line N.24.c.0.8. to N.24.a.1.6. AAA At 6.20.a.m. artillery will put shrapnel barrage on same line at which hour leading Infantry will be closed up to it AAA Barrage lifts at 6.24.a.m. and advance at rate of 100 yards in 4 minutes until it reaches line N.24.d.8.6. to N.24.b.9.4. where it forms protective barrage for 8 minutes and then stops AAA 4.5" Hows and 18 pdrs. will bombard SUGAR FACTORY from 5.40a.m. to 6.40a.m. AAA On conclusion of both operations RUVE will consolidate and hold line SUGAR FACTORY inclusive (joining with 17th Division) East of BEAULENCOURT and joining 42ndDiv at Southern end of REINCOURT AAA BURA will take over positions vacated by RUVE as already ordered AAA Contact aeroplane will call for flares at daylight and subsequently at odd hours 7.a.m. 9 a.m. etc. AAA ACKNOWLEDGE AAA Addsd. All recipients JEZU Order No.210

JEZU

9.p.m.

A.F.MACDOUGALL.
Major,
for. Lieut-Col. G.S.

Certified True Copy

ADJUTANT,
21st BN. MACHINE GUN CORPS.

MESSAGES AND SIGNALS.

Urgent operations

21 Div.   10.20p.m.   5.45.a.m.

To:-   21 M.G. Battn.

/   29   /   AAA

21Div. Order No.219 AAA The enemy are holding REINCOURT BEAULENCOURT le TRANSLOY MORVAL aaa N.Z.Div. have taken BAPUME and are astride Bapume - Peronne Road AAA 42 Div are in N.4.c. and 10.a. AAA 17th Div hold high ground N.35 N.28.N.22.AAA All available arty will bombard BEAULENCOURT until 2a.m. Aug 30 when 110 Bde will send forward fighting patrols to ascertain situation as regards the village and occupying if found empty AAA 110 Bde will endeavour to resume advance till 4th objective early tomorrow Aug 30th when 4th objective taken 110 Bde will remain in position until further orders sending forward of 1 coy and 1 section of M.Gs to LABDA COPSE to form flank defence facing N.AAA After crossing Bapume Peronne Road 17th and 38th Divs only will follow up retreating enemy leaving LABDA COPSE on their left and 21 Div will come into Corps reserve about LE TRANSLOY AAA 64 Bde and 62 Bde will remain in present positions until further orders AAA 64 Bde will be ready to occupy YELLOW CUT positions, at short notice AAA Cyclist Coy and troop Div.Cav.remain under orders of 110 bde AAA DIV.H.Q. closes GRANDCOURT 12 noon and opens same hour in bank M.9.c.8.AAA
ACKNOWLEDGE.

21St.Div.
10.20.p.m.

Certified True Copy
J Hamilton Capt

ADJUTANT,
21st BN. MACHINE GUN CORPS.

APPENDIX "B".

MEDICAL ARRANGEMENTS.

1. LOCATION OF MEDICAL POSTS.

	Right Bde.	Centre Bde.	Left Bde.
(a) Front Regtl. Aid Posts.	Q.28.c.6.7.	Q.16.c.8.2.	Q.8.b.5.1.
(b) Support " " "	Q.26.b.4.7.	Q.8.c.0.5.	Q.2 Central.

   At each of these places is a Medical Officer with Orderly, Bearers, Stretchers etc.

(c) Bearer Posts.	Q.21.c.3.9.	Q.15.c.2.8.	Q.8.b.5.0.
	Q.28.c.6.7.	Q.14.c.1.8.	Q.2.c.3.2.

   R.A.M.C. Bearers with stretchers are situated at these places, and carry stretcher cases or assist walking wounded when necessary to the next Post in rear or from next Post in front. They are under the orders of the Bearer Officer.

   (d) Collecting Posts.   ENGLEBELMER P.11.b.3.4.
                            (Q.25.a.5.9)

   This is where the walking wounded cases are collected. From this they are marched down, or carried by transport, to the Corps Walking Wounded Dressing Station (i) or other field hospital.

   (e) & (f). Advanced Dressing Stations. ENGLEBELMER, Q.25.a.5.9.
                                          MAILLY MAILLET, P.12.d.6.6.
   There is one Medical Officer or more with R.A.M.C. Staff at each of these places. Cases are evacuated by Motor Ambulances from these places to (g) Main Dressing Station at ACHEUX, P.13.a.4.3.

   (h) Corps Gas Centre & Walking Wounded Collecting Post.

   All gassed cases should be sent here - CLAIRFAYE, O.29.b.6.5., either direct, with cases of slight wounds, or through a Regimental Aid Post or Advanced Dressing Station.

   (i) Corps Walking Wounded Dressing Station.

   Slight cases able to walk go to above (CLAIRFAYE), or to this, N.18.d Central. Sign boards at intervals and sentries will indicate the route.

2. In the event of the Advanced Dressing Station and Collecting Posts becoming untenable due to alteration in the Front System, the Advanced Dressing Station for the Centre and Left Brigades will fall back on BEAUSSART or ACHEUX. The A.D.S. for the Right Brigade will similarly fall back on HEDAUVILLE or FORCEVILLE.

---oOo---

21 Bn MG Corps
US 7
September
1918

On His Majesty's Service

The Officer i/c,
A.G's Office,
The Base.

War Diary
1.7.18

WAR DIARY / INTELLIGENCE SUMMARY

Army Form C. 2118.

September 21st Bn M.G. Corps 1918

Place	Date	Hour	Summary of Events and Information	Remarks and references to Appendices
YPRES	12th	9.20 AM	A Coy report Barrage put down by 16 guns in conjunction with 21st Div Attack 220 successful and lots of Enemy casualties caused	
		9 PM	21st Div Order No. 221 Received	
		10 PM	A Coy O.O. 22 received	
		10.15 PM	9 guns of A Coy attached 110th 2nd Bde at N15.d.2.6. — B Coy Staff 4 Vickers & M12.a.5 — C Coy Staff	
			62nd Inf Bde. HQ at Quarry M.15.a.99. — 3 guns Div Reserve 64 BO at Bussy NK1.72.	
			Casualties 1 O.R Wounded. — Course Major JR Hastings to be proceeded UK & Chad Camera	
	2nd Sept	9.30 AM	B Coy in attack — Rest under Lieut JA Kirkham M.C. at I.4 B.D.A Copse in O.B.C with 1st E.Yorks — Running Rt to Lt	
			on line of Raintree N10.c.31. to N22.c.04. — 6 of 4 Qt at N.16.a.32. & 1 Sub.	
		10 AM	A Coy in sepn history explained — M.G. Barrage — consisting with the successfully carried out —	
		12.5 PM	C Coy HQ at N27.d.0.0. attached 62nd Inf Bde.	
		10.30 PM	Div Order No 223 Received. — Div in Corps Reserve.	
		10.30 PM	When 9 x 765 received	
			Casualties 1 O.R Wounded.	

WAR DIARY September 1918 21.B. R.G.6/3.

Sheet 2

Army Form C. 2118.

Place	Date	Hour	Summary of Events and Information	Remarks and references to Appendices
LE SARS	3		Div in Corps Reserve. — Quiet day — Cleaning firearms etc — Lieut L.J. Southard and Lieut E.C. Plath returned from Cameiro	
M.15.A.Central		10.25 pm	Div Order No 223 Received — General Left WEIBERT M.C. returned from Leave — 2nd Lt. J.R. Evans and Capt J. Boswell and 26 O.R. Ranks joined	Copy attached
—	4		Div in Corps Reserve — Quiet day	Copy attached
—	—	7.45 pm	Div Order No 224 Received	
—	—	9 am	Situation of Div — A Coy attached 110th Inf Bde at TULLEN H&F FARM N.13.d.9.9. — 3 Sects in Lewis Posn. 1 Sect N.7.6.5.4.	
—	—		C Coy attached 63rd Inf Bde — Coy HQ Fabechere N.27.c.t.d — 3 Sects in Div Reserve at Quarry M.15.a.	
—	—		B Coy attached 14th Inf Bde — Coy HQ destroches N.9.c.2.3. 3rd section N.8.a.3.5.	
—	—	12 noon	62 Inf Bde and C Coy moved to O.21.c.20 near GUEDECOURT	
			Casualties	
	5	8.30 am	Also O. Order No 115 and Adden: Pack Rd Issued	
MORVAL	—	2 pm	Adv Bn HQ closed at M.15.a and opened at T.10.6.09. — Transpt. Lines moved to ECCAREE	
—	—		D Coy in Div Reserve moved to MORVAL P.11.c.5.7 — A Coy moved with 110th Inf Bde to HQ U.14.a.3.5 — C Coy moved with 63rd Inf Bde to HQ U.11.c.16. — B Coy moved with 64 Inf Bde to HQ U.8.a.2.H.	
—	—	7 pm	War Gx 935 received	
—	—	7.10 pm	Div Order 225 received	
—	5/6		21st Div relieved 38th Div in front line — Approx ETRICOURT — MAMANCOURT	

WAR DIARY Sept 21st Bn L.G.C.

Army Form C. 2118.

Sheet - 3

or

INTELLIGENCE SUMMARY.

(Erase heading not required.)

Place	Date	Hour	Summary of Events and Information	Remarks and references to Appendices
MORVAL T.b.O.9.	6	10AM	B'ly was - log HQrs at X Rds V.14.b.4.	1/H C/L
	-	5.30PM	Wire G.X.87a received S.H - German Boot was found in a coal dump at BAZAUME but might near the coal	V/H C/L
	-		dump to left by enemy may contain a Bomb.	1/HQ C/L
	-	8PM	Div Order 226 received	Bu extra toi 1/HQ C/L
	-	9.15PM	Wire V.S.89 received to D'Coy	647 extra toi 1/HQ C/L
	-	11.10PM	C'Coy wire - attached 62 Inf Bde by HQrs V.10.d.10. (that is V.g.SW) all positions in STRASBOURG TRENCH V.7 c and	V/H C/L
	-		V.13 t - to the N. of but 2' Lincoln Reg - 2n the W. of but 2' Lancaster to 3 others Bn. Reserve	1/HQ C/L
	-	Casualties nil - Decease 1.O.R. to Base unfit adventures Service 1 O.R. joined from Base	1 HRpt 7 1/H C/L
	7th	9.45AM	Liu Wire 9.X.89h received	Cpy Note 12 H Coys
	-	10AM	Wire V.R. 32.fact to 3 Coys	
	-	10.30PM	Reserve Bn. HQrs: 146y Reserve HQ: moved from ZEPARS to MORVAL S.A.T.H. SHOWER ROAD T.13.a.5.2.	V/H C/L
	-	12.noon	Reserve Post established at V.14.c.2.h X Rds	1/HQ C/L V/H C/L
	-	1PM	Adjt Bn HQrs cloud at T.10.b.0.9. and opened at Sunken Road V.10.d.7.6.	V/HQ C/L
Sunken Road V.10.d.7.6.	-	6PM	D by. was log HQ V.17.a.0.2. - B Coy V.9.d.30.15. - C'Coy V.17.d.90.50. - A Coy V.8.a.27.	1st C/L Cpy note 12 H Coys
	-	9.15PM	L/U Order No 227 Received	
	-		Casualties 1.O.R wounded - 2.O.R's wounded Sick - Cpt A.L. Harvey to G.H.Q. Army School Camera probation -	V/H C/L

WAR DIARY September 1918 21st Bn R of Fus.
INTELLIGENCE SUMMARY.

Army Form C. 2118.

Sheet 4

Place	Date	Hour	Summary of Events and Information	Remarks and references to Appendices
Sumlin R.A.	8-	9 A.M.	Rear Bn HQ and Coy Rear HQ moved from MIRVA - SAILLY Road to V.3.C.20.30.	1/Lt J.P.R.P.—
V.10.d.76.	-		Position of Coys as shown — Quiet day —	1/Lt J.P. C/R.
MESNIL	-	8 P.M.	War Bn HQ moved from Sunken Road to Mesnil V.4.b.9.0.	1/Lt J.P. C/R. Coy. Cdrs. 1/Lt J.P. C/R.
-	-	11 P.M.	S.10 Order No. 228 received.	1/Lt J.P.—
-	9-	9 A.M.	Bg shew Coy HQs at V.10.A.4.2 — all Coys in chags — hugs Bothwick met round walking forward	3/Lt J.P.— 1/Lt J.P. C/R.
-	-	4 P.M.	S.10 Order No. 229 Received.	1/Lt J.P. C/R.
-	-		Casualties — 10. O.R. Wounded — 2. O.R. Sounds Self — Lieut G.Col Hilary Ithugar MC Howard MC went ahead	1/Lt J.P. C/R.
-	10-	8 A.M.	Position of Coys A Coy with 110. Inf Bde in towed over B HQ Escolaries V.12.c.14 — B Coy with 64 Inf Bde in	1/Lt J.P. C/R.
-	-		Div Reff — Coy HQ at ENQUANTECOURT V.10.a.27. — C Coy with 62. Inf Bde in Div Re. at ETRICOURT	1/Lt J.P. C/R.
-	-		Coy HQ V.7.d.32. — D Coy Hdle forward Bn HQ V.10 — Bn HQs at V.12.C.17	1/Lt J.P. C/R.
-	-	11.20 A.M.	Wire from 9x 963 received	1/Lt J.P. C/R.
-	-	3. P.M.	Operation Order No. 16 Bn issued.	1/Lt J.P. C/R.
-	-	8 P.M.	Div Order No. 230 received	1/Lt J.P. C/R.
-	-	10.40 P.M.	Wire 9x 987 Received	1/Lt J.P. C/R.
-	-		Casualties 2/Lt H. Fairhurst B.C. Wounded — 1.O.R. Wounded for —30 R. Wounded — 5. O.R. Sounds Self etc.	1/Lt J.P. C/R.
-	-		Officers to Bn Lts. T.J. Bush. — H.E. Cobb. — J.L. Harmer — 2/Lts ASTRUTRAM. — W. FAULKNER — E.R. HARRIS M.C. — M.M. Jones	1/Lt J.P. C/R.

WAR DIARY or INTELLIGENCE SUMMARY

Army Form C. 2118.

Sheet 5 Sept 1918. 2/1 Bn. L.C. Cp.

Place	Date	Hour	Summary of Events and Information	Remarks and references to Appendices
MESNIL	11th	8 A/M	Quiet night - No change in line.	
—	—	3 P.M	Memo C. 9/5 received	
—	—	3.37pm	A Cy sent 2 patrols to front on L. edge of GENIN WELL COPSE - No other information of Bosh movements in their sector.	
—	—	—	with instructions at W.23.d.4.1 - No 3 on South Road W.B.6. road to Mesnil at Sunk rd at W.17.d.9.5 that M.G.	
—	—	—	Posts are Bde Reserve about BHQ - Coy HQ. W.17.b.6.2.	
—	—	8.20pm	Memo A.K/108/10 received.	
—	—	—	2. Lieut T.O. WATTS - 2 Lieut D. MANN M.C. wounded Capt W.H. SIMPSON went on leave	
—	—	—	Casualties 7 O.R.'s wounded - 10 O.R missing - 5 O.R wounded (at duty) 3 drowned	
—	12th	8 A/M	Coy relieved. A Cy with 110" Inf Bd # by 1/4th V.13.62 2nmds Bn - B/y with 6/2 Bn 2/y at V.14 Znmds Inf	
—	—	—	B/y with ? - C/y attached 1/62 2/y Bde at ETRICOURT - Du Riseun - 2/6 attd 2 wounded D.	
—	—	9 P.M	Lys Battn sent 2/10 Front Line	
—	—	12.30 P.M	Memo A.K/108/13 received	
—	—	—	Casualties 3 O.R.'s wounded - Lieut A.A.T. SEARLE rejoined from leave decrease PO Eggs	
—	13	7pm	Derations Order No 47 issued — Marshall to Erockbarn	
—	—	8pm	A Company carried out harassing fire on CHAPPEL CROSSING, TRACK No. b.50 + SUNKEN ROAD W.5d.	
—	—	—	Casualties 2 O.R. killed 4 O.R wounded, 3 O.R wounded (gas) Increase 33 O.R. joined from base	
—	14th	10 am	Major Bathurst and Brand Liaison and objectmt passage...	

Sheet. 6.

September, 1918. 21st Battⁿ M. Gun Corps Army Form C. 2118.

WAR DIARY
INTELLIGENCE SUMMARY

Place	Date	Hour	Summary of Events and Information	Remarks and references to Appendices
MESNIL	14	6am	Enemy attempted raid on trench South of CHAPEL HILL; 2 guns had good targets	At front
"	"	6pm	Enemy planes very busy	"
"	"		Casualties — 1 O.R. wounded (gas) 4 O.Rs evacuated	"
"	15		Harassing fire carried out at intervals during day & night	"
"	"	4pm	21st Divisional Special orders received	Copy attached
"	"	4.30pm	21st Divisional order No. 231 received	Copy attached
"	"		Casualties 3 O.Rs killed 2 O.R wounded	"
"	16	2am	Ammunition dump bombed at W23a & W16d 9.2	"
"	"	9.30am	Major Borthwick attended Divisional conference	"
"	"		Harassing fire carried out at intervals during day & night	"
"	"	3pm	21st Div order No. 233 received	Copy attached
"	"	4.30pm	Remaining order No. 44 received	Copy attached
"	"	6pm	Order No. AX/565/0 received	Copy attached
"	"		Casualties — 2 O.R. wounded.	
"	17	9am	Order No. AX/581/0 received	Copy attached
"	"	10am	Order No. AX/592/0 received	Copy attached
"	"	11am	Order No. AX/579/0 received	Copy attached
"	"	3pm	Order No. AX/59t/0 received	Copy attached

Sheet 7

WAR DIARY
or
INTELLIGENCE SUMMARY

Army Form C. 2118.

September 1918
21st Batt. M. Gun Corps

Place	Date	Hour	Summary of Events and Information	Remarks and references to Appendices
MESNIL	17	4am	Order N°AX/588/0 received	Copy attached Ap. Sheet
		4am	Heads to Walker returned from musketry course. Heads to Barbough reported from leave	Ap Sheet
		7am	Order N°AX/589/0 received	Copy attached Ap Sheet
			21st Div. G 301 received	Ap Sheet
		10am	Cpl Walker L.O.R. wounded	
		11am	21st Div. G. 217 received	Ap Sheet
		1pm	A.M.G.O, bn H.G.O, hold conference at B.H.Q	Copy attached Ap Sheet
		4.30pm	21st Div G.17 received	Ap Sheet
	18	9am	Div order N° 23t received	Ap Sheet
			2nd Lieut E.L Steele killed — Lieut R.H Shaman Heads to Backwick wounded. In Heads to McHugh — D McHugh	
		3.0R	Killed 21 O.R wounded 4 O.R missing	Copy attached Ap Sheet
		2.0R	wounded at duty	
		15am	10 bendigoes N°19 received	Copy attached Ap Sheet
			Lieut V.T Sanderson went on leave	
		11.50am	O.O. 49 cancelled	Copy attached
	19	4pm	21st Div order N°235 received	Ap Sheet
		5.0	10 Div order N°50 received	Ap Sheet

Sheet 8

WAR DIARY
or
INTELLIGENCE SUMMARY

September 1918
2nd M. Gun Batt.

Army Form C. 2118.

Place	Date	Hour	Summary of Events and Information	Remarks and references to Appendices
MESNIL	19	6 a.m.	Order AX/62/10 received	Copy attached
"	"	6 p.m.	Special order G.30 received	"
"	"	"	Casualties 2 O.R. killed 30 O.R. wounded	
"	20	8 a.m.	"A" & "B" Companies withdrawn to "M"S.P.L.	
"	"		C & D Companies heavy barrage & aerial attack made by 33rd Div	
"	"		Casualties NIL	
"	"		Lieut. G.W. Sayliss A.A.& S sent to Hqrs to East Q	
"	"	2.0 P.M.	Evacuated Camels	Copy attached
"	20	Mid-day	36 Div Special orders received	"
"	21	11 am	Attended a Conference at DOULLENS	
			Major Nurring returned from M.G. School	
"	"	8 am	C & D Companies withdrawn to MESNIL	
"	"		Capt. A.J. Pack Lieut J.W. Bennett & Lieut W. Walker joined from Base also 23 ORs	
"	"		1 O.R. evacuated	
"	22		Lieut J.S. Reypeth (India Office) to interview	
"	23		All companies out of the line	
"	"		Lieut A.S. Whickam admitted to hospital	
"	"		Lieut E.D. West & A.S. Bodie joined from Base	
"	"		Companies busy with general organization	
"	24	5 pm	21st Division Order No. 236 received	Copy attached
"	25	11 am	Order G.306 received	"

Sheet 9.

Army Form C. 2118.

WAR DIARY or INTELLIGENCE SUMMARY

September 1918 21st M. Gun Batt"

(Erase heading not required.)

Instructions regarding War Diaries and Intelligence Summaries are contained in F. S. Regs., Part II. and the Staff Manual respectively. Title pages will be prepared in manuscript.

Place	Date	Hour	Summary of Events and Information	Remarks and references to Appendices
MESNIL	21st	9am	Operation order No. 61 issued	Copy attached
—	—	11am	21st Div. G.418 received	II
—	—	—	All coys continue training for the line	
—	—	—	Major Cuth. Howard M.C. returned from leave. 23 O.R.'s joined from Base	
—	23rd	—	Lieut. C.R. Macan M.C. proceeded on leave. 1 O.R. evacuated	
—	25th	10am	Conference — Coy Commanders at Battn Orderly Room.	
—	—	12:30pm	All Companies move forward	
—	—	—	Casualties 3 O.R.'s wounded	
—	26th	—	2nd Lieut. B.W. Kay returned from leave. 1 O.R. evacuated to Reinforcement Camp	Copy attached
—	—	10am	21st Div. Order No. 237 received	II
—	—	11am	Forty of S. Batt. 67 received	
—	—	6pm	Operation order No. 52 issued	
—	27th	10am	Batt. H.Q. moved to V36 — Sheet 57c S.E.	
—	—	11am	21st Div. G.498 received	
—	—	—	Casualties 20 O.R.'s killed 9 O.R.'s wounded. 1 O.R. missing	
—	—	—	Capt. W.M. Simpson returned from leave	

Sheet 19

WAR DIARY / INTELLIGENCE SUMMARY

September 1918 21st M. Gun Batt'n

Army Form C. 2118.

Place	Date	Hour	Summary of Events and Information	Remarks and references to Appendices
Inno	28th	11.55am	G.X 5157 received	
—	—	6.35am	G.X 5176	
—	—	6.35am	Enemy counter attacked 6 Company report 3 guns destroyed by shell fire & one captured	
—	—	1.30pm	Adm order No. 238 received	Copy attached
—	29th		Company working with Infantry Brigade. D Company to Div reserve	
—	—	11am	21st Divisions order No. 129 received	Copy attached
—	—		Casualties: Major R.P. Godfrey wounded. 11 O.Rs wounded. gas	
—	—		Feb H.D. St Rich ME Scott N.3 Scotland 1 OR — gas (Al duty)	
—	30th	3.15am	To India Office and will go to A.G. Shrapnel Hospital 18th picgh	
—	—	3.15am	M. Gun Batt" HQ moved to B33d Central 2.4.6.5.7.9.8.6	
—	—	10am	Enemy not met, to leave of Canal, one patrol told M.G. Company advanced	
—	1st	12.30pm	L/Cpl C. McKerron granted 7 days leave to PARIS	
—	1st	1.15pm	21st Div order No. 240 received	Copy attached
—	1st	7.31pm	21st Div order No. 241	
—	1st	9am	21st Div G. 5/67 received	

Copy No.7.

"A"Coy. O.Order 22.

Ref.Map 1.20,000
    57c S.W.

1. In connection with operations of flank formations JONE will capture SUGAR FACTORY N.24. tomorrow morning. Zero hour will be 2 a.m.

2. Action of M.Gs.
Nos.1 and 4 Sections and 1 Section of "B" Coy will barrage as follows.
   (a) Annihilating barrage on SUGAR FACTORY and road for 2oo yds W of it from Zero to Zero plus 10.
   (b) Creeping barrage in slopes of hill O.19.a. and N.24.c. from Zero plus 12 to Zero plus 40.

In addition No.3 Section will carry out slow harassing fire on LE TRANSLOY from Zero plus 10 to Zero plus 40.
no firing is to be carried out S.W. of a line drawn S.E. & N.W. through N.30 central.

3. When the SUGAR FACTORY is captured LOFO will probably occupy to line of the road between BEAULENCOURT and SUGAR FACTORY. O.C. No.3 Section will liaison with O.C. LOFO regarding consolidation of this line at the direction of O.C. LOFO.

4. ACKNOWLEDGE.

1.9.18
                                 R.T.ASSHETON.
                                    Major
                     Commanding "A"Coy 21st.M.G.C.

Copies to:-

1	No.1Section	5......	110th.Inf.Bde.
2	" 2 "	6......	JOKE
3	" 3 "	7......	21stM.G.C.
4	" 4 "	8......	"B"Coy.M.G.C.
		9......	FILE

CERTIFIED TRUE COPY.

Capt. & Adjt.
21st.Battalion Machine Gun Corps.

TELEGRAM.

	Words	
URGENT OPERATIONS PRIORITY.	Sent At.................m To................. By.................	

BUMA	RORU	5th Corps.	15th Sqn.R.A.F.
BURA	JEKU	5th Corps R.A.	Div.Cyclist Coy.
RUVE	JEMU	17th Div.	Div.Cav.Troop.
WUMA	FOLO	42nd Div.	
JENU	A/Q	38th Div.	

/ 1st / AAA

JEZU Order No.221. AAA The 4th and 5th Corps are carrying out a series of operations tomorrow September 2nd AAA In conformity with verbal instructions already given AAA RUVE will capture SUGAR FACTORY N.24.Central AAA At 2 a.m. Artillery Barrage will come down on line N.24.a.1.7. to N.18.d.1.3. and will lift at 2.12 a.m. AAA Barrage will move at rate of 100 yards in 4 minutes until line N.24.d.0.1. to 0.19.c.0.6. is reached where it will form protector for 8 minutes and then cease AAA After capture of SUGAR FACTORY RUVE will push force not to exceed one Company to about 0.19.d. Central with object of preventing withdrawal of garrison of LE TRANSLOY AAA In conjunction with main attack to be delivered later in morning BURA will capture LOBDA COPSE AAA 17th. Div will be attacking ROCQUIGNY crossing Main Road just SE.of LE TRANSLOY at 6.15 a.m. AAA 42nd. Division will attack VILLERS AU FLOS and pushing on towards BARASTRE with Zero hour 5.15.a.m. AAA Artillery barrage for BURAS attack will come down on the line N.18.d.2.0. to N.18.b.2.6. at 5.15 a.m. AAA Barrage will lift at 5.18 a.m. and move at rate of 100 yds in 3 minutes until line 0.19.b.0.5. 0.13.d.5.0. 0.13.d.6.9. is reached, where it will form a protector for 9 minutes and then cease. AAA After capture of LABDA COPSE BURA will effect junction with 42nd Div. at Cross Roads 0.13.a.2.4. AAA When 42nd Div. move forward to their 2nd objective BURA will establish post at 0.13.b.4.0 and will send patrol to get in touch with 42nd Div at 0.13.b.9.1. AAA BURA will also establish line from LABDA COPSE to SUGAR FACTORY and get in touch with RUVES force in 0.19.d. Central. AAA O.C. M.G. Battn will arrange M.G. barrages to co-ordinate with Artillery Barrages AAA Artillery arrangements other than detailed above will appear in Artillery Orders AAA Contact Aeroplane will call for flares at daylight and subsequently at odd hours 7 a.m. 9 a.m. etc. AAA ACKNOWLEDGE AAA Addsd. Recipients JEZU Order No.220.

JEZU

8.15 p.m.

H.C.FRANKLYN
Lieut-Col. G.S.

CERTIFIED TRUE COPY

Capt. & Adjt.
21st Battalion Machine Gun Corps.

TELEGRAM.

		Words	
URGENT			
OPERATIONS		Sent	
PRIORITY		At....................m	
		By....................	
		To....................	

BUMA	RORU	5th Corps	15th Sqn.R.A.F.
BURA	JEKU	5th Corps R.A.	Div.Cyclist Coy.
RUVE	JEMU	17th Div.	Div.Cav.Troop
WUMA	FOLO	42nd Div.	
JENU	A/Q	38th Div.	

/ 2nd / AAA

JEZU Order No.222 AAA 17 Div are holding general line O.32.central. O.19.b. and d. central. LABDA COPSE AAA 42 Div. are holding line O.13.b.3.1. thence Eastern-Ridge of VILLERS-AU-FLOS to high ground in O.8.central AAA These Divisions will be advancing in ROCQUIGNY and BARASTRE tonight or tomorrow morning AAA JEZU comes into Corps Reserve AAA RUVE will relieve forward Bn. of BURA to-night September 2nd/3rd AAA RUVE will then hold SUGAR FACTORY and LABDA COPSE maintaining touch with 42 Div. at O.13.b.3.1. AAA RUVE will also garrison defences of BEAULENCOURT AAA RUVE will maintain at least 1 Bn. in Bde. Reserve in valler West of main BAPUME - PERONNE Road AAA BURA including HOWI will be prepared to hold general line N.22.central. N.10.central. AAA Bde. will be disposed between this line and LUISENHOF FARM Road AAA BUMA will move to area near LES BOEUFS this evening AAA One M.G.Coy will remain affiliated to each Bde. AAA R.E. Pioneers etc. will remain in present accommodation AAA Further orders will be issued as regards Div.Arty.AAA Completion of movements and reliefs will be reported by wire to JEZU H.Q. AAA Acknowledge AAA Addsd recipients JEZU Order No.221.

JEZU

6.15.p.m.

H.C.FRANKLYN.
Lt.-Col. G.S.

Certified True Copy
/Hamilton Capt
ADJUTANT.
21st BN. MACHINE GUN CORPS.

TELEGRAM.

21st M.G.Battn.

GX.765   2   aaa

The following from General SHUTE 5th Corps begins aaa My warmest congratulations to you on your operations of the last few days aaa Please convey my appreciation and thanks to all under your command for the rapid and thorough manner in which they carried out the many and difficult tasks assigned to them aaa The great results obtained by the Division were due to the skill of the Commander and the dash of the men aaa Ends

21st Division.   (Sgd) H.F.McDOUGALL, Major,
                                            General Staff.
7.40 p.m.

Certified True Copy
V. F. Sammlin Capt. ADJUTANT,
21st BN. MACHINE GUN CORPS.

TELEGRAM.

```
URGENT            :     Words     :
OPERATIONS        : ---------------:
PRIORITY          :     Sent      :
                  : At..............m:
                  : By.............. :
                  L To.............. :
```

BUMA	RORU	5th Corps	15th Sqn.R.A.F.
BURA	JEKU	5th Corps R.A.	Div.Cav.Troops.
RUVE	JEMU	17th Div.	Div.Cyclist Coy.
WUMA	FOLO	42nd Div.	
JENU	A/Q	38th Div.	

/   3rd   /   AAA

JEZU Order No.223 AAA General line reached by our troops is Eastern edge of VAUX WOODS to Railway West of YTRES AAA Probably enemy line of resistance is CANAL de L'ESCAUT to BANTEUX and HINDENBURGH Line AAA Corps will continue the advance tomorrow to the general line W.22.Central - Q.32.d. AAA JEZU will remain in Corps Reserve AAA BUMA Group will move to area about O.20 and O.21 tomorrow 4th inst. so as to clear LE TRANSLOY by 10 a.m. AAA BUMA will establish observation posts in the Trench System East of ROCQUIGNY as soon as vacated by 17th Div and will be prepared to hold this line between O.35.c.0.0. and O.16.c.0.0. in case of necessity AAA Following distances will be maintained on line of march AAA 200 yds between Coys and 500 yards between Battns. AAA BUMA will notify JEZU position of new H.Q. as soon as possible tomorrow AAA RUVE and BURA will probably not move but BURA will be ready to move at one hours notice AAA Div.Cav. and Div.Cyclists will remain in present positions ready to move at one hour's notice AAA 'Q' will issue orders for move of BUMAS Transport AAA Acknowledge AA Addsd recipients JEZU Order No.222

JEZU

10.25 p.m.

                                  A.F.MACDOUGALL
                                            Major
                                for Lt.Colonel.G.S.

CERTIFIED TRUE COPY.

[signature]

                                        Capt. & Adjt.
                   21st Battalion Machine Gun Corps.

TELEGRAM.

	Words	
PRIORITY	Sent	
	At....................m	
	By....................	
	To....................	

BUMA	RORU	5th Corps.
BURA	JEKU	5th Corps. R.A.
RUVE	JEMU	17 Div.
WUMA	FOLO	38 Div.
JENU	A/Q	15 Sqn.R.A.F.

/ 4 / AAA

JEZU Order No.224.AAA 38th Div and 17th Div are reported at 7 p.m.
to have troops across CANAL DU NORD but not yet across
EQUANCOURT Trench System AAA JEZU will relieve 38th Div tomorrow
Sept 5th AAA BUMA Group will relieve advanced guard Brigade
Group 38th Div.AAA BURA will relieve supporting Brigade and RUVE
reserve Brigade AAA BUMA will keep in touch with situation of
leading Brigade tomorrow AAA If advance during Sept.5th is carried
across NURLU - FINS Road BUMA will move to vicinity of
CANAL DU NORD during afternoon AAA BURA Group will move tomorrow
morning to reach West of SAILLY SAILLISEL by 1.p.m. and have
dinners there AAA Any orders for BURA will be sent to BUMA H.Q.
O.31.b.3.3. after 11 a.m. AAA RUVE Group will be prepared to move
at one hour's notice after 9 a.m. AAA Distances for Infantry on
the march 500 yards between Battalions and 200 yards between
Coys AAA Div.Cav. and Cyclists and two sections GILE have been
ordered to report BUMAS H.Q tomorrow morning and will come under
BUMAS Orders AAA 21Div.Arty reverts to JEZU AAA Orders for move of
Units not mentioned above will be issued later AAA Div.H.Q.closes
LE SARS 2.30.p.m. and opens LES BOEUFS same hour AAA Acknowledge
AAA ADDSd all concerned.

JEZU

7.45 p.m.

Certified True Copy
J Hamilton Capt
ADJUTANT,
21st BN. MACHINE GUN CORPS.

H.C.FRANKLYN
Lt.Col.G.S.

Copy No. 15   S E C R E T.

21st. Bn. M.G.C. OPERATION ORDER No. 45.

Ref. Maps:
57.c.S.W. 1/20,000.
57.c.S.E. 1/20,000.   5th. Sept. 1918.
----

1.   The 21st. Division will relieve the 38th. Division today, 5th. September.

2.   "C" Coy. 21 Bn.M.G.C. will remain attached to 62 Inf.Bde.
       "B" Coy.   "   "   "   "   64   "
       "A" Coy.   "   "   "   "   110   "
       "D" Coy.   "   will remain in Divisional Reserve and will move with Battn.H.Q's.

3.   Battalion Headquarters will close at LE SARS at 2. 0 p.m. and open at Divl.H.Q's. same hour until exact location of new Battn.H.Q's. is known.

4.   Companies Forward will wire Battalion Headquarters exact location of their new Company Headquarters as soon as possible.

5.   Administrative Instruction No. 1 is issued with this Order.

6.   A C K N O W L E D G E.

                                        V. F. Saunders
                                        Capt. & Adjt.
                                   21st. Battn. Machine Gun Corps.

Issued to:

Copy No. 1 .. O.C. "A" Coy. (Fwd).
          2 .. "   "B" Coy.   "
          3 .. "   "C" Coy.   "
          4 .. "   "D" Coy.   "
          5 .. "   "A" Coy. (Rear).
          6 .. "   "B" Coy.   "
          7 .. "   "C" Coy.   "
          8 .. "   "D" Coy.   "
          9 .. "   H.Q8s. Coy.
         10 .. Commanding Officer.
         11 .. Quartermaster.
         12 .. Signalling Officer.
         13 .. 21st. Div. 'G'.
         14 .. File.
      15/16 .. War Diary.

Copy No. 16.   S E C R E T.

21st. Bn. M.G.C. OPERATION ORDER No. 45.

Ref. Maps:
 57.c.S.W. 1/20,000.
 57.c.S.E. 1/20,000.   5th. Sept. 1918.
----

1. The 21st. Division will relieve the 38th. Division today, 5th. September.

2. "C" Coy. 21 Bn.M.G.C. will remain attached to 62 Inf.Bde.
   "B" Coy.   "   "   "   "   64   "
   "A" Coy.   "   "   "   "   110   "
   "D" Coy.   "   will remain in Divisional Reserve and will move with Battn.H.Q's.

3. Battalion Headquarters will close at LE SARS at 2. 0 p.m. and open at Divl.H.Q's. same hour until exact location of new Battn.H.Q's. is known.

4. Companies Forward will wire Battalion Headquarters exact location of their new Company Headquarters as soon as possible.

5. Administrative Instruction No. 1 is issued with this Order.

6.   A C K N O W L E D G E.

                                                    [signature]
                                                    Capt. & Adjt.
Issued to: 21st. Battn. Machine Gun Corps.

Copy No. 1 .. O.C. "A" Coy. (Fwd).
         2 .. "   "B" Coy.   "
         3 .. "   "C" Coy.   "
         4 .. "   "D" Coy.   "
         5 .. "   "A" Coy. (Rear).
         6 .. "   "B" Coy.   "
         7 .. "   "C" Coy.   "
         8 .. "   "D" Coy.
         9 .. "   H.Qs. Coy.
        10 .. Commanding Officer.
        11 .. Quartermaster.
        12 .. Signalling Officer.
        13 .. 21st. Div. 'G'.
        14 .. File.
     15/16 .. War Diary.

MESSAGES AND SIGNALS.

JEZU

Recd at 7.30 p.m.
5.9.18
21st Div.

TO:- 21st Battn. M.G.C.

The whole of the MANANCOURT ETRICOURT valle and ST MARTINS WOOD is impregnated with mustard gas As few troops as possible will be located in the localities until they are reported clear AAA All stagnant water will not be used either for drinking or washing.

21 Div.   7 p.m.

MESSAGES AND SIGNALS.

JEZU

7.10.p.m.
5.9.18

PRIORITY.

TO:- 21st Battn. M. G. C.

/ 5 / AAA

21Div Order No.225 AAA Situation remains as already issued to Bdes
AAA 62nd Bde will carry out active patrolling during tonight and
tomorrow AAA If resistance of enemy opposite Div front shows signs
of slackening 62 Bde will push forward advanced guard and be
prepared to follow with remainder of Bde AAA Advance will continue
until objective W.22. C.0.4. REVELON W.10.central is reached when
orders for fresh advance will be issued from Div H.Q. AAA 62 Bde will
not engage in serious attack unless fresh instructions are issued AAA
Successive Bde report centres will be established by Div Signals
whenever further advance is made at cross roads V.14.b. AAA Cross Road
V.18.c. AAA HEUDECOURT SQUARE AAA Sunken road W.18.c.8.2. AAA 64 Bde
be prepared to hold line ST MARTINS WOOD LE MESNIL in ARROAISC but
as counter attack by enemy across CANAL DU NORD is unlikely efforts
will be concentrated on keeping troops fresh AAA 110 bde will remain
as at present AAA 64 Bde and 110 bde will not advance without orders
from Div.H.Q. AAA 21 Div. Arty takes over from 38 Div.Arty.tonight.
AAA 62 Div Arty. remains covering sector AAA Acknowledge AAA
Addressed all concerned.

21 Div.   6.50 p.m.

Certified True Copy
V Hamilton Capt
ADJUTANT,
21st BN. MACHINE GUN CORPS.

MESSAGES AND SIGNALS

JEZU PRIORITY 6.9.18

Handed in at 21 Div.   8 p.m.   Received 8.40 p.m.

TO:- 21st BATTN. M.G.C.

          /   6   /   AAA

21Div Order 226 AAA Situation at 7.30 p.m. AAA 12 Div hold V29 with troops in cutting V.30 AAA 17 Div are reported to hold trench P.36.b. and d. and V.6.b. and d. AAA 62Bde hold NURLU - FINS road in V.23. and V.17. with advanced troops in SOREL-LE-GRAND AAA Position about FINS uncertain AAA 62 Bde Group will continue advance tomorrow AAA Main guard will move forward at 6 a.m. AAA 1st Objective Old BROWN LINE W.22.g. W.16.central W.10.a.00. W.9.a.8.9. AAA 2nd Objective N. end of PEZIERE VAUCELETTE FARM CHAPEL crossing 64Bde group will move forward by stages or ready order until EQUANCOURT trench system is occupied when further orders will be issued AAA 110 Bde group will remain in present position AAA Next bound when ordered will be to area just E. of CANAL DU NORD AAA Res M.G. Coy will assemble V.20.a. and b. by 8 a.m. tomorrow and will maintain officer at report centre V.14.b.8.3. AAA Div H.Q. will move to Q.5.c.3.2. at an hour to be notified later AAA Acknowledge AAA Addsd recipients order number 225.

From. 21st Div.   8 p.m.

CERTIFIED TRUE COPY.

Capt & Adjt.
21st Battalion Machine Gun Corps.

MESSAGES AND SIGNALS.

TO:- O.C."D"Coy. (Forward)

VS 29   6   AAA

You will assemble your coy at V.20 a. and b. by 8 a.m. tomorrow 7th inst and will maintain an Officer at Report Centre Div V.14.b.8.a.3. and await orders AAA DIV HQ's will move to U.5.c.32. at a time to be notified later AAA BN.HQs will move forward tomorro place and time to be notified later.

FOLO.   V.F.SAMUELSON
                                          Capt.& Adjt.

                    CERTIFIED TRUE COPY.

                    [signature]

                                    Capt. & Adjt.
                    21st Battalion Machine Gun Corps.

TELEGRAM.

	: Words. :
URGENT	: --------------- :
OPERATIONS	: Sent. :
PRIORITY to	: At.................m:
64th Bde.	: To................:
	: By................:

BUMA   WUMA   FOLO
BURA   RORU
RUVE   "Q"

GX. 894.   /   7th   /   AAA

Reference 21 Div Order No.226 AAA When BUMA has occupied whole of 1st Objective BURA will move one Battalion to occupy SOREL LE GRAND AAA When BUMAS Reserve BN moves forward from 1st objective BURA will move one Battn to about W.8.central and another to about W.20.a. and c. maintaining one Battn. in SOREL AAA When BUMA reports whole of 2nd objective captured BURA will dispose Brigade so as to be able to occupy 1st objective in case of need or to take up advance tomorrow AAA RUVE will probably move to ground E. of CANAL DU NORD this evening so all preparations should be made AAA Reserve M.G. Coy. will move in future when leading Brigade H.Q. moves and will maintain liaison Officer with later AAA Acknowledge.

JEZU

9.45 a.m.

                          H.C.FRANKLYN.
                          Lt.Col. G.S.

CERTIFIED TRUE COPY.

[signature]

                    Capt. & Adjt.
21st. Battalion Machine Gun Corps.

MESSAGES AND SIGNALS.

TO:- O.C."D"Coy.

VS 32   7   AAA

The Coy in Divisional Reserve will in future move with the
leading Bde HQs and maintain liaison officer with the Bde.HQs
AAA You will move your Company forthwith to about V.17.d.
route via EQUANCOURT AAA On arrival you will report to G.B.C.
62nd Inf Bde at Cross Roads V.18.c.19. and receive orders AAA
When 62nd Bde are relieved or another Bde. passes through
and becomes leading Brigade you automatically come under the
orders of that Bde AAA This Company will only operate under
orders from DIV HQs which will come through the Bde.HQs or
this Office.

FOLO.

10.15 a.m.   V.F.SAMUELSON
                                          Capt. & Adjt.
                             21st Battalion Machine Gun Corps.

                    CERTIFIED TRUE COPY.

                                          Capt. & Adjt.
                             21st Battalion Machine Gun Corps.

TELEGRAM.

URGENT OPERATIONS PRIORITY to 64th Bde. 62nd Bde.	Words .... Sent At............m To............ By............

BUMA	RORU	5th Corps.	15 Sqn. R.A.F.
BURA	JEKU	5th Corps R.A.	
RUVE	JEMU	12th Div.	
WUMA	FOLO	17th Div.	
JENU	A/Q	38th Div.	

/ 7th / AAA

JEZU Order No.227. Reports tends to show that enemy is holding line Q.35. - W.5. - W.11. - CHAPEL HILL - VAUCELLETTE FARM - PEIZERE in some strength AAA Third Corps hold SAULCOURT - GUYENCOURT - W.28.Central AAA 17th Div. hold trench line W.3. Q.32. AAA 62nd Bde hold general line of BROWN Line W.22.c. W.9.b. AAA 62nd Bde will send forward advanced guards at 6 a.m. tomorrow to try and make good second objective AAA If enemy's resistance has slackened advanced guards will be supported AAA No serious attack will be undertaken without reference to Div.H.Q. AAA Brigadier 62nd Bde. will support his advanced guards with 94 and 95 Bdes R.A. which are placed under his orders AAA M.Gs will be freely used firing from the high ground on each flank AAA Reserve M.G.Coy will be used by 62nd Bde for this purpose AAA Arty and M.Gs will be freely used for Harassing AAA 64th and 110th Bdes will remain as at present AAA 64th Bde. will carry out necessary reconnaicsances with a view to relieving 62nd Bde. tomorrow night AAA 110th Bde will reconnoitre EQUANCOURT trench system with a view to future occupation AAA ACKNOWLEDGE AAA Addsd recipients JEZU Order No.226.

JEZU
8 p.m.

H.C.FRANKLYN
Lt.Col.G.S.

CERTIFIED TRUE COPY

Capt. & Adjt.
21st Battalion Machine Gun Corps.

TELEGRAM.

URGENT OPERATIONS PRIORITY TO 62nd and 64th Bdes. 110th.Bde.	: Words : --- : Sent : at...............: : To...............: : By...............:

BUMA	RORU	5th Corps	15th Sqn R.A.F.
BURA	JEKU	5th Corps R.A.	
RUVE	JEMU	17th Div.	
WUMA	FOLO	38th Div.	
JENU	A/Q	58th Div.	

/ 8th / AAA

21st Div. Order No.228. AAA 58th Div. hold YELLOW line E.5.b. & d.
W.29.b. & d. AAA 17 Div hold trench line W.3. Q.32 with outposts in
front AAA 62 Bde. Held YELLOW Line W.24.c. Knoll at W.23.central
REVELON Farm with patrol in GENIN WELL COPSE No.2. AAA 64 Bde.
will attack tomorrow at 4 a.m. in conjunction with 17 Div on their
left. AAA 58 Div. will not be attacking tomorrow but will keep
PEIZIERE under heavy bombardment from 4 a.m. to 4.15 a.m. and
from 5.15 a.m. to 6 a.m. AAA Objectives for 64 Bde. are CHAPEL
Hill and high ground in W.11.d. AAA 17 Div are attacking HEATHER
SUPPORT and HEATHER TRENCH as far South as W.5.c.7.1. and W.5.d.1.2.
respectively AAA After capture of objectives 17 Div. will work down
these two trenches to obtain touch with 64 Bde. on Div.Boundary AAA
Barrage for CHAPEL HILL attack opens at Zero on line W.18.b.0.1.
W.18.a.2.9. lifts at Zero plus 15 and moves at 100 yards in 4 minutes
to line W.18.b.7.8. W.12.c.9.5. then jumps to Railway X.13.a.2.6.
X.7.a.0.2. for 8 minutes and burts of fire until Zero plus 60 AAA
Barrage for W.11.d. attack opens on line W.18.a.2.8. W.17.a.7.8.
lifts at Zero plus 15 mins. and moves at rate of 100 yds in 4
minutes until line W.12.c.2.4. W.11.a.7.4. is reached and then
stops AAA Other Artillery arrangements in Arty.Orders AAA Reserve
M.G.Coy is transferred from 62 to 64 Bde and will be used for
barrage work and harassing fire AAA After capture of CHAPEL HILL
64 Bde will push patrols ɴᴏʀᴛʜᴡᴀʀᴅs towards VAUCELLETTE FARM which will
be occupied in absence of resistance AAA 110 Bde. will have 2 Battns.
in vicinity of and ready to occupy EQUANCOURT Trench System by
6 a.m. tomorrow AAA Remaining Battn. will move to neighbourhood
of SOREL LE GRAND AAA 62 Bde. will be withdrawn gradually under
orders from Div.H.Q. to MANANCOURT and ETRICOURT and ground just
East of CANAL AAA Acknowledge AAA Addsd all concerned.

JEZU

10.10 p.m.

H.C.FRANKLYN.
Lt.Col.G.S.

CERTIFIED TRUE COPY.

Capt. & Adjt.
21st Battalion Machine Gun Corps.

TELEGRAM			
URGENT	: Words :		
OPERATIONS	:----------:		
PRIORITY	: Sent		
TO BDES.	: at............m:		
	: To.................		
	: By................		

BUMA	RORU	5th Corps	15 Sqn.R.A.F.
BURA	JEKU	5th Corps R.A.	
RUVE	JEMU	17th Div.	
WUMA	FOLO	38th Div.	
JENU	A/Q	58th Div.	

/ 9th / AAA

21st Div.Order No.229. AAA 58th Div.hold YELLOW LINE up to W.23.d.8.0. AAA 17 Div hold HEATHER SUPPORT from W.11.a.5.0. northward AAA 64 Bde. holds trench from W.18.b.0.3. along LOWLAND SUPPORT to junction with 17 Div AAA Following attacks will take place tomorrow AAA 64 Bde. will unless attack delivered at 5.30 p.m. succeeded attack in conjunction with 17 Div. at 4 a.m. AAA Objective of 17 Div. LOWLAND AND HEATHER TRENCHES AAA Objective of 64 Bde. CHAPEL HILL thence along CAVALRY TRENCH and LOWLAND TRENCH to junction with 17 Div. at W.12.a.0.0. AAA 58 Div. will attack EPEHY And PEIZIERE at 5.15 a.m. AAA At same hour 64 Bde and 110 Bde. will advance under a creeping barrage and occupy YELLOW LINE AAA 64 Bde. from CHAPEL HILL to RAILTON - VAUCELLETTE FARM Road exclusive AAA 110 Bde from this road inclusive to South-ern Div. Boundary where touch must be obtained with 58 Div. AAA When PEIZIERE is reported captured by 58 Div 110 bde. will detail parties to work along RAILTON - PEIZERE Rly occupying "T" heads and join up with 58 Div. at Bridge W.30.a.9.7. AAA At 5.45 a.m. barrage will come down on line W.18.d.4.7. K.13.a.0.3. and will creep South-Eastwards until clear of VAUCELLETTE FARM AAA 64 Bde. will detail patrols to follow barrage down CAVALRY TRENCH and CAVALRY SUPPORT AAA Progress down these trenches will be made good by blocks AAA If and when VAUCELLETTE FARM is entered 64 Bde. will send garrison to occupy it AAA M.Gs. and Stokes Mortars will be freely used to asist consolidation of final objectives and help to resist counter-attacks AAA All above barrages will move at the rate of 100 yds in 4 minutes AAA Details of lifts and Heavy Arty. support will appear in Arty Orders AAA 64 Bde. will arrange M.G. barrages for attack Reserve M.G. Coy being placed at their disposal AAA 110 Bde will relieve 62 Bde. in BROWN LINE and at Knoll W.23.Central tonight under arrangements between Brigadiers AAA 110 Bde. will be prepared to occupy REVELON FARM and No.1 Copse if vacated by forward move of troops of 64 Bde AAA On relief 62 Bde to MANANCOURT - ETRICOURT Area AAA Acknowledge AAA Addsd recipients Order 228.

JEZU.
8 p.m.

H.C.FRANKLYN.
Lt.Col.G.S.

CERTIFIED TRUE COPY

Capt. & Adjt.
21st Battalion Machine Gun Corps.

TELEGRAM.

| URGENT OPERATIONS PRIORITY TO 64 and 110 BDES. | Words
 Sent
 At................m
 To................
 By................ |

BUMA	RORU	5th Corps	15th Sqn.RAF
BURA	JEKU	5th Corps R.A.	
RUVE	JEMU	17th Div.	
WUMA	FOLO	38th Div.	
JENU	A/Q	58th Div.	

G.X.963. / 10th / AAA

Warning Order AAA Attack on CHAPEL HILL did not succeed this morning AAA 110 Bde. will relieve 64 Bde tonight AAA 110 Bde. will also be prepared to advance under a barrage and occupy the YELLOW LINE from CHAPEL HILL to Southern Div. Boundary AAA On relief of 64 Bde. will move to EQUANCOURT Trench System with one Battn. about SOREL LE GRAND AAA ACKNOWLEDGE AAA Addsd Recipients JEZU Order No.229.

JEZU

11.20 a.m.

A.F.MACDOUGALL
Major
for Lt.Col. G.S.

CERTIFIED TRUE COPY.

Capt. & Adjt.
21st Battalion Machine Gun Corps.

Copy No. 10   S E C R E T.

21st. Bn. M.G.C. OPERATION ORDER No. 46.

Ref. Map 57.c.S.E. 1/20,000.   10th. September 1918.

1. Confirming instructions issued to Machine Gun Company Commanders this morning, the following moves and redistribution will take place on night 10th/11th. Sept.-

2. "A" Coy. less 1 Section will take up following positions:

    1 Section ... attached 1st. Wilts. Regt.
    1 Section ... in vicinity of REVELON FARM.
    1 Section ... in BROWN LINE.

1 Section already detailed will remain under orders of 7th. Leicester Regt.

3. On completion of above moves, "C" Coy. will withdraw to ETRICOURT and come under the orders of B.G.C. 62nd. Inf.Bde.

4. "B" Coy. will withdraw to EQUANCOURT LINE under orders of B.G.C. 64th. Inf.Bde.

5. "D" Coy. with dispositions as follows come under the orders of B.G.C. 110th. Inf.Bde:-

    3 Sections ... in W.23.a. for Barrage purposes. Barrage Line: VAUCELLETTE FARM - CHAPEL CROSSING.
    1 Section ... in W.23.a. for direct fire on to VAUCELLETTE FARM and PEZIERE - VAUCELLETTE FARM Ridge.

6. Completion of above moves will be wired to Battalion H.Q. by code word "O.K."

7. Machine Gun Companies to acknowledge.

                                                V.F. Samuels
                                                Capt. & Adjutant.
                                        21st. Battn. Machine Gun Corps.

Issued to:

    Copy No. 1 ... O.C. 'A' Coy. Fwd.
             2 ... O.C. 'B' Coy. "
             3 ... O.C. 'C' Coy. "
             4 ... O.C. 'D' Coy. "
             5 ... 21st. Div. 'G'.
             6 ... 62nd. Inf.Bde.
             7 ... 64th. Inf.Bde.
             8 ... 110th. Inf.Bde.
             9 ... File.
       10-11 ... War Diary.

TELEGRAM.

Urgent Operations priority to 64 & 110 Bdes.	Words .... Sent At................m To.................. By..................

BUMA	RORU	5th Corps	15 Sqn. R.A.F.
BURA	JEKU	5th Corps R.A.	
RUVE	JEMU	17th Div.	
WUMA	FOLO	38th Div.	
JENU	A/Q	58th Div.	

/ 10th / AAA

21 Div Order No.230 AAA 58th Div are reported to hold TOTTENHAM POST and WOOD FARM otherwise position of flank Divs. remains unchanged AAA 64 Bde. line is as given in Order No.229 of yesterday AAA 110 Bde will advance under a barrage and make good the whole of the YELLOW LINE within the Div. Sector tonight affecting junction with 58 Div on Southern Boundary AAA Barrage will come down on line W.23.d.6.4. to W.17.d.6.6. will lift at Zero plus 10 minutes and advance at rate of 100 yds in five minutes until line W.24.d.6.4. to W.18.d.6.6. is reached and remain stationary here for 10 minutes and then cease AAA Other Artillery arrangements in Artillery orders AAA 110 Bde will use Reserve M.G.Coy for barrage and this Coy. will now come under their orders AAA 110 Bde. will relieve 64 Bde in line tonight AAA After relief 64 Bde. will be accommodated in and about EQUANCOURT Trench System with one Battn. near SOREL AAA Letter on policy for immediate future follows AAA Acknowledge AAA Addsd recipients JEZU Order 229.

H.C.FRANKLYN.
Lt.Col.G.S.

JEZU

7.30 p.m.

CERTIFIED TRUE COPY.

Capt. & Adjt.
21st Battalion Machine Gun Corps.

MESSAGES AND SIGNALS.

JEZU PRIORITY   FOLO
                                                        10.9.18.

Handed in at 21st DIV.   10.30 Received 10.35

TO:→   21st. M.G. BATTN.

GX987   10th.   AAA

Ref D 0230 AAA ZERO Hour 3 a.m. 11th.inst.

FROM: 21st.Div

       10.15 p.m.

                    CERTIFIED TRUE COPY.

                           V F Sannahn

                                Capt. & Adjt.
              21st. Battalion Machine Gun Corps.

POSITION CODE CALLS.

in reference to attached War Diary.

UNIT	STATION CODE CALL	UNIT	STATION CODE CALL
21 Div.H.Q.	JIXU	21 DIVL.ARTY.H.Q.	WUMA
62nd Inf.Bde.H.Q.	BUMA	94 Bde.R.F.A.	JUFU
12/13 N.F.	MOHI	"A" Battery	JUGA
1st. LINCS.	JOKE	"B" do.	JULA
2nd. LINCS	JOPE	"C" do.	JURA
62 LTM.Batty.	LILI	"D" do.	JUVA
64th Inf.Bde.H.Q.		93rd Bde.R.F.A.	JUQU
1 E.YORKS.	HOWI	"A" Battery	JUDU
9 K.O.Y.L.I.	HOLI	"B" do.	JUBU
15 D.L.I.	QOJO	"C" do.	JUFU
64th LTM.Batty.	LIVI		
		95th.Bde.R.F.A.	JUJA
110th Inf.Bde.HQ	HUVE	"A" Battery	JUZA
		"B" do.	JUNA
6 LIECTR.REGT.	JONE	"C" do.	JUKA
7 do do	JOKE	"D" do.	JUSA
1 WILTS REGT	LOFO		
110 LTM Batty.	LIXU	315 Bde.R.F.A.	GUMA
		"A" Battery	GUKA
21st M.G.BATTN.	FOLO	"B" do.	GUSA
"A" Coy	FOTO	"C" do.	GUNA
"B" Coy	FOGA	"D" do.	GUWA
"C" Coy	FOHO		
"D" Coy	FOVO		

62nd Inf.Bde.
64th. :
110th : :
C.R.A.
C.R.E.
D.M.G.C.
"Q"
Signals.

SECRET.
21 Div.
G.985.

POLICY FOR IMMEDIATE FUTURE.

1.   As soon as the YELLOW LINE has been made good and junction effected with the 58th Division about W.24.d.8.0. and with the 17th Division about W.11. Central, the general policy is :-

   (a)   To keep touch with the enemy, so that advantage may be taken of any weakening of resistance.

   (b)   To make all preparations for subsequent operations which will probably be on a more extended scale than those carried out recently.

   (c)   To harass the enemy with all available means.

   (d)   To improve the defences in the Divisional Boundary.

2.   As regards (a) constant patrolling will be carried out and if any opportunity presents itself of improving our position in the CHAPEL HILL area, it will be taken advantage of.
Fighting patrols will be used in likely places (e.g. along Railway in W.24.d. and along Sunken Road W.18.d.) for rounding up prisoners.

3.   As regards (b) information will be communicated to those immediately concerned.

As regards 1(c) Stokes Mortars, Machine Guns and Artillery will be freely used both by day and night to harass the enemy's communications, centres of resistance and of accommodation.

Details as to Gas-projector attacks will be issued later.

4.   As regards 1 (d):-

Infantry Garrisons will deepen the trenches where necessary and repair the wire entanglements.

The C.R.E. will detail:-

   (a)   One Field Coy. R.E. to make REVELON FARM into a strong point for a garrison of one Coy.

   (b)   One Field Coy. R.E. will be employed on renovating the BROWN LINE

/(c)........

(c) One Coy. Pioneers will wire CAVALRY SUPPORT and LOWLAND SUPPORT.

(d) One Coy. Pioneers will construct strong points in the EQUANCOURT Trench System.

5. (a) The forward Brigade will be responsible for the defence of the Sector up to and including the BROWN LINE.

(b) The Supporting Brigade (less 1 Battalion) will be responsible for the defence of the GREEN LINE (EQUANCOURT System) and will be ready to occupy it at one hour's notice.
The B.G.C. forward Brigade will have the call on the Battalion supporting Brigade (Located near SOREL LE GRAND) for counter-attacking to regain any portion of the BROWN LINE or for forming a defensive flank either to the East or West of this line. Except in case of great urgency this Battalion will not be used without reference to Divisional Headquarters.

(c) The Brigade in ETRICOURT - MANANCOURT Area will be in Divisional Reserve.

H.C. FRANKLYN.
Lieut. Col.
General Staff
10th September, 1918.   21st Division.

CERTIFIED TRUE COPY.

Capt. & Adjt.
21st Battalion Machine Gun Corps.

O.C. "A" Coy. (Fwd).
O.C. "B" Coy.   "
O.C. "C" Coy.   "
O.C. "D" Coy.   "

SECRET.

AX/505/0.

POLICY FOR IMMEDIATE FUTURE.

1. As soon as the YELLOW LINE has been made good and junction effected with the 58th. Division about W.24.d.8.0. and with the 17th. Division about W.11.central, the general policy is:-

   (a) To keep touch with the enemy, so that advantage may be taken of any weakening of resistance.

   (b) To make all preparations for subsequent operations, which will probably be on a more extended scale than those carried out recently.

   (c) To harass the enemy with all available means.

   (d) To improve the defences in the Divisional Sector.

2. As regards 1 (b), information will be communicated to those immediately concerned.

   As regards 1 (c), Stokes Mortars, Machine Guns and Artillery will be freely used both by day and night to harass the enemy's communications, centres of resistance and of accommodation.

   Details as to Gas-projector attacks will be issued later.

   Company Commanders will carry out harassing fire on all available occasions, and on tracks in enemy lines at night. B.Gs.C. will be shown suggested targets to be engaged, and a copy sent to Battalion Headquarters.

3. (a) The forward Brigade will be responsible for the defence of the Sector up to and including the BROWN LINE.

   (b) The supporting Brigade (less 1 Battalion) will be responsible for the defence of the GREEN LINE (EQUANCOURT System), and will be ready to occupy it at one hour's notice.
   The B.G.C. forward Brigade will have the call on one Battalion supporting Brigade (located near SOREL LE GRAND) for counter-attacking to regain any portion of the BROWN LINE or for forming a defensive flank either to East or West of this line. Except in case of great urgency, this Battalion will not be used without reference to Divisional Headquarters.

   (c) The Brigade in the ETRICOURT - MANANCOURT Area will be in Divisional Reserve.

/4 ......

-2-

4. The Reserve Divisional Machine Gun Company will remain at the orders of B.G.C. forward Brigade.

[signature]

11th. Sept. 1918.
Capt. & Adjutant.
21st. Battn. Machine Gun Corps.

Copies to:

62nd. Inf. Bde.
64th. Inf. Bde.
110th. Inf. Bde.
21st. Div. 'G'.
Commanding Officer.
File.
War Diary (2).

SECRET.

To:-
All Os.C. Coys.(Forward).
Advanced Bn. H.Q.
Rear Bn. H.Q.   AX/508/13.
Signals.

      I herewith give below a list of Code Calls which will come into force midnight 13th/14th September.
      All other Code Calls are cancelled, and any copies Companies are in possession of will please be returned to Battalion Headquarters on the 14th inst.
    ACKNOWLEDGE.

V. F. Sanders

Capt. & Adjt.,
21st Bn. Machine Gun Corps.

12.9.18.

21st Division - Station Code Calls.

Name of Unit.	Code Calls after midnight 13/14 Sept.	Name of Unit.	Code Calls after midnight 13/14 Sept.
21st Division HQ.	ZOWU	21st D.A.C.	KAVE
		X/21 T.M.Battery.	ZIFO
62nd Inf.Bde.HQ.	DADE	Y/21 T.M.Battery.	ZIQA
12/13 Northd Fus.	DULI		
1st Lincoln Regt.	VESE	21st Bn.M.G.Corps.	ZEJU
2nd Lincoln Regt.	VEZA	"A" Company.	REMA
62nd Light T.M.Bty.	SUJE	"B" Company.	RENU
64th Inf.Bde. HQ.	BASU	"C" Company.	ZELO
1st East Yorks Regt.	NORU	"D" Company.	ZEFI
9th K.O.Y.L.I.	LOJE		
15th Durham L.I.	SIQE	14th North'd Fus(P).	DUFA
64th Light T.M.Bty.	SUFA		
110th Inf.Bde.HQ.	VUFE	C.R.E.	ZOKI
6th Leicester Regt.	GEKA	97th Field Coy.R.E.	SUJA
7th Leicester Regt.	GEHE	98th -do-	SULU
1st Wilts. Regt.	LAPU	126th -do-	GUSE
110th Light T.M.Bty.	GUVA		
		21st Div. Signal Coy.	JESO
21st Divl.Arty.HQ.	LODE		
94th Bde.R.F.A.	DUME	A.D.M.S.	ZOHO
"A" Battery.	DUNO	63rd Field Ambulance.	HUWO
"B" Battery.	PUJO	64th -do-	HUKE
"C" Battery.	PULA	65th -do-	HUHA
"D" Battery.	PUFU	D.A.D.O.S.	ZOTE
95th Bde. R.F.A.	PUQI	21st Divl. Train.	ZODU
"A" Battery.	PUWE	No. 1 Company.	MOKU
"B" Battery.	PUKO	No. 2 Company.	MOHI
"C" Battery.	PUHU	No. 3 Company.	MOTO
"D" Battery.	PUTA	No. 4 Company.	MODA

War Diary

SECRET.   Copy No. 10

21st Battn. Machine Gun Corps
OPERATION ORDER No. 47.

13th September 1918.

1.   "C" Company, attached 62nd Infantry Brigade, will relieve "D" Company in Divisional Reserve tonight, 13th/14th September, and be attached to the Brigade in Forward Area.

     "D" Company will return to ETRICOURT, and come under the orders of B.G.C., 62nd Infantry Brigade.

2.   Lieut. CHAMBERLAIN and 1 N.C.O. per pair of guns, will remain at the gun positions tonight, and return to Company Headquarters on the 14th inst. when the relieving Officer is quite satisfied that everything is correct.

3.   Completion of relief will be reported to Battalion Headquarters by code word "SALLY" by wire and runner.

4.   "D" Company's rations will be delivered at "C" Company Headquarters, ETRICOURT by 6 a.m., 14th inst.

5.   All other details of relief will be arranged between Company Commanders concerned.

                                       V.F. Samuelson
                                       Capt. & Adjt.,
                                 21st Battn. Machine Gun Corps.

DISTRIBUTION.

Copy No. 1 .. "D" Coy. (Forward).)
        2 .. "D" Coy. (Rear).   ) To acknowledge.
        3 .. "C" Coy. (Forward).   )
        4 .. 62nd Infantry Brigade.)
        5 .. 110th   "   "   )
        6 .. "G" 21st Division.   ) For information.
        7 .. Quartermaster.   )
        8 .. Commanding Officer.   )
        9 .. File.
   10 & 11 .. War Diary.

TELEGRAM.

URGENT
OPERATIONS
PRIORITY to
110th and
19th Inf. Bdes.

Words
Sent.
at.........................m
To...........................
By..........................

DADE	JESO	V Corps H.A.
BASU	ZOHO	17th. Div.
VUFE	ZODU	33rd. Div.
LODE	A/Q	38th. Div.
ZOKI	A.P.M.	15th. Sqn. R.A.F.
DUFA	V Corps	19th Inf. Bde.
ZEJU	V Corps R.A.	58th. Div.

ZOWU Order No.231 AAA VUFE will be relieved by HASA in the line tonight 15th/16th instant under arrangements to be made between Brigadiers concerned AAA On relief VUFE will take over accommodation vacated by HASA AAA Coys. of ZEJU will not be relieved AAA 2 Sections SULU at present attached to VUFE will revert to ZOKI at 8 p.m. today AAA No movement will take place before dark AAA Completion of relief will be reported to these Headquarters AAA Command of Sector passes to GOQE on completion of relief AAA Ack AAA Adsd all concerned.

ZOWU.

4 p.m.

G. TOOTH Captn.
for Lt.Col.G.S.

CERTIFIED TRUE COPY.

21st DIVISION SPECIAL ORDER.

Sunday, 15th September 1918.

We have been detailed to retake a considerable portion of the line which the Troops of this Division defended in so gallant a manner on March 21st as to call for special mention in the Commander-in-Chief's despatches.

The recapture of this historic ground will be a magnificent sequel to the great achievements of this Division during the past six months.

I am certain that all ranks will again show that fine spirit of determination and self-sacrifice which was so conspicuous on March 21st and following days; that every man will go forward with the one resolve to reach and hold the objective assigned to him, and that we shall add this crowning victory to the long list of successes which we have obtained during the recent fighting, and which have already made this Division one of the most famous in the British Expeditionary Force.

Good Luck.

(Sgd) DAVID G. M. CAMPBELL,
Major General,
Commanding 21st Division.

Certified true copy

SECRET   Copy No....7....

21st DIVISION ORDER No.233.

Ref. Map.Sheet 57.c.S.E.
1/20,000.
                                                        16th September 1918.

1.   The enemy is holding the general line CHAPEL HILL,
VAUCELLETTE FARM, PEIZIERE, EPEHY, in considerable strength but,
it is believed, in little depth.

2. (a)   The Vth Corps is attacking on a date which has been
     communicated to those concerned and at a Zero hour which will
     be notified later, in conjunction with the Fourth Army and
     other Armies to the South.

   (b)   The 58th Division (173rd Brigade on left) will be
     attacking on our right during first phase of operations, i.e.,
     up to and including capture of POPLAR TRENCH. The 12th
     Division (37th Infantry Brigade on left) will be attacking on
     our right from POPLAR TRENCH to the RED LINE and to the
     exploitation line (marked blue on map).

   (c)   The 17th Division will be attacking on our left and will
     include FIVES TRENCH in their objective.

3. (a)   The 21st Division will capture successively the BROWN,
     GREEN and RED lines (see Map).

   (b)   The 62nd Infantry Brigade will capture the BROWN and
     GREEN lines.

   (c)   The 110th Infantry Brigade on the right and the 64th
     Infantry Brigade on the left will capture the BROWN line. RED.

   (d)   The 110th Infantry Brigade will exploit, with previously
     detailed Companies, up to the BLUE line, to protect the left
     flank of the 12th Division, under arrangements to be made
     between the B.G.C. 110th Infantry Brigade and the B.G.C.
     37th Infantry Brigade.

   (e)   The 64th Infantry Brigade will exploit up to the BLACK
     line (One or more Coys. being definitely detailed for this
     purpose), with the idea of rounding up prisoners and capturing
     material. When this has been done, Units detailed for
     exploitation will return to the RED line.

   (f)   Immediately after the 110th Infantry Brigade has passed
     through the 62nd Infantry Brigade, this latter Brigade will
     collect one Battalion into Divisional Reserve in the
     neighbourhood of LINNET VALLEY.

   (g)   There will be a pause of 18 minutes on the BROWN line
     and of 15 minutes on line of road running from POPLAR
     TRENCH to TARGELLE TRENCH and thence by BEET FACTORY (see
     Barrage Map). The length of pause on the GREEN line will be
     notified later.

                                                        /4........

- 2 -

4. Liaison posts will be established with neighbouring Units as follows :-

(a) Between 62nd Infantry Brigade and 173rd Infantry Brigade at X.20.c.2.0.

(b) Between 62nd Infantry Brigade and 17th Division at S.E. Corner of BIRCH TREE COPSE X.13.b.3.1.

(c) Between 110th Infantry Brigade and 37th Infantry Brigade at X.22.c.4.3. and X.23.c.5.5.

(d) Between 64th Infantry Brigade and 17th Division at junction of BEET TRENCH and CHAPEL STREET.

(e) Between 110th Infantry Brigade and 64th Infantry Brigade at junction of MEUNIER TRENCH and LEITH WALK.

These Liaison posts will be joint posts and will consist of one Platoon found by each Unit concerned.

5. Five Brigades of Field Artillery will support the attack of the 21st Division, in addition to Heavy Artillery; of these, three Brigades will support the attack of the 62nd Infantry Brigade and all five Brigades of the 110th and 64th Infantry Brigades.

Barrage tables will be issued separately.

Other Artillery arrangements will appear in Artillery Orders.

6. The attack of the 62nd Infantry Brigade will be supported by a barrage fired by :-

Three Coys. of 21st Battalion Machine Gun Corps.

Two   :   :33rd.   :   :   ;

The attack of the 110th Infantry Brigade will be supported by a barrage of One Machine Gun Company and of the 64th Infantry Brigade by the barrage of 8 Machine Guns.

Each Infantry Brigade will have one Machine Gun Company to cover its advance by direct fire and to assist in consolidation.

Orders for the above will be issued to all concerned by O.C., 21st Battalion Machine Gun Corps.

7. (a) 8 Stokes Mortars of the 19th Brigade are placed at the disposal of the 62nd Infantry Brigade for a hurricane bombardment at Zero.

(b) One Supply Tank is allotted to 110th Infantry Brigade and one Supply Tank to 64th Infantry Brigade. These tanks will be used in the first instance for carrying forward Stokes Mortars and ammunition for use in the RED line.

/8......

- 3 -

8. The O.C. 15th Squadron R.A.F. will be arranging for a contact aeroplane to call for flares as early as possible after daylight and subsequently at odd hours (i.e., 7 a.m., 9.am, 11 a.m., etc.)

RED flares will be used.

Flares will be lit by the foremost troops at the above hours or at any other hour, when called for by the contact aeroplane, sounding a Klaxon Horn.

The aeroplane signal to denote the assembly of enemy to counter-attack is the dropping of a Red Smoke Bomb over the place where the enemy is seen.

9. Headquarters will be established as follows :-

(a) Divisional Headquarters ..LE MESNIL en ARROUAISE.

(b) 62nd Infantry Brigade Headquarters .. W.21.c.0.0.

(c) 110th Infantry Brigade H.Q. in first instance at W.21.c.0.0. and subsequently at W.18.d.0.2.

(d) 64th Infantry Brigade Headquarters in first instance at Railway Cutting W.23.b. and subsequently at W.18.c.7.5.

10. Watches will be synchronized by an Officer from Divisional Headquarters between 7 p.m. and 8 p.m. on Z. minus 1 day.

11. Acknowledge.

Lieut.Colonel.
General Staff.
21st Division.

Issued through Signals at

	Copy No.		Copy No.
62nd Inf. Bde.	1	A.P.M.	12
64th " "	2	Vth Corps.	13-14.
110th " "	3	Vth Corps R.A.	15
C.R.A.	4	Vth Corps H.A.	16
C.R.E.	5.	12th Div.	17
Pioneers.	6	17th Div.	18
D.M.G.C.	7	33rd Div.	19
Signals.	8	58th Div.	20
A.D.M.S.	9	15th Sqn. R.A.F.	21
Train.	10.	War Diary	22
A/Q	11.	File	23

S E C R E T.   Copy No. 18

                    21st Battn. Machine Gun Corps
                      OPERATION ORDER No. 48.
                      ─────────────────

                                              16th September 1918.
Ref. Map Sheet:
57c.S.E., 1/20,000.
────────────────

1.   The enemy is holding the general line CHAPEL HILL -
   VAUCELLETTE FARM - PEIZIERE - EPEHY in considerable strength,
   but it is believed in little depth.

2. (a) The Vth Corps is attacking at an hour and date to be
       notified later, in conjunction with Armies to the South.

   (b) The 58th Division (173rd Infantry Brigade on left) will
       be attacking on our right during the first phase of
       operations, and the 12th Division (37th Infantry Brigade
       on left) to the RED LINE and to the Exploitation Line.

   (c) The 17th Division will be attacking on our left.

3.   The objectives of 21st Division, and Inter-Brigade and
   Divisional Boundaries, are marked on attached map (issued to
   Machine Gun Companies only.)

4. (a) The 62nd Infantry Brigade will capture the BROWN and
       GREEN LINES.

   (b) The 110th Infantry Brigade on the right, and 64th
       Infantry Brigade on the left, will capture the RED LINE.

   (c) The 110th Infantry Brigade will exploit up to the BLUE
       LINE to protect the Left Flank of the 12th Division.

   (d) The 64th Infantry Brigade will exploit up to the BLACK LINE
       with the idea of rounding up prisoners and capturing
       material.   When this has been done, Units will return to
       the RED LINE.

   (e) There will be a pause of 18 minutes on the BROWN LINE,
       and of 15 minutes on line of road running from POPLAR
       TRENCH to TARGELLE TRENCH, and thence by BEET FACTORY.
       The length of pause on GREEN LINE will be notified later.

5.   Liaison Posts will be established with neighbouring Units
   at the following points:-

       X.20.c.2.0.
       S.E. Corner of BIRCH TREE COPSE, X.13.b.3.1.
       X.22.c.4.3.
       X.23.c.5.5.
       Junction of BEET TRENCH and CHAPEL STREET.
       Junction of MEUNIER TRENCH and LEITH WALK.

       These Liaison Posts will consist of one Platoon from
   each Unit concerned.

6.   Five Brigades of Field Artillery will support the attack
   in addition to Heavy Artillery.

                                                /7..........

7. ACTION OF MACHINE GUNS.

The 21st Battalion, and two Companies of 33rd Battalion, Machine Gun Corps, will co-operate as follows:-

(a) "D" Company, 21st Battn. and "A" & "C" Companies 33rd Battn. will support the attack of 62nd Infantry Brigade on to the BROWN LINE by Barrage Fire as shown on attached time table.

(b) On completion of above Barrage, "A" & "C" Companies, 33rd Battn., will remain in Battery positions until further orders.
"D" Company, 21st Battn., will move to positions on PEIZIERE RIDGE in X.19.a & c., and will carry out direct overhead fire in support of the attack on the RED LINE.

(c) "A" & "B" Companies, 21st Battn., will come under the orders of B.G.C. 110th and 64th Infantry Brigades respectively for the attack on, and consolidation of the RED LINE.

(d) "C" Company 21st Battn., less 2 Sections, will come under the orders of B.G.C. 62nd Infantry Brigade for the attack on and consolidation of the BROWN LINE. 8 Guns will be placed on VAUCELLETTE FARM SPUR in X.13.c for direct overhead fire in support of the attack on the RED LINE.
As soon as the RED LINE is captured or the attacking Infantry are consolidating a definite line, these guns will take up defensive positions as follows:-

2 Guns at W.24.d.3.6. firing N.E.
2 Guns at W.18.d.3.9. firing E. & N.E.
2 Guns at W.24.a.8.8 firing E. & S.E.
2 Guns at W.24.b.9.9 firing N.E.

(e) The 8 guns of "C" Company, 21st Battn., on VAUCELLETTE FARM SPUR, and 16 Guns of "D" Company on PEIZIERE RIDGE must be prepared to support the attack on the RED LINE by indirect methods if found necessary on account of smoke or fog.

(f) All Forward Guns will be used with the utmost boldness, and every opportunity taken of ground from which direct overhead fire can support the attack.

(g) All Barrage Calculations, and a Certificate that all necessary calculations are complete, will be forwarded to reach Battalion Headquarters by 12 noon, 17th inst.

(h) S.A.A. Dumps have been formed as follows:-

RAILWAY CUTTING (W.23.a). 50,000 (in addition to 50,000 already there.)
W.16.d.9.2. .. .. 100,000.

(i) Pack Saddlery has been increased to the following scale:-

"A", "B" & "D" Companies .. 32 Sets.
Sets are held in Battalion Reserve.

Where possible, limbers should be used in preference to Pack Trains.

/8..........

-3-

8. 8 Stokes Mortars of 19th Infantry Brigade are placed at the disposal of 62nd Infantry Brigade for a hurricane bombardment at zero.

9. One supply tank is allotted to 110th Infantry Brigade, and one to 64th Infantry Brigade for transporting Stokes Mortars and S.A.A. for use in RED LINE.

10. The Aeroplane Signal to denote the assembly of enemy to counter-attack is the dropping of a Red Smoke Bomb over the place where the enemy is seen.

11. Headquarters will be established as follows:-

Divisional HQ.)   LE MESNIL - EN-ARROUAISE.
21st Bn.MGC.)

62nd Infantry Bde.   W.21.c.0.0.

110th   -do-   In first instance, W.21.c.0.0.
                        Subsequently .. W.18.d.0.2.

64th   -do-   In first instance, RAILWAY CUTTING W.23.b.
                       Subsequently, .. W.18.c.7.5.

12. Watches will be synchronised by Company Commanders at their nearest Brigade Headquarters at 8 p.m. and 9 p.m. on Zero minus one day.

13. A C K N O W L E D G E.

A. Humphry   Lieut for
                                       Major,
Commanding 21st Battn. Machine Gun Corps.

DISTRIBUTION.

Copy No. 1 .. O.C. "A" Coy.(F'd).
         2 .. O.C. "B" Coy. (F'd).
         3 .. O.C. "C" Coy.(F'd).
         4 .. O.C. "D" Coy.(F'd).
         5 .. O.C. "A" Coy.33rd MG.Bn.
         6 .. O.C. "C" Coy.33rd MG.Bn.
         7 .. 62nd Inf. Bde.
         8 .. 64th Inf. Bde.
         9 .. 110th Inf. Bde.
       10 .. 21st Division 'G'.
       11 .. O.C. 33rd M.G.Bn.
       12 .. O.C. 17th M.G.Bn.
       13 .. O.C. 58th M.G.Bn.
       14 .. O.C. 12th M.G.Bn.
       15 .. Commanding Officer.
       16 .. Intelligence Officer.
       17 .. File.
   18 & 19 .. War Diary.

SECRET.

To:-
  O.C. "A" Coy. Fwd.   AX/365/0.
  O.C. "C" Coy. "
  110th. Inf. Bde.)
  62nd. Inf. Bde.) for information.
  21st. Div. 'G'.)

        Confirming instructions issued to Coy. Commanders concerned today, the following guns will be withdrawn from the line tonight, 16/17th. inst. on completion of relief by 62nd. Inf. Bde.

"A" Coy. - (4 guns in LOWLAND SUPPORT.
             (4 guns in GENIN WELL COPSE.
             (4 guns in BROWN LINE, W.9.d.8.8.

"C" Coy. -   8 guns in RAILWAY CUTTING, W.23.a.

        These guns will return to a position of readiness near SOREL LE GRAND; the exact location will be wired to Battn. Headquarters. These guns will be prepared to occupy defensive positions in the BROWN LINE at one hour's notice if required.

                                             Lieut. & A/Adjutant.
                                     21st. Battn. Machine Gun Corps.

16th. September, 1918.

MESSAGES & SIGNALS.

TO:- ALL COYS. FORWARD.

AX/581/0   17   AAA

Ref. Order No.48 para 12 AAA For 8 p.m. and 9 p.m. read between 5 p.m. and 6 p.m. AAA

FROM. 21st. Bn.M.G.C.

CERTIFIED TRUE COPY.

War Diary.

SECRET.

AX/579/0.

In continuation of 21st. Battn. M.G.C. Operation Order No. 48:-

1. **INTELLIGENCE.**

    The Divisional Intelligence Officer will be at P. of W. Cage, V.18.c.1.9. All Maps, papers, documents and soldbuchers (Pay Books) from enemy dead will be forwarded to Companies respective Brigade H.Q.
    Identity Discs will be left on dead.
    Papers will not be collected from prisoners.

2. **S.A.A.**

    There is an advanced Divisional Dump at W.28.b.0.9 containing 90 boxes S.A.A. (M.G.).
    This should be drawn before drawing from new dump at W.21.b.3.3.

3. **PETROL TINS.**

    Every effort must be made to salve and send back empty petrol tins. Holes to facilitate pouring water out must not be made.

4. **TRANSPORT LINES.**

    Transport Lines will remain in present positions.

5. **CASUALTIES.**

    Estimated casualties will be forwarded to Battalion H.Q. as early as possible.

6. **STRAGGLERS POSTS.**

    Stragglers Posts will be established on the NURLU - FINS Road.

7. **ANTI-TANK MINEFIELDS.**

    Gaps in these minefields will be marked with a Notice Board on each side.

8. **LIGHT SIGNALS.**

    S.O.S.   Vth. Corps.   ...   GREEN/RED/GREEN.
    "   3rd. Corps.(on Right) ...   RED/RED/RED.

    Coloured Very Lights will be used as follows:-

    RED   ...   "We are here".
    GREEN   ...   "Lengthen range".

/9 ......

-2-

9. COMMUNICATIONS.

Personnel allotted to each Company: 1 N.C.O. & 2 men.

By wire.

Section Officers will make use of the Signal arrangements of the Infantry Battalion with which they are operating or the Infantry Battalion nearest to their position.

By hand.

Full use will be made of Brigade Despatch Riders. If for any reason this is impracticable, Companies can make use of the Runner Posts established at CUTTING in W.23.a. and at V.17.b.7.2.

Runner Post will open at CUTTING in W.23.a. at 9 p.m. 17th. inst.

Barrage Coys.

The 2 M.G.Coys. attached to this Battalion for Barrage purposes will make use of wire already laid into Headquarters at CUTTING in W.23.a.

Arrangements for "D" Coy.

Arrangements for "D" Coy. communications during Barrage will be made and O.C. "D" Coy. informed as soon as completed.

Use of telephone.

As far as possible, messages will be sent and telephone conversations avoided during operations.

10. BARRAGE FOR ATTACK ON RED LINE.

Targets, times and rate of fire for supporting the attack on the RED LINE and areas to be exploited will be issued to Company Commanders concerned direct.

17th. September, 1918.   A. Huxley Lieuxfor
                          Major.
                          Commanding 21st. Bn. Machine Gun Corps.

Distribution:

All recipients of 21st. Bn. M.G.C. O.O. No.48.

To:- O.C. "A" Coy.Fwd.
    O.C. "C" Coy.Fwd.
    "G"21st Division.)
    110th Inf.Bde.   )For information.
    62nd Inf.Bde.   )

SECRET.

AK/582/0.

    The following M.Gs. of "A" & "C" Coys. 21st Battn. Machine Gun Corps now in the Line will be withdrawn tonight under arrangements to be made by Company Commanders with B.G.Cs. concerned.

"A" Coy.-   4 guns in W.2.3.c.

"C" Coy.-   8 guns in Railway Cutting, W.2.3.a.

                                                A. Huxley Lieut.
                                               Lieut. & A/Adjutant,
17th September,18. 21st Battalion Machine Gun Corps.

BARRAGE TIME TABLE FOR ATTACK ON BROWN LINE.

Battery.	Battery Position.	Target.	Time.	Rate of fire.	Remarks.
"D" Coy., 21 Bn. MGC.	X.13.c.5.8.	Trench immediately EAST of VAUCELLETTE FARM from X.13.c.8.8. - FOOTBALL TRENCH - LEITH WALK (incl).	Z. to Z. plus 14 minutes.	1 belt per gun every 2 minutes.	On cessation of fire, act as in para.2.
"A" Coy., 33 Bn. MGC.	~~RAILWAY CUTTING, X.23.a.~~ W.23.b.5.9.	LEITH WALK (incl) - X.19.a.95.10. (incl).	Z. to Z. plus 20 minutes.	-do-	Remain in Battery Pos^ns.
"C" Coy., 33 Bn. MGC.	W.23.c.5.7.	X.19.a.95.10 (incl). - Southern Divisional Boundary.	Z. to Z. plus 24 minutes.	-do-	-do-

NOTE: No fire will be directed WEST of Grid Line running N. and S. through X.19.central.

SECRET.

AX/584/0.

O.C. "C" Coy. Forward. With tracing.
O.C. "D" Coy.   "   "   "
62nd. Inf. Bde.)
64th. Inf. Bde.)
110th. Inf. Bde.) for information.
21st. Div. 'G'.)

Reference 21st. Bn. M.G.C. Operation Order No. 48 and AX/579/0 dated 17-9-18, para. 10.

Attached is tracing shewing Time Table of Artillery Barrage in support of attack on the RED LINE.

8 guns of "C" Coy. and 16 guns of "D" Coy. will support this attack from positions selected by Os.C. Coys.
The following areas require particular attention:

By "C" Coy.- S.W. approaches to VILLERS GUISLAIN. Sunken Road (LEITH WALK) from X.15.a.2.2. to X.15.c.9.0. High ground in X.9.c. and X.15.a. and b.

By "D" Coy.- MEATH POST and vicinity. LIMERICK TRENCH. PARRS TRENCH. X.21.d. LIMERICK POST.

The 58th. Battn. M.G.C. are also engaging X.21.d. and area about X.20.central, with one Company to each area.

All fire will as far as possible be direct overhead. The greatest care will be taken that a sufficient clearance is assured over the heads of the attacking Infantry. The Machine Gun Barrage should be at least 400 yards E. of the Field Artillery Barrage (shewn on attached tracing).

On completion of above M.G. Barrage:

(i) The 8 guns of "C" Coy. will take up positions laid down in O.O. No. 48, para. 7 (d), and will come under the orders of B.G.C. 62nd. Inf.Bde. O.C. "C" Coy. will report to 62nd. Inf.Bde.H.Q. as soon as guns are in position.

(ii) "D" Coy. will assemble in LINNET VALLEY with the 2nd. Bn. Lincoln Regt. and will come under the orders of B.G.C. 62nd. Inf. Bde. O.C. "D" Coy. will report to 62nd. Inf.Bde. H.Q. as soon as Company is concentrated.

A. Huxley Lieut /for
Major.
Commanding 21st. Bn. Machine Gun Corps.

17th. September, 1918.

Second Operation
Barrage Table issued with 21 D.A. O.O. 5

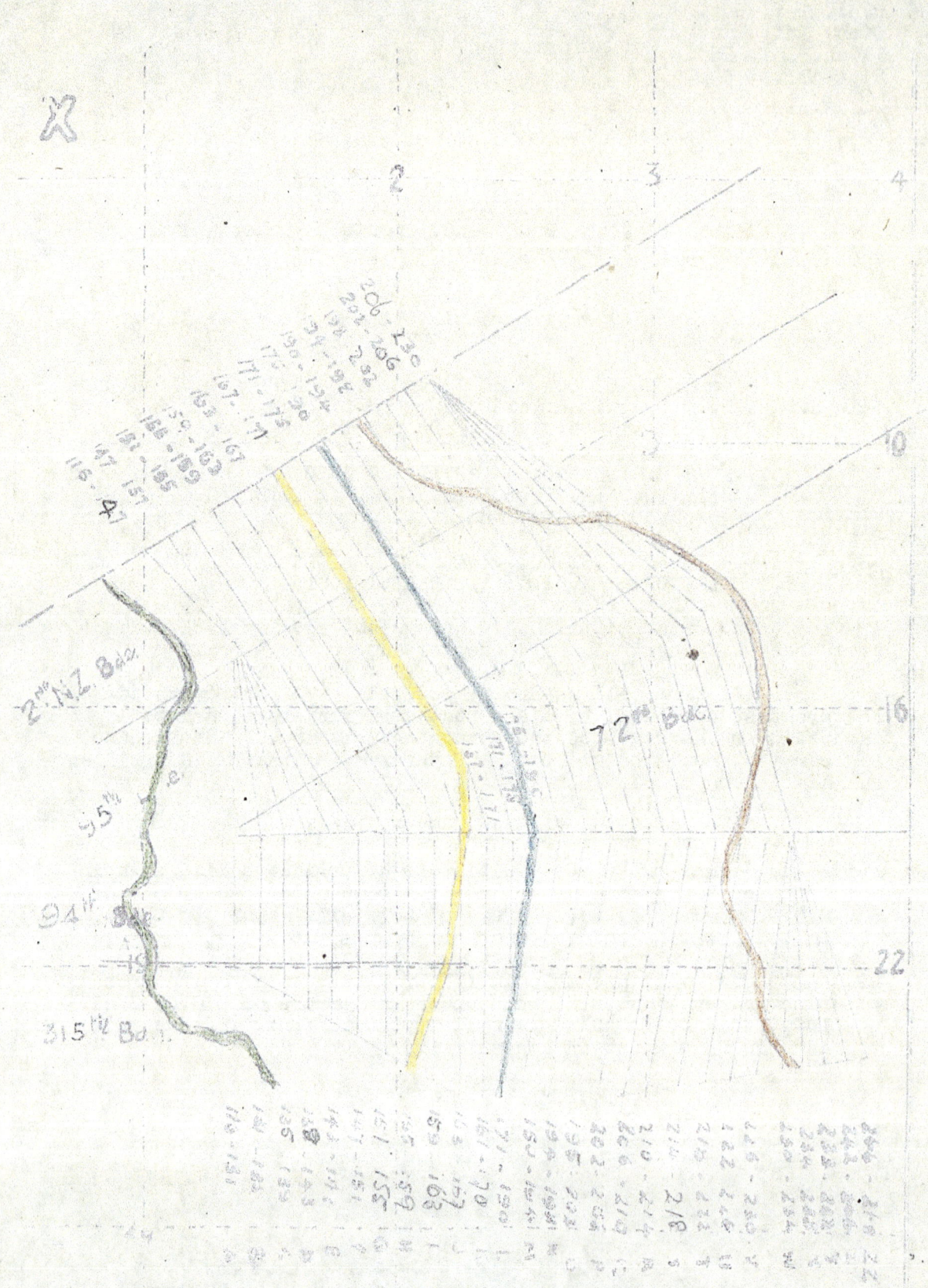

War Diary.

SECRET.

AX/588/0.

ADDENDA to 21st. Bn. M.G.C. O.O. No. 48.

1. During the present operations the Support Trench running from X.8.d.8.3. through X,9.c. - X.15.b. to X.15.d.7.4 will be known as "MEUNIER SUPPORT."

2. One squadron low flying Bristol fighting planes are being detailed to co-operate in the Infantry attack forward from the GREEN LINE and will engage any enemy who appear to be holding up the advance.

3. ZERO hour has been fixed as 5.20 a.m. on 18th. Sept.

                                                      Major.
                      Commanding 21st. Bn. Machine Gun Corps.

17th. September, 1918.

Distribution:

All recipients of 21st. Bn.M.G.C. O.O. No. 48.

SECRET.

To:-
   O.C. "A" Coy. 33rd Bn.M.G.C.
   O.C. "C" Coy.   "
   33rd Bn.M.G.C. (for information)

AX/589/0.

      As soon as notification is received that the BROWN LINE has been captured by this Division, 33rd Bn.M.G.C. Headquarters will be informed.

      "A" and "C" Coys. 33rd Battalion will then withdraw to assembly positions under 33rd Bn. arrangements.

              (sgd.)   A.HUXLEY Lieut.
                               for.
                                   Major.
           Commanding 21st Battn. Machine Gun Corps.

17th.September,1918.

SECRET.
21 Div.
G. 501.

62nd Inf. Bde.
64th :   :
110th :   :
C.R.A.
C.R.E.
D.M.G.O. ✓
Pioneers.

1. Zero hour has been provisionally fixed as 5.20.A.m. on 18th inst.

2. The hour definitely fixed will be communicated by telephone by either saying "Orders hold good" or by indicating the hour decided on by saying the number of minutes before or after 5.20.A.m. that may be fixed.

3. For instance, should 6.A.m. be the hour finally fixed, plus 40 will be telephoned to you.

If 5.A.m. is the hour finally fixed, minus 20 will be telephoned to you.

4. This information will be confirmed by D.R.L.S.

5. Acknowledge.

A.I. Macdougall. Major.
for H. Col.

General Staff.
17th September 1918. 21st Division.

SECRET.

21 Div.
G.212.

62nd Inf Bde.
64th   :
110th   :
C.R.A.
C.R.E.
D.M.G.C.
Pioneers.

Reference 21 Div. G. 201 of to-day.

"ORDERS HOLD GOOD."

Acknowledge.

[signature] Macdougall, Major
General Staff,
21st Division.

17.9.1918.

21st. DIVISION SPECIAL ORDER.

Friday, 20th. September, 1918.

      The successes gained by the Division in the recent fighting, which culminated in the magnificent and successful attack carried out on September 19th, will probably never be surpassed by any Division in the British Army.

      That any Division, after suffering the heavy casualties this Division suffered, whilst breaking up the almost overwhelming attacks of the enemy, should be capable, with practically no respite, of passing to the offensive and, during a months hard and continuous fighting, of carrying out one brilliant attack after another would, previously, have been considered totally impossible.

      It has, however, been accomplished by this Division in no uncertain manner.

      It has only been accomplished because of the splendid "esprit de corps" which animates all ranks, and the "Will to win" which every officer, N.C.O. and man throughout the Division has so clearly shown.

      You have set yourselves a tremendous standard and you now have to live up to that standard.

      This will require the best that every man can give.

      That you will succeed in doing so I have no doubt at all.

(sgd) David G. H. CAMPBELL.

Major-General.
Commanding 21st. Division.

SECRET.
21 Div.
G. 217.

All recipients of Divl. Order No.233.

THE FOLLOWING ADDENDA ARE ISSUED TO
21st DIVISION ORDER 233.

<u>Para 6.</u> add "When the barrage to cover the advance of the 110th Infantry Brigade has been fired, the Reserve Machine Gun Company will assemble with one Battalion 62nd Infantry Brigade (see para 3 (f)) in LINNET VALLEY and will report completion of assembly to 62nd Infantry Brigade Headquarters, through whom any fresh orders will be sent."

<u>At end of para 8.</u>
add "One Squadron low flying Bristol fighting planes are being detailed to co-operate in the Infantry attack forward from the GREEN LINE and will engage any enemy who appear to be holding up the advance."

<u>Appendix "A".</u>
Add to para 3 sub-para (2).
"The Reserve Battalion of the 62nd Infantry Brigade will move by 'B' Group tracks. Arrangements will be made between B.Gs.C. 62nd and 64th Infantry Brigades to avoid clashing."

<u>Add new para 5.</u>
"The boundary in the assembly area between 64th and 110th Infantry Brigades will be a line running due East and West through W.24.a.0.5."

<u>Appendix 'C'.</u>
Add new para 5.
"5. Two Sections, 126th Field Coy. R.E. after completing work of making gaps in the minefield will be at the disposal of the B.G.C. 62nd Infantry Brigade for the purpose of constructing two strong points on the VAUCELLETTE FARM RIDGE."

Macdougall. Major
for
Lieut.Colonel,
General Staff,
21st Division.

17th Sept. 1918.

ZERO hour has been fixed as 5.20 A.M. on 18th Sept.

TELEGRAM.

URGENT
OPERATIONS
PRIORITY
TO BRIGADES.

Words Sent.
AT............
To............
By............

+++++
DADE	DUFA	A/Q	17 Div.
BASU	ZEJU	5th Corps.	33 Div.
VUFE	JESO	do R.A.	38 Div.
LODE	ZOHO	do H.A.	58 Div.
ZOKI	ZODU	12th Div.	15 Sqn R.A.F.

/ 18 / AAA

ZOWU Order No.234. AAA 58 Div. are holding FIR SUPPORT and are advancing at 7.45 p.m. to recapture POPLAR TRENCH AAA 12 Div are trying to make good ROOM TRENCH this evening AAA 17 Div hold BEET TRENCH in touch with our left and GAUCHE WOOD AAA VUFE hold road in X.20 b and d. with advanced line on SPUR X.15.c. . . AAA BASU hold RED LINE objective throughout AAA Boundary between 17 and 21 Divs will now run from X.8.a.6.3. to W.18.Central AAA VUFE will take over PLANE TRENCH from DADE tonight AAA DADE will hold VAUCELLETTE FARM RIDGE from Southern boundary to SKITTLE ALLEY inclusive with two Battns taking over Northern portion from 17 Div AAA Remaining Battn. less two Coys. in Reserve behind their left AAA BASU will hold RED line and will use all resources of Brigade for this purpose AAA DADE will place two Coys. at disposal of BASU for purpose of holding supporting positions West of BEET FACTORY AAA R.E. and Pioneers will construct a line of posts on general line PLANE TRENCH - Spur in X.20.a. West of BEET FACTORY - FIVES TRENCH AAA A continuous line of wire will be put out to cover these posts beginning in the North AAA VUFE will be prepared to carry out attack on LIMERICK POST and RED line tomorrow morning AAA Orders for this later AAA Acknowledge AAA Added. all concerned.

ZOWU

8 p.m.

Lt.Col. G.S.

Copy No. _____ .   S E C R E T.

21st. Bn. M.G.C. OPERATION ORDER No.49.

Ref. Map:
57.c.S.E. 1/20,000.   18th. September, 1918.
----

1.   An attack on LIMERICK POST and MEATH POST and the RED LINE will be carried out by 110th. Inf. Bde. tomorrow from the SUNKEN ROAD in X.20.b. and d.

2.   The guns of "D" Coy. from positions in FOOTBALL TRENCH 8 guns of "A" Coy. in PLANE TRENCH will support the attack with overhead covering fire as follows:-

   "D" Coy.- All available guns will engage LIMERICK POST and Trenches in X.21.d.

   "A" Coy.- 8 guns will engage MEATH POST, LIMERICK TRENCH and PARRS TRENCH in X.21.b.

   No fire will be directed WEST of Grid Line running N. & S. through X.21.central.

3.   The Artillery Barrage (marked BLUE) will be put down at Zero EAST of YELLOW LINE on line marked "L", attached tracing.   It will remain there until Zero plus 8 minutes, when it will creep forward at the rate of 100 yards in four minutes.
   Machine Gun fire will open at Zero and cease fire at Z. plus 16 minutes.

4.   Companies will ascertain Zero hour from respective Brigadiers.

5.   M.G. Companies to acknowledge.

                                     A. Huxley Lieut for
                                                      Major.
Issued at 10 p.m. to: Commanding 21st. Bn. M. G. Corps.

Copy No. 1 .. O.C. "A" Coy.)
         2 .. O.C. "D" Coy.) with tracing.
         3 .. 62nd. Inf. Bde.
         4 .. 110th. Inf. Bde.
         5 .. File.
     6 & 7 .. War Diary.

MESSAGES & SIGNALS.

	Sent	
ZEJU	At 12.15. a.m.	ZEJU
	To 62 Bde.	19.9.18.
	By A.E.B.	

TO:- ZEFI.

---   19   AAA

O.O. No.49 cancelled.

From.-ZEJU.

CERTIFIED TRUE COPY.

S E C R E T.

Copy No......7

21st DIVISION ORDER No.235.

Ref. Sheet 57.c. 1/40,000.

19th September 1918.

1. The Division (less Artillery) will be relieved in the line by the 33rd Division (less Artillery) tonight 19th/20th September, 1918.

   Reliefs and moves to rest areas will take place in accordance with attached Table.

2. All details will be arranged between Brigadiers concerned.

3. (a) The Machine Gun Companies attached to 64th and 110th Infantry Brigades will be relieved under arrangements to be made between B.G's.C. 64th, 110th, 19th and 98th Infantry Brigades.

   (b) The remaining Machine Gun Companies will be relieved under arrangements to be made between O's.C. 21st and 33rd Battalions Machine Gun Corps.

   (c) On relief, Machine Gun Companies will stage with affiliated Brigades for the night 19th/20th inst, and will move to final rest area in Valley U.6.c and d. on 20th inst. No restrictions as to time. 21st Battalion Machine Gun Corps Headquarters will not move.

4. On completion of relief, the Field Artillery at present covering the Divisional Sector will come under the orders of G.O.C. 33rd Division.

5. The relief of Field Companies R.E. and Pioneer Battalion will be arranged between C's.R.E. On relief, Field Companies R.E. and Pioneer Battalion will remain in present locations..

6. The relief of Field Ambulances will be arranged between A.D's.M.S.

7. All movement of Infantry and Horse Transport will be by cross-country tracks where available.

8. Completion of reliefs and moves will be reported to Divisional Headquarters.

9. Command of Sector passes to G.O.C., 33rd Division on completion of Infantry relief.

/10......

- 2 -

10.   Divisional Headquarters will not move.

11.   A C K N O W L E D G E.

A.M.Macdougall. Major
for.
Lieut.-Colonel.
General Staff.
21st Division.

Issued through Signals at 3.30 p.m.

	Copy No.		Copy No.
62nd Inf. Bde.	1	D.G.O.	13
64th " "	2	Vth Corps.	14-15
110th " "	3	Vth Corps R.A.	16
C.R.A.	4	Vth Corps H.A.	17
C.R.E.	5	58th Div.	19
Pioneers.	6	12th Div.	20
D.M.G.O.	7	17th Div.	21
Signals.	8	33rd Div.	22
A.D.M.S.	9	38th Div.	23
Train.	10	15th Sqn. R.A.F.	24
A/Q	11	War Diary.	25
A.P.M.	12	File.	26.

Copy No. 16   S E C R E T.

21st. Bn. M.G.C. OPERATION ORDER No. 50.

Ref. Map:
57.c.S.E. 1/20.000.   19th. Sept. 1918.

1. The 21st. Division (less Artillery) will be relieved by the 33rd. Division on the night 19/20th. inst.

2. The guns of "A", "B" and "C" Coys. 21st. Bn. M.G.C. will be relieved by 2 Coys. of the 33rd. Bn. M.G.C. under arrangements made direct between Coy. Commanders concerned.

3. On relief or withdrawal, Companies will return to concentration areas as follows:-

   "A" Coy .. with 110th. Inf.Bde .. ETRICOURT - MANANCOURT.

   "B" Coy (plus 2
   guns "D" Coy)   " 64th.   "   .. area in Squares V.14, 15 and 9.

   "C" Coy .. with 62nd.   "   .. area between SOREL LE GRAND and NURLU-FINS Road.

   "D" Coy (less 2 guns) will withdraw on completion of relief of 110th. Inf.Bde. to area between SOREL LE GRAND and NURLU-FINS Road.

4. Company Seconds-in-Command will arrange direct with Os.C. Coys. regarding Transport requirements.

5. Arrival in new area will be reported by code word "ASSHETON."

6. On the 20th. inst. all Companies will move to final Rest area in Valley U.6.c. and d.
   Companies will not arrive in new area before 4 p.m.

7. M.G.Companies to acknowledge.

                                            Lieut. & A/Adjutant.
                                            21st. Battn. Machine Gun Corps.

Distribution:
Copy No. 1 .. O.C. "A" Coy. Fwd.   9 .. 62nd.Inf.Bde.
         2 .. "   "   "   Rear. 10 .. 64th.   "
         3 .. "   " "B" Coy. Fwd. 11 .. 110th. "
         4 .. "   "   "   Rear. 12 .. 21st. Div. 'G'.
         5 .. "   " "C" Coy. Fwd. 13 .. Quartermaster.
         6 .. "   "   "   Rear. 14 .. File.
         7 .. "   " "D" Coy. Fwd. 15 .. War Diary.
         8 .. "   "   "   Rear, 16 .. "   "
                                   17 .. 33 Bn. M.G.C.

War Diary.

AX/621/O.

O.C. "C" Coy. Forward.
O.C. "D" Coy.   "

        Reference para. 6 of 21st. Bn. M.G.C. Operation Order No. 50 of today's date:

        Please note that under instructions received from Divisional H.Q. you will remain in your present location until further orders.

        Acknowledge by wire.

19th. Sept. 1918.
                            Lieut. & A/Adjt.
                 for O.C. 21 Bn. Machine Gun Corps.

Copy of Telegram received from General SHUTE d/ 18.9.18.

I am instructed by the Army Commander to convey his most hearty congratulations and thanks to all Units of the Vth Corps on their splendid performance today AAA It is unnecessary for me to say how proud I am of what all ranks have done AAA

21 Div
G. 300.

To all concerned.

Forwarded for communication to all ranks.

A.F.MACDOUGALL, Major
General Staff
21st Division.

19.9.18.

CERTIFIED TRUE COPY.

SECRET.   Copy No. 7......

21st DIVISION ORDER NO. 236.

Ref. Sheet 57.c.
1/40,000   23rd September 1918.

1.   The Division (less Artillery) will relieve the 17th Division (less Artillery) in the left Sector of the Vth Corps front on the night 25th/26th inst. Moves and reliefs will take place in accordance with attached table.

2.   All details will be arranged between Brigadiers concerned.

3.   Machine Gun reliefs will be arranged between O's C. 21st and 17th Battalions Machine Gun Corps.

4.   Reliefs of Field Companies R.E. and Field Ambulances will be arranged between C's R.E. and A.D's M.S. respectively.

5.   All Defence Schemes, Aeroplane Photographs etc. will be taken over.

6.   Completion of reliefs will be reported to Divisional Headquarters.

7.   Command of the Sector passes to G.O.C. 21st Division on completion of the Infantry Relief.

8.   Divisional Headquarters will remain in the present location but will eventually move to V.4.b. at an hour and date to be notified later.

9.   Acknowledge.

                                                    A.I. MACDOUGALL, Major
                                                               for
                                                              Lieut. Colonel.
                                                               General Staff.
                                                              21st Division.

Issued through Signals 7.30 p.m. to:-

	Copy. No.		Copy No.
62nd Inf Bde.	1	D.G.O.	13
64th " "	2	Vth Corps	14-15
110th " "	3	Vth Corps R.A.	16
C.R.A.	4	Vth Corps H.A.	17
C.R.E.	5	5th Division.	18
Pioneers.	6	33rd Division.	19
D.M.G.C.	7	17th Division.	20
Signals.	8	38th Division.	21
A.D.M.S.	9	15th Sqn. R.A.F.	22
Train	10	War Diary	23
A/Q	11	File.	24
A.P.M.	12		

                              CERTIFIED TRUE COPY.

SECRET.

21 Div.
G.396.

PROCEEDINGS OF CONFERENCE HELD AT DIVISIONAL
HEADQUARTERS, 23rd SEPT, 1918.

Present:-

  B.G.C. 62nd Inf. Bde.
  B.G.C. 64th " "
  O.C. 110th." "
  C.R.A.
  C.R.E.
  D.M.G.C.
  A.A.Q.M.G.
  O.C.Signals.

1. The Divisional Commander explained the situation and the reasons for the Division again going into the line in relief of 17th Division.

2. The Divisional Commander said that he did not intend that the 64th Infantry Brigade, which would be in support, to take over the dispositions at present held by support Brigade, 17th Div. The dispositions of the 64th Infantry Brigade would be as follows:-

  1 Battalion. ... V.3.
  1 " ... Q.32.
  1 " ... V.6.

3. Combing Out.

The Divisional Commander wished Brigadiers to go into the question of combing out all men at present employed in transport lines, band etc. He said that he wished every man who is not essential for transport etc. to be available to take his place in the line.

4. Attack on Strong Points.

The Divisional Commander said that the Corps Commander had pointed out that most of the casualties suffered by the 33rd Division in their recent attacks had been caused through Brigades attacking strong points by driblets instead of forming a proper plan by which strong points could be attacked with sufficient force using trench mortars etc.,

5. Gas.

The Area which the Division is taking over has been subjected to a certain amount of gas shelling during the last few days. The Divisional Commander wished the Brigadiers to ensure that proper gas discipline is observed.

6. Tracks.

B.Gs.C. 62nd and 64th Inf Bdes pointed out that the tracks laid out for recent operations crossed sunken roads in such a way that in wet weather it was extremely difficult for troops to get up the banks. The C.R.E. said he would take this matter in hand.

7. The B.G.C. 64th Inf Bde considered, that, when one Brigade had to leap-frog through another Brigade in the attack, it was advisable to detail a Company from the Reserve Battalion to mop up any points that might not have been cleared by the first attacking Brigade in order that the troops making the second attack

/should......

-2-

should not be delayed. This method was employed by the 64th Inf. Bde. in the recent attack and was fully justified. The Divisional Commander agreed.

8. The B.G.C. 62nd Inf Bde suggested that when all three Brigades were taking part in an attack, the Division should lay down orders the times for marching to the assembling positions and also the time by which the assembly of each Brigade was to be completed. The Divisional Commander agreed.

9. Communications.

The Divisional Commander considered that during recent operations communications had not been entirely satisfactory.

O.C. Signals said that this was not due to Brigades but entirely to technical faults which he hoped had now been rectified. He suggested that only Infantry and Artillery Brigades, M.G. Companies and the liaison Heavy Artillery Brigade should be allowed to use Divisional Exchanges. Instructions will be issued on this point.

In order to lessen the traffic on telephone and telegraph lines, it was suggested that Divisional and Brigade Operation Orders whould be sent by D.R.

B.G.C. 62nd Inf Bde said that he found communication with flank Brigades was very difficult during recent operations.

The Divisional Commander said that during moving warfare it would be impossible to lay lateral lines for this purpose and that the Corps Cyclists attached to Brigades should be used for this purpose.

B.G.C. 64th Inf Bde said that during recent operations the three lines laid from Division to Brigades were too close together and that one shell broke them all. O.C. Signals said that this matter had been taken up.

10. Greatcoats.

Brigadiers were averse to taking greatcoats into the line. The A.A.& Q.M.G. said that leather jerkins would be available tomorrow and Brigadiers said that they would like them issued.

The Divisional Commander said that in his opinion it was essential that everything should be done for the men's comfort in the present case but that he left the matter entirely in the hands of the Brigadiers.

A.F. MACDOUGALL, Major
For Lt. Col.
General Staff,
21st Division.

23.9.18.

CERTIFIED TRUE COPY.

Copy No. 13. 　　　　　　　　　　　　　　　　　　　　　　　　SECRET.

21st. Bn. M.G.C. OPERATION ORDER No. 51.

Ref. Map:
57.c.S.E. 1/20.000.　　　　　　　　　　　　　　　24th. September, 1918.

1. The 21st. Division, less Artillery, will relieve the 17th. Division in the GOUZEAUCOURT Sector on the night 25/26th. Sept.

2. The 21st. Bn. M.G.C. will relieve guns of the 17th. Bn. as follows:-

   (a) "A" Coy. will relieve 4 guns at each of the following positions:

   　　W.6.d.central.　　W.11.a.central.　　W.5.a.2.2.

   4 guns will be placed in SUNKEN ROAD in W.9.d. as Bde.Reserve.

   (b) The guns of "C" Coy. will be placed in selected areas by Sections, under arrangements made between B.G.C. 62nd. Inf.Bde. and O.C. "C" Coy.

   (c) "B" Coy. will relieve 16 guns of 17th. Bn. in Barrage Positions in W.4.b.

   (d) "D" Coy. will place 16 guns in positions in W.4.d. for Barrage purposes.

   Further instructions will be issued regarding paras. (c) and (d) above.

3. All other arrangements will be made between Company Commanders direct.

4. Completion of above moves and reliefs will be wired to Battalion H.Q. by code word "THOMSON".

5. Battalion H.Q. will remain in present location but will move at an hour and date to be notified later to approximately V.4.a.

6. ACKNOWLEDGE.

　　　　　　　　　　　　　　　　　　　　　　　　Lieut. & A/Adjt.
　　　　　　　　　　　　　　　　　　　21st. Battalion Machine Gun Corps.

Distribution:

Copy No. 1 .. O.C. "A" Coy.　　　　Copy No. 8 .. 21st. Div. 'G'.
　　　　2 .. "   "B" Coy.　　　　　　　　　9 .. 17th. Bn. M.G.C.
　　　　3 .. "   "C" Coy.　　　　　　　　　10 .. 33rd. Bn. M.G.C.
　　　　4 .. "   "D" Coy.　　　　　　　　　11 .. File.
　　　　5 .. 62nd. Inf.Bde.　　　　　　　　12 .. War Diary.
　　　　6 .. 64th. Inf.Bde.　　　　　　　　13 .. "   "
　　　　7 .. 110th. Inf.Bde.

SECRET.

21 Div.
G. 418.

62 Inf Bde.
64 " "
110 " "

PLAN FOR ATTACK ALONG QUENTIN RIDGE AND ON GONNELIEU.
----

1. This attack will be carried out by the 64th and 110th Infantry Brigades, probably on night 27th/28th at a Zero hour about 3.30 a.m.
    Simultaneously the 33rd. Division will be attacking VILLERS GUISLAN and the 5th Division CEMETRY and FUSILIER RIDGES (probably from the North)

2. The objectives :-

    (a) Dotted Green Line.

    (b) Red line.

    (c) Blue Line.

    are shown on attached Map.
    Inter-Divisional boundaries are shown Black and Brigade Boundaries Brown.

3. It is proposed that the initial barrage line shall be as shown dotted black on Map.
    All posts in front of this line or within the safety limit would have to be withdrawn previous to Zero.

4. 64th Infantry Brigade would take over area South East of Inter-Brigade Boundary on night Y/Z
    62nd Infantry Brigade would take over as far East as Railway inclusive on same night.

5. It is suggested that the 64th Infantry Brigade would require one Battalion for Green dotted and Red lines and two Battalions for GONNELIEU and Blue line, and that 110th Infantry Brigade would require 6 Companies for Green dotted line and for Green Switch and neighbouring trenches, 4 Companies for Red line and two in Reserve.

6. Probably half an hours pause would be required on Red line.
    Is any pause required on the Green dotted line? It is considered advisable to get away from the GAUCHE WOOD Area as soon as possible.

7. Four Tanks will be available. Their suggested lines of advance are shown Yellow on Map.

    The 110th Infantry Brigade will detail a special party to accompany the most Westerly Tank, in order to "MOP UP" the LOOP TRENCH in R.31.b.

/8..........

8. Four Brigades R.A. will be available for barrage, also four Machine Gun Companies.
One Machine Gun Company will be attached to 64th Infantry Brigade and one Machine Gun Company to 110th Infantry Brigade for consolidation purposes.

9. GOUZEAUCOURT will be kept under bombardment by heavy artillery and 6" Newton Mortars throughout the operation and will be mopped by up by 62nd Infantry Brigade from the East at a time to be detailed later.

10. Brigadiers will forward any suggested alterations or additions to the above as soon as possible.

xxxxMACRONGALLYxMajor

H.E.FRANKLYN Lt.Col.
General Staff,
21st. Division.

24.9.18.

Copies to:-
   C.R.A.
   D.M.G.C.
   "B" Coy. Tanks.

CERTIFIED TRUE COPY.

SECRET.   Copy No.7......

                    21st Division Order No.237.

                                                26th September 1918.

Ref: Map 57.C. S.E. 1/20,000
----

1.   In conjunction with operations to the North, the
   21st Division will:-

   (a)   Capture AFRICAN TRENCH from trench junction
            Q.35.a.6.5. to the Northern Divisional Boundary.

   (b)   Advance along QUENTIN RIDGE and capture GONNELIEU
            at the same time that the 33rd Division on the right
            attacks VILLERS GUISLAIN.

2.   The date for attack (a) and the probable date for attack
            (b) have been communicated to all concerned. The
            Zero hour for each will be notified later.

3. (a)   The attack on AFRICAN TRENCH will be carried
            out by one Battalion, 62nd Infantry Brigade
            supported by one Brigade R.F.A. and 12 - 6" Newton
            Mortars.
               This attack will be made in conjunction with
            the 13th Infantry Brigade (5th Division) on the
            left.

   (b)   The ground for 300 yards East of AFRICAN TRENCH
            will be cleared of the enemy by specially detailed
            parties, after which these parties will return to
            the trench.

   (c)   Details of an indirect Machine Gun Barrage will
            be notified separately.

4. (a)   The attack along QUENTIN RIDGE will be carried
            out by the 64th and 110th Infantry Brigades.

   (b)   One Battalion 64th Infantry Brigade on the
            right and the 110th Infantry Brigade on the left
            will capture successively the dotted Green and
            Red lines, after which two Battalions 64th Infantry
            Brigade will pass through the 110th Infantry
            Brigade and take GONNELIEU Village, connecting with
            the 5th Division who will be attacking FUSILIER
            and CEMETRY RIDGES from the N.W.

   (c)   The 64th Infantry Brigade will make good the
            Brown line as a final objective.

   (d)   The 110th Infantry Brigade will detail parties
            to "mop up" the Quarry in R.31.c. and the loop trench
            in R.31.b.
               "Green Switch" and "QUENTIN ALLEY" will be held
            as a defensive flank against GOUZEAUCOURT, until
            this latter place has been captured.
               GREEN LANE and GREEN SWITCH will also be held as
            a supporting line to the final objective.

                                                /(e).......

(e) After the capture of VILLERS TRENCH the 64th Infantry Brigade, when they renew their advance will arrange ti leave a garrison in it connecting with the 33rd Division on the right and the 110th Infantry Brigade on the left.

5. After the capture of the Brown line orders may be received for the exploitation of success to the Green Line. If GOUZEAUCOURT has been cleared and sufficient notice is received, this exploitation will be carried out by the 62nd Infantry Brigade; otherwise orders will be issued for one Battalion 110th Infantry Brigade on the right and one Battalion 64th Infantry Brigade on the left to undertake this operation.

6. The 62nd Infantry Brigade will keep constant touch with the enemy in GOUZEAUCOURT (particularly at Zero plus two hours) by means of patrols and will be prepared to reinforce these patrols and occupy the village if the enemy shows signs of evacuating it.

Liaison will be arranged by 62nd Infantry Brigade with the two Newton Mortar Batteries which will be bombarding GOUZEAUCOURT so that their fire can be stopped earlier than Zero plus two hours, if required. (see para 9)

7. Liaison Posts will be established as follows:-

(a) Between 64th Infantry Brigade and the 33rd Division at the Cemetery X.2.d.9.9. and on the Boundary in GLASS STREET.

(b) Between 64th Infantry Brigade and 5th Division at road junction R.27.a.9.1.

These Liaison posts will be joint posts and will consist of one Platoon found by each Unit concerned.

8. (a) Four Brigades R.F.A. will support the attack along QUENTIN RIDGE.
Barrage Tables will be issued separately.

(b) Heavy Artillery to support the attack will be :-

3 Batteries 6" Howitzers.
1 Battery   8"   "
1   "   9'2" "
1   "   60 pdrs.

(c) The tasks of the Heavy Artillery will be to bombard the Red line and GONNELIEU until the approach of the Infantry.

(d) When it becomes necessary to lift off GONNELIEU all except 1 - 6" Howitzer Battery and the 60-pdr Battery will be engaged on counter-battery work. The 6" Howitzer Battery will fire on BANTEUX SPUR and the 60 pdr Battery on the area round TURNER CRATER (R.34.d.)

/9.(a).........

9. (a) 18 - 6" Newton Mortars will bombard GOUZEAUCOURT particularly the Eastern outskirts from Zero till Zero plus two hours.

   (b) 6 Newton Mortars will put down a hurricane bombardment on the trenches in R.31.d. from Zero to Zero plus 4 minutes and will then lift and join in the bombardment of GOUZEAUCOURT.

10. (a) 1½ Machine Gun Companies will cover the advance of the 64th and 110th Infantry Brigades by an indirect barrage.

    (b) Two Machine Gun Companies will engage the area between the main Railway and GOUZEAUCOURT from Zero till Zero plus two hours.
    One Machine Gun Company is allotted to 64th Infantry Brigade and one Company to 110th Infantry Brigade for consolidation purposes.

    (c) Eight machine guns will remain with the 62nd Infantry Brigade.

11. Four tanks will assist the advance along QUENTIN RIDGE and the capture of GONNELIEU. They will afterwards rally west of the Village and will be prepared to assist the troops detailed to make an immediate counter-attack against GONNELIEUm should this be necessary.

12. The O.C. 15th Squadron, R.A.F. will be arranging for contact aeroplanes to call for flares during daylight. The call for flares will be the sounding of a Klaxon Horn.
    Red flares will be used.
    Only the foremost troops will light flares when the aeroplane calls.
    The aeroplane signal to denote the assembly of enemy to counter-attack is the dropping of a redsmoke bomb over the place where the enemy is seen.

13. Watches will be synchronised by an Officer from Divisional Headquarters between 5 p.m. and 6 p.m. on the evening before the attack.

14. ACKNOWLEDGE.

                                Sgd. H.I.FRANKLYN
                                    Lieut. Colonel.
                                    General Staff,
                                    21st Division.

Issued at 9 a.m. to:-

	Copy No.		Copy No.
62 Inf. Bde.	1	A.P.M.	12
64 " "	2	5th Div.	13
110 " "	3	17th Div.	14
C.R.A.	4	33rd Div.	15
C.R.E.	5	38th Div.	16
Pioneers	6	V.Corps	17 - 18
D.M.G.C.	7	V.Corps R.A.	19
Signals	8	V.Corps H.A.	20
A.D.M.S.	9	B Coy. Tanks	21
Train	10	War Diary	22
A/Q	11	File.	23

CERTIFIED TRUE COPY.

SECRET.

21Div.
G.467.

All Recipients of Divl. Order No. 237.

The following amendments and addenda will be made to 21st Division Order No.237.-

Para 5 will be amended to read:-

"As soon as the protective barrage lifts, previously detailed fighting patrols will advance with the object of capturing prisoners and feeling their way towards the Green Line. If these patrols do not meet with resistance they will be supported and the Green Line made good, if possible.
If patrols meet resistance there is no question of attacking the Green Line, but a properly organised operation will be arranged by the Divisional Commander to take place at a later date. This operation will probably be carried out by the 62nd Infantry Brigade: in any case fresh orders for this operation will be issued."

Add new sub-para (c) to para 7:-

"(c). Between 110th Infantry Brigade and 1st Devons (Right Battalion, 5th Division) at R.26.a.8.1. where reserve line crosses main road"

H.I.FRANKLYN

Lieut. Colonel.
General Staff
21st. Division.

26.9.18.

CERTIFIED TRUE COPY.

Copy No. 16   S E C R E T.

21st. Bn. M.G.C. OPERATION ORDER No. 52.

Ref. Map:
57.c.S.E. 1/20.000.   26th. September 1918.
----

1.   In conjunction with operations to the North, the
   21st. Division will -

   (a) Capture AFRICAN TRENCH from Q.35.a.6.8. to Northern
       Divisional Boundary.

   (b) Advance along QUENTIN RIDGE and capture GONNELIEU at the
       same time that the 33rd. Division on the Right attacks
       VILLERS GUISLAIN.

2.   The attack on AFRICAN TRENCH will be carried out by
   1 Battalion 62nd. Inf.Bde. in conjunction with the 5th. Divn.
   on the Left. The ground for 300 yards East of AFRICAN TRENCH
   will be cleared of the enemy by specially detailed parties,
   after which these parties will return to the trench.

3.   "B" and "D" Coys. 21st. Bn. M.G.C. will support
   (a) attack as shown in Barrage Time Table No. 1.

4.   (a) The attack along QUENTIN RIDGE will be carried out
   by 64th. and 110th. Inf.Bdes.

     (b) One Battalion 64th. Inf.Bde. on the Right and 110th.
   Inf.Bde. on the Left will capture successively the Dotted
   GREEN and RED Lines, after which two Battalions 64th. Inf.Bde.
   will pass through 110th. Inf.Bde. and take GONNELIEU,
   connecting with 5th. Division who will be attacking FUSILIER
   and CEMETERY Ridges from the N.W.

     (c) The 64th. Inf.Bde. will make good the BROWN LINE as
   a final objective.

     (d) 110th. Inf.Bde. will "Mop up" the QUARRY in R.31.c.
   and the Loop Trench in R.31.b.

        GREEN SWITCH and QUENTIN ALLEY will be held as a
   defensive flank against GOUZEAUCOURT until this latter place
   has been captured.

5.   After the capture of the BROWN LINE orders may be
   received for the exploitation of success to the GREEN LINE.
   If GOUZEAUCOURT has been cleared and sufficient notice is
   received, this exploitation will be carried out by the 62nd.
   Inf.Bde; otherwise orders will be issued for one Battalion
   110th. Inf.Bde. on the Right and one Battalion 64th. Inf.Bde.
   on the Left to undertake this operation.

                                                   /6 ....

6. The 62nd. Inf.Bde. will keep constant touch with the enemy in GOUZEAUCOURT (particularly at Zero plus 2 hours) by means of patrols and will be prepared to reinforce those patrols and occupy the village if the enemy shows signs of evacuating it.

7. Liaison Posts will be established as follows:-

   (a.) Between 64th. Inf.Bde. and 33rd. Division at the Cemetery X.2.d.9.9 and on the Boundary in GLASS STREET.

   (b) Between 64th. Inf.Bde. and 5th. Division at road junction R.27.a.9.1.

   These liaison posts will be joint posts and will consist of one Platoon found by each unit concerned.

8. "D" Coy. and 8 guns of "C" Coy. plus 2 Coys. 17th. Bn. M.G.C. will support (b) attack as shown on Barrage Time Table No. 2.

9. "A" Coy. will be affiliated to 110th. Inf.Bde. for consolidation of objectives under orders of B.G.C. 110th. Inf.Bde.

10. "C" Coy. less 8 guns will be affiliated to 62nd. Inf.Bde. under orders of B.G.C. 62nd. Inf.Bde.

11. A C K N O W L E D G E.

Issued at 8 p.m.

Lieut. & A/Adjt.
21st. Battalion Machine Gun Corps.

Distribution:

Copy No. 1 .. O.C. "A" Coy.   Copy No. 12 .. Commanding
         2 ..   "B" Coy.   Officer.
         3 ..   "C" Coy.   13 .. Intell.Offr.
         4 ..   "D" Coy.   14 .. Quartermaster.
         5 .. 62nd. Inf.Bde.   15 .. File.
         6 .. 64th.   "   16 .. War Diary.
         7 .. 110th. "   17 .. "   "
         8 .. 21st. Div. 'G'   18 ..
         9 .. 5th. Bn. M.G.C.   19 ..
        10 .. 17th. Bn. M.G.C.
        11 .. 33rd. Bn. M.G.C.

SECRET.

AX/719/0.

In continuation of 21st. Bn. M.G.C. Operation Order No. 52:-

1. Four tanks will assist the advance along QUENTIN RIDGE and the capture of GONNELIEU. They will afterwards rally west of the village and will be prepared to assist the troops detailed to make an immediate counter-attack against GONNELIEU, should this be necessary.

2. The aeroplane signal to denote the assembly of enemy to counter-attack is the dropping of a red smoke bomb over the place where the enemy is seen.

3. Watches will be synchronised by an Officer from respective Brigade Headquarters between 5 p.m. and 6 p.m. on the evening before each attack.

Lieut. & A/Adjt.
21st. Battn. Machine Gun Corps.

To:
All receipients of 21 Bn. M.G.C. O.O.No.52.

21st. Battn. Machine Gun Corps.   BARRAGE TIME TABLE No. 1.

Coy.	Battery Position.	Target.	Time.	Rate of fire.	Remarks.
"B" 8 guns.	W.4.b. and d.	Q.36.a.2.0. - Q.30.d.3.3.	Zero to Zero plus 35 minutes.	1 belt per 2 mins. for 10 minutes. 1 belt per 3 mins. for 25 minutes.	On completion, pass to B.G.C. 64th. Inf. Bde.
"B" 8 guns.	- do -	Q.36.a.45.20 - Q.30.d.1.3.	- do -	- do -	- do -
"D" 8 guns.	W.4.b. and d.	Q.36.a.3.2. - Q.30.c.7.3.	- do -	- do -	On completion, move to Barrage Positions in W.6.d. to support attack (b)
"D" 8 guns.	- do -	Q.36.a.1.2. - Q.30.c.4.3.	- do -	- do -	- do -

ZERO hour will be *[signature]*

AMENDMENT to 21st. Bn. M.G.C. Barrage Time Table No. 2.

Ref: "B" Coy. 17th. Bn. M.G.C.

Rate of fire:

For: "1 belt per gun per 3 mins. for 12 mins, then 1 belt per 5 mins."

Read: "1 belt per gun per 2 mins. for 12 mins, then 1 belt per 5 mins."

To:
All recipients of 21 Bn.M.G.C. O.O. No.52.

21st. Bn. Machine Gun Corps.   BARRAGE TIME TABLE No. 2.

Coy.	Battery Position.	Target.	Time.	Rate of fire.	Remarks.
"D" Coy. 21 Bn.MGC. 16 guns.	W.5.b.6.5.	R.32.a.3.0. – R.32.d.3.0.	Zero – Zero plus 12 mins.	1 belt per gun per 2 mins.	Lift on to 2nd. Barrage Line.
		R.32.a.8.9. – R.32.b.1.0.	Zero plus 12 – Z. plus 60.	1 belt per gun per 5 mins.	Cease fire and remain in Battery Positions in Divl Reserve, and be prepared to engage targets between GOUZEAUCOURT and the Railway.
"C" Coy. 21 Bn.MGC. 8 guns.	CHAPEL ALLEY.	R.3.c.05.70 – R.32.d.3.2.	Zero – Zero plus 12 mins.	1 belt per gun per 2 mins.	Lift on to 2nd. Barrage Line.
		R.33.c.5.1. – R.32.d.9.8.	Zero plus 12 – Z. plus 76.	1 belt per gun per 3 mins.	Cease fire and remain in Battery Positions under orders of 62 Inf.Bde.
"A" Coy. 17 Bn.MGC	W.11.d. & W.12.c.	Q.36.d.8.6 – R.25.c.4.4.	Zero – Zero plus 120 mins.	1 belt per gun per 2 mins for 12 mins, then 1 belt per 5 mins.	These guns can be withdrawn at the discretion of Coy.Cmdrs. at Zero plus 120.
"B" Coy. 17 Bn.MGC.	W.11.b. & W.12.c.	Q.36.d.5.8 – R.25.c.1.4.	Zero – Zero plus 120 mins.	1 belt per gun per 3 mins for 12 mins, then 1 belt per 5 mins.	– do –

Zero hour will be notified later.

S E C R E T.

21st Battalion M.G.Corps.

ADMINISTRATIVE INSTRUCTION No.1.

1. PRECAUTIONS AGAINST GAS.

    (a) Any man whose clothes have been impregnated with gas will be sent to the Baths at V.4.c.6.2. where they will be given a bath and change of clothing.
    (b) Bottles for carrying the iron ration of carbonate of soda have now been issued. These bottles are hard to replace and care must be taken that they are not lost or thrown away.

2. SALVAGE.

    (a) All Salvage collected will be sent to First Line Transport lines.
    (b) It is important that all perishable stores, such as rifles, machine guns, etc., should be salved as soon as possible M.G.belts, Lewis gun drums and petrol tins are also urgently required.

3. VETERINARY.

    At several places, German notices bearing the following words have been found:-

              ACHTUNG
          PFERDE LAZARETT
            RAUDE;
    (Translation:- Beware - Veterinary Hospital - MANGE)

    These places should be avoided.

4. IDENTITY DISCS.

    Cases frequently occur of both identity discs being taken off bodies. The green identity disc must never be removed, but must be buried with the body.

Distribution.

All Companies (Forward)
    -do-   (Rear)
    -do-   Quartermaster.

S E C R E T.

APPENDIX 'A' to 21st.Dn. M.G.C. O.O. No.52.

ADMINISTRATIVE ARRANGEMENTS.

1. AMMUNITION.

    (a) A.R.P. is at P.32.b.5.6.
    (b) S.A.A. & Grenade dumps are at:-

        V.4.c.9.0.
        W.2.c.9.4.
        W.13.b.7.6.

2. WATER.

A water-point (pipe supply) will be opened at DESSART WOOD, W.2.c.

3. PACKS, TRENCH SHELTERS ETC.

Greatcoats and trench shelters will be collected and stacked on a lorry route and left in charge of a small guard. Positions to be reported to Divisional H.Q.

4. STRAGGLERS POSTS.

D.A.P.M. will arrange for a line of Straggler Posts on the road V.6.d. - V.35.a. Straggler Collecting Post - V.35.central.

SECRET.

APPENDIX 'B' to 21st. Bn. M.G.C. O.O. No.52.

MISCELLANEOUS.

1. **LIGHT SIGNALS.**

    (a) S.O.S. Signal for Vth. Corps will remain Green/Red/Green.

    (b) S.O.S. Signal for IV Corps on our Left is Red/Green/Red.

    (c) Coloured Very Lights will be used as follows:-

    RED - "We are here."

    GREEN - "Lengthen range."

2. **DISTINCTIVE MARKS.**

    The following will wear a knot of white tape on the left shoulder strap:

    (a) The Right Battalion of the 64th. Inf.Bde. (detailed to attack Green dotted and Red lines).

    (b) The 4th. King's Regiment (Left Battalion, 33rd. Div).

    (c) The Battalion of the 110th. Inf.Bde. detailed to capture the Red Line.

    (d) The Left Battalion 64th. Inf.Bde. detailed to capture GONNELIEU.

    (e) The 1st. Devons (Right Battalion 5th. Division).

3. The pass word to be used by the Right of the 5th. Divn. and the left of this Division so as to ensure recognition will be the word "THRUSH".

4. **HEADQUARTERS.**

    Divisional Headquarters will be at V.4.b.2.5.
    64th. Inf.Bde. Headquarters   .. X.7.c.0.7.
    110th. Inf. Bde.   ..   .. W.18.a.3.8.

SECRET.

21 Div.
G.498.

All recipients of Div. Order No.237.

      Reference para.1 (b) of 21st Division Order No.237 dated 26th September, 1918.

      This operation will NOT take place tonight, but will probably take place on night 28th/29th instant.

                       A.F.MACDOUGALL, Major
                          for Lt.Col.
                       General Staff
                       21st. Division.

27th September, 1918.

CERTIFIED TRUE COPY.

TELEGRAM.

URGENT
OPERATIONS
PRIORITY TO
    Bdes
       H.I.F.

Words

Sent.
At.....................
To.....................
By.....................

DADE	LODE	33rd. Div.
BASU	ZEJU	5th Corps.
VUFE	5th Div.	15th. Sqn. R.A.F.

G.X.5151. / 28 / AAA

IVth Corps report that enemy have withdrawn from their front AAA
DADE has occupied AFRICAN TRENCH and is pushing patrols towards
GOUZEAUCOURT AAA If patrols sent by VUFE meet no resistance VUFE will
occupy line GREEN LANE GREEN SWITCH getting touch with 5th Division
at R.26.a.9.1. AAA When this line made good by VUFE patrols will be
sent to BROWN LINE but no advance in force until touch established
with 5th Division on left AAA When 5th Division have occupied FUSILIER
RIDGE and if patrols still report no resistance VUFE will make good
BROWN LINE and send patrols to GREEN LINE AAA In addition to above
VUFE will send one special reconnoitring patrol at once to KITCHEN
CRATER and another to GONNELIEU to report if enemy occupy these places
or not AAA When VUFE has occupied GREEN LINE GREEN SWITCH and when
patrols have reached BROWN LINE DADE will assemble Brigade in
GOUZEAUCOURT VALLEY assusming that GOUZEAUCOURT is found empty AAA
DADE will be prepared on receipt of orders to move through VUFE and
occupy GREEN LINE AAA BASU will be at half hours' notice to move AAA
Ack AAA Addsd to all concerned.

                                       H.I. FRANKLYN.
                                        Lieut. Colonel.
                                        General Staff.

ZOWU
11.35 a.m.

CERTIFIED TRUE COPY.

MESSAGES AND SIGNALS.

ZOWU

Received
At 7.30 p.m.
From. 21 Div.

TO:- 21 M.G.BATTN.

GX526   /   28   /   AAA

2 Coys 17 Battn M.G.C. attached to you will rejoin their own Battalion forthwith AAA Addressed 21 M.G.Battn. repeated 17 Divn.

From.- 21 Div.
Timed. 6.15 p.m.

CERTIFIED TRUE COPY.

TELEGRAM.

			Words
D.R.L.S. 5th Div.			Sent.
S.D.R. 33rd. Div.		At................	
H.I.F.		To................	
		By................	

DADE	JESO	33rd Div.	15 Sqn. R.A.F.
BASU	ZOHO		Cyclist Troop
VUFE	DUFA	V Corps.	
LODE	A/Q	V Corps R.A.	
ZOKI	5th Div.	V Corps H.A.	
ZEJU		"B" Coy Tanks	

-	/ 28th /	AAA

ZOWU Order No.238 AAA Enemy have withdrawn opposite Vth and IVth Corps fronts but to what extent is not yet known AAA ZOWU has been ordered to capture BROWN and GREEN LINES early tomorrow morning AAA VUFE will attack on right and DADE on left AAA Dividing line between Brigades R.31 R.33. R.36.central AAA //33rd. Division will be attacking VILLERS GUISLAN and GREEN LINE in conjunction with us. AAA 5th Division will be attacking FUSILIER and CEMETERY RIDGES and subsequently BANTEUX AAA Two Tanks will work with VUFE and two Tanks with DADE AAA The former rendezvous X.8.a.1.9. and latter R.25.d.2.0. about 11 p.m. AAA Right paid Tanks will work via Cemetery X.2.d. KITCHEN CRATER TURNER CRATER and clear GREEN LINE AAA Left pair tanks work round each side GONNELIEU and down GLASGOW TRENCH and prepared to deal with BANTEUX SUPPORT if Infantry in difficulties AAA All Tanks rally KITCHEN CRATER after operations where available for immediate counter-attack AAA Artillery starting line for barrage X.2.d.3.5. to R.26.d.3.8. AAA Barrage moves 100 yards in six minutes to BROWN LINE and 100 yards in four minutes from BROWN to GREEN LINE AAA Barrage will be amended and added to according to most Easterly line reached by Infantry this evening AAA Barrage Tables issued to Brigades show other details AAA One M.G.Coy. will accompany each Brigade AAA Unless otherwise detailed for Barrage for attack on BROWN LINE will come down at 3.30 a.m. and for attack from BROWN to GREEN LINE at 5.50 a.m. AAA Ack. AAA Addsd all concerned.

ZOWU
7.30 p.m.

H.I.FRANKLYN
Lieut. Colonel
General Staff.

CERTIFIED TRUE COPY.

TELEGRAM.

URGENT &OPERATIONS
PRIORITY to 3 Bdes.

Words
Sent
At..................
To..................
By..................

DADE	JESO	V Corps
BASU	ZOHO	V Corps R.A.
VUFE	DUFA	V Corps H.A.
LODE	A/Q	15 Sqn.R.A.F.
ZOKI	5th Div. Divl. Cyclist Troop	
ZEJU	33rd Div.	

— / 29th / AAA

ZOWU Order No.239 AAA Owing to success of both flanks today it appears probable that the enemy will withdraw shortly from our immediate front AAA Active patrolling will be carried out by VUFE and DADE tonight AAA If GONNELIEU and BROWN LINE are entered by patrols without resistance either tonight or tomorrow they will at once be occupied in force and patrols pushed on to GREEN LINE AAA If GREEN LINE is occupied by patrols this line will also be occupied in strength and patrols pushed down towards CANAL AAA Boundary between Brigades Sunken Road at R.26.c.3.0 - R.32.Central - R.34.Central - R.36. Central AAA Patrolling must be carried out by strong fighting patrols and minor resistance must be overcome AAA Patrols must be sent out at least once every hour and be particularly active just before Dawn AAA All available Heavy Artillery and Field Howitzers will bombard GONNELIEU from 4.5. a.m. to 5 a.m. and then cease AAA DADE will inform Div.H.Q. by 3 a.m. if bombardment is not to take place owing to their being in occupation of village AAA Any barrage required by Brigades for patrols to work under will be arranged with affiliated Artillery AAA DADE will have call on 122 Brigade as well as 79th Brigade for this purpose AAA BASU will remain in present positions till further orders AAA Ack, Addsd all concerned.

H.I.FRANKLYN.
Lieut. Colonel.
General Staff.

ZOWU
10.10. p.m.

CERTIFIED TRUE COPY.

SECRET.

21Div.
G.567.

nd Inf. Bde.　　D.M.G.C.　　Signals.
th   "   "　　　"Q"
0th "   "　　　A.D.M.S.
.R.A.　　　　　　A.P.M.
.R.E.　　　　　　Cyclist Sqn.

FORECAST OF FUTURE POLICY.

The following forecast is given as a guide only:-

1. The Corps on our right with IInd American Corps is to cross the Canal today and capture GOUY and LE CATELET, after which the Australian Corps will pass through and take BEAUREVOIR, the American Corps forming a defensive flank from GOUY through S.23 Central to the Canal at S.13.d.

2. On the completion of this operation the 38th Division will cross the Canal and relieve the Americans holding the defensive flank.

3. Meanwhile, the 33rd. Division will push forward its right and bridge the Canal, between VENDHUILLE and HONNECOURT, and relieve the left Brigade 38th Division.

4. The 38th. Division will then capture LA TERRIERE. The remainder of 33rd. Division will cross the Canal and occupy the general line LA TERRIERE - HONNECOURT (both inclusive)

5. By this time the IVth Corps on our left should have captured BANTEUX and BANTOUZEELE and the 21st Division should be on the GREEN line.

6. When the above situation, or something akin to it has arisen, the 21st Division will cross the Canal and occupy the HINDENBURG LINE between RANCOURT FARM and BANTOUZEELE both exclusive.
The 33rd Division will assist this operation by attacking Northwards towards S.3. and S.4.central, should any resistance be met with.

7. The C.R.E. is making arrangements to construct bridges over the Canal at:-
　　　　　S.1.d.4.9.
　　　　　S.1.b.9.4.
　　　　　M.31.b.2.2.
and to provide means for an Infantry party to be thrown across to cover the bridging operations.

8. The forward Divisional Boundaries will be issued shortly on a Map.

9. It is not yet possible to allot tasks to Brigades, but it is probable that after the capture of the GREEN Line by the 62nd and 110th Infantry Brigades the 64th Infantry Brigade will take over the Divisional front with the 110th Infantry Brigade in Support and 62nd Infantry Brigade in Reserve.

10. The route of supply for the Division will be :-

FINS - GOUZECOURT - VILLERS GUISLAN or GONNELIEU to BANTOUZEELE.

H.I.FRANKLYN
Lt. Colonel.
General Staff,
21st. Division.

29th September 1918.

CERTIFIED TRUE COPY.

MESSAGES AND SIGNALS.

TO:- 21 M.G.BATTN.

/ 30. / AAA

21 Div. order No.240 AAA Prisoners state that enemy will withdraw to dsitance of 4 kilometres E. of canal AAA When GREEN Line has been made good on Divl. front 62 Bde and 110 bde will send forward to canal seize crossings and establish bridgeheads on E.bank AAA 64 Bde will move to just W. of QUENTIN RIDGE forthwith and will be prepared on receipt of orders to advance through 110 Bde and 62 Bde cross Canal and occupy HINDENBURG LINE between RANCOURT FARM and BANTOUZEELE both exclusive AAA Report centres will be established at KITCHEN CRATER in R.33.c. TURNER QUARRY ARNOLD QUARRY AAA 62 Bde. will transfer cyclists to 64 Bde when later takes up advance AAA Addsd. all concerned AAA Ack.

From 21 Div.

Time 12.10 p.m.

CERTIFIED TRUE COPY.

MESSAGES AND SIGNALS

Handed in 21st.Div.   7.30 p.m.   Recd at 8.15 p.m.

TO:- 21 M.G.BATTN.

/   30.   /   AAA

21 Div Order No.241 AAA 110 Bde on right and 62 Bde on left will continue to hold GREEN LINE AAA Front line to be held thinly and Brigades disposed in depth AAA 64 Bde will remain in present positions AAA Patrols will be sent to Canal bank tonight accompanied by R.E. AAA If any bridges are found to be repairable and hostile fire permits R.E. will carry out repairs protected by Infantry patrols on E. bank AAA Risk of heavy casualties will NOT be run AAA If any bridges are foudd intact or are repaired by R.E. post will be established on W. bank to cover bridge with fire and so prevent demolition by enemy AAA If patrols can cross canal they will work towards HINDENBURG LINE to report if enemy hold this line or not AAA All troops E. of GREEN LINE except those detailed to guard bridges or to occupy tactical points selected by Brigadiers will be withdrawn before daylight AAA Troopstto be rested as much as possible tonight and tomorrow unless situation changes AAA Acknowledge AAA Addsd all concerned.

FROM.- 21 Div.
Time. 7.30 p.m.

CERTIFIED TRUE COPY.

Sheet 1.

Army Form C. 2118.

WAR DIARY or INTELLIGENCE SUMMARY.

(Erase heading not required.) 21st M. Gun Batt.

October 1918

Place	Date	Hour	Summary of Events and Information	Remarks and references to Appendices
Toure	1st	—	Enemy in position East of Canal. C. Company claim good results from direct shooting	
"	"	—	Casualties Nil.	
"	2nd	—	Casualties 5. O.Rs evacuated. 1.O.R. Sick.	
"	"	1600	21st Div. G.X. 689 received.	Copy attached
"	2nd	1100	General situation unaltered. C.O. went round line	
"	3	930	21st Div order No 212 received	
"	"	12.30	G.X. 662 received	
"	"	1600	21st Div. order No 213 received.	
"	"	—	Operation Order No 53 issued	
"	"	—	C.O. went round line	
"	"	—	Tents A.O. Williams & W. Munday, T.C. Wild & C.L. Williams joined from base	
"	"	—	34 O.Rs joined from base	
"	4th	—	Immediate front quiet. Banks bombing own.	
"	"	—	Capt V.T. Lapsley on M.C. & Joined from leave	
"	"	—	Lieut T. Cartwright evacuated Sick.	
"	5th	0900	Enemy withdrawing on Corps front.	
"	"	1205	21st Div order No 214 received	

Sheet 2

Army Form C. 2118.

WAR DIARY
INTELLIGENCE SUMMARY

October 1918.

of 21.-M. Gun. Batt.

Place	Date	Hour	Summary of Events and Information	Remarks and references to Appendices
Line	5th	1100	Operation Order No. 54 issued. Copy attached	
Gouzeaucourt	—	2100	21st Div. orders No. 245 received	
GOUZECOURT	—	—	Major W.M. Stuart & Lieut G. Fell & S.M. Bourdon joined from Base	
"	6th	0900	21 O.R.s joined from Base	
"	"	0900	Patrols fighting on	
"	"	1000	G X 763 received Copy attached	
"	"	—	Lieut L. Evans wounded. 1 O.R. wounded & 1 O.R. wounded accidentally	
"	7th	1030	Conference at 110th Brigade H.Qrs. C.O. attended	
"	"	1130	Batt. H.Qrs. moved to M 32 b.	
GRATTE PANCHE FARM.	—	—	1 O.R. wounded. Lieut J.B. Ruffert to Indian Army	
"	—	2200	P No 70 issued Copy attached	
"	—	1930	21st Div. orders No. 276 received	
"	8th	0930	Batt. H.Qrs. moved to sunken road M 35 b.	
"	—	—	Attack very successful, enemy withdrawing	
"	—	1700	21st Div. order G X 807 received	
"	—	—	Major J.C. Botham & leave to U.K. Lieut J.W. Mandy wounded. 5 O.R. wounded 1 O.R. missing 1 O.R. evacuated	

Army Form C. 2118.

Sheet III

WAR DIARY for October 1918
INTELLIGENCE SUMMARY. 21st M.G. Battn

(Erase heading not required.)

Place	Date	Hour	Summary of Events and Information	Remarks and references to Appendices
GRATTE PANCE FARM	9th	0915	O/X F38 received	Copy attached
		—	Companies reorganising	
	10th	—	1 O.R. wounded	
WALINCOURT	—	16.00	Bn. HQ. moved to WALINCOURT	
	11th	—	Battn. resting and refitting. BGGS Corps to visit Coy. WALINCOURT and A Coy CAULLERY	
		17.00	Co. attended G.O.C's conference at Serancourt	
		19.00	Capt DUNCAN & 2/Lt HACON returned from leave in UK. 2/Lt McKERNON returned from PARIS leave	
	12th	0900	2 NCOs to M.G.C. Base Depot for Junior NCO's course at GRANTHAM	
		—	10 O.R. struck off strength sick	
		—	21st Division Special order issued	Copy attached
	13th	—	2/Lt TRISTAM rejoins from Hospital	
		—	Companies resting	
		16.15	Church parade held by Rev Marsh C.F.	
	14th	0830	Companies began training	
		—	2/Lt SCOTT & 16 O.Rs proceeds to ST VALERY Rest camp	

WAR DIARY
INTELLIGENCE SUMMARY
for October 1918
21st M.G. Battn.

Army Form C. 2118.
Sheet IV

Place	Date	Hour	Summary of Events and Information	Remarks and references to Appendices
WALINCOURT	14	14.00	CO & O.Cs B&C Coys proceeded to INCHY to confer int. CO 17th M.G. Battn. regarding a barrage to be carried out int. hat Battn. Zero day had not known as yet.	OC/S
—	—	—	Final arrangements now up to in abeyance.	OC/S
—	15	—	Lieut. G.H.B. McRuffie struck off strength — joins Indian Army.	OC/S
—	15	—	A hot still day. Companies training. 2nd Lt T. HUNTER awarded MC	OC/S
—	16	—	2nd Lts HOLMES & McKERRON embarked for tour of duty at GRANTHAM	OC/S
—	16	—	Heather brighter. Companies training. Nothing of interest to note.	OC/S
—	17	09.30	2nd Lt H.J.PARKER F.C. WISE M.E. CAMBRAY joined Battn. int. to O.Ro.	OC/S
—	17	—	Companies continued training. Weather turn finer.	OC/S
—	18	—	A brighter day. Co. & Officers attended demonstration of signal Rockets at 15 hours	OC/S
—	18	18.00	21st Divn. G.46. Instructions for forthcoming operations received. Copy attached	OC/S
—	19	19.00	Division orders No SS issued	OC/S
—	19	09.00	B&C Coys proceeded to INCHY preparatory to firing barrage to support attack of 7th Divn on 20th.	OC/S
—	—	10.00	CO proceeded to INCHY in connection int. the above operation returning at 15 hrs	OC/S

Sheet I

WAR DIARY for 91st M.G. Batt.
or
INTELLIGENCE SUMMARY. October 1918

Army Form C. 2118.

(Erase heading not required.)

Place	Date	Hour	Summary of Events and Information	Remarks and references to Appendices
WALINCOURT	20th	0200	B+C Coys fired barrage in support of 17th Div attack on high ground near AMERVAL	
"	"	0400	B+C Coys returned to INCHY	
"	"	"	Casualties 6 ORs wounded	
"	"	14.30	Co. attended Conference at Div.	
"	"	1500	Lieut. Elson proceeds to join 1/8 Notts. & Derby Regt.	
"	"	1800	Administrative Instruction No 4 issued	
"	21st	"	A bright day. Reports received that 17th & 38th Divs. has gained objectives. Copy attached	
"	21	"	CO. attended Conference at GOC Divn	
"	"	13.00	D Coy moved to INCHY	
"	"	1800	21st Divn Operation Order No 247 received	Copy attached
"	"	"	Administrative Instruction No 5 issued	—
"	"	"	Operation Order No 5b issued	—
"	22	09.00	Batt. HQrs moves to INCHY Co. & OC. "C" Coy reconnoitres for positions for Barrage to be fired on 23rd to support attack details in 21st Div Order No 247 above.	
"	"	01.00	B & D Coys moved up to NEUVILLY. Prior to Batts. positions taken	
"	"	"	Capt. Capt. R. Ball M.C. proceeded on leave to U.K.	

/15.

Sheet VI

WAR DIARY
INTELLIGENCE SUMMARY

October 1918   2/1st Bat'n M.G. Corps

Army Form C. 2118.

Place	Date	Hour	Summary of Events and Information	Remarks and references to Appendices
INCHY	22		Very heavy rain in morning but afternoon & evening has been & dry	
	23	0100	Enemy barrage returned with & caused casualties to troops assembling	
		0200	Zero for attack "C" Coy fired barrage on Emerling & Cross Rds in OUVILLERS. attack appeared to be going well	
		0600	Batn HQ moved to NEUVILLY	
NEUVILLY		0605	Coy & 10 kept forward & found junk offensive captured & our troops moving forwards VENDEGIES au BOIS	
			A Coy here operating with 151 Div. B Coy with 64 Bde & D Coy with 62 Bde	
			C Coy in reserve Cy	
			On capture of red dotted line "C" Coy now moved up to consolidate	
		1200	Capture of VENDEGIES au BOIS reported complete	
		1600	Attack carried owing to Right Division unable to keep pace of Coy attacks	
		1600	GX 161 Received	
		1700	GX 167 Received	
		2100	21 Div Order No 248 Received	
		2200	GX 169 Received	

Sheet VII

WAR DIARY or INTELLIGENCE SUMMARY October 1918   21st Battn M G Corps

Army Form C. 2118.

Place	Date	Hour	Summary of Events and Information	Remarks and references to Appendices
Nr NEUVILLY	23		D Coy with 62 Bde obtained many targets which they engaged. Convoys, Cavalry	
—	—		B Coy observed an enemy gun limber & opened fire on the horse killing them	
—	—		The gun was subsequently captured.	
—	—		Lieut G.O. FAIRLIE M.C. & Lieut A.O.H SEARL rejoined from M.G. School	
—	—		CASUALTIES wth 5 ORs	
—	—		Canadian 1 OR kills 7 OR wounded 1 OR missing	
NEUVILLY	24	0400	The attack was resumed under good weather conditions	
			"C" Coy fired barrage on to sunken road in F2 & F3 a and various road	
			junctions in MAIRETZ au BOIS F36. Other companies acted with the same	
			Brigades	
		0800	Battn HQ moved to ORILLERS	
			POIX du NORD had been captured by fine objective of the attack. The	
			sunken road through X11 a, 1c + X17 b,t,d was not reached in this	
			attack	
		1500	Battn HQ moved to VENDEGIES au BOIS	
VENDEGIES au BOIS		1500	21 Div order no 249 Red Copy attached	

Army Form C. 2118.

WAR DIARY or INTELLIGENCE SUMMARY

21st Bn. M.G. Corps

West V... October 1918

(Erase heading not required.)

Place	Date	Hour	Summary of Events and Information	Remarks and references to Appendices
VENDEGIES	24	01.00	Attack for sunken road sort of LOUVIGNIES launched later than plan. The objective had been reached.	
		23.00	21st Div Order No 250 received. Copy attached	
			Casualties 2/Lt A.O. WILLIAMS wounded 2 O.R. killed 35 O.R. wounded 1 O.R. wounded (gas) 1 O.R. missing	
VENDEGIES	25		Our front line ran along sunken road X.11 a.t.c. and X.17 b.t.d. Orders were to push out patrols from 62 & 64 Bdes towards LOUVIGNIES. These were driven in. B Coys Reserve section took places on right flank which was doubtful & made it secure. On the attack B Coy Carried out check carrier fire.	
			D Coy had 4 guns on road X.28 a. or b. X.27 b.95.55. 4 on high ground X.22 cent. 4 on line of road X.27 b.30 to X.27 a.5.e 4 reserve guns in X.22 d. 9.1.16 (incl ruddles) enemy concentration. B Coy places 2 guns X.3.d.3.3. 2 guns X.10 b.25.40. 4 guns on spur X.24E. 2 guns () X.17d.3.6 & () X.17c.7.4. A Coy with 110th Bde in Reserve	
			C Coy has 8 guns in GREEN LINE & in mass	

Army Form C. 2118.

WAR DIARY
INTELLIGENCE SUMMARY
Sheet IX
October 1918
21st Batt. M.G. Corps

(Erase heading not required.)

Place	Date	Hour	Summary of Events and Information	Remarks and references to Appendices
VENDEGIES	25	10.00	21 A.I. Order No 251 received	Copy attached
		16.00	21 A.I. Order No 252	
		—	GX No 219 Received	
		20.00	GX No 228	
			"C" Coy eight Vickers guns now placed at disposal of 110th Bde to form night defensive flank	
			110th Bde relieved 62nd & 64th Bdes B Coy withdrew to VENDEGIES D Coy to POIX DU NORD less 1 Section remaining at X28a
			Casualties Lt Pawlton Wounded (gas)
			Major L.C. BORTHWICK returned from leave
	26	01.00	Barrage put down to assist Divn on our lines to establish posts successfully established	Copy attached
			Three posts here not	
		16.00	21 A.I. Order No 253 received	Copy attached
		15.00	Operation Order No 57 issued	
			Day passed quietly at Vendée	
		21.00	Relief by 1st Divn complete & Batt Hq moved to NEUVILLY	

Sheet X

WAR DIARY
INTELLIGENCE SUMMARY. 21st Battn M.G.C.

October 1918

Army Form C. 2118.

Place	Date	Hour	Summary of Events and Information	Remarks and references to Appendices
NEUVILLY	26	21:00	A Coy moved to NEUVILLY B Coy to INCHY with 64 Bde C Coy AMERVAL	
			with 110th Bde D Coy with 69th Bde to NEUVILLY	
			Lieuts T. MATHEWS, A.H. BONNER and 2/Lt FAIRHURST MC. Joins Battn	
			1 OR evacuated sick	
	27		Companies resting and refitting. Day passed quietly.	
		12:00	38 OR Reinforcements arrived	
			o/c F.O CLEMENTSON proceeds to 12th Battn MANCHESTER Regt & to attend	
			Off strength	
			a bright day. C.O. attended conference at Division. Copy attached	
	28	22:00	21 Aust 25th received	
			OO. No 58 issued	
			Administrative Instructions No 5	
			5 OR struck off strength sick	
	29	09:00	Another bright day. Companies moved up to where 17th Divn in front of	
			POIX du NORD A Coy in about Reserve. B Coy to man guns &	
			Intermediate zone C Coy on right with 110th Bde D Coy left with 62 Bde	

Army Form C. 2118.

Sheet XI

WAR DIARY for INTELLIGENCE SUMMARY.

October 1918. 21st Battn. M.G.C.

(Erase heading not required.)

Place	Date	Hour	Summary of Events and Information	Remarks and references to Appendices
VENDEGIES	29th	1200	Batn HQrs moved to VENDEGIES & near HQrs to OVILLERS	
"	"	2200	Relief of 1st Australian completed	
VENDEGIES	30th	0900	A Type day. Situation fairly quiet. Coy "C" + "D" Heat round line in morning and "B" to Aircraft in afternoon.	
"	"		NAVY G.347 Received	Copy attached
"	"		Day passes quietly	
"	"		Casualties reported on 29th. 3 O.R. killed 1 O.R. died of wounds 1 O.R. wounds (gas) 1 O.R. wounded 1 O.R. wounded (at duty) 1 O.R. found	
"	31st	0900	Heather inclined to rain. Coy "C" + "D" heat to transport lines & return.	
"	"	1400	C.O. visits forward Companies. Situation remains unchanged & fairly quiet.	
"	"	2000	Enemy Artillery very active shelling VENDEGIES & OVILLERS	
"	"	2100	21 Div Order No 255 received	Copy attached

LIEUT-COLONEL
COMMANDING 21st BN. MACHINE GUN CORPS.

War Diary.

21st Br. Machine Gun Corps.

October 1918.

MESSAGES AND SIGNALS.

Handed in at 21 Div. 10.8 a.m. Received 10.50 a.m.

TO:- 21st. M.G.BATTN.

GX 689. / 2 / . AAA

Until further orders only 8 M.Gs. will be attached to each Bde. AAA Remaining M.Gs. will revert to 21 M.G.Battn. and will be used for defence of BANTEUX SPUR AAA Addsd. 62 Bde. 110 Bde and 21 M.G.Battn.

FROM. 21st. Division.

Place & Time 10.40

CERTIFIED TRUE COPY.

SECRET. Copy No....7.....

21st Division Order No.242.

2nd October, 1918.

Ref: Sheet 57.c.S.E. 1/20,000

1. The 110 Infantry Brigade will take over the front now held by the 62nd Infantry Brigade on the night 3rd/4th October.
   Relief to be complete by 0200 hours.

2. On relief, 62nd Infantry Brigade will withdraw to the area Q.34. Q.35. W.4. and W.5.
   62nd Infantry Brigade will report as soon as possible the proposed location of their Headquarters.

3. All details of relief will be arranged between Brigadiers.

4. Machine Gun Reliefs will be arranged by O.C. 21st Battalion Machine Gun Corps.

5. Completion of relief will be reported to Divisional Headquarters.

6. A C K N O W L E D G E.

A.F.MACDOUGALL,
Major.for
Lieut. Colonel
General Staff
21st Division.

Issued through Signals at
1930 hours to :-

	Copy No.		Copy No.
62 Inf Bde.	1	A.P.M	12
64 " "	2	D.G.O.	13
110 " "	3	V Corps.	14 - 15
C.R.A.	4	V Corps R.A.	16
C.R.E.	5	V Corps H.A.	17
Pioneers	6	37th Div.	18
D.M.G.C.	7	33rd Div.	19
Signals	8	17th Div.	20
A.D.M.S.	9	15 Sqn.R.A.F.	21
Train	10	War Diary	22
A/Q	11	File.	23

CERTIFIED TRUE COPY.

TELEGRAM

Urgent operations　　　　　　　Words
Priority to　　　　　　　　　　Sent
3 Bdes.　　　　　　　　　At.....................
　　　　　　　　　　　　　To.....................
　　　　　　　　　　　　　By.....................

DADE	JESO	38th Div.
BASU	ZOHO	V Corps.
VUFE	DUFA	V Corps. R.A.
LODE	A/Q	V. Corps H.A.
ZOKI		33rd Div. 15 Sqn. R.A.F.
ZEJU		37th Div. Div. Cyclists.

- / 3rd / AAA

ZOWU Order No.243 AAA The 50th. Division have reached Northern outskirts of CATELET and GOUY and are to attack high ground S.28. S.29 this evening AAA 38th Div will then relieve them and will tomorrow attack LA TERRIERE and clear crossings for 33rd Div. at OSSUS AAA 33rd. Div will then cross Canal and form offensive flank facing North between LA TERRIERE and HONNECOURT AAA C.R.A. and M.G. Bn will keep HINDENBURG LINE and ground between it and 300 yards E. of Canal under steady continuous fire during these operations AAA VUFE will keep touch with the enemy tonight with patrols endeavouring to pass patrols across Canal on rafts AAA Patrols to withdraw before daylight. AAA VUFE will be prepared from tomorrow inclusive as pressure from South increases to push patrols across Canal and to support them AAA C.R.E. will arrange for bridges to be thrown across whenever and wherever VUFE obtains lodgement on East bank AAA BASU will be prepared to cross by these bridges or via HONNECOURT and establish themselves in HINDENBURG LINE within Div. Boundaries AAA Cyclist Sqn comes under orders of BASU from tomorrow inclusive AAA O.C. will report BASU H.Q. during morning AAA Ack AAA Addsd all concerned.

　　　　　　　　　　　　　　　　　H.I.FRANKLYN
　　　　　　　　　　　　　　　　　　Lieut. Colonel
　　　　　　　　　　　　　　　　　　General Staff

ZOWU
1800 Hours.

CERTIFIED TRUE COPY

SECRET.   Copy No......

                21st Battn. Machine Gun Corps
                 OPERATION ORDER No. 53.
                 ─────────────
                                      3rd October 1918.
Ref. Map Sheet
57c.S.E., 1/20,000.
─────────────────

1.   The 110th Infantry Brigade will take over the front now held by 62nd Infantry Brigade on night 3rd/4th October.

2.   On relief, 62nd Infantry Brigade will withdraw to Q.34, Q.35, W.4, W.5.

3.   "C" Coy. 21st Bn.M.G.C., will withdraw its 16 guns to W.5.a.4.7. No movement will take place except under cover of darkness.

4.   Completion of above move will be wired to Battalion H.Q. by code word "HOWARD".

5.   16 Guns of "D" Coy. will remain in position on BANTEUX SPUR for harassing fire by day.

6.   "A" Coy. will remain affiliated to 110th Infantry Brigade.

7.   Machine Gun Companies to ACKNOWLEDGE.

                                    [signature]

                                    Lieut. & A/Adjt.,
                          21st Battalion, Machine Gun Corps.
                          ─────────────────────────

DISTRIBUTION.

Copy No. 1 .. O.C. "A" Coy.(F'd).
          2 .. O.C. "C" Coy.(F'd).
          3 .. O.C. "D" Coy.(F'd).
          4 .. O.C. "C" Coy.(Rear).
          5 .. O.C. "D" Coy.(Rear).
          6 .. Quartermaster.
          7 .. 62nd Infantry Brigade.
          8 .. 64th   do.   do.
          9 .. 110th   do.   do.
         10 .. 21st Division 'G'.
         11 .. File.
    12 & 13 .. War Diary.

TELEGRAM.

URGENT OPERATIONS
PRIORITY to 3 Bdes.

Words
Sent
At....................
To....................
By....................

DADE	JESO	38th Div.
BASU	ZOHO	V Corps.
VUFE	DUFA	V Corps R.A.
LODE	A/Q	V Corps H.A.
ZOKI	33rdDiv.	15Sqn.R.A.F.
ZEJU	37th Div.	Div. Cyclist Troop.

- / 5th / AAA

ZOWU Order No.244 AAA All indications show enemy have withdrawn opposite Corps front AAA Aeroplanes report HINDENBURG LINE appears deserted AAA 33rd Div reported to have patrol in or near LA TERRIERE AAA VUFE will establish bridge-head round outskirts of BANTOUZELLE forthwith under cover of which C.R.E. will throw bridges to take Infantry in fours AAA When this objective made good VUFE will occupy more extended bridge-head as follows AAA ARNOULD QUARRY - C.T. through M.33.a. and M.27.d. - HINDENBURG SUPPORT Line from M.27.d.3.5. to M.27.b.0.3. thence via RED FARM to Canal AAA Fighting patrols will then be sent to HINDENBURG SUPPORT Line between RANCOURT FARM exc. and M.27.d. AAA This line will be occupied by VUFE as soon as made good by patrols but VUFE will continue to hold bridge-head strongly until further notice AAA BASU will move heads of leading Battns. to BANTEUX forthwith and will start crossing the Canal as soon as VUFE has made good larger bridge-head AAA Objectives for BASU as follows AAA HINDENBURG SUPPORT line from RANCOURT FARM exclusive to M.27.d. if not already made good by VUFE AAA Line of road MONTECOUVEZ FARM - BONNE ENFANCE FARM within Divl. Boundaries AAA When latter objectives made good patrols will be sent to MASNIERES BEAUREVOIR Trench System to ascertain if occupied by enemy or not AAA Minor resistance must be overcome by VUFE and BASU AAA Touch must be obtained and kept with 33rd Div AAA Care must be taken to protect left flank throughout operations until 37th Div. are up in line AAA DADE will move to area R.28.c.&.d. R.29.c.&.d. R.23. as soon as vacated by VUFE and BASU AAA One M.G. Coy. with each Bde. AAA Successive Report centres will be established by Divl. Signals at ARNOULD QUARRY GRATTE PANCHE FARM and ARDISSART FARM AAA AckAAA Addsd all concerned.

ZOWU

1205 hrs.

H.I.FRANKLYN
Lieut. Colonel
General Staff

CERTIFIED TRUE COPY

SECRET.   Copy No. 11...

                    21st Battn. Machine Gun Corps
                    OPERATION ORDER No. 54.
                    ─────────────────────

                                              5th October 1918.
Ref. Map Sheet
57c.S.E., 1/20,000.
─────────────────────

1.   Advanced Battalion H.Q. will close at present location
        at 15 hours today, and open same time at Sunken Road,
        W.6.b.5.4.

2.   Rear Battalion H.Q. and Rear Coys. H.Q. will move
        forthwith to W.2.b. and W.3.a, under Lieut. A. HUXLEY's orders.

        Capt. VIBERT will proceed forthwith to select Transport
        Lines.

                                        V.F. Samuelson
                                           Capt. & Adjt.,
                                        21st Battn. Machine Gun Corps.
                                        ─────────────────────

DISTRIBUTION.
─────────────

Copy No. 1 .. O.C. "A" Coy. (F'd).
          2 .. O.C. "B" Coy. (F'd).
          3 .. O.C. "C" Coy. (F'd).
          4 .. O.C. "D" Coy. (F'd).
          5 .. O.C. "A" Coy. (Rear).
          6 .. O.C. "B" Coy. (Rear).
          7 .. O.C. "C" Coy. (Rear).
          8 .. O.C. "D" Coy. (Rear).
          9 .. Quartermaster.
         10 .. File.
   11 & 12 .. War Diary.
         13 .. 21st Division

MESSAGES AND SIGNALS.

URGENT OPERATIONS
   PRIORITY.

TO :- 21st. M.G.BATTN.

/   5th   /   AAA

ZOWU Order No.245 AAA Line reached today not yet certain but we hold BONNE ENFANCE FARM M.24.c. M.17.d. AAA Aeroplane report enemy seen retiring from BEAURE-VOIRE line this evening AAA Advance will be resumed tomorrow Oct.6th AAA BASU will act as advanced guard Brigade AAA First objective line of road N.33.d. and B. - HAUT FARM - HURTEBISE farm AAA 2nd objective WALINCOURT village and high ground N.18.a. with patrols into FERVAL CHATEAU and SELVIGNY AAA Touch will be gained if possible on Flank at conclusion of each bound but advance must not be delayed for this purpose AAA 78th Brigade R.F.A. come under direct orders of BASU for tomorrow AAA VUFE will act as supporting Brigade and will move to line MONTECOUVEZ FARM - BONNE ENFANCE FARM as soon as BASU has completely cleared BEAUREVOIR front line AAA DADE will be reserve Brigade and will move to HINDENBURG SUPPORT LINE as soon as VUFE has completely cleared this line AAA Policy for BASU will be to manouvre enemy out of positions they may be holding and to act vigoursly without engaging Brigade in frontal attack on strong positions AAA 38th Div. on our right are being directed on High ground in O.27.central AAA Objective for 37th Div. not yet known AAA Acknowledge AAA Addsd all concerned.

FROM :- ZOWU
        20.45

CERTIFIED TRUE COPY.

MESSAGES & SIGNALS.

Handed in at 21Div.   1530   Received 1550.

TO:- 21 M.G.BATTN.

GX 762   /   6   /   AAA

It is possible that the enemy may attempt fraternisation and movement of troops under cover of the white flag AAA No notice is to be taken of the white flag except in the case of absolute surrender any enemy attempting fraternisation are to be made prisoners.

FROM.-ZOWU

CERTIFIED TRUE COPY.

MESSAGES AND SIGNALS

TO:- 21Div"G" All Coys 21stM.G.Battn. A & B Coys 17th M.G.Battn 110, 62 & 64 Inf.Bdes.

P.70   /   7   /   AAA

Machine guns will cooperate as follows AAA A Coy 21st. Bn. affiliated 110 bde AAA B Coy affiliated 64 Bde AAA D Coy affiliated 62nd Bde AAA C Coy 21st Battn and A & B Coys 17th Bn M.G. Battn will fire barrages as follows AAA FIRST phase NIL AAA Second phase AAA C Coy 21 M.G. location M.36.a.2.5. barrage N.26.c.0.3. to N.26.d.8.8. zero to zero plus six AAA one belt 3 minutes AAA Second task AAA Barrage N.26.a.5.2. to N.26.b.4.6. zero plus six to zero plus eighteen AAA 1 belt 3 minutes AAA A & B Coys 17th M.G.Battn location M.36.a.3.8. AAA Barrage N.26.c.1.9. to N.26.b.8.2. zero to zero plus 6 AAA 1 belt 3 mins AAA Second task AAA Barrage N.26.a.1.5. to N.20.d.9.1. zero plus six to zero plus thirty AAA 1 belt 3 mins AAA Third task barrage N.25.b.8.7. to N20.d.4.4. zero plus 30 mins to Zero plus 36 AAA 1 belt 3 mns AAA Fourth task B Coy only AAA Barrage N.20.c.3.6. to N.20.b.4.4. zero plus 36 to zero plus 46 AAA 1 belt 5 mins AAA Third phase AAA "C"Coy will move to high ground in N.21.a.&.b. to engage to engage targets which may appear AAA Zero hours have been communicated to all concerned AAAendsAAA

FROM:- ZEJU
Time 22 hours.
                                    Sgd.A.J.Pack
                                    for O.C. ZEJU

CERTIFIED TRUE COPY

MESSAGES AND SIGNALS

TO:- 21Div"G" All Coys 21st M.G.Battn. A & B Coys 17th M.G.Battn
110, 62 & 64 Inf.Bdes.

P.70 / 7 / AAA

Machine guns will cooperate as follows AAA A Coy 21st. Bn.
affiliated 110 bde AAA B Coy affiliated 64 Bde AAA D Coy affiliated
62nd Bde AAA C Coy 21st Battn and A & B Coys 17th Bn M.G.
Battn will fire barrages as follows AAA FIRST phase NIL AAA
Second phase AAA C Coy 21 M.G. location M.36.a.2.5. barrage
N.26.c.0.3. to N.26.d.8.8. zero to zero plus six AAA one belt 3
minutes AAA Second task AAA Barrage N.26.a.5.2. to N.26.b.4.6.
zero plus six to zero plus eighteen AAA 1 belt 3 minutes AAA
A & B Coys 17th M.G.Battn location M.36.a.3.8. AAA Barrage
N.26.c.1.9. to N.26.b.8.2. zero to zero plus 6 AAA 1 belt 3 mins AAA
Second task AAA Barrage N.26.a.1.5. to N.20.d.9.1. zero plus six
to zero plus thirty AAA 1 belt 3 mins AAA Third task barrage
N.25.b.8.7. to N20.d.4.4. zero plus 30 mins to Zero plus 36 AAA
1 belt 3 mns AAA Fourth task B Coy only AAA Barrage N.20.c.3.6.
to N.20.b.4.4. zero plus 36 to zero plus 46 AAA 1 belt 5 mins AAA
Third phase AAA "C" Coy will move to high ground in N.21.a.&.b.
to engageto engage targets which may appear AAA Zero hours have
been communicated to all concerned AAAendsAAA

FROM:- ZEJU
Time 22 hours.

Sgd.A.J.Pack
for O.C. ZEJU

CERTIFIED TRUE COPY

SECRET.   Copy No...7.....

                    21st Division Order No.246.

                                              7th October, 1918.

Ref: Map 1/20,000, 57 B.S.W.

1.   The Third and Fourth Armies have been ordered to
attack the enemy opposite their fronts on 8th October, 1918

2.   The 21st Division will attack with :-

   (a) First Objective   ...   GREEN LINE

   (b) Second Objective   ...   RED LINE

   (c) Third Objective   ...   BLUE LINE

3. (a) The 38th Division will be attacking on the right
   of the 21st Division with :-

        First Objective   ...   VILLERS OUTREAUX

        Second Objective   ...   MALINCOURT - WALINCOURT MILL
                                       - O.25.central.

   (b) The 37th Division will be attacking on the left
   of the 21st Division with :-

        First Objective   ...   BEAUREVOIR - MASNIERES Trench
                                       System

        Second Objective   ...   Ridge running Northwards
                                       from BURTEBISE FARM

        Third Objective   ...   BRISEUX WOOD.

        FOURTH OBJECTIVE   ...   High ground in O.11.b.

   (c) The 38th Division will advance from their first
   to the second objective at 0800 hours.

   (d) The 37th Division will push straight on to their
   third objective after the capture of the second objective
   (0638 hours) and from the third to the fourth objective
   at 1000 hours.

4. (a) The attack on the first objective will be carried out
   by the 64th Infantry Brigade on the right and the
   110th Infantry Brigade on the left.
        The Inter-Brigade Boundary is shown "BLACK" on map.
        Zero for this attack will be at 0100 hours.

   (b) The attack on the second objective will be carried out
   by the 110th Infantry Brigade.
        Zero for this attack will be 0515 hours.

   (c) The attack on the third objective will be carried out
   by the 62nd Infantry Brigade.
        Zero for this attack will be 0800 hours.

                                              /d.........

(d) After the capture of the third objective, the 62nd Infantry Brigade will send patrols :-

   i. To the Eastern Edge of GARD WOOD.

   ii. SORVAL CHATEAU.

   iii. SELVIGNY VILLAGE.

   The Cyclist Squadron, which is placed at the disposal of 62nd Infantry Brigade, should be used for this purpose. Standing Patrols will remain in the above place if found unoccupied, and Reconnoitring Patrols pushed on towards CAULLERY.

5. Liaison Posts will be establised as follows :-

   (a) Between the 64th Infantry Brigade and 38th Division at Road Junction T.3.a.9.1.

   (b) Between 110th Infantry Brigade and 37th Division at HURTEBISE FARM.

   (c) Between 62nd Infantry Brigade and 37th Division at bend in Sunken Road N.12.c.0.5.

   (d) Between 62nd Infantry Brigade and 38th Division at STAR Roads 0.25.central.

   These liaison Posts will be joint posts and will consist of One Platoon found by each Unit concerned.

6. (a) Five Field Artillery Brigades will support the attack of the 21st Division.

   (b) Barrage Tables will be issued separately.

   (c) Targets for Heavy Artillery will appear in Artillery Orders.

   (d) The village of WALINCOURT and the high ground in N.18 will be kept under smoke from 0800 hours till the approach of the 62nd Infantry Brigade necessitates lifting.

   (e) the 94th Brigade R.F.A. will come under the direct orders of the B.G.C. 62nd Infantry Brigade for the attack on the third objective and will not take part in the barrage for this attack.

7. (a) Three Machine Gun Companies will put down a barrage for the attack on the second objective.

   (b) One Machine Gun Company will support the advance of the 62nd Infantry Brigade by direct fire from the ridge in N.27 and N.21.

   (c) One Machine Gun Company is allotted to each Infantry Brigade for consolidating objectives when gained.

/8.......

-3-

8.   Six Tanks (Mark V) will assist in the attack; of these:-

(a)   Four Tanks will assist the advance of the 110th Infantry Brigade on the second objective.

(b)   Two Tanks will be available for 64th Infantry Brigade after daylight, for clearing up ANGLES CHATEAU area, if this has not already been done.

(c)   On the completion of these tasks Tanks will rally by pairs at each of the following places :-

    ARDISSART FARM
    Rd. junc. N.26.a.8.9.
    Rd. junc. N.20.c.4.9.

All six Tanks will advance from these places with the supporting troops of the 62nd Infantry Brigade, as they pass through and will be used for clearing up "pockets" of the enemy during the advance to the third objective.

9.   The 15th Squadron R.A.F. will be calling for flares as soon as possible after daylight and subsequently at 0900, 1100 hours etc.,

10.   Divisional Headquarters will close at REVELON FARM at 0700 October 8th and will re-open at M.32.b.7.1. at the same hour.

11.   A C K N O W L E D G E.

                          H.I.FRANKLYN
                          Lieut. Colonel
                          General Staff
                          21st Division.

Issued at 1930 hours through
Signals to :-

	Copy No.		Copy No.
62nd Inf. Bde.	1	A.P.M.	12
64 " "	2	17th Div.	13
110 " "	3	37th Div.	14
C.R.A.	4	38th Div.	15
C.R.E.	5	33rd Div.	16
Pioneers	6	V Corps.	17
D.M.G.C.	7	V Corps R.A.	18
Signals	8	V Corps H.A.	19
A.D.M.S.	9	"B" Coy 11th Bn	
Train	10	Tanks	20
A/Q	11	15th Sqn	21
		War Diary	22 -23
		File.	24

certified true copy

MESSAGES AND SIGNALS

URGENT OPERATIONS
PRIORITY.

Handed in at 1112   Received 1225.

GX 827   /   8   /   AAA

TO:- 21 M.G.BATTN.

The 17th Div will pass through 62 Bde early tomorrow morning and resume the advance AAA When the 17 Div have passed through orders will be issued to Bdes to concentrate in the following areas DADE in squares N.17-23 & 29 AAA BASU squares N.28.27 & 32 AAA VUFE squares N22.21 & 20 AAA M.G.Companies reorganized with affiliated Bdes AAA Cyclists will reorganise with DADE and will not be transferred without further orders AAA 17th and 21st DA's come under orders of G.O.C. 17 Div. on completion of relieve AAA Acknowledge AAA Addsd DADE, BASU, VUFE, ZEJU, reptd LODE, ZOKI, "Q" ZODU, ZOHO.

From 21st. Division.

CERTIFIED TRUE COPY.

MESSAGES AND SIGNALS.

PRIORITY. Handed in at 21 Div. Office. Received at 10.5.

TO:- 21 M.G. BATTN.

GX 838 / 9 / AAA

Ref. GX827 of 8th inst units will reorganise forthwith in their present locations and will not concentrate into Bde groups AAA

FROM 21 Div. Time 0915.

Certified true copy

21st DIVISION SPECIAL ORDER.

Saturday, 12th October 1918.

The Army & Corps Commanders have requested me to convey to all Troops under my command their high appreciation of the magnificent success gained by the 21st Division during the past few days.

I personally, have nothing to add to what I have already told you, namely that I was confident you would live up to the tremendously high standard you had already set yourselves. That you intend to do so is clearly proved by your success in the recent fighting, especially as your success has been gained in the face of the greatest difficulties.

I would ask all ranks to note the ruthless havoc wrought by the enemy on the person and property of defenceless women and old men. You are fighting a vicious beast and you must treat him as such. The enemy is rapidly reaching the end of his tether and it is up to you to see that his final defeat is as complete as possible.

What you suffered in the early days of the year the enemy is suffering now with, moreover, the prospect of an overwhelming defeat staring him in the face.

Good luck.

Major-General
Commanding 21st Division.

War Diary

S E C R E T.

21st. Battn. M.G.Corps Administrative Instructions No.4. for forthcoming Operations.

1. **FIRST LINE TRANSPORT.**

    (a) "B" Echelon will in the first instance move with Coys.

    (b) When Coys. move forward "B" Echelon will concentrate in J.28.b.&.d.

2. **S.A.A.SECTION,D.A.C.**

    (a) S.A.A.Section D.A.C. will move to square P.1.b. on 21st. inst.

3. **AMMUNITION.**

    (a) Fireworks and Grenades required to be carried on the man will be issued to Bdes. at INCHY on the 21st. inst.
    (b) 17th Div.S.A.A. and Grenade Dump is at J.27.c.8.2.
    A Forward Dump will be established at K.2.b.3.1.
    The dumps may be drawn on by this Battan. after Zero.

4. **WATER.**

    There are waterpoints at INCHY, MONTIGNY, J.33.b.2.6., J.26.b.7.3. & J.26.b.5.7.
    17th Division are arranging for supply and policing of Water points which will be prepared on the River SELLE.

5. **STRAGGLERS.**

    D.A.P.M. will arrange for a line of Straggler Posts to be in position by Zero hour on the LE CATEAU - SOLESMES road.
    Stragglers Collecting post K.9.a.2.7.

6. **PRISONERS OF WAR CAGE.**

    Prisoners of War cage will be established at K.9.a.2.7. at Zero hour.

7. **CIVILIANS.**

    Arrangements are being made by O.C. 21st. Div. Train to feed all civilians.

V.F. Samuelson

Capt. & Adjt.
21st. Battn. Machine Gun Corps.

20/10/18.

Distribution.-

All Os.C.Coys.
Quartermaster.
21st Division "Q"
File
War Diary (2)

SECRET.

Reference.- 21st. Bn.M.G.Corps Administrative Instructions
             No.4 for forthcoming operations.

The following amendments will be made :-

Para.2. Line.2.   for 21st. inst. read 22nd. inst.,

Para.3.(a) Line.2. for 21st.inst., read 22nd. inst.,

Para.3.(b) Line1. for J.27.c.8.2. read J.23.c.2.6.

                              J. F. Samuelson
                                      Capt. & Adjt.
21/10/18.   21st. Battn. Machine Gun Corps.

Distribution.-
All recipients 21st Bn.M.G.Corps Administrative Instructions No.4.

SECRET.   Copy No. 8

       21st Battn. Machine Gun Corps
          OPERATION ORDER No. 55.

                                    18th October 1918.

Ref. Map Sheets:
57b.S.W. & 57b.N.E.

1.   "B" & "C" Coys. will proceed by route march on the
        19th inst. to INCHY, leaving present area at 09.00 hours,
        and reporting to O.C., 17th Battn. Machine Gun Corps,
        immediately on arrival.

2.   Both Coys. are placed at the disposal of O.C., 17th
        Battn. M.G.Corps to carry out Barrage fire from the 19th inst.

3.   After carrying out Barrage fire, these Coys. will
        not move forward, but will remain in INCHY area until further
        instructions are received from H.Q. 21st Battn. M.G.Corps.

4.   All Coy. Surplus Stores will be dumped at Barn,
        N.30.b.56. (Road Junction) by 08.00 hours, 19th inst.

5.   Rations for the 19th and 20th will be carried.

6.   Location of respective Coy. H.Q. will be wired Battn.
        H.Q. as soon as possible.

7.   ACKNOWLEDGE.

                                    V. T. Samuelson
                                        Capt. & Adjt.,
                                    21st Battn. Machine Gun Corps.

DISTRIBUTION.

Copy No. 1 .. O.C. "B" Coy.
        2 .. O.C. "C" Coy.
        3 .. 'G', 21st Division.
        4 .. 17th Bn. M.G.Corps.

SECRET.   Copy No...7.....

21st Division Order No. 247.

21st October, 1918.

Ref : Maps 1/20,000

Sheets 57 b. N.E., 51 a.S.E.

1.   The Third and Fourth Armies, in conjunction with other operations, have been ordered to attack the enemy on October 23rd. at an hour which has been notified to all concerned.

2.   The V Corps will be attacking with 38th Division on the right and 17th Division on the left. The objectives for these operations were given in the map accompanying 21st Division G.F.No.1.

3.   (a) On October 23rd at an hour which has been notified to all concerned the Third and Fourth Armies will renew the attack.
     (b) The 33rd Division will attack on the right and the 37th Division on the left of the 21st Division.

4.   The 21st Division will be the left Division of the Vth Corps and will attack in a North Easterly direction with successive objectives:-

     (a) Red dotted line.
     (b) Red Line.
     (c) Green dotted line.
     (d) Green Line.
     (e) Brown Line.

5.   (a) The 64th Infantry Brigade on the right and 110th Infantry Brigade on the left will capture the Red dotted line, Red Line and Green dotted Line.
     (b) After the capture of the green dotted line the 110th Infantry Brigade will establish posts beyond VENDEGIES Village so as to assist the advance of the 62nd Infantry Brigade.
     (c) The 62nd Infantry Brigade will pass through the two leading Brigades and capture the Green and Brown lines.
     (d) After the capture of the Brown Line the 62nd Infantry Brigade will exploit through and beyond the BOIS DE GIAGEON. The Cyclist Squadron which is placed at the disposal of the 62nd Infantry Brigade should be used for this purpose.

6.   Liaison posts will be established as follows :-
     (a) Between 64th and (19th Infantry Brigade) 33rd Division.
         On Red dotted line at corner of fence E.30.c.7.5. om
         On Red line .... F.19.c.8.5.
         On Green dotted Line. ..   ..   .. F.19.b.9.9.

     (b) Between 62nd Infantry Brigade and (19th Infantry Brigade) 33rd Division.
         On Green Line at Road Junction   .. ..F.9.c.8.5.
         Between 62nd Infantry Brigade (100th Inf.Bde.)33rd Division
         On Brown Line at LES TUILERIES Road junction.

     (c) Between 110th Infantry Brigade and 37th Division
         On Red Line at corner of fence .. .. E.12.c.6.0.

     (d) Between 62nd Infantry Brigade and 37th Division.
         On Brown Line at SALESCHES Station.

/Liaison......

-2-

Liaison Posts will be joint posts and will consist of one Platoon found by each Unit concerned.

7. (a) Five Field Artillery Brigades will support the attack of the 21st Division.
(b) Four Field Artillery Brigades will support the advance of the 64th and 110th Infantry Brigades.
The Barrage will consist of two thirds of the 18 pdrs. firing shrapnel with 10% smoke and one third of the 18 pdrs. firing H.E. 100 yards in advance of the shrapnel Barrage.
Four 4.5." Howitzers and Heavy Artillery will deepen the barrage in advance of the 18 pdrs, special attention being paid to sunken roads and the outskirts of villages.
(c) 4t.5" Howitzers will fire smoke on the general line of the River HARPIES during the advance of the 64th and 110th Infantry Brigades from the Red Line.
(d) The 94th Brigade R.F.A. is placed under the orders of the B.G.C. 62nd Infantry Brigade to support his attack.
This Brigade will not be employed with barrages detailed in sub-para (b) above.
(e) 6 Mobile Trench Mortars are placed at the disposal of the 62nd Infantry Brigade.

8. (a) One and a half Machine Gun Companies will support the advance of the 64th and 110th Infantry Brigades with an indirect Machine Gun barrage.
(b) One Machine Gun company will be affiliated to each Infantry Brigade. 8 guns of the Company allotted to the 62nd. Infantry Brigade will not join this Brigade until after firing the barrage detailed in sub-para (a).
(c) These Machine Gun companies are to be used for offensive action. i.e. supporting the advance by direct fire as well as for consolidation purposes.

9. Two tanks are allotted to the 64th Infantry Brigade and 1 Tank to 110th Infantry Brigade for the purpose of clearing the village of OVILLERS.
One Platoon of Infantry will be detailed to accompany each Tank.
After OVILLERS has been "mopped up" Tanks will rally at the CHATEAU F.13.a.

10. The 15th Squadron R.A.F. will be calling for flares as soon as possible after daylight and subsequently at 0090, 1100 hrs etc.,

11. Divisional Headquarters will be at INCHY during the first stages of the operations, subsequently moving to about K.2.b.2.2. and then along the general line of the Brigade report centres (detailed in 21st. Division G.F.No.3.)

12. ACKNOWLEDGE.

Sgd. H.I.FRANKLYN.
Lieut.Colonel.General Staff,
21st. Division.

Issued at 1330 hrs through Signals to :-

	Copy No.			Copy No.
62nd Inf. Bde.	1		Vth Corps.	14 - 15
64th do. do.	2	@	Vth Corps. R.A.	16
110th do. do.	3	@	Vth Corps. H.A.	17
C.R.A.	4	@	17th Div.	18
C.R.E.	5		33rd Div.	19
@ Pioneers.	6		37th Div.	20
D.M.G.C.	7	@	38th Div.	21
Signals.	8	@	15 Sqn.R.A.F.	22
@ A.D.M.S.	9		11th Tank. Battn.	23
Train	10		War Diary.	24
@ A/Q.	11		File.	25
A.P.M.	12			
@ D.G.O.	13			

Map showing objectives follows.

SECRET.

21 Div.
G. 104.

All recipients of Div.Order No.247.

The following amendments will be made to 21st Division Order No. 247 :-

Para 3 (b). will be amended to read :-

"The 33rd Division will attack on the right of the 21st Division and the 5th Division on the left of the 21st Division as far as the Green Dotted Line, where the 37th Division will pass through and continue the attack on our left."

Para 5 (d). will be amended to read :-

"After capture of the Brown Line, 62nd Inf.Bde., will exploit as far as the road running South Eastwards from GHISSIGNIES through Squares X.11 X.17, and a Reconnoitring Patrol will be sent into LOUVIGNIES + LES QUESNOY.

The Cyclist Squadron which is placed at the disposal of the 62nd Infantry Brigade will be used for this purpose".

Add to para 5 sub-para (e).

"As soon as the Red Line has been captured, the 64th and 110th Inf. Bdes., will each re-organise one Battalion so that assistance may be sent to the 62nd Inf.Bde.if required at a later period.

After the capture of the Green Dotted Line, the 64th Inf.Bde. will re-organise and concentrate a second Battalion. The two Battalions thus re-organised will be prepared in case of need to form a defensive flank between the spur in F.10.c. and the River HARPIES in F.16.d.

If these Battalions are not required to form this defensive flank they will move forward so as to occupy the Green Line as soon as this line is vacated by the 62nd Inf.Bde.

The 110th Inf.Bde., will take over the S.E. portion of the Green Dotted Line from the 64th Inf. Bde. The Battalion 64th Inf.Bde. thus relieved will move forward in support of remainder of Brigade.

The 110th Inf.Bde., will be prepared to hold the Green Dotted and Red Lines, or to move forward on receipt of orders from Divisional Head quarters in support of 64th Inf.Bde".

Para 6 (c). will be amended to read :-

"Between 110th Inf.Bde., and 5th Division.
On Green Dotted Line at corner of Fences F.7.a.1.6".

Para 6 (d). will be amended to read :-

"Between 62nd Inf.Bde. and (111th Inf.Bde) 37th Div.
On Brown Line at SALESCHES Station".

Para 8 (a).
For "1½ M.G.Coys" read "1 M.G.Coy".

Para 8.(b). will be amended to read.
"One M.G.Coy.will be affiliated to each Inf.Bde".

Para 9 will be amended to read.
"Three tanks have been detailed to assist in the clearing of the village of OVILLERS. These Tanks will work round the outer edges of the Village and will be ready to assist the Infantry to "mop up" where required.

When OVILLERS has been cleared up, the Tanks will move forward and provided that they can cross the River HARPIES, will assist the 62nd Inf. Bde. in the capture of the Brown and Green Lines".

21.10.1918.

(sgd). H.I.Franklyn.
Lt-Colonel. General Staff.
21st Division.

```
                                                          S E C R E T.
                                                             21 Div.
                                                             G. 197.
```

To all recipients of Div. Order No. 247.

    Divisional Head Quarters close Walincourt and open INCHY (J.22.a.4.3.) at 5.p.m. October 22nd.1918.

                                    (sgd). A.F.Macdougall.
                                               Major.
                                           General Staff.
21.10.1918.   21st Division.

                  CERTIFIED TRUE COPY.

War Diary

SECRET.

21st Battn. Machine Gun Corps Administrative Instructions No.5.

Sheet 57b.N.E.

1. "B" Echelon Transport of the Battalion will assemble at J.28.b. & d. by 1400 hrs 22nd. October.

2. Rations will be issued from new Transport Lines on the 22nd inst.,

3. "D" Coy. and Battalion Headquarters "B" Echelon will be ready to move from present area at 0900 hours 22nd. inst.,

Lieut. A. Huxley will issue the necessary orders re starting point and be in command of the convoy.

V. F. Saunders
Capt. & Adjt.

21/10/18.   21st. Battn. Machine Gun Corps.

Distribution.-

All Os.C.Coys.
"D"Coy. (Rear)
21st. Division "Q"
Quartermaster.
War Diary (2)
File.

SECRET.   Copy No. 4

                21st Battn. Machine Gun Corps
                     OPERATION ORDER No. 56.
                     ─────────────────────
                                               21st October 1918.

Ref. Maps 1/20,000.
Sheets 57b.N.E., 51.A.S.E.
─────────────────────────

1.   The Third and Fourth Armies, in conjunction with other
       operations, have been ordered to attack the enemy on October
       23rd, at an hour which has been notified to all concerned.

2.   The Vth Corps will be attacking with 38th Division on
       the right and 17th Division on the left. The objectives
       for these operations were given in the Map accompanying
       21st Division G.F.No. 1.

3. (a)   On October 23rd, at an hour which has been notified
           to all concerned, the Third and Fourth Armies will renew
           the attack.

   (b)   The 33rd Division will attack on the right, and the
           37th Division on the left of the 21st Division.

4.   The 21st Division will be the left Division of the Vth
       Corps, and will attack in a North Easterly direction with
       successive objectives:-

               (a) Red dotted line.
               (b) Red line.
               (c) Green dotted line.
               (d) Green line.
               (e) Brown line.

       Maps herewith.

5. (a)   The 64th Infantry Brigade on the right, and the 110th
           Infantry Brigade on the left will capture the Red Dotted Line,
           Red Line, and Green Dotted Line.

   (b).   After the capture of the Green Dotted Line, the
           110th Infantry Brigade will establish posts beyond VENDEGIES
           Village, so as to assist the advance of the 62nd Infantry
           Brigade.

   (c)   The 62nd Infantry Brigade will pass through the two
           leading Brigades and capture the Green and Brown Lines.

   (d)   After the capture of the Brown Line, the 62nd Infantry
           Brigade will exploit through and beyond the BOIS DE GLAGEON.
               The Cyclist Squadron which is placed at the disposal
           of the 62nd Infantry Brigade should be used for this purpose.

                                                        /6......

-2-

6. (a) "C" Coy. 21st Bn.MGC. will support the advance of the 64th and 110th Infantry Brigades with an indirect Machine Gun Barrage.
On the capture of the Red Line, "C" Coy. will take up defensive positions on the Red Dotted Line, and on capture of Green Line will take up defensive positions on the Red Line.
Orders for move will be issued by O.C. 21st Battn. M.G.C. direct.

"A" Coy. is affiliated to 110th Infantry Brigade.
"B" Coy. is affiliated to 64th Infantry Brigade.
"C" Coy. will be in Divisional Reserve.
"D" Coy. is affiliated to 62nd Infantry Brigade.

A.B. & D.
(b) These Machine Gun Companies are to be used for offensive action, i.e., supporting the advance by direct fire, as well as for consolidation purposes.

7. The 15th Squadron, R.A.F. will be calling for flares as soon as possible after daylight, and subsequently at 09.00, 11.00 hours etc.

8. Divisional Headquarters will be at INCHY during the first stages of the operations, subsequently moving to about K.2.b.2.2, and then along the general line of the Brigade Report Centres (detailed in 21st Division G.F.No.3).

9. Battalion Headquarters will close at WALINCOURT at 09.00 hours, and open at INCHY, J.23.c.20.60 at same hour on the 22nd October 1918.

V.F. Samuelson
Capt. & Adjt.,
21st Battn. Machine Gun Corps.

DISTRIBUTION.

Copy No. 1 .. O.C. "A" Coy.)
        2 .. O.C. "B" Coy.) To acknowledge.
        3 .. O.C. "C" Coy.)
        4 .. O.C. "D" Coy.)
        5 .. Quartermaster.
        6 .. 'G', 21st Division.
        7 .. Commanding Officer.
        8 .. 2nd in Command.
        9 .. 62nd Inf. Bde.
       10 .. 64th Inf. Bde.
       11 .. 110th Inf. Bde.
       12 .. File.
   13 & 14 .. War Diary.

Priority.

To:- ZEJU. BADE. BASU. VUEE.

GX 161.   23/10/1918.

"ZEJU will move two Sections from Reserve Coy. to GREEN Line forthwith aaa These Sections will reconnoitre positions but will not occupy them unless necessary aaa Two Sections Res.Coy. will remain on RED Line aaa Whole Coy. will probably be required to fire a barrage to assist advance tomorrow aaa Acknowledge aaa Addsd.ZEJU reptd.3 Bdes.

        From........ZOWU.
        Time........1600 hrs.

                      (sgd).A.F. Macdougall.
                      Major.
                      General Staff.
                      21st Division.

CERTIFIED TRUE COPY.

TELEGRAM.

Urgent.   Words.
Operations   A R M Y
priority to   To...........................   -Y23 X 18 - U.
Brigades.   At...........................   T E L E G R A P H S
                   By...........................
(sgd).H.I.V., Lt-Col.

DADE	LODE	ZEJU	ZODU	17 Div.	5th Corps.
BASU	ZOKI	A/Q	5th Div.	37 Div.	
VUFE	DUPA	ZOHO	33 Div.	15 Sqn.	

G.X. 162   c / 23 / AAA.

Zowu Warning Order aaa   Advance will be resumed to-morrow by Zowu aaa
Objective line of road X.24.a.9.0. GRAND GAY FARM to Halt X.11.a.5.5.
AAA Right Div. Boundary from X.29.Cent. to Cross Roads S.3.b.8.7. aaa
Left Div. Boundary from X.6.a.0.2. M.31.b.3.0. M.26.b.5.0. M.21.c.3.0.
aaa Inter Brigade Boundary POIX SPINNING MILL to road junction X.28.d.1.4.
just inclusive to right Brigade thence straight line to X.22.d.6.5.
South of road to X.17.b.3.1. thence straight line to M.33.c.0.8.   aaa
BASU will attack on right and DADE on Left aaa   Jumping off line depends
on progress of DADE to-day aaa After capture of objective advance guards
will be sent forward to make as much ground as possible towards
JOLIMETZ - LE QUESNOY Road aaa Cancelling previous instructions BASU
will now take over GREEN line on right Brigade front and VUFE on left
Brigade front as soon as vacated by DADE aaa   BASU will push forward troop
troops to protect right rear of DADE during latters advance today
and will take over right Brigade front from DADE on final line
reached tonight aaa VUFE will be disposed tonight between GREEN Line
inclusive and RED line exclusive and will be in Div.Reserve tomorrow aaa
Further orders later   Acknowledge.

                                    (sgd). H.I.Franklyn.
                                           Lieut-Colonel.
                                           General Staff.
                                           21st Division.
ZOWU.
1400.

CERTIFIED TRUE COPY.

TELEGRAM.

URGENT OPERATIONS
PRIORITY 3 BDES.
D.M.G.C.

H.I.F. Lt-Col.

DADE	ZOKI	ZEJU	ZODU	17 Div.	V Corps.
BASU	LODE	A/Q	5 Div.	37 Div.	
VUFE	DUFA	ZOHO	33 Div.	15 Sqn.R.A.F.	

— / 23 / AAA

ZOWU Order No. 248 AAA Ref.Warning Order G.X.162 of today AAA Advance is being continued tomorrow AAA 33rd Division attack LANDRECIES - LE QUESNOY Road AAA 37 Division attack high ground North of GHISSIGNIES AAA BASU on right and DADE on left will attack with first objective line of road from X.29.c.7.7. to X.21.b.7.1. AAA Second objective line of road from rd. junc. X.24.a.9.0. GRAND GAY FARM to Halt X.11.a.5.5. AAA Advance to first objective under barrage AAA No barrage for advance beyond first objective AAA Artillery starting line 300 yards in advance of road F.9.c.6.6. F.2.a.3.5. AAA Barrage dwells on starting line for 8 minutes and then advances at rate of 100 yards in 4 minutes AAA Protector beyond first objective for 8 minutes and then cease AAA No barrage for right Brigade through Village of POIX DU NORD AAA BASU will pick up barrage on far side of village AAA Advance through village will be calculated at rate of 100 yards in 4 minutes AAA Reserve Coy. Machine Guns will barrage 400 yards ahead of Artillery AAA One M.G.Coy. remains with each Brigade AAA 95th Bde.R.F.A. will support advance from first to second objectives and keep liaison with BASU and DADE H.Q. AAA Second objective will be consolidated in depth when captured AAA Liaison post with 33rd Div. at rd. junc. X.24.a.9.0. and with 37th Div. on rly. at X.5.c.9.5. AAA After capture of objectives all three Divs., will send advanced guards forward to make good outpost zone AAA 33 Div. to FUTOY and JOLIMETZ AAA 37th Div. to East of LE QUESNOY AAA Objective for ZOWU Adv.Guards main JOLIMETZ - LE QUESNOY Road aaa VUFE will act as Adv.Guard leading troops crossing Green Line at 0700 hours and advancing through BASU and DADE after capture of second objective aaa 95th Bde.R.F.A. will support advance of VUFE AAA Most important for VUFE to protect right of 37th Div. during advance AAA Ack AAA addsd.all concerned.

(sgd).H.I.Franklin.
Lieut-Colonel.
General Staff.

ZOWU.
20.30.hrs.

CERTIFIED TRUE COPY.

MESSAGES & SIGNALS.

TO:- DADE. LODE. ZEJU. ZODU. 17 Div. V.Corps.
BASU. ZOKI. A/Q. 5 Div. 37 Div.
VUFE. DUFA. ZOHO. 33 Div. 15 Sqn.

Senders No.	Day of Month.	
GX.169.	23	AAA

Ref. ZOWU Warning Order G.X.162 Inter-Bde. Boundary for rd. junction. X.28.d.1.4. read rd. junc. X.28.c.1.4.

From :- ZOWU.

(sgd). G. TOOTH.
Capt.

CERTIFIED TRUE COPY.

MESSAGES & SIGNALS.

Urgent Operations
Priority 3 Bdes.

To:-	DADE	LODE	ZEJU	ZODU	17 Div.	V Corps.
	BASU	ZOKI	A/Q	5 Div.	37 Div.	
VU	VUFE	DUFA	ZOHO	33 Div.	15 Sqn.R.A.F.	

Senders No.   Day of Month.
G.X. 249.   24.   AAA

ZOWU Order No. 249 AAA BASU on right and DADE on left will attack and capture second objective this afternoon AAA Arty(?) comes down at 15.00 hrs. on line 300 yards in front of LES TULLERIES - SALESCHES Rd. on right Bde. front and about 400 yards in front of this road on left Bde. front aaa Exact Arty. starting line has been given to those concerned AAA Barrage lifts at 16.12 hrs and advances at rate of 100 yards in 3 mins. until 500 yards beyond objective and then ceases AAA Heavy Arty. will bombard objective and orchards west of objective from Zero till safety compels lift AAA H.A. then lifts on to high ground 500 yards beyond objective for 20 mins. and then ceases AAA Ack.

From :- ZOWU.
Time :- 14.40.

(sgd). A.F.Macdougall.
Major.
for Lieut-Colonel.

CERTIFIED TRUE COPY.

TELEGRAM.

Words.

URGENT
OPERATIONS
PRIORITY 3 BDES.

Sent.

To..........................
At..........................
By..........................

		HIP.			
DADE	LODE	ZEJU	ZODU	17 Div.	
BASU	ZOKI	A/Q	5 Div.	37 Div.	V Corps.
VUFE	DUFA	ZOHO	33 Div.	15 Sqn.R.A.F.	

G.K. / 24 / AAA

ZOWU Order No 250 AAA It is considered possible that the enemy may withdraw from opposite our front tonight AAA BASU and DADE will send out patrols at Dawn to search ground between our present front line and line of orchards about 1000 yards N.E. of it AAA If no enemy encountered these patrols will be supported and patrols sent on again to line of road through CROIX ROUGE and into LOUVIGNIES AAA If still no enemy encountered DADE and BASU will NOT be required to send patrols further AAA VUFE will have two Companies between Brown Line and POIX inclusive by 0700 hrs. tomorrow Oct.25th AAA Remainder of Bde. will be disposed in depth and obtain as much rest as possible until leading Coys. are ordered to move. AAA VUFE will keep close touch with the situation through BASU and DADE H.Q. AAA If patrols report no enemy on this side of line of orchards VUFE will order leading Companies to advance and take over work of patrolling from DADE and BASU AAA These two Coys. will patrol by bounds and will support patrols on conclusion of each bound. AAA VUFE will support leading Coys. by remainder of Bde. making good as first objective line of JOLIMETZ - LE QUESNOY Rd. AAA When this road made good patrols will be sent forward to Railway but no further advance except by patrols until ordered from Div. H.Q. AAA If BASU and DADE encounter enemy it is not the Div. Comdr's intention to make ground by fighting AAA Divs. on flanks will be taking similar action AAA One Bde. R.F.A. will be held in readiness and come under orders of VUFE if latter moves forward AAA One troop Cyclists will be sent to report to each Bde. about 0800 hrs tomorrow and will be used to get touch with the enemy if Inf. patrols fail to do so AAA Div. H.Q. closes NEUVILLY 10.00 and re-opens OVILLERS same hour AAA Ack.

ZOWU.
22.15.hrs.

(sgd). H.I.Franklyn.
Lieut-Colonel.

CERTIFIED TRUE COPY.

TELEGRAM.

Urgent
Operations
priority
to Bdes. HIF.

Words.
Sent.
At.........................
To.........................
By.........................

DADE	LODE	ZEJU	ZODU	17 Div.	
BASU	ZOKI	A/Q	5th Corps.	33rd Div.	15th Sqn. R.A.F.
VUFE	DUFA	ZOHO	5th Div.	37th Div.	

/ 25 / AAA

ZOWU Order No 251 AAA If VUFE does not pass through DADE and BASU today VUFE will relieve DADE and BASU tonight 25/26 inst AAA Details will be arranged Brigadiers AAA On relief DADE will withdraw to the area between the BROWN and GREEN Lines both exclusive AAA Basu will withdraw to the area between the GREEN Line and VENDEGIES both inclusive AAA DADE will be prepared to hold the BROWN Line or to form a defensive flank facing S.E. AAA BASU will be prepared to hold the GREEN line AAA DADE will hold two Battalions in readiness to move at quarter hours notice and BASU will hold one Battalion ready to move at half hours notice AAA Reserve M.G.Coy. will be disposed for the defence of the GREEN Line AAA Completion of relief will be reported to ZOWU AAA Ack.

ZOWU.
0910.

(sgd). A.F.Macdougall. Major
for Lieut-Colonel.

CERTIFIED TRUE COPY.

MESSAGES & SIGNALS.

Service Instructions :-   YO Urgent Operations.
25.

21 Div. Order No. 252 AAA In conjunction with operation by 33rd Divn.
110th Bde. will establish outpost zone tonight in front of present line aaa
Fighting patrols will be sent forward under creeping barrage to establish
platoon posts approximately in following places aaa S.13.d.0.4.
X.18.b.9.4. X.13.b.7.6. X.11.d.8.8. X.11.b.5.4. X.11.b.1.9. aaa Barrage
will come down at 0100 hrs. Oct. 26th on line S.19.b.0.7. to X.11.b.0.5.
will pause for 8 minutes and then advance at 100 yds. in 4 minutes until
300 yards clear of posts given above and then cease aaa At dawn
reconnoitring patrols will be sent forward to line of orchards S.W. and
S. of LOUVIGNIES AAA   If no enemy encountered action detailed in 21 Divn.
Order No. 250 of yesterday will be adopted aaa If enemy encountered
reconnoitring patrols will be withdrawn aaa Relief of 64th Bde and 62nd
Bde must be completed by 23.59 hrs. so as to facilitate above operation aaa
Whole Cyclist Squadron comes under 110 Bde after relief aaa Ack aaa
Addsd. all concerned.

From...... 21 Div.
Time...... 15.50. hrs.

CERTIFIED TRUE COPY.

MESSAGES & SIGNALS.

Prefix.S.M. Code. 1620. Words.34.
Service Instructions :- YU.
Handed in at 21 Divn. Office 1550   Received 1701.
To:-
    21st M.G.Battn.

| G.X. 219 | / 25/ | / | AAA. |

21 M.G.Battn. will place eight guns from Res.Coy. at disposal of 110 Bde for defence of right flank aaa Details of attachment will be arranged between 21 M.G.Battn and 110 Bde.

From.21 Divn.
Time.1550.

CERTIFIED TRUE COPY.

SECRET.

Words.
To..........................
At..........................
By..........................

DADE	LODE	ZEJU	ZODU
BASU	ZOKI	A/Q	JESO
VUFE	DUFA	ZOHO	

GX 228 / 25/ AAA.

Warning Order AAA ZOWU less LODE will be relieved by 17th Division less Arty. tomorrow and night 26/27 inst AAA DADE and BASU will be relieved by 50 and 51 Inf. Bdes. respectively. AAA Reliefs to be complete by 1530 hrs. AAA VUFE will be relieved by 52nd Inf.Bde. AAA On relief BASU to INCHY DADE to NEUVILLY VUFE to OVILLERS and AMERVAL AAA 3 Coys. ZEJU will be billeted with affiliated Bdes. AAA ZEJU H.Q. and Res.Coy. to NEUVILLY AAA ZOKI will arrange reliefs of Field Coys. R.E. and DUFA AAA Addsd. DADE, BASU, VUFE, ZEJU, ZOKI repeated LODE DUFA, A/Q, JESO, ZOHO, ZODU.

ZOWU.
1930.

(sgd).A.F.Macdougall.
Major.
for Lieut-Colonel.
General Staff.

CERTIFIED TRUE COPY.

SECRET.   Copy No. 11.
              21st DIVISION ORDER NO. 253.
Ref. Sheets 57 B and 51 a.
      1/40,000.   26th October, 1918.

1.   The Division (less Artillery) will be relieved by the 17th Division (less Artillery) to-day and night 26/27th October, in accordance with attached table.
2.   All details of relief will be arranged between Brigadiers.
3.   Reliefs of Field Coys., R.E. Pioneers and Field Ambulances will be arranged between Cs.R.E. and A.Ds.M.S.
4.   Machine Gun reliefs will be arranged between Os.C. 21st and 17th Machine Gun Battalions.
5.   Completion of relief will be reported to Divisional Head Quarters.
6.   Command of the Sector and the Artillery in it will pass to G.O.C. 17th Division on completion of the Infantry relief.
7.   Divisional Headquarters close at OVILLERS and open at NEUVILLY at 1600 hrs. October 26th. 1918.
8.   Acknowledge.

                                          (sgd). H.I. Franklyn.
                                                  Lieut-Colonel.
                                                  General Staff.
                                                  21st Division.

Issued through Signals at 13.30.

	Copy. No.		Copy. No.
62nd Inf. Bde.	1.	21st Battn. M.G.C.	11.
64th " "	2.	D.G.O.	12.
110th " "	3.	Train.	13.
C.R.A.	4.	21st M.T.Co.	14.
C.R.E.	5.	5th Corps.	15 - 16.
Pioneers.	6.	Vth Corps H.A.	17.
"Q"	7.	Vth Corps R.A.	18.
Signals.	8.	17th Div.	19.
A.D.M.S.	9.	33rd Div.	20.
A.P.M.	10.	37th Div.	21.
		38th Div.	22.
		15th Sqn. R.A.F.	23.
		O.C.D Sqn. N.I.H.	24.
		War Diary.	25.
		File.	26.

CERTIFIED TRUE COPY.

TABLE TO ACCOMPANY 21st DIVISION ORDER NO.253.

Serial No.	Unit.	From.	To.	Relieved by.	Route.	Remarks.
1.	62nd Inf. Bde.	Support.	NEUVILLY.	50th Inf. Bde.	CROSS COUNTRY TRACKS.	Relief to be complete by 15.30.hours.
2.	64th Inf. Bde.	Reserve.	INCHY.	51st Inf. Bde.		
3.	110th Inf.Bde.	Line.	OVILLERS & AMERVAL.	52nd Inf. Bde.		Relief not to commence before dark.
4.	21st Bn.M.G.C.	Line.	2 Coys. NEUVILLY. 1 Coy. INCHY. 1 Coy. OVILLERS or AMERVAL. H.Q. NEUVILLY.	17th Bn. M.G.C.		

NOTES :-

A. All movement by day will be by Platoons at 100 yards interval and all precautions will be taken against observation by enemy aircraft.

B. When troops have to march on roads, they will move in file. Transport moving by road will adhere to traffic routes laid down.

SECRET.   Copy No. 12

21st Battalion Machine Gun Corps.

OPERATION ORDER No. 57.

Ref. Maps 1/20,000
Sheets: 57b.N.E. & 51.a.S.E.   26th October, 1918.

1.   21st Division less LODE will be relieved by 17th Division on the night 26/27th. inst.

2.   21st. Battalion Machine Gun Corps will be relieved as follows :-

   "A" Coy. 21st Battn. M.G.C. - by - "A" Coy. 17th Battn. M.G.C.
   "B" Coy.   do.   do.   do.   do.   "D" do.   do.   do.   do.
   ("C" Coy.   do.   do.   do.)
   ((8 guns in Green Line))   do.   "C" do.   do.   do.   do.
   (8 guns now with 110thInf.Bde.do. "B" do.   do.   do.   do.
   "D" Coy. 1 Section 21 Bn.M.G.C.do. "B" do.   do.   do.   do.

            The remaining 3 Sections will be withdrawn on completion of the relief of the 62nd Bde.

3.   All arrangements for the relief will be made by Company Commanders concerned.

4.   Completion of relief will be telephoned to Battn.H.Qrs. by Code word ORLREET.

5.   After the relief companies will march to billeting areas as follows :-

   "A" Coy. Divisional Reserve.   NEUVILLY.
   "B" "   Affiliated 64th Inf.Bde. INCHY.
   "C" "   do.   110th "   "   OVILLERS & AMERVAL.
   "D" "   do.   62nd   "   "   NEUVILLY.

            Billets for "A" Coy. will be arranged by Adjutant 21st. Battn. Machine Gun Corps and for the remaining Coys. by the Bdes. to which they are affiliated.

6.   ACKNOWLEDGE.

                              (Sgd). A.J. PACK.
                                    Lt. & Asst.Adjt.
                     for Lieut.Colonel. Commanding 21st.Bn.M.G.Corps.

DISTRIBUTION.

	Copy. No.		Copy No.
O.C. "A" Coy.	1	62nd. Inf.Bde.	9
do. "B" "	2	110th. do. do.	11
do. "C" "	3	64th do. do.	10
do. "D" "	4	File	12
Quartermaster.	5	War Diary	13 - 14
"G" 21st Division	6	O.C.17th Bn.M.G.C.	15
Commanding Officer.	7		
Second-in-Command.	8		

SECRET.　　　　　　　　　　　　　　　　　　　　　　Copy No...11......

21st Division Order No.254.

Ref. Maps 57.B. and 51.A. 1/40,000.　　　　　　28th October, 1918.

1. The Division (less Artillery) will relieve the 17th Division (less Artillery) in the Left Sector of the V Corps front on October 29th and night 29th/30th October, 1918. in accordance with the attached Table.

2. All details of the relief will be arranged between Brigadiers.

3. Boundary between 62nd and 110th Infantry Brigades will be :-
K.28.c.0.2. - K.22.d.6.5. - thence along road (inclusive to 62nd Inf. Bde.) to K.17.b.3.2. - S.7.b.0.0.

4. (a) Field Coys. R.E. and Pioneers reliefs will be arranged between Cs.R.E.
Field Coys. R.E. 21st. Division will not leave present billets until 15.30 hours October 29th.

(b) Field Ambulance Reliefs will be arranged between A.Ds.M.S.
Field Ambulances, 21st Division, will move with the Infantry Brigades to whom they are attached.

5. Machine Gun reliefs will be arranged between Os.C. 21st and 17th Battalions, Machine Gun Corps.

6. Completion of reliefs will be reported to Divisional Headquarters.

7. Command of the Sector and the Artillery in it will pass to the G.O.C. 21st Division on completion of the Infantry relief.

8. Divisional Headquarters close at NEUVILLY and open at OVILLERS at 16.00 hours October 29th.

9. Acknowledge.

　　　　　　　　　　　　　　　　　　　(Sgd.) S.TOOTH. Capt.
　　　　　　　　　　　　　　　　　　　　for. Lieut.Colonel
　　　　　　　　　　　　　　　　　　　　General Staff,
　　　　　　　　　　　　　　　　　　　　21st. Division.

Issued through Signals
at 19.30 hours to :-

	Copy No.		Copy No.		Copy No.
62 Inf. Bde.	1	A.D.M.S.	9	17th Division	18
64 : :	2	D.A.P.M.	10	33rd do.	19
110 : :	3	D.M.G.C.	11	37th do.	20
C.R.A.	4	D.G.O.	12	38th do.	21
C.R.E.	5	Train.	13	Sqn.R.A.F.	22
Pioneers.	6	21 M.T.Coy.	14	Div. Cyclists.	23
"Q"	7	V Corps	15 - 16	War Diary.	24
Signals.	8	V Corps H.A.	17	File.	25
		V Corps R.A.	18	Div. Rec. Camp	26

CERTIFIED TRUE COPY.

SECRET.   OPERATION ORDER NO. 58   COPY NO............
           21st BATTALION, MACHINE GUN CORPS.
           ---o---o---o---o---

Ref.Maps 1/40,000
Sheets. 57 B & 51 A.   28th October, 1918.

1.   The Division (less Artillery) will relieve the 17th Division
        (less Artillery) in the left Sector of the Vth Corps Front on October
        29th and night 29/30th October.1918.

2.   All details of relief will be arranged between Company
        Commanders concerned.

3.   Boundary between 62nd and 110th Infantry Brigades will be
        X.28.c.0.2. - X.22.d.6.5. - thence along road (incl. to 62nd Inf
        to X.17.b.3.2. - S.7.b.0.0.

4.   "A" Coy. 21st Bn. M.G.Corps will relieve "C" Coy. 17th Bn. M.G.Cor
        "B" "   "   "   "   "   "   "D" "   "   "   "
        "C" "   "   "   "   "   "   "A" "   "   "   "
        "D" "   "   "   "   "   "   "B" "   "   "   "

5.   "A" Company will be in Divisional Reserve and march in rea
        of 62nd Inf.Bde: from NEUVILLY.
        "B" Company will move with 64th Inf.Bde.
        "C"   "   "   "   " 110th "   "
        "D"   "   "   "   " 62nd   "   "

6.   Battalion Headquarters will close at NEUVILLY at 1200 hou
        and open at VENDEGIES at F.7.c.8.7. same hour.

7.   Completion of relief will be reported to Battalion Head
        Quarters by code word "HILDA".

8.   Major Borthwick, O's.C. Companies and 1 Officer per Compa
        will report Head Quarters, 17th Battalion, M.G.Corps, F.7.c.8.7. at
        11.00 hours to take over accommodation, etc., of relieving Companie

9.   All S.A.A., Photos, Defence Schemes etc., will be taken ov
        and receipts given.

                                                    10.....

- 2 -

(a). All movement EAST of VENDEGIES will be by equivalent of Platoons at 100 yards interval.
   All precautions will be taken against observation by enemy aircraft.
(b). Attention is directed to this Office letter H.268 of the 28th inst reference movements on road.   These instructions will be strictly complied with.
(c). Transport moving by road will adhere to traffic routes laid down.

ACKNOWLEDGE.

V F Saunders

Capt. & Adjutant.
28.10.1918.   21st Battalion, Machine Gun Corps.

DISTRIBUTION.
                          Copy No.

O.C., "A" Coy.   1.
O.C., "B" Coy.   2.
O.C., "C" Coy.   3.
O.C., "D" Coy.   4.
Quarter Master.   5.
Commanding Officer.   6.
"G" 21st Division.   7.
62nd Inf.Bde.   8.
64th Inf.Bde.   9.
110th Inf.Bde.   10.
2nd in command.   11.
17th Bn., M.G.Corps.   12.
War Diary.   13 & 14.
File.   15.

SECRET.

21st BATTALION, MACHINE GUN CORPS.

ADMINISTRATIVE INSTRUCTION No. 5.

---o---o---o---o---

1. **TRANSPORT.**
"A" Echelon will proceed with Companies to the Line.
"B" Echelon will take over accommodation of corresponding Companies of 17th Battalion, Machine Gun Corps at E.23.b.8.1.
Lieut. A.J. Pack will report to the Adjutant, 17th Battalion M.G.C. at above at 10.00 hours and take over all Rear Head Quarters. Each Company will detail a representative to report to Lieut. A.J. Pack at 10.30 hours at E.23.b.8.1. to take over respective Transport Lines.
"B" Echelon will accompany respective Companies to OVILLERS and then proceed to E.23.b.8.1.

2. **S.A.A. & GRENADES.**
The Main Div. Dump will be at E.24.a.5.5.
Advanced Div. Dump will be at F.8.a.7.2.

3. **RATIONS.**
Rations will be issued from new Transport Lines. The Quarter Master will send the necessary personnel to go ahead to issue rations to Companies by 14.30 hours. Companies will send necessary transport.

4. **ACCOMMODATION.**
Tents and Trench Shelters in OVILLERS Area will be taken over and receipts taken and given.

5. **BATHS.**
Baths at VENDEGIES & POIX will be available for this Division.

6. **WATER POINTS.** Water Points have been established as follows:-
4 Water Troughs at F.13.a.9.7.
2 " " " F.13.d.4.5.
4 " " " F.7.c.3.8.
2 " " " F.7.c.3.9.

7. **BILLETS.**
(a). Care must be taken that all billets are left scrupulously clean.
(b). Billeting certificates must be rendered in the usual way. As it will probably not be possible to give the name of the owner, the name of the street and the number of the billet will be entered on the certificate.

V.F. Samuelson
Capt. & Adjutant.
21st Battalion, Machine Gun Corps.

28.10.1918.

DISTRIBUTION.
O.C., "A" Coy.
" "B" "
" "C" "
" "D" "
Quarter Master.
Commanding Officer.
Lieut. A.J. Pack.

62nd Inf. Bde.
64th Inf. Bde.
110th Inf. Bde.
"Q" 21st Division.
War Diary (2).
File.

62 Inf. Bde.
64 : :
110 : :

SECRET.

21 Div.
G.347.

1. The Offensive will probably be resumed about November 4th or 5th.

2. (a) The advance will be due Eastwards through the FORET DE MORMAL.
   (b) The probable Northern Boundary will be from cross roads X.11.c.9.0. along grid line to M.12.c.0.0. and to U.7.c.0.0.
   (c) The probable Southern boundary will be from X.24.c.0.0. - S 22.c.0.0. - South of LOCQNIGNOL and then practically due East.

3. (a) The first phase of the operations will be undertaken by the 38th Division on the right and the 17th Division on the left.

   (b) The task allotted to these two Divisions will probably be an advance of 8,000 yards.

   (c) The 33rd Division on the right and the 21st Division on the left will follow up the leading Divisions and will be prepared to go through them and take up the advance, probably on Z plus 1 day.

4. The present idea is that zero for the attack of the 38th Div and the 17th Div. shall be about 07.30 hours.

5. The 17th Division will be relieving this Division 24 hours previous to Zero, i.e. either on the night November 2nd/3rd or on the night 3rd/4th.

6. The above is to be regarded as a forecast only and it is not yet possible to particularize further.

7. With a view to assisting the forming up of the 17th Division for an attack in daylight, the following steps will be taken by this Division :-

   (a) The road from X.24.a.9.0. - X.11.c.9.0. will be prepared to accommodate ten Coys Infantry.
   In the Right Brigade Sector this will be done by digging a continuous trench along the general line of the road.
   In the Left Brigade Sector by digging "cubby-holes" into the Eastern face of the Sunken Road.

   (b) A new trench to accommodate ten Coys Infantry will be dug along the general line of the ditch from X.24.a.5.0. - X.17.c.9.7. and behind the stream from X.17.c.9.7. - X.17.a.2.9.
   This work (starting tonight October 30th/31st) is being carried out under the orders of the C.R.E.
   O.C. 98th Field Company R.E. is in charge of the work in the Right Brigade Sector, and O.C. 97th Field Company R.E. in the Left Brigade Sector.
   The Pioneer Battalion is beginning this trench tonight, but additional Infantry working parties will be required tomorrow night, October 31st/November 1st, and the next night, November 1st/2nd. These will be supplied by the 62nd and 110th Infantry Brigades, three Companies, totalling not less than 250 men, will be detailed by each Brigade.

/Field.........

Field Company Commanders concerned will call at Brigade Headquarters tomorrow morning, and arrange details.

(c) The chain of Strong Points are being added to and improved by the R.E. These will be used to accommodate a portion of the Reserve Brigade, 17th Division.

(d) B.Gs.C. 62nd and 110th Infantry Brigades will do all in their power to improve forming up facilities in their respective areas, so as to assist the 17th Division.

                      (Sgd.) H.I. FRANKLYN
                                Lieut. Col.
                           General Staff,
                           21st. Division.

30th October, 1918.

Copies to C.R.A.
          C.R.E.
          "Q"
          D.M.G.C.

CERTIFIED TRUE COPY.

SECRET.   Copy No....11......

21st DIVISION ORDER No. 255.

Ref. 57.A.S.E. & 51.S.W.
   1/20,000   31st October, 1918.

1. The Divisional and Brigade Boundaries will be readjusted on the night 1st/2nd November, as under :-

Northern Divisional Boundary.

   K.10.d.6.0. - thence due East along grid line between K.11. and K.17, S.8. and S.14, etc.,

Southern Divisional Boundary.

   K.24.c.0.0. - S.26.b.0.9. - T.25.a.0.4.

Inter-Brigade Boundary.

   K.18.a.6.0. - K.17.d.6.0. - ARBRE de la CROIX (inclusive to 110th Infantry Brigade) - thence original boundary.

2. The following reliefs will be carried out on the night 1st/2nd November :-

(a) The 110th Infantry Brigade will extend its right to the new Divisional Right Boundary, relieving troops of the 38th Division.

(b) 62nd Infantry Brigade will extend its right to the new Inter-Brigade Boundary, relieving troops of the 110th Infantry Brigade.

(c) All troops of the 62nd Infantry Brigade North of the new Divisional Left Boundary will be relieved by the 37th Division.

3. All details of relief will be arranged between Brigadiers concerned.

4. No reliefs will commence before 18.00 hours November 1st. and will be complete by 04.00 hrs. November 2nd.

5. Completion of reliefs will be reported to Divisional Headquarters.

6. A C K N O W L E D G E.

                           (Sgd.) A.F.MACDOUGALL, Major.
                                         Lieut.Colonel.
                                         General Staff.
Issued through Signals at 19.30hrs.   21st. Division.

	Copy No.		Copy No.		Copy No.
62nd Inf. Bde.	1				
64th " "	2	D.G.O.	12	38th Div.	21
110th " "	3	Train.	13	15th Sqn.R.A.F.	22
C.R.A.	4	21st M.T.Coy.	14	Div. Cyclists.	23
C.RE.	5	Vth Corps.	15 - 16	Div.Rec.Camp.	24
Pioneers.	6	Vth Corps H.A.	17	War Diary	25
"Q"	7	Vth Corps. R.A.	18	File.	26
Signals.	8	17th Div.	19		
A.D.M.S.	9	37th Div.	20		
D.A.P.M.	10				
D.M.G.O.	11				

CONFIDENTIAL.

WAR   DIARY

OF

21st Battn. Machine Gun Corps.

FROM:- 1st November 1918.   TO:- 30th November 1918.

Sheet I.

WAR DIARY
or
INTELLIGENCE SUMMARY.

November 1918

21st Battn M.G.C.

Army Form C. 2118.

Place	Date	Hour	Summary of Events and Information	Remarks and references to Appendices
VENDEGIES	1st	1100	Co. Hars. Found line. Dispositions A Coy. Stn. Reserve at VENDEGIES (East) of POIX and 3 paws. to GREEN LINE forward sector with 10th Bde. hat 12 guns in depth in forward zone + 4 guns in reserve occupying a position of readiness with 62 Bde hat 8 guns in forward zone and 8 guns in position of readiness. Day passed quietly. Hostile shelled at intervals otherwise. B Coy 3 paws guns on right. C Coy in right forward zone + D Coy left sector. 2 Post in N. or Post in	copy attached
		2100	Ammn order No 256 received	
		11/E	O.R. evacuate sick	
		11/E	H.V. SCOTT returns from Rest camp.	
	2nd	0930	A. Kit Day. Conference of Coy Commas at H.Q.	
		1000	Co. attended conference with G.O.C. Divn	
			Operation Order No 59 and Administrative order No 6 issued	copy attached
		1700	2/Lt G.H. MEADOWS and C.J. NEILL joins Battn with 36 O.R.	

Army Form C. 2118.

WAR DIARY / INTELLIGENCE SUMMARY

NOVEMBER 1918   21st Battn. M.G.C.

(Erase heading not required.)

Place	Date	Hour	Summary of Events and Information	Remarks and references to Appendices
VENDEGIES	2	1500	21 Div order No 287 received	Copy attached
		2000	Battn relieved by 17th Battn. M.G.C. Battn HQ moved back to NEUVILLY. A&B Coys to NEUVILLY. C Coy to OVILLERS. D Coy to VENDEGIES. Relief carried out quietly without casualties.	
NEUVILLY	3	1100	Day passes quietly. Companies resting. C.O. attended conference at Bde. and refitting. Weather very wet.	
		1800	Operation order No 60 issued with Administrative Instructions No 718. Copy attached	Copy attached
	4		Zero day for attack by Third Army 17th Corps attacked with 38th Divn on right. Weather bright & clear. The companies were disposed - A Coy in Divnl. Reserve. B Coy attached to 64th Bde. C Coy with 110th Bde. D Coy with 62nd Bde. First reports state attack going well.	
		1000	Companies moved to POIX to essentials preparatory to pushing through 17th Divn on 5th.	
		1600	Battn HQ opened at POIX du NORD. A Coy reserved at POIX. B Coy concentrates A15c.4.1 with C Coy and D Coy at D16a.3.5	
		2350	21st Div order No 258 received	Copy attached
POIX				

Sheet III

Army Form C. 2118.

WAR DIARY
or
INTELLIGENCE SUMMARY.

(Erase heading not required.)

November 1918
91st Battn. M.G.C.

Place	Date	Hour	Summary of Events and Information	Remarks and references to Appendices
POIX	5	0900	Very hot day. Owing to rapid progress of Infantry & with resistance & effort 62nd Bde. Hve. Bde. captured successively the GREEN, BLACK & YELLOW Lines. Whole Hve. pushes across the river & posts established.	
		1300	Battn. Hqrs. moved to LOCQUIGNOL when A Coy. Hqrs. also established. B.C.& D. Coys. reserved in Bde. Reserve at LA TÊTE NOIRE.	
LOCQUIGNOL		1400	Lt. G.O. FAIRLIE proceeds on leave to U.K.	
		2100	91 Stn. Order No. 259 issued.	Copy attached
			The rain pours continuously throughout the night making progress almost impossible.	
		0900	The morning opens very hot and progress very difficult. Craters in roads make transportation much deranged. Later in the day some progress was made & B.& D. Coys also reached C Coy.	
LOCQUIGNOL			A Coy moves to LA TÊTE NOIRE when B.& D. Coys also remain. C Coy moves to BERLAIMONT	
		1700	Lieut A.H. BONNER proceeds to INDIA OFFICE for interview.	

Army Form C. 2118.

WAR DIARY
or
INTELLIGENCE SUMMARY.

(Erase heading not required.)

November 1918 21st Battn NZC

Place	Date	Hour	Summary of Events and Information	Remarks and references to Appendices
LOCQUIGNOL	6	1500	Progress towards JOLIMETZ line began. "C" Coy had no S[?]ilition at U22c89 Not sent to U22.c.7.7 & No 16 Sect to BERLAIMONT C Coy right Coy. Our U22.b.t.d above artillery fire was coming. They also answered our U22.b.t.d above artillery fire on high ground E of AYMERIES 20,000 men in Call from Infantry to fire on high ground all ram fires to support of the attack. Capt H.H. SIMPSON & J. BOSWELL promoted to GHQ m.g school for course Lt H.E. CHAMBERLAIN proceeded on special leave. Lt M.E. CAMBRAY proceeded on special leave.	
		1700	91 other ranks, No 260 recruits Copy attached	
LOCQUIGNOL	7th	0530	Advance continued. The day's objective was BEAUFORT. Weather very dull and misty but no rain	
		0900	Battn HQ moved to BERLAIMONT	

Army Form C. 2118.

Sheet V
WAR DIARY
or
INTELLIGENCE SUMMARY. 9th Battn M.G.C.
NOVEMBER 1918
(Erase heading not required.)

Place	Date	Hour	Summary of Events and Information	Remarks and references to Appendices
BERLAIMONT	7	09.30	31 Jun. G.B. 101 received	copy attached
		1000	A Coy moved to AULNOYE. 110th Inf. Bde. attacked Railway at 6730 two "C" Coy guns barrage of 8 guns in support of the attack. Two other sections proceeded in rear of the attacking Infantry & took up positions on high ground 1/30 a 5.15 to support the advance. After barrage the other two sections took up positions on the right flank, flank being respectively & nearest them during the advance. Owing to left flank being met exposed No. 1 & 3 sections eventually formed a defensive flank to V.14.a. & V.15 a. and 1104 came to reserve at BACHANT. Visibility was bad throughout and good targets were scarce. 6/s Bde. passed through 110th Bde and progressed towards BLUE LINE. B Coy covered the advance by direct fire. D Coy remained in reserve with 62 Bde at AYMERIES.	

Sheet VI

Army Form C. 2118.

WAR DIARY
or
INTELLIGENCE SUMMARY.

NOVEMBER 1918
21st Batt. M.G.C.

(Erase heading not required.)

Place	Date	Hour	Summary of Events and Information	Remarks and references to Appendices
BERLAIMONT	7	1400	Capt. C.R. BALL M.C. returned from leave	
			Casualties 5 O.R. wounded 1 O.R. wounded gas	
		1800	21 Lts. O/R. returns No 261 returns	
		2100	19th Divn. passed through 21st Divn. A Coy remains at AULNOYE. 2 Coy attached	
			B & C Coys returned to BERLAIMONT. D Coy remains at AYMERIES	
	8		very wet day.	
			A Coy wet day Companies resting and refitting. A Coy moves back to BERLAIMONT. Nothing of interest to report	
	9		Another bright day. Companies refitting	
		1600	News received that enemy had retired opposite Corps Front 19 Div	
			gained touch with enemy E of River THURE	
			day passed quietly	

Army Form C. 2118.

Sheet VII

WAR DIARY or INTELLIGENCE SUMMARY.

November 1918. 21st Battn MGC

(Erase heading not required.)

Place	Date	Hour	Summary of Events and Information	Remarks and references to Appendices
BERLAIMONT	10		Companies noting notice of about to resort 90 OR Reinforcements arrived. ONCO 6 trumpeters at GRANTHAM 21 Air Order 9162 Recvd	
		23.50		Copy attached
	11	10.00	Battn HQ move to BACHANT with A+B Coys C Coy moves to ROPSEY D Coy remained at ANNERIES GX 607 Recvd stating "Hostilities will cease at 11.05 hours Copy attached Troops ants nine Crossed ground quietly & without acclamation	
BACHANT		19.00	21 Air Order No 263 recvd 21 Air Special Order received Copy of Corps Commanders Congratulatory message recvd	Copy attached
BACHANT	12ª	10.00	Battn HQ A+B Coys move to ANNERIES. Nothing of interest to report	
ANNERIES	13ª		Companies training to having to posts in afternoon Have to note Lt A.J. HEBBER MN Proceeded for Course of Instn at GRANTHAM	

Lt Col 21 Battn MGC

Army Form C. 2118.

Sheet No. 1

WAR DIARY
or
INTELLIGENCE SUMMARY.

(Erase heading not required.)

November 1918
21st Battn M.G.C.

Place	Date	Hour	Summary of Events and Information	Remarks and references to Appendices
AMERIES	14th	10.00	Col. L. Ashe proceeds to ROPSEY to view "C" Coy. returned later	
		10/11	21 Div At 889 received	copy attached
			V.S. P. issued	
			Day passed quietly	
AYMERIES	15th	11.00	Battn HQ A.B.+D Coys moved to BERLAIMONT	
		12.00	2/Lieut P. DALTON joins Battn. 2/Lt ENGLISH returns from leave	
BERLAIMONT	16th	09.00	Companies training in morning not spots in afternoon. Nothing of interest to report	
	17th	10.30	Special Church service held in Battn theatre. Day passes quietly	
		15.00	GX Mo 684 received copy attached	
	18th	13.00	"C" Coy reports Battn at BERLAIMONT from ROPSEY	
			2/Lt PITT admitted to hospital	

Army Form C. 2118.

Sheet IX

WAR DIARY
or
INTELLIGENCE SUMMARY.

November 1918 31st Battn M.G.C.

(Erase heading not required.)

Place	Date	Hour	Summary of Events and Information	Remarks and references to Appendices
BERLAIMONT	19th		Companies training. 2/Lt J.H.D. KIRTLEY joins	
	20th		Companies training. 2/Lt E.R. HARRIS MC MM proceeds on leave to UK	
	21st		Companies training. 17 OR Reinforcements joins	
	22nd		Companies training. Nothing of interest to note	
	23rd		— do — — do —	

Army Form C. 2118.

WAR DIARY
or
INTELLIGENCE SUMMARY.

(Erase heading not required.)

Shut-I
November 1918.
21 Bn M.G. Corps

Instructions regarding War Diaries and Intelligence Summaries are contained in F. S. Regs., Part II. and the Staff Manual respectively. Title pages will be prepared in manuscript.

Place	Date	Hour	Summary of Events and Information	Remarks and references to Appendices
BERLIMONT	24th		Coy training. Church parade. 2nd Lt. M.E. CABRY reported from Base. Field W.K. 50 O.R's evacuated sick.	V.7.1./p.
"	25th		—do— —do— 2nd Lt. W.E. Champlin.	
"	26th		Coy training. 2nd Lt. S.H. GABBELL and 10 O.R. joined.	
"	27th		Coy training & Batt'n Drill	
"	28th		Coys & Batt'n drill. Cont. at PACK animal work etc.	
"	29th		Ordinary training. 2nd Lt H.V. Scott admitted to hospital. 2nd Lt. J.D. McAdam proceeded 1/Rifle School.	
"	30th		Coy training. 60 O.R's proceeded CAMBRAI for Divisional Rest Camps. Ordinary training and games. 2nd Lt. Ewe Dent field Lieut to W.K. 30 O.R. joined from Div Reception Camps.	1/R2 apx

J.F. [signature]
LIEUT-COLONEL,
COMMANDING 21st Bn. MACHINE GUN CORPS.

SECRET.   Copy No. 11

21st Division Order No. 256.

Ref: Sheets 57.B. and 51.A.
     1/40,000   1st. November, 1918.

1. The Division (less Artillery) will be relieved by the 17th Division (less Artillery) on the night 2nd/3rd November in accordance with attached Table.

2. All details of relief will be arranged between Brigadiers.

3. Reliefs of Field Coys. R.E., Pioneers and Field Ambulances will be arranged by Cs.R.E. and A.Ds.M.S.
   Field Ambulances will remain in their present locations.

4. Machine Gun reliefs will be arranged between Os.C. 17th and 21st Machine Gun Battalions.

5. No movement of troops will take place before 17.00 hrs November 2nd.

6. Completion of relief will be reported to Div.H.Q.

7. Command of the Sector and of the Artillery in it will pass to G.O.C. 17th Division on completion of the Infantry Relief.

8. Divisional Headquarters close at OVILLERS and open at NEUVILLY at 15.30 hours, November 2nd.

9. A C K N O W L E D G E.

                                    (Sgd) A.F.MACDOUGALL, Major
                                                for
                                            Lieut. Colonel.
                                            General Staff,
                                            21st. Division.

Issued through Signals at
19.30 hours to :-

	Copy No.		Copy No.
62 Inf. Bde.	1	21st M.T.Coy	14
64 " "	2	V Corps.	15 - 16
110 " "	3	V Corps H.A.	17
C.R.A.	4	V Corps R.A.	18
C.R.E.	5	17th Div.	19
Pioneers	6	33rd Div.	20
"Q"	7	37th Div.	21
Signals	8	38th Div.	22
A.D.M.S.	9	15th Sqn.R.A.F.	23
D.A.P.M.	10	Div. Cyclists.	24
D.M.G.C.	11	Div. Rec. Camp.	25
D.G.O.	12	War Diary.	26
Train.	13	File.	27

                    CERTIFIED TRUE COPY.

Table to accompany 21st Division Order No. 256.

Serial No.	Unit	From	To	Relieved by	Route	Remarks.
1.	62 Inf. Bde.	Line Left.	VENDEGIES-OVILLERS Bde.H.Q. & 1 Bn. OVILLERS. 2 Bns. & T.M.Bty. VENDEGIES.	52nd. Inf. Bde.	VENDEGIES - OVILLERS - AMERVAL.	(a) Head of 52nd Inf.Bde. leaves OVILLERS at 17.00 hours. (b) Reserve Bn. 110 Inf. Bde. will leave POIX at 17.00 hours. (c) Reserve Bn. 62 Inf. Bde. will leave POIX at 17.30 hours. (d) Support Bn. 62 Inf. Bde. will withdraw as soon as head of 51st Inf. Bde. reaches POIX. (e) Head of 51st Inf. Bde. leaves NEUVILLY at 17.00 hours.
2.	110 Inf. Bde.	Line Right.	OVILLERS-AMERVAL Bde.H.Q. & 2 Bns. & T.M.Bty. OVILLERS 1 Bn. camp between OVILLERS & AMERVAL	52nd Inf. Bde.		
3.	64 Inf. Bde.	VENDEGIES.	NEUVILLY.	50th Inf. Bde.		Head of 64 Inf.Bde. to leave VENDEGIES at 17.00 hrs. Rear parties to be left to hand over. Transport of 64 I.B. will leave VENDEGIES at 17.00 hrs. and march via CROIX - FOREST - MONTAY
4.	21st Bn.M.G.C.	Line.	H.Q. & 2 Companies NEUVILLY 1 Coy. VENDEGIES. 1 Coy. OVILLERS.	17th M.G.Bn.		
5.	F.Coys. R.E.	Line.	Camps near DUKE'S WOOD	F.Coys R.E. 17th Divn.		
6.	H.Q. & 1 Coy. Pioneers.	VENDEGIES.	NEUVILLY.	Pioneers 17th Divn.		As for 64 I.B. Inf. will follow 64th Inf. Bde. Transport will follow 64 I.B.transport.
7.	2 Coys. Pioneers.	VENDEGIES.	Camp in DUKE'S WOOD.			

NOTE. Attention is directed to 21st Division G.285 dated 27.10.18.

SECRET.   Copy No. 16

21st Battalion Machine Gun Corps
OPERATION ORDER No. 59

Ref: Sheets 57.B &
51.A. 1/40,000   2nd November, 1918.

1. 21st Division (less Artillery) will be relieved by 17th Division (less Artillery) on night 2nd/3rd November.

2. Machine Gun Coys. will be relieved as follows :-

   "C" & "D" Coys. 21st. Bn. by "C" & "D" Coys. 17th Battn.
   Particulars of relief of "A" & "B" Coys will be issued later.

3. Details of relief will be arranged by Company Commanders concerned.

4. On completion of relief Coys. will move to billeting area as follows :-

   H.Q., "A" & "B" Coys to ..   NEUVILLY.
   "C" Coy.   ..   ..   OVILLERS.
   "D" do.   ..   ..   VENDEGIES.

5. Billets for H.Q's., "A" & "B" Coys. will be arranged by Adjutant 21st Bn. M.G.C.
   O.C. "C" Coy. will arrange billets with Staff Captain 110th Bde.
   "D" Coy. will take over billets at in VENDEGIES at present occupied by "A" Coy.

6. No movement of troops will take place before 17 hours Nov. 2nd.

7. Route for Transport "A" & "B" Coys will be via CROIX - FORET - MONTAY.

8. An Officer from each Company will report completion of Relief to Battn. Headquarters at VENDEGIES as soon as possible after relief.

9. Battalion Headquarters will close at VENDEGIES and open at NEUVILLY on completion of relief.

10. A C K N O W L E D G E.

                                          Capt. & Adjt.
                                   21st. Battn. Machine Gun Corps.

Distribution.	Copy No
All Coys. (Forward)	1 - 4
All Coys. (Rear)	5 - 8
21st Division "G"	9
Quartermaster	10
17th Battn. M.G. Corps.	11
Commanding Officer.	12
64th Inf. Bde.	13
62nd Inf. Bde.	14
110th Inf. Bde.	15
War Diary	16 - 17
File	18.

SECRET.   2nd November, 1918.

                    21st. Battalion Machine Gun Corps.

                    ADMINISTRATIVE INSTRUCTIONS No.6.

1. BILLETS.

   O.C. "A" & "B" Coys.(Rear) will detail an Officer or representative to report Adjutant at Area Commandant's Office NEUVILLY at 10.30 hours.
   All billeting in VENDEGIES and OVILLERS will be close billeting. There will be no accomodation for Orderly Rooms, or Quartermaster Stores and Transport personnel will occupy Bivouacs near their horse lines.

2. TRANSPORT.

   "C" & "D" Coys "B" Echelon Transport will rejoin Companies under orders to be issued by Company Commander concerned.
   H.Q's, "A" & "B" Coys. "B" Echelon Transport will leave present camp at 13.30 hrs. under orders of Lieut. Huxley.

3. BATHS.

   O.C. "D" & "C" Coys will arrange Baths with Staff Captain 110th Inf. Bde at VENDEGIES.

4. CANVAS.

   All Canvas issued to Coys. from Q.M. Stores will be handed over to O.C. "C" Coy (Rear) and receipts obtained.

5. RATIONS.

   Rations will be issued from Camp OVILLERS at 11.30 hrs.

                                        V. F. Sanderson
                                              Capt. & Adjt.
                                    21st. Battn. Machine Gun Corps.

DISTRIBUTION.

All recipients of 21st. Bn.
Administrative Instructions No.5.

SECRET.   Copy No...11......

21st DIVISION ORDER NO.257.

Ref: Maps Sheets 51.A.S.E. 51 S.W.   2nd November, 1918.
          57.B. N.E. 57.A.N.W.
          1/20,000

1. The First French Army and the Fourth, Third and First British Armies are resuming the offensive on a date which has already been notified to those concerned.

2. These operations will be carried out in two phases :-

    (a) As far as the Vth Corps is concerned, the first phase (i.e. operations on "Z" Day) will be carried out by the 38th Division on the right and the 17th Division on the left, with final objective the GREEN LINE.

    (b) The second phase (i.e. operations on Z plus 1 day) will be carried out by the 33rd Division on the right and the 21st Division on the left, with final objective the DOTTED BROWN LINE.

    (c) The 37th Division will be operating on the left of the 17th Division and the 5th Division on the left of the 21st Division.

3. The objectives for both first and second phases, also Inter-Divisional Boundaries are shown on attached Map.

4. The final objective for the first phase is the GREEN LINE In the event of the 17th Division not reaching this line, the 21st Division will, on Z plus 1 day, pass through them and continue the advance from the most forward line reached by 17th Division, wherever this line may be.

5. (a) The 62nd Infantry Brigade is detailed to capture the BLACK LINE, but, if the 17th Division have only reached the RED LINE or just beyond, it will be the task of the 62nd Infantry Brigade to take the GREEN LINE instead.
    The 62nd Infantry Brigade must, therefore, have plans prepared for the capture of either the GREEN LINE or the BLACK LINE.

    (b) The 64th Infantry Brigade is detailed to capture the YELLOW LINE.

    (c) the 110th Infantry Brigade is detailed :-

    (i) To capture the BROWN DOTTED LINE, if 17th Division take the GREEN LINE, and in consequence, 62nd Infantry Brigade attack the BLACK LINE.

                                    OR

    (ii) To capture the BLACK LINE, if 62nd Infantry Brigade have to attack the GREEN LINE in place of the 17th Division.
    The 110th Infantry Brigade, must, therefore, have plans prepared for the capture of either the BROWN DOTTED LINE or the BLACK LINE.

-2-

6. The following time table is given as a guide; every effort is to be made to avoid being behind time. As there is no barrage, and as it is of the utmost importance to push on rapidly in order to secure bridgeheads over the River SAMBRE, it is not incumbent upon Brigades to wait, if circumstances allow them to push on in advance of the time table. Such advance will be made irrespective of the progress of flank Divisions.

No advance in force, however, will be made Eastwards from the River SAMBRE, until Zero plus 8 hours, unless troops of the Division on either flank are up in line.

Patrols, however, should be sent on as soon as possible after securing bridge-heads, towards the BROWN DOTTED LINE :-

Arrive BLACK LINE	Zero plus 3 hours.
Leave " "	" " 3½ "
Arrive YELLOW LINE	" " 7 "
Leave " "	" " 8 "
Arrive BROWN DOTTED LINE	" " 10½ "

7. (a) Although definite objectives have been allotted to Brigades, it is the duty of the Brigade detailed to capture the BLACK LINE, if little or no opposition is being encountered, to push on as fast as possible towards the River SAMBRE and to seize bridge-heads.

(b) 64th Infantry Brigade will then move forward in support and will either pass through and capture the YELLOW LINE, if the Leading Brigade is held up, or if the YELLOW LINE has been secured, continue the advance to the BROWN DOTTED LINE at the sheduled time.

(c) If the River SAMBRE is crossed in advance of flank Divisions efforts will be made to clear bridge-heads for them by operating against the enemy's flanks.

8. As soon as a Brigade has captured its objective, and as soon as the next Brigade has passed through, it will re-organise and concentrate by Companies as soon as possible. It will then be prepared either to hold the line it has captured, or to push on, at short notice, in support of the leading Brigade, orders for such advance will be issued from Divisional Headquarters.

9. After the capture of the final objective, the leading Brigade will exploit to the Eastern edge of the Village of BACHANT and under cover of this exploitation will establish an outpost zone covering their front.

10. (a) Five Brigades of Field Artillery will be available to cover the advance. There will be no barrage unless Brigades meet such stubborn resistance that they are unable to advance without one, a barrage will then be arranged from Divisional Headquarters.

(b) One Section of 18-pdrs will be detailed to accompany each of the Leading Battalions of the Leading Infantry Brigade. One Brigade R.F.A. will also be placed under the orders of each Infantry Brigadier from the time his Brigade takes up the advance.

(c) The remainder of the Field Artillery will move and act under orders of the Divisional Commander.

/11..........

- 3 -

11.   The O.C. 21st. Battalion Machine Gun Corps will detail one Machine Gun Company to be affiliated to each Infantry Brigade.
        The remaining Machine Gun Company will be in Divisional Reserve.

12.   Divisional Headquarters will be at POIX on Z/Z plus 1 Night, and will move to FUTOY at an hour to be notified later. Subsequent moves will be made along the Divisional line of Report Centres.

13.   A c k n o w l e d g e.

                            (Sgd).   H.I.FRANKLYN.
                                     Lieut. Colonel.
                                     General Staff.
                                     21st. Division.

Issued through Signals at
13.30 hours to :-

	Copy No.		Copy No.
62 Inf. Bde.	1	M.T.Coy	14
64 " "	2	V Corps.	15 - 16
110 " "	3	V Corps H.A.	17
C.R.A.	4	V Corps R.A.	18
C.R.E.	5	5th Div.	19
Pioneers.	6	17th Div.	20
"Q"	7	33rd Div.	21
Signals.	8	15 Sqn. R.A.F.	22
A.D.M.S.	9	Div. Cyclists.	23
D.A.P.M.	10	Div. Rec. Camp.	24
D.M.G.C.	11	War Diary.	25
D.G.O.	12	File.	26
Train.	13		

CERTIFIED TRUE COPY.

SECRET.   Copy No. 16

21st Battn. Machine Gun Corps
OPERATION ORDER No. 60.

3rd November 1918.

Ref: Map Sheets 51.A.S.E., 51 S.W.,
57.B. N.E., 57.A. N.W.
1/20,000.

---

1. The First French Army, and the Fourth, Third and First British Armies are resuming the offensive on a date which has been notified to all concerned.

2. These operations will be carried out as far as the Vth Corps is concerned, in two phases:-

    (a) First Phase.   "Z" Day.

    38th Division on Right.
    17th Division on Left.

    Objective - GREEN LINE.

    (b) Second Phase.   "Z" plus 1 day.

    33rd Division on Right.
    21st Division on Left.

    Objective - DOTTED BROWN LINE.

    (c) The 37th Division will be operating on the Left of the 17th Division.
    The 5th Division will be operating on the Left of the 21st Division.

3. The objectives for both phases and Inter-Divisional Boundaries have been issued to all concerned.

4. Objectives.

    BLACK LINE   ..   62nd Inf. Bde.
        or
    GREEN LINE   ..   If 17th Division only reach RED LINE.

    YELLOW LINE   ..   64th Inf. Bde.

    BROWN DOTTED LINE   ..   110th Inf. Bde.
        or
    BLACK LINE   ..   If 62nd Inf. Bde. attack GREEN LINE.

5. The following time table is given as a guide only:-

    Arrive BLACK LINE   ..   Zero plus 3 hours.
    Leave   "   "   ..   "   "   3½   "
    Arrive YELLOW LINE   ..   "   "   7   "
    Leave   "   "   ..   "   "   8   "
    Arrive BROWN DOTTED LINE   ..   "   " 10½   "

    If circumstances allow, Brigades will push forward irrespective of progress of Flank Divisions, and Bridge Heads over the SAMBRE established.
    No advance in force Eastwards of River SAMBRE will be made until Zero plus 8 hours, unless troops of Divisions on the flanks are up in line.

/6........

- 2 -

6. Five Brigades of Field Artillery will cover the advance. There will be no barrage unless Brigades meet with stubborn resistance.
   One Section of 18-pdrs will be detailed to accompany each of the leading Battalions of the leading Infantry Brigade.

7. Machine Guns will operate as under:-

   (a) "D" Company will assist in the consolidation of objective (GREEN or BLACK LINE) of 62nd Infantry Brigade. Particular attention will be paid to the Left Flank.

   (b) "B" Company will support the attack of 64th Infantry Brigade on to the YELLOW LINE. Guns should be handled boldly, and every effort taken of ground to obtain direct shooting.

   (c) "C" Company will support the attack of 110th Infantry Brigade on to the BROWN DOTTED LINE with 2 Sections in close support for offensive action as well as consolidation. The remaining 2 Sections will be held in Company Reserve, and be prepared to supplement fire according to the requirements of B.G.C. 110th Infantry Brigade.

   (d) "A" Company will be in Divisional Reserve, and be prepared to operate under the direct orders of O.C., 21st Battn. M.G.C.

8. Battalion Headquarters will close at 14.00 hours "Z" day at NEUVILLY, and open at same hour at POIX, F.4.a.0.5. It will probably move to FUTOY, at an hour to be notified later.
   Subsequent moves will be along the Divisional line of Report Centres.

9. Line of Report Centres will be as follows:-

FUTOY, S.14.d.9.5,	Known as	FT.
INSTITUTE FORESTIER, S.24.d.3.3.	" "	IF.
On H.T. Road at T.21.a.7.0.	" "	CR.
LA TETE NOIRE at T.24.c.5.4.	" "	TN.
BERLAIMONT at U.20.d.6.7.	" "	BL.
Near ETREE, West of BACHANT at U.18.c.1.6.	" "	ET.

10. A C K N O W L E D G E. (MG. Corp only)

                                    Lieut. Colonel,
                        Commanding 21st Battn. Machine Gun Corps.

DISTRIBUTION.

Copy No. 1 .. O.C. "A" Coy.
         2 .. O.C. "B" Coy.
         3 .. O.C. "C" Coy.
         4 .. O.C. "D" Coy.
         5 .. 62nd Inf. Bde.
         6 .. 64th Inf. Bde.
         7 .. 110th Inf. Bde.
         8 .. 21st Division 'G'.
         9 .. 5th I   M.G. Bn.
        10 .. 33rd   "   "
        11 .. Commanding Officer.
        12 .. 2nd in Command.
        13 .. 21st Div. Signals.
        14 .. File.
     15 & 16 .. War Diary.

SECRET.   Copy No. 10

21 Bn. M.G.C. ASSEMBLY INSTRUCTION No. 1.

Ref Map:
 Sheet 57.c.   3rd. November 1918.
----

1.   Companies will move with affiliated Brigades.
"A" Coy. in Divisional Reserve will leave present area
at 12.30 hrs. and march to POIX, arranging billets under
Coy. arrangements.
     Attention is drawn to Administrative Instructions
No.7, para. 1.

2.   Rear Battn. H.Qrs. Coy. will march in rear of "A" Coy.
leaving billets at 12.30 hrs., and move to F.3.a.7.4.

3.   O.C. "A" Coy. must keep in close touch with Advanced
Battn. H.Q. in future moves.

                                            Capt. & Adjutant.
                                       21st. Battn. Machine Gun Corps.

Issued to:

   Copies 1 - 4 ... All Os.C. Coys.
   Copy No. 5   ... H.Qrs. Coy.
             6   ... Quartermaster.
             7   ... Commanding Officer.
             8   ... 21st. Div. 'G'.
             9   ... War Diary.
            10   ...   "   "
            11   ... File.

SECRET.

21st Battalion Machine Gun Corps.
ADMINISTRATIVE INSTRUCTIONS No.7.

1. TRANSPORT   3rd November, 1918.

"B" Echelon will move with Coys. on Z day, until they start to advance to assembly positions, when they will concentrate at F.3.a.7.4.
If circumstances permit "B" Echelon will move to the neighbourhood of FUTOY on Z day, but orders will be issued at above map reference.

2. AMMUNITION AND GRENADES.

(a) A.R.P. will be at S.7.a.
(b) Div. Grenade Dump is at X.27.d.9.9. and F.8.a.4.1. The advanced Grenade Dump will be formed by 17th Division at S.21.a.5.9.
(c) A Dump will be formed at LOCQUIGNOL as soon as possible, but Brigades must be prepared to come on to the normal system of supply as outlined in this Office letter S.100 dated 17/10/18.

3. RATIONS.

Rations for the 6th November can be drawn from F.3.a.7.4. by Coys. at 14.00 hrs.
Men will go into action carrying rations for Z plus 1 day.

4. ROADS.

Transport not actually moving with troops will move East of POIX DU NORD by the road ARBRE DE LA CROIX - F.6.a.7.9. - X.24.a.9.0. - S.26.a.3.1. The ENGLEFONTAINE - BAVAY road South west of S.26.a.3.1. has to be kept clear for the right Division.
Transport will whenever possible move off the roads.

5. PACK TRANSPORT.

After entering the FORET DE MORMAL Coys. will be prepared to send up all ammunition and supplies by Pack Transport.

6. PACKS & BLANKETS.

All Blankets will be stored at the Battn. Dump NEUVILLY (Bn.HQ's) by 09.00 hrs.

7. PRISONERS OF WAR CAGE.

Prisoners of War Cage will be established at S.17.a.8.8.

8. CASUALTIES.

Attention is again called to the importance of reporting estimated casualties as early as possible.
A rough estimate only is required first and true figures as soon as possible afterwards.

                                                                 Capt. & Adjt.
                                     21st. Battn. Machine Gun Corps.

DISTRIBUTION.

All recipients of Administrative Instructions No.6.

SECRET.

A.879/O.

Ref. 21 Bn. M.G.C. Operation Order No. 60.

MISCELLANEOUS.

1. MEDICAL ARRANGEMENTS.

Cases will be evacuated in the first instance to:

(i) Corps Main Dressing Station FOREST.
(ii) Corps Walking Wounded Station FOREST.
then to C.C.Ss. at CAUDRY.

Should the Corps Main Dressing Station and Walking Wounded Station move, they will be located at ENGLEFONTAINE.

2. LIGHT SIGNALS.

The following Light Signals will be used:

(a) RED Very Light to signify "We are here".
(b) GREEN " " " " "Lengthen Range".
(c) GREEN/RED/GREEN rifle grenade signal to signify "S.O.S".

V.J. Samuelson
Capt. & Adjutant.
21st. Battalion Machine Gun Corps.

3rd. Nov. 1918.

To:
All recipients 21 Bn. M.G.C. O.O. No.60.

War Diary

SECRET.

A.878/O.

All recipients of 21st. Bn. M.G. Corps Order No. 60.

The following amendment will be made to para. 9, line 4.

"C.R" Report Centre will now be established at road junction R.27.a.3.9. and NOT as therein stated.

V. F. Sanxxx
Capt. & Adjt.
21st. Battn. Machine Gun Corps.

3/11/18.

SECRET.

21st. Battalion Machine Gun Corps.

ADMINISTRATIVE INSTRUCTION No.8.

3rd November, 1918.

1. **TENTS AND TRENCH SHELTERS**

    Tents and Trench Shelters now occupied by Units will be struck and handed over to Area Commandant before moving off tomorrow.

2. **PROTECTION OF CIVILIAN PROPERTY.**

    As a consequence of the present operation, many French people have been forced to leave their homes and abandon the whole of their possessions. Many of these homes lie in the area occupied by British Troops, who therefore become trustees to the French people for their abandoned property.

    The Army Commander exhorts every Officer, Warrant Officer, Non-commissioned Officer and Man in the Third Army to do all in his power to protect the homes and property of our Allies who are fighting our common enemy.

    This order will be constantly brought to the notice of all troops in the Third Army.

3. **RAILWAY STORES, REMOVAL OF.**

    A.R.O. 489 is republished for information :- "The practice of removing permanent material such as sleepers and rails, the property of railways, for the construction of dugouts, gun emplacements, or any other purpose, is forbidden.

    Assurances on this subject have been given to the French and Units must realize that if the Stations and the line are to be ready at short notice this practice must cease at once "

4. **DAMAGE TO TREES.**

    As the country in advance of the present area, in which horse lines are situated, has many valuable orchards, the following Order is republished. Great care is to be exercised to prevent any unnecessary damage to trees, and to ensure that this Order is complied with :-

    When the occupation of Orchards etc., by mounted troops is necessary, horses will on no account be tied to trees ; and care must be taken to tether them whenever possible, out of reach of any trees.

    Cases have occured where the trunks of trees have been barked all round by horses being tied to them or by the horses themselves eating the bark, with the result that the trees perish.

    To protect them from such injury, sacking or some similar material will invariably be wrapped round the trunks.

5. **HAY AND STRAW.**

    Arrangements have been made for the S.S.C. to purchase Hay and Straw in the captured areas and to issue sufficient to make up the full ration. Hay and Straw found in the captured area will therefore not be used without authority from the S.S.C.

    V.F. Saunders,
    Capt, & Adjt.
    21st. 1Battn. Machine Gun Corps.

DISTRIBUTION.

To all recipients of
Administrative Instruction No.7.

TELEGRAM

URGENT ⟶ OPERATIONS
PRIORITY 3 Bdes.

Words
Sent
At......................
To......................
By......................

DADE	ZOKI	ZOHO	V Corps	17th Div.
BASU	DUFA	D.A.P.M.	V Corps H.A.	33rd Div.
VUFE	"Q"	ZEJU	V Corps R.A.	15 Sqn. R.A.F.
LODE	JESO	ZODU	5th Div.	Div. Cyclists.

— / 4 / AAA

ZOWU Order No.258 AAA Ref Order No.257 AAA Front line 17th Div. not definitely ascertained but believed to run S.30.b.Central - T.19.c.5.0. - T.19.c.2.9. - T.13.c.5.9. - T.13.a.0.5. - T.13.a.0.9. AAA Left of 38th Div. believed in S.30.a. AAA 37th Div. believed in BIG WOOD T.1.2.7. and 8 AAA DADE will capture GREEN LINE tomorrow morning working S.E. with right on ROUTE DE LA FLAQUETTE and clearing LOCQNIGNOL from North and East AAA DADE will cross line of road running N.E. through S.18.c.a. & b. at 05.00 hours AAA VUFE is detailed to capture BLACK LINE timing advance so as to cross GREEN LINE at 08.00 hours AAA BASU is detailed to capture YELLOW LINE timing advance to cross BLACK LINE at 11.00 hours AAA DADE will reform after capture of GREEN LINE and will be prepared to advance across River SAMBRE moving on orders from Div. H.Q. AAA Above times only to be taken as a guide if real opposition is met AAA It is of supreme importance that crossings over River SAMBRE should be seized at earliest possible moment therefore if little or no opposition leading Brigade will push on as rapidly as possible to BLACK and YELLOW LINES until opposition is met when next Brigade will pass through AAA Rear Brigades must keep touch during advance with Brigade next in front but must avoid getting crowded on top of it AAA Barrage for DADE will be arranged in accordance with Appendix "F" Order No.257 AAA Artillery starting line T.19.d.3.8. - T.14.b.6.5. At 05.30 hours AAA Barrage will move S.E. AAA Otherwise arrangements detailed in Order No.257 hold good. AAA Ack.

H.I.FRANKLYN Lt.Col.
G.S.

ZOWU
23.10 hrs.

CERTIFIED TRUE COPY.

TELEGRAM

Words

S.D.R.
to Bdes.   Sent
H.I.F.   At.........................
                To.........................
                By.........................

DADE	ZOKI	ZOHO	V Corps	17 Div.
BASU	DUFA	D.A.P.M.	V Corps R.A.	33rd Div.
VUFE	"Q"	ZEJU	V Corps H.A.	15 Sqn. R.A.F.
LODE	JESO	ZOFU	5th Div.	Div. Cyclists.

ZOWU Order No.259 AAA The advance is progressing on whole Army front and on front of flank armies AAA Orders have been received that no respite is to be allowed the enemy AAA DADE will capture the remainder of YELLOW LINE as soon as possible and will push patrols down to river in U.16.a. AAA DADE will also establish bridgehead tonight on line U.21.d.0.7. - U.21.d.9.2. - U.27.d.5.8. and thence back to river AAA Under cover of bridgehead C.R.E. will throw bridges over SAMBRE exact positions selected will be notified later AAA VUFE will advance tomorrow so as to pass advanced troops of DADE holing bridgehead at 05.30 hrs AAA VUFE will capture successively BROWN DOTTED LINE AAA Ridge running through V.21. and V.15 Central to be known as RED LINE AAA Main AVESNES - MAUBEUGE Road to be known as BLUE LINE AAA BASU will support VUFE and will start crossing river when leading troops of VUFE reach BROWN DOTTED LINE probably about 07.30 hrs AAA BASU will occupy BROWN DOTTED LINE when vacated by VUFE AAA DADE will be in Divisional Reserve AAA One Brigade R.F.A. under VUFE finding advanced sections with Battalions AAA DADE will transfer Cyclists and Mobile Mortars to VUFE AAA Div. Signals will establish Report Centre B.L. VUFE will establish B.T. and New Report Centre at V.16.c.3.2. to be known as R.E. AAA One M.G.Coy affiliated to each Brigade AAA One Section R.E. and One Coy Pioneers under VUFE AAA Acknowledge AAA Added all concerned.

(Sgd) H.I.FRANKLYN.
Lt.Col.
General Staff.

ZOWU
20.00 hrs.

CERTIFIED TRUE COPY.

TELEGRAM

SDR Bdes
33rd.Div.
5th Div.
H.I.F.

Words

Sent

To..................
At..................
By..................

DADE	DUFA	ZEJU	5th Corps H.A.	15 Sqn R.A.F.
BASU	"Q"	ZODU	5th Div.	Div. Cyclists.
VUFE	JESO	5th Corps.	17th Divn.	
LODE	ZORO	5th Corps. R.A.	33rd. Divn.	
ZOKI	D.A.P.M.			

— / 6 / AAA

ZOWU Order No.260 AAA 33rd. Divn believed to be on BROWN DOTTED LINE
AAA 5th Divn. held BROWN DOTTED LINE from U.11.a.Cent. Northwestwards
AAA Enemy were still in S. portion of PONT SUR SAMBRE at 14.00 hrs. AAA
Advance will be continued tomorrow AAA VUFE will begin advance under
barrage AAA Barrage will come down on Artillery starting line 300 yds
in advance of an parallel to main road in U.17.d. U.23.b. U.24.c. at
0545 hrs AAA Barrage rests on above line for 8 mins and then advances
at rate of 100 yards in 4 mins. for 1000 yards and will then cease AAA
Barrage will skep village of BACHANT AAA VUFE will continue advance to
RED LINE AAA BASU will move so as to begin crossing River SAMBRE at
o5.30 hrs and will take up advance from RED LINE or earlier if VUFE
held up AAA BASU will make good successively the BLUE LINE and village
of BEAUFORT and will establish outposts on line W.16.Cent. W.22.Cent.
AAA If VUFE held up BASU will make progress by working round S. flank
AAA Owing to probable delay in crossing the River SAMBRE by 5th
Div. Brigades must take precautions to guard their left flank AAA
One Brigade R.F.A. under BASU AAA VUFE will transfer cyclists and
Mobile Mortars to BASU when latter takes up advance AAA VUFE will lay
Div. Signal line to ET and BASU from E.T. to R.E. and to new report
centre X Roads W.13.d.1.1. to be known as H.F. AAA Acknowledge AAA
Addsd all concerned.

H.I.FRANKLYN.
Lt.Col.

ZOWU
2010 hrs.

CERTIFIED TRUE COPY.

TELEGRAM

Urgent operations
priority to
Bdes. HIF.

Words
Sent
At.....................
To.....................
By.....................

DADE	DUFA	ZEJU	5th Div.
BASU	"Q"	ZODU	17th Div.
VUFE	JESO	V Corps	33rd Div.
LODE	ZOHO	V Corps R.A.	15 Sqn. R.A.F.
ZOKI	D.A.P.M.	V Corps H.A.	Div. Cyclists.

— / 7 / AAA

ZOWU Order No.261 AAA 17th Div. will advance through front line at 21.00 hours tonight AAA After 17th Div. have taken over Brigades will be withdrawn to billets AAA VUFE and BASU to BERLAIMONT DADE remains AYMERIES AAA BASU will start withdrawing from positions finally reached at 05.00 hours tomorrow AAA VUFE will withdraw as soon as 50th Bde. have taken up a position in support to front line tonight AAA Troops withdrawing must give way to troops of 17th Div. on roads and tracks and bridges AAA Div.H.Q. remains BERLAIMONT AAA Brigades will report completion of moves AAA Ack AAA Addsd all concerned.

(Sgd.) A.F.MACDOUGALL
Major for Lt.Col
General Staff
ZOWU.
21st Division.

CERTIFIED TRUE COPY.

MESSAGES AND SIGNALS.

TO :- ZEJU.

G.B.101.   /   7   /   AAA

As soon as BASU has reached BLUE LINE VUFE will move one
Battn to high ground V.22 to be prepared to protect left flank
of BASU from counter attack coming down on valley V.12 V.11
AAA Remaining Battn. VUFE to be disposed in depth with head on
RED LINE AAA Ack AAA Addsd VUFE Rept. DADE BASU ZEJU.

FROM : ZOWU
Time.- 08.35

<u>CERTIFIED TRUE COPY.</u>

MESSAGES AND SIGNALS.

TO:- 21 M.G.Bn.

| | / | 10 | / | AAA |

ZOWU Order No.262 AAA ZOWU will move tomorrow as follows AAA BASU plus 1 field Amb. to LIMONT FONTAINE head to cross river at 08.45 hrs and whole route to be clear of AULNOYE STA by 10.30 hrs AAA Route AULNOYE STA - POT DE VIN (D.9) AAA ZEJU less 2 Coys to BACHANT head to cross river at 10.00 hrs AAA Route AULNOYE - AYMERIES AAA DUFA to BACHANT head to cross river at 10.30 hrs AAA Route same as for ZEJU AAA VUFE plus one field Coy. R.E. and 1 Coy. ZEJU to BEAFORT head to cross river at 12.45 hrs and whole group to be clear of AULNOYE STA by 14.30 hrs AAA Route as for BASU AAA VUFE will relieve and take over outposts of 52 bde 17 Div AAA 1 field Coy. R.E. will remain in BERLAIMONT for the construction of bridges AAA On Nov.12th DADE will move to BASHANT and ZEJU less 2 Coys and DUFA will move to AYMERIES AAA Further orders will be issued for these moves AAA Completion of moves will be reported to Div.H.Q. AAA Div. H.Q. will NOT move until Nov.12 AAA Ack AAA Added all concerned.

21 Div. 23.25.

CERTIFIED TRUE COPY.

21st DIVISION SPECIAL ORDER.

Monday, 11th November 1918.

The work which the Division has done, whilst helping to win the great series of victories which have forced GERMANY to sue for peace, has been surpassed by no Division and equalled by few, if any, in the whole of the Allied Armies.

The record of the Division during the past eight months is absolutely unique.

Every Officer, N.C.O., and Man who has ever belonged to the 21st Division may well be proud of the fact, and especially those who fought so doggedly through the dark days of the Spring, and early Summer, and then returned to the attack with a spirit which no troops in this world could have surpassed.

Proud indeed may you be, and proud indeed am I to have the honour of commanding such a glorious Division during the greatest epoch making period in the history of the whole world.

Peace is not yet ensured and, until it is, I confidently rely on every Officer, N.C.O., and Man so training himself that, whatever the result of the peace negotiations may be, you will be prepared to live up to the magnificent reputation which you have so rightfully and worthily earned and which will cause the name of the 21st DIVISION to be remembered and honoured as long as our Empire exists.

David M. Campbell
Major General,
Commanding 21st Division.

"C" Form
MESSAGES AND SIGNALS.

Army Form C. 2123
(In books of 100.)

No. of Message............

PSB ....0845.... Words 47

Charges to Collect

Service Instructions

YU. PRIORITY.

Handed in at .... Office .... m. Received .... m.

TO 21 Bn.M.G.C.

*Sender's Number	Day of Month	In reply to Number	A A A
G.X.607.	11		

Hostilities	will	cease	at
11.00 hrs	today	Nov	11th
AAA	Defensive	precautions	will
be	maintained	AAA	There
will	be	no	intercourse
of	any	description	with
the	enemy	AAA	Moves
ordered	in	Divisional	Order
No.262	will	take	place
AAA	Ack.		

FROM PLACE & TIME   21 Div.   08.30 hrs.

* This line should be erased if not required.

21 Div.
G.620.

Copy of telegram received from LIEUT-GENERAL C.D.SHUTE,
Commander of Vth Corps, timed 10.52 hrs. dated today :-

On the signature of the Armistice I wish to convey to all Ranks of the Vth Corps my most sincere and cordial congratulations on their gallantry and enduranceAAA No task has been too ardous for you AAA No difficulty too great for you to surmount AAA You have always been in the forefront of the advance AAA The prominent part taken by the Vth Corps in the defeat of the enemy has only been rendered possible by the gallant and unselfish manner in which every Officer N.C.O. and man in the Corps has played up for the common good AAA The Command of such troops has been an honour for me which I shall always remember AAA

                                          A.F.MACDOUGALL, Major.
                                                  General Staff.
11th November 1918.   21st. Division.

CERTIFIED TRUE COPY.

TELEGRAM.

Priority to 62 Bde.
D.M.G.C. Pioneers
C.R.E. & Train.

Words
Sent
At........................
To........................
By........................

| - | / | 11 | / | AAA |

DADE	DUFA	ZEJU	5 Div.
BASU	"Q"	ZODU	17 Div.
VUFE	JESO	V Corps.	33 Div.
LODE	ZOHO	V Corps H.A.	15 Sqn. R.A.F.
ZOKI	D.A.P.M.	V Corps R.A.	

ZOWU Order No. 263 AAA Following moves will take place tomorrow AAA
DADE will move to BACHANT head to pass cross roads U.22.c.5.8. at
09.30 hours AAA Route cross roads U.17.d.7.2. - U.24.a.0.0.-
BACHANT AAA ZEJU less two Coys. to AYMERIES head to pass road junction
U.18.c.4.1. at 09.30 hours AAA Route cross roads U.17.d.7.2. -
U.17.d.5.6. - Aymeries AAA DUFA to AYMERIES head to pass road junction
U.18.c.4.1. at 10.15 hours AAA Route same as for ZEJU AAA One
Field Coy. R.E. now in BACHANT will NOT move AAA ZODU to BACHANT NOT
to cross River SAMBRE before 14.00 hours AAA Completion of moves will be
reported to Div. H.Q. AAA Div. H.Q. close at BERLAIMONT and open at
BEAUFORT at 11.00 hours Nov.12th AAA Ack AAA Addsd all concerned.

A.F.MACDOUGALL, Major
for Lt.Col.
General Staff.

ZOWU
17.00 hrs.

CERTIFIED TRUE COPY.

21 Div.
G.625.

To all recipients 21st Div. Order No.263.

Reference 21st Division Order No.263, Divisional Headquarters will now open at AULNOYE and not as therein stated.

11/11/18.

A.F.MACDOUGALL, Major
General Staff
21st Division.

CERTIFIED TRUE COPY.

MESSAGES AND SIGNALS.

To:- O.C. "A" - "B" - "D" & "H.Q." Coys.
"C" Coy. "G" 21st Div.

V.S.73.   14.   AAA

The Battn. less "C" Coy will move to BERLAIMONT 15th inst AAA
Coys. will leave present area as follows AAA Bn.H Q's
11.00 hrs. "D" Coy 11.05 hrs. "A" Coy.11.15 hrs. "B" Coy. 11.20
hrs AAA Coys. are responsible for moving all kit including
blankets but Limbers must not be overloaded and two journeys
made where necessary AAA Usual billet certificates to be
returned rendered H.Qrs by 10.00 hrs AAA Strict march discipline
to be observed AAA Coys will detail 1 Officer Mounted 2 N.C.O's
on Bicycles to report Lieut. PACK Bn.H.Qs. at 08.45 hrs to
proceed ahead to Billet AAA Lieut. PACK will detail one
above N.C.O's to be at BRIDGE 11.10 hrs to guide Coys. to
Billet area AAA Bn.H.Qrs. will close at AYMERIES at 10.30 hrs and
open BERLAIMONT at same hour AAA Acknowledge

From :- H.Qrs. 21st Bn. M.G.C.
Time 21.10 hrs.

CERTIFIED TRUE COPY.

MESSAGES AND SIGNALS.

TO :- 21st. M.G.C.

GX684.   17th   AAA

The fourth Army having now taken over the front of the Third Army all picquets and examining posts will be withdrawn forthwith AAA The Coy. of the M.G.Battn. at present attached to 110th Bde will rejoin the M.G.Battn. under arrangements to be made by D.M.G.C. AAA Addsd 110th D.M.G.C. repeated 62 Bde. 64th Bde. A.P.M.

From 21 Div.   14.35 hrs.

CERTIFIED TRUE COPY.

C O N F I D E N T I A L.

WAR DIARY

OF

21st Batt. Machine Gun Corps.

FROM:- December 1st.   TO:- December 31st 1918.

WAR DIARY December 1918 21st Bn. O Corps
INTELLIGENCE SUMMARY
Army Form C. 2118.

(Erase heading not required.)

Place	Date	Hour	Summary of Events and Information	Remarks and references to Appendices
BERLIMONT	1st to 4th		Battn. Training and Sports	
	5th		½ Battn. marched to Pont-sur-Sambre and saw His Majesty King George in person on his way to front area.	
	6th to 11th		Battn. Training and preparation for the move to Cambrai Area. – O.O. 61 issued (Appx attchd)	
	12th		Battn. marched to VENDEGIES – Weather very bad – V.S. 28 issued re Cambrai ie funeral.	
VENDEGIES	13th		Battn. marched to INCHY	
INCHY	14th 15th 16th		Battn. Drafted and cleaned up the Billets & Fighting equipmt.	
	17th		Battn. Entrained and embarked for BREILLY at 06.00 hrs arriving BREILLY 15.10 hrs Battn. Transport marched under orders of 8 to 110 Inf Bde to VILLERS-OUTRÉAUX	
BREILLY	18th		Battn. Les Infant. commenced to clean up and away Billets. Battn. Transport marched to TINCOURT (en route along 110 Bde) & To – Lt/ TITU REEVE DSO RCA reported & took over command of Battn.	
– do –	19th		Battn. Les Infant. cleaned Billets etc. Battn. Transport marched to PROYART	

Army Form C. 2118.

WAR DIARY
or
INTELLIGENCE SUMMARY.
(Erase heading not required.)

Instructions regarding War Diaries and Intelligence Summaries are contained in F. S. Regs., Part II. and the Staff Manual respectively. Title pages will be prepared in manuscript.

Place	Date	Hour	Summary of Events and Information	Remarks and references to Appendices
BREILLY	20th		Batt? transport marched to GUY	
"	21st		Batt? personnel to carried on with improving Billets.	
"	22nd		Batt? transport marched into BREILLY at 14.20 hrs after 4 days very wet and bad weather march.	
"	24th		Batt? training and sports.	
"	25th		Christmas day - End by had dinner and a Batt? Concert at night.	
"	26th to 31st		Batt? training and Route march.	

J. Reeve,
LIEUT-COLONEL,
COMMANDING 21st BN. MACHINE GUN CORPS.

SECRET.   Copy No. 11.

21st. Bn. M.G.C. OPERATION ORDER No. 61.

Ref. VALENCIENNES,
ST.QUENTIN and AMIENS
1/100000.
Sheet 51, 1/40,000.   9th. December, 1918.
----

1. The Battalion will move to the CAVILLON Area by Bus and Route March between the 12th. December and 17th. December.

2. Distances laid down in Amendments to S.S.724 (republished in Battalion Orders dated 23rd. Nov. 1918) will be observed in all marches connected with the move.
   A distance of 100 yards will be left between Coy. personnel and Coy. Transport, when marching as a Battalion.

3. The Battalion will march out of BERLAIMONT on the 12th. Dec., in the following order:-

   Battn.H.Qrs, "C" Coy. "B" Coy. "A" Coy. "D" Coy.

   Head of column to pass Starting Point, Road junction U.21.c.5.9 at 09.00 hours.
   The Battalion will halt the night 12th/13th. Dec. at VENDIGES. Route to be taken: LOCQUIGNOL.

4. The Battalion will move from VENDIGES to INCHY on the 13th. December, via NEUVILLY, and remain there until the 17th. Dec., when it will embus for BREILLY.
   Further orders will be issued re above moves, as regards hours of movements.

5. All Battalion Transport will be brigaded with 110th. Bde. and will move by road from INCHY to BREILLY. Special orders will be issued re this move.

6. Special Administrative Instructions will be issued.

7. A C K N O W L E D G E.

                                                    [signature]
                                                    Capt. & Adjt.
                                              21st. Battn. Machine Gun Corps.

Distribution:

    Copy No. 1 .. O.C. "A" Coy.
             2 .. O.C. "B" Coy.
             3 .. O.C. "C" Coy.
             4 .. O.C. "D" Coy.
             5 .. O.C. HQs Coy.
             6 .. Quartermaster.
             7 .. Commanding Officer.
             8 .. Major Borthwick.
             9 .. 21st. Division.
            10 .. War Diary.
            11 ..   "   "
            12 .. File.

War Diary

SECRET.

ADMINISTRATIVE INSTRUCTIONS in connection with
21st. Battalion Machine Gun Corps Order No.61.

1. GROUP.

On arrival of 110th Infantry Brigade at INCHY on the 16th December, the Battalion will come under the orders of B.G.C. 110th Inf. Bde. for remainder of Move.
The Battalion Transport will move with the Transport of 110th Inf. Bde. and Personnel will embus with personnel 110th Inf. Bde.
Further orders will be issued re above Moves.

2. EMBUSSING.

Further Orders will be issued.

3. SUPPLIES.

Rations will be issued at BERLAIMONT 11th inst. for
    consumption on the 12th Inst.,
Rations will be issued at VENDEGIES 12th inst. for
    consumption on the 13th inst.,
Rations will be issued at INCHY 13th inst., for
    consumption on the 14th inst.,
Rations will be issued at INCHY 14th inst., for
    consumption on the 15th inst.,
Rations will be issued at INCHY 15th inst., for
    consumption on the 16th inst.,
Rations will be issued at INCHY 16th inst. for
    consumption on the 17th inst.,
Rations will be issued at INCHY 17th inst., for
    consumption on the 18th inst.,
Rations will be issued at BREILLY 18th inst., for
    consumption on the 19th inst.,

The Rations that are being issued at INCHY for consumption 18th inst., will be carried under Battalion arrangements for personnel embussing.
The road party Rations will be issued to respective Company Transports on the 16th inst., for 17th & 18th insts., to be carried when they move.
Personnel embussing on the 17th inst., will have breakfast before embussing, and each man must embus with a midday haversack ration. Tea will be issued on arrival at BREILLY.

4. BLANKETS.

All Blankets (2 per man) will be sent to Quartermaster's Stores by 07.30 hrs. 12th inst., to be conveyed by motor lorry to VENDIGES when they will be re-issued. Each bundle rolled in tens must be duly labelled distinctly with Co.-Section, in BLOCK letters.

/All.........

-2-

All Blankets will again be conveyed on the 13th inst., by Lorry to INCHY, time and place to be dumped, will be issued later, but instructions re labelling etc., must be carried out.

On the 17th inst., each man will embus with 2 Blankets for use on the journey.

Transport Personnel will carry 2 Blankets per man on the Limbers to new Area.

5. **OFFICERS' VALISES.**

Coys. will convoy own Officers Valises as far as INCHY and from INCHY to BREILLY they will be carried on a Lorry under Battalion arrangements. Place and time to be dumped will be notified later.

Officers who are on Leave and will not rejoin the Unit before the 21st inst., will have their valises sent by Coy. Transport all the way, but those who are on leave, and will rejoin by the 21st inst., will be taken on bus from INCHY.

Each Officer must have as small a Valise as possible on the Bus, as accommodation will not be great.

6. **MEDICAL ARRANGEMENTS.**

A Medical Officer from the 64th Field Ambulance is being attached to the Battalion for duty from 11th - 14th December.

7. **MARCH DISCIPLINE.**

Strict March Discipline will be maintained on the line of march.

8. **LEAVE.**

All Ranks embarking up to and including 19th inst., will proceed via CAMBRAI, after which they will entrain AILLY-SUR-SOMME, hour of reporting Battn.H.Q's will be notified later.

All Ranks returning from Leave etc., will be directed to AILLY-SUR-SOMME on and after the 15th inst., under Div. arrangements.

9. **CANTEEN.**

A Supply of Canteen Stores will be available at the main Divisional Canteen at BOVELLES. Until the arrival of Transport the Divisional Canteen Officer will deliver stores to units on application from Regimental Canteens.

10. **STORES.**

All dixies etc., for Coy. cooking until the arrival of Transport will be carried on the busses by Coys.

/11.........

11. DRESS.

Battle Order - Steel Helmets - Box Respirators will be worn on line of march from BERLAIMONT to INCHY.
Mens' valises will be carried by Companies.
On the 17th inst., Personnel will embus Full Marching Order - 2 Blankets and Midday Haversack Ration.

12. BILLETS AND BILLET CERTIFICATES.

All Billets and Stables to be left scrupulously clean, and usual certificate sent to Battn. H.Q's 1 hour before marching out that this has been done.
List of Billets occupied will be sent Bn.H.Q's as under:

Occupation of BERLAIMONT to Bn.H.Q's by 14.00 hrs. 11th inst.,
: : VENDIGES. : : : : 18.00 : 12th :
: : INCHY : : : : 12.00 : 16th :
in each case up to time of marching out, including all Transport Personnel.
Each Coy. will detail 1 N.C.O. and 3 men to report to Lt. TATLOW at Bn. H.Q's at 08.30 hrs. on the 12th inst., to remain behind and clean up anything that is required. This party will rejoin the Battalion when work is completed.
Lt. TATLOW will report Adjutant 09.00 hrs. 11th inst., for special instructions.

13. ADVANCE PARTIES.

Each Coy. will detail 1 N.C.O. (including Bn.H.Q's.) to report Bn. H.Q's at 07.30 hrs. 12th inst., on Bicycles to go ahead for Billets.
Lieut. WARD will report Bn. H.Q's (mounted) at same hour to go ahead to Town Major VENDIGES and get accommodation

----

Capt. & Adjt.
10/12/18.   21st. Battn. Machine Gun Corps.

SECRET.

21st Battalion Machine Gun Corps.

SPECIAL INSTRUCTIONS re "Staging of Battn. Transport"

1. The Battalion Transport will be grouped with 110th Inf. Bde. and come under the orders of Brigade Transport Officer at INCHY on the 17th inst., Hour of move will be notified later.

2. The strictest march discipline will be maintained on the line of march and special attention paid to distances, namely, 100 yards between Units and 50 yards between each 12 to 13 vehicles.

3. Capt. W.C.VIBERT,MC. will be in charge of the column and arrange with Brigade Transport Officer re advance Billeting Party etc.,
   During the staging period care must be taken to ensure that billeting certificates (i.e. payment) are rendered before the Battalion leaves.
   An Officer will invariably be detailed by the Brigade Transport Officer to investigate and settle with the Maire any claims which may be made.

4. LOADING.

   Special attention will be paid to the loading of all vehicles, on no account are vehicles to be over-loaded.
   No personnel will be allowed to ride on Vehicles except those authorised.
   Each vehicle must have a brakesman.
   Sick or lame animals which have to be left on the line of march will be taken to the nearest Supply Railhead and left with a guard. In all cases two days Rations will be left for men and animals.
   Particulars of any animals left behind should be wired to Bn. H.Q's BREILLY from the Railhead at which they are left.

5. RATIONS.

   Rations for consumption 17th & 18th inst., will be issued at INCHY on the 16th inst.,
   Rations for consumption 19th inst. will be issued TINCOURT 18th inst.,
       :   :   :   20th. : : :   : PROYART 19th :
       :   :   :   21st. : : :   :BLANGY GLISSY
                                                             LONGEAU . 20th :
       :   :   :   22nd. : : :   : BREILLY   21st :

DRESS.

    Battle Order - Steel Helmets - Box Respirators will be worn on the line of march.
    Mons valises will be carried on Limbers.

/7..........

-2-

7. STAGING AREAS.

        Night 17/18th inst.,   ...   VILLERS OUTREAUX
        "   18/19th   "   ..   TINCOURT.
        "   19/20th   "   ..   PROYART.
        "   20/21st.   "   ..   GLISY - LONGEAU.
        "   21/22nd.   "   ..   BREILLY.

    Route to be taken each day will be issued by the Brigade Transport Officer.

8. MEDICAL ARRANGEMENTS.

    There will be a Medical Officer moving with each Brigade Group, and arrangements made re evacuation of sick from each Staging area under his orders.

10/12/18.   Capt. & Adjt.
                21st. Battalion Machine Gun Corps.

SECRET.   Copy No. 13

                        21st Battn. Machine Gun Corps.
                        OPERATION ORDER No. 62.
                        ─────────────────────

                                                    15th December 1918.
Ref. Map Sheet 57.B.,
            (VALENCIENNES,
1/100,000   (LENS,
            (AMIENS.
────────────────────────

1.   The 21st Battn. Machine Gun Corps, less Transport, will move by bus to BREILLY on the 17th inst. from INCHY.

2.   All busses will be consecutively numbered in chalk on the left hand side, from front to rear.
        Coys. will distribute their Officers among their respective busses.
        Each bus will carry 25 Officers and Other Ranks.
        Road space per bus is 10 yds. Coys. will therefore be able to estimate their respective forming up positions in the convoy prior to embussing.
        To avoid overlapping, Coys. will send representatives at least a quarter of an hour before the embussing hour, to locate their respective busses.
        It is estimated that the journey will take about 8 hours.

3.   Battalion Headquarters will close at AUDENCOURT at 05.00 hrs 17th inst., and open at BREILLY one hour after arrival of busses.

4.   Busses allotted Coys. and route to be taken, are shown on attached table.

5.   Special orders re Transport Move will be issued separately.

6.   Attention is drawn to Administrative Instructions issued 10.12.18, para. 11, lines 4 & 5.

7.   In order that a hot meal can be provided for the men on arrival at BREILLY, Os.C. Coys. including Headquarters Coy., will send 3 Coy. Cooks (including Officers' Cook), with dixies and tea ration, to report Q. M. Stores at AUDENCOURT at 05.00 hrs. 17th inst., and this party will be conveyed by a special lorry in advance of the Battalion.
        O.C. "C" Coy. will detail one Subaltern Officer to accompany this party.

8.   Each Coy. will have to carry its own Officers' valises on the busses allotted.

9.   There will be halts on route, which will be sounded by one long blast on whistle to debus, and two long ones to embus. Men must not be allowed to enter any shops or to go a long way from busses at halts, as they will only be short halts.

                                                    /10........

10.   Only two limbers per Coy. must be used to convoy Officers' kits etc. from billets to Embussing Point, and these must be clear of Embussing Point by 05.40 hours.

11.   A C K N O W L E D G E.

(signature)
Capt. & Adjt.
21st. Battn. Machine Gun Corps.

Distribution:

    Copy No. 1 ... O.C. "A" Coy.
            2 ... O.C. "B" Coy.
            3 ... O.C. "C" Coy.
            4 ... O.C. "D" Coy.
            5 ... O.C. H.Qs.Coy.
            6 ... Quartermaster.
            7 ... -
            7 ... Commanding Officer.
            8 ... Medical Officer.
            9 ... 21st. Division.
           10 ... 110th. Inf. Bde.
           11 ... File.
        12/13 ... Diary.

TABLE to accompany 21st. Bn. M.G.C. Order No. 62 for embussing 17-12-18.

Coy.	Time to commence embussing.	Nos. of Busses.	Embussing Point.	Route.	Debussing Point.	To embark on
Battn. H.Q.	06.00 hrs	88 - 90	J.22.a.8.2 to J.22.a.8.6 (Sheet 57b).	CAMBRAI - BOIS LATEAU - GOUZEAUCOURT - METZ - RUYAULCOURT - BAPAUME - ALBERT - AMIENS - DREUIL - BREILLY.	BREILLY - DREUIL Road. Head of convoy, Rd. junction W. exit of Village.	BREILLY.
A.	-do-	91 - 94 and ½ 95	-do-	-do-	-do-	-do-
C.	-do-	½ of 95 96 - 99	-do-	-do-	-do-	-do-
D.	-do-	100 - 104	-do-	-do-	-do-	-do-
B.	-do-	105 - 108	-do-	-do-	-do-	-do-

West

21st Batn MGC

WAR DIARY
or
INTELLIGENCE SUMMARY. for January 1919

Army Form C. 2118.

Place	Date	Hour	Summary of Events and Information	Remarks and references to Appendices
BREUIL	1st		Training & Sports	
	2		do	
	3		do	
	4		do	
	5		do	
	6		do	
	7		do	
	8		do	
	9		Batn team won Divisional Cross Country Race	
	10		Officers cadre to hen	
	11		Church Parade	
	12		Batn Cross Country Championship Won by B Coy	
	13		Training & Sports	
	14-18		do	

Army Form C. 2118.

WAR DIARY
or
INTELLIGENCE SUMMARY.

(Erase heading not required.)

21st Bn. 10 G.C. January 1919

Place	Date	Hour	Summary of Events and Information	Remarks and references to Appendices
BREILLY	19/20/21		Bath. Training & Sports	
	22		Boxing Competition commenced in Battn.	
	23		continued	
	24		To semifinals held	
	25		Boxing finals & General Sports	
	26		First Battn. Football Competition	
	27		Battn. Training & General Sports	
	28/29		to	
	30		First Annual Dinner Officers 21st Battn.	
	31		General Sports	

Lieut-Colonel,
Commanding 21st Bn. Machine Gun Corps.

C O N F I D E N T I A L.

WAR DIARY

OF

21st Batt. Machine Gun Corps.

FROM:- 1st February 1919.   TO:- 28th February, 1919.

Army Form C. 2118.

WAR DIARY
or
INTELLIGENCE SUMMARY.
(Erase heading not required.)

21st Battn. M.G.C.

for February 1919.

Place	Date	Hour	Summary of Events and Information	Remarks and references to Appendices
BREILLY SUR SOMME	1st		Major W.M. Stuart & Major S.C. Thompson M.C. & 23 Other Ranks proceeded for Demobilization.	A.S.C. 2nd Lt
	2nd		V Corps Cross Country Runs. Vignacourt. Won by this Battalion, who also supplied the fastest man home. Capt. O.A. Palmer. 33226. 2 Other ranks joined from Base.	
	3rd		Nothing of interest to note. Very cold ypresse frozen over.	
	4th		Maj. L.C. Borthwick, Lt. J.F. Burke & 2nd Lt. J.D.W. Kirtley proceeded on Leave to U.K.	
	5th		P.T. Sgt. Instructor attached. (S.I. Rogers).	
	6th		Lieut. W.H. Baillie, 2nd Lieut. F.C. Wise & 50 Other ranks. Proceeded for Demobilization. Capt. J. Boswell proceeded on 7 days Special Leave to U.K.	
			2nd Lieuts. S.C. Slaymaker and J.C. Wild and 3 other ranks proceeded to V Corps School for Beginners Course in Motor Engineering. 1 other rank demobilised whilst on Leave in U.K.	
	7th		2nd Lieut. G.D. Meadows (Educational Instructor) & V Corps School Proceeded for Demobilization.	A.S.C. 2nd Lt
	8th		Lieut. A.J. Pack assumed duties of Adjutant.	

Army Form C. 2118.

WAR DIARY
or
INTELLIGENCE SUMMARY.

(Erase heading not required.)

Instructions regarding War Diaries and Intelligence Summaries are contained in F. S. Regs., Part II. and the Staff Manual respectively. Title pages will be prepared in manuscript.

Place	Date	Hour	Summary of Events and Information	Remarks and references to Appendices

Army Form C. 2118.

WAR DIARY
or
INTELLIGENCE SUMMARY.
(Erase heading not required.)

21st Bn. M.G.C. for February 1919

Instructions regarding War Diaries and Intelligence Summaries are contained in F. S. Regs., Part II. and the Staff Manual respectively. Title pages will be prepared in manuscript.

Place	Date	Hour	Summary of Events and Information	Remarks and references to Appendices
BRIFFY SUR SOMME	18th		Nothing of interest to note	
	19th		2/Lt J. D. W. KIRTLEY rejoined from leave	
	20th		Lts G. H. GOBELL, A. H. BONNER, T. HYNTER, 2/Lt A. S. TRISTRAM & 38 other Ranks proceeded by rail from AILLY-SUR-SOMME to join 55th Div for Army of Occupation	
	21st		Maj. L. C. BORTHWICK rejoined from leave.	
	22nd		Nothing of interest to report.	
	23rd		2/Lt VICKERS M.C. proceeded for demobilisation	
	24th		Capt. T. MATTHEWS MC ceased to understudy/attend to for corporal course.	
	25th		Reorganisation of Bn into One Coy + H.Q. - Nothing of interest to note	
	26th		Maj. BORTHWICK proceeds on 2 months leave to England	
	27th		Nothing of special interest. Lt T. G. BURKE rejoins from leave	
	28th		Nothing to report	

J Reeve Capt.
O.C. 21st Batt M.G.C.

H.Q.,
   21st Division.

S. 908.

           Herewith War Diary for the month
of March.

           Please acknowledge receipt.

                                    [signature] Capt [signature]

                         Lieut. Colonel,
           Commanding 21st Bn. Machine Gun Corps.
                         ─────

3rd April 1919.

WAR DIARY or INTELLIGENCE SUMMARY

Army Form C. 2118.

March 1919
21st Bn. MFC

Place	Date	Hour	Summary of Events and Information	Remarks and references to Appendices
BREILLY SUR SOMME	1st		2/Lt BOURDIN & WILLIAMS proceeded on leave.	
	2nd		C.O. proceeded on leave. Church parade in the Mairie.	
	3rd		Mobilization Stores sent to LONGPRÉ in 20 limbers. 48 animals to HORNOY under 2/Lt DALTON	
	4th		Capt W.H. SIMPSON returns from leave.	
	5th		9 Riders & 46 R.D. animals sent off to DIEPPE under 2/Lt TELL. 22 limbers to Canal park	
	6th		42 animals despatches. 2/Lt HARRIS MC NM proceeded to take charge at LONGPRÉ	
	7th		Lt BENNELL returned from leave.	
	8th		2/Lt NEILL proceeded to England with draft of 19 demobilises, 7 on leave men. 14th Bn. Northumberlands further arrived at BREILLY.	
	9th		Lt BENNELL proceeded to LONGPRÉ with 7 vehicles.	
	10th		2/Lt G. TELL returns from DIEPPE	
	11th		Lt P. DALTON proceeded to DIEPPE	
	12th		Capt W.H. SIMPSON took over command of Corporate Corps.	
	13th		Lt BENNELL & 28 O.R. proceeded for demobilisation.	
	14th		Nil.	
	15th		2/Lt G. FELL proceeded on leave	
	16th		Maj. HARDINGE proceeded on special leave to U.K. Capt BOSWELL proceeded with animals to CANDAS.	
	17th		2/Lt WILLIAMS returns from leave.	

WAR DIARY
or
INTELLIGENCE SUMMARY.
(Erase heading not required.)

Army Form C. 2118.

Place	Date	Hour	Summary of Events and Information	Remarks and references to Appendices
BRIEULT-SUR-SOMME	18th		2/Lt Bourdin returned from leave. 2/Lt H. Fairhurst proceeded on leave to Paris.	
	19th		Capt Boswell returned from Candas.	
	20th		To Achiete then proceeded on leave.	
	21st		All demobilisation & leave stopped.	
	22nd		Lt T. Matthews returned from course (Commercial)	
	23rd		2/Lt S.C. Slaymaker & Wild returned from course (engineering).	
	24th		2/Lt H. Fairhurst returned from Paris. 2/Lt R. Harris & S.M. Bourdin proceeded to join 62nd Bn. M.G.C. 2/Lt M.E. Cambery & J.C. Wild to 51st Bn. M.G.C.	
	25th		Notice sent to Lt P. Dalton & 2Lt G Fell to join 62nd Bn. M.G.C. on completion of leave.	
	26th		Capt Boswell, Lts Matthews, Burke, & 2Lt Williams, Slaymaker & 4 O.R's proceeded to join 61st Bn. M.G.C.	
	27th		Nil	
	28th		Lt Fairlie proceeded to V Corps Horse Camp Bourdon with 14 x mules.	
	29th		CO & 2/Lt Neill returned from leave. Draft of 116 O.R. under Lt Fairhurst proceeded to join 61st Bn M.G.C.	
	30th		Maj. C.M. Howard & 2/Lt Neill proceeded to join 61st Bn. M.G.C.	
	31st		Nil	

R.W. Prestine Lieut-Colonel
Commanding 3rd Bn. Machine Gun Corps.

www.ingramcontent.com/pod-product-compliance
Lightning Source LLC
Chambersburg PA
CBHW081424300426
44108CB00016BA/2294